D1823287

Metaphysics and Transcendence

In the light of advances in cosmology, mathematics and logic in the twenty-first century, metaphysics is in need of a fundamental overhaul. From standpoints in the humanities, modernism made exaggerated or unwarranted claims for reducing or removing transcendence. Such claims cannot now be justified in the light of discoveries at the frontiers of the sciences, although previous ways of depicting transcendence were frequently crude and unsustainable.

Metaphysics and Transcendence takes up this story for the future. Arthur Gibson presents a new metaphysics with a genealogy based on counter-intuition and locates counter-intuition and complexity at the foundations of truth. Having devised fresh concepts on the basis of the new frontiers of science and philosophy, the author presents original explanations of transcendence arguing that just as we need revolutionary and original ways of depicting the physical world, so it is with such topics as God, miracles, the resurrection, the source and identity of consciousness and reason itself.

Metaphysics and Transcendence is set to stimulate future philosophical, scientific and religious discussion in its challenge to philosophy and theology to 'get real', to come out of institutionalised pigeonholes and to recognise that metaphysics and transcendence are highly creative subjects.

Arthur Gibson is Reader in Logic and Metaphysics at the University of Surrey, Roehampton, and Visiting Fellow of the Cambridge University Lauterpacht Research Centre for International Law, Faculty of Law. He is the author of *God and the Universe* (Routledge, 2000).

Routledge Studies in Religion

Metaphysics and Transcendence

Arthur Gibson

 Routledge
Taylor & Francis Group

LONDON AND NEW YORK

First published 2003
by Routledge
11 New Fetter Lane, London EC4P 4EE

Simultaneously published in the USA and Canada
by Routledge
29 West 35th Street, New York, NY 10001

Routledge is an imprint of the Taylor & Francis Group

© 2003 Arthur Gibson

Typeset in Baskerville by
The Running Head Limited, Cambridge
Printed and bound in Great Britain by
Antony Rowe Ltd, Chippenham, Wiltshire

British Library Cataloguing in Publication Data
A catalogue record for this book is available from the British Library

Library of Congress Cataloging in Publication Data
Gibson, Arthur, 1943–
    Metaphysics and transcendence/Arthur Gibson.
      p. cm.
    Includes bibliographical references (p.) and index.
    1. Philosophical theology. 2. Metaphysics. I. Title.
BT40.G53 2003
110—dc2.   2003043130

ISBN 0-415-32128-X

For Gerard Gibson

Contents

Acknowledgements

Thanks to Joe Whiting at Routledge for promoting this book project. I much appreciate the special care and quality of attention that Carole Drummond and David Williams (of The Running Head) have conferred on *Metaphysics and Transcendence*.

Due acknowledgement is given to the following publishers for use of some material (which has been revised and extended) drawn from the following chapters. Chapter 2: 'Ockham's world and future', in J. Marenbon (ed.) *History of Philosophy*, III: *Medieval Philosophy* (London: Routledge, 1998): 329–67. Chapter 7: 'Logic of the resurrection', in S. E. Porter *et al.* (eds) *Resurrection* (Sheffield: Sheffield Academic Press, 1999): 166–94. Chapter 8: 'God's semantic logic: some functions in the Dead Sea Scrolls and the Bible', in S. E. Porter and C. Evans (eds) *The Scrolls and the Scriptures* (Sheffield: Sheffield Academic Press, 1997): 68–106. Chapter 9: 'Modern philosophy and past mentality', in M. A. Hayes *et al.* (eds) *Religion and Sexuality* (Sheffield: Sheffield Academic Press, 1998): 22–48. Chapter 10: 'Relations between rhetoric and philosophical logic', in S. E. Porter and D. Stamps (eds) *Rhetorical Criticism and the Bible* (New York: Continuum/ Sheffield Academic Press, 2002): 100–31.

Part I
The problem

Introduction

Beginning philosophy

If life were a dog, the tale of philosophy should not wag it. If life were a ship, its philosophical rudder should hold a key to successful routes to truth.

Bernard Williams (2002) has demonstrated that relations between 'truth' and 'truthfulness' are more unstable in our cultural genealogy than our contemporary philosophy allows. He develops his own fine version of a genealogy of truthfulness, which is a descendant of Nietzsche's composition of genealogy.

This book presents new metaphysics with a genealogy based on counter-intuition.[1] Counter-intuition embodies the principle that the identity and occurrence of truthfulness are often unpredicted, especially when we have confidence that we know what it is. In certain respects, this is the formulation of the genealogy of surprise, of wonder, though I argue that – upon recognising this, it has a consequence: we need to go further than phenomenological survey. Our history, in respect of truth, shows that indoctrination and fabrication have the upper hand as influences and servants of tradition, institutionalism and rationality.

The present book supposes that we are more irrational than we have realised. We are irrational animals. That is, Aristotle was wrong to maintain that we are rational animals. Of course, we can reason; but we are not naturally logical. Animals are non-logical, in that they have no capacity to reason. Truth is counter-intuitive in relation to much of our natural disposition in reasoning. Even without particular traditions writers express concerns about counter-intuitive consequences. For example, Raymond Geuss (2002: 147) observes that: 'One major psychological motivation for introducing and holding fast to the concept of a subjective "right" is a fear of the counter-intuitive consequences of a certain type of consequentialism, particularly utilitarianism.' Traditional academies of taste have tended to intertwine their assumptions about culture with the attempts to identify logic, which are sometimes questionable in ways that we recognise, and also concerning aspects of which we have inadequate perception.

In these perspectives, a concern to furnish a philosophy of understanding includes an attempt to explore and construct contents for understanding. Accordingly, this expands the idea of content and context principles to go beyond methods in philosophy and its logic to procure the concepts of conditions for understanding. In analytical philosophy it is customary to remain within the scope of questions that consider, for example, '*how* we know a thing', and '*what* the criteria are for understanding'. Within such imperial ivory tower foci – so the politically correct version goes – the *content* of what we know, and *what* we understand, are said to belong to other subjects, such as science and economics, etc. This division of labour is speculative, however. Rule-following is not itself a criterion by which to discover the meaning of life.

An alternative philosophy does not have to put aside method and logic. The present book resists the idea that there is no objective basis for reasoning.[2] Nevertheless, just as there are basic controversies among philosophers that dispute what a concept is and what understanding is, the present study will engage in producing its own versions of such matters, partially generated by attention to the contents of subjects and the possibility of understanding them. It is worth trying something different. We still have to struggle with abstract problems – for fresh reasons – and get beyond them. We may wish to leave the past behind, though to do this we may need to go back to it, perhaps even to the third millennium BC, to regain some neglected perspectives. This involves counter-intuitive recognition of differences, similarities and connections. I argue that the tasks of the philosopher and of the historian can relevantly coincide at this juncture. Methods in analytical philosophy can be applied to the actual world, be it past or present. This challenge is akin to that of the historian, in keeping with Quentin Skinner's (1988: 247) formulation:

> The primary task is therefore that of trying to recover a particular context of presuppositions and other beliefs, a context that serves to exhibit the utterance in which we are interested as one that was rational for that particular agent, in those particular circumstances, to have held to be true.

The world and philosophy have improved enormously in some respects. That people who are not rulers now have choice, freedom and moral autonomy are unprecedented developments; yet we still have dictators who are morally as diabolical as some of those were five thousand years ago. That science and technology have advanced is of course marvellous; nevertheless, with regard to public morality and science, there are unresolved issues concerning integrity.[3]

In the extraordinary growth of information and concepts in widely different subjects, we are ignorant of what a philosophy of understanding would be. This has two levels: (a) the logic of what it is to understand; and (b) the content of a philosophy that tackles the larger questions. Many technical philosophies are of no interest to most people outside of philosophy. Some people and certain philosophers do not believe that (a) concerns or applies to practical problems that trouble people, whilst this book does so believe. It is incorrect to conclude that technical philosophy does not apply to pragmatic issues because it is true to suppose that philosophy has discredited transcendence and is self-referential. Some philosophy is self-referential; yet that is a state of play or self-examination, for better or for worse. Such self-concern – where it is taken to be the death-knell for its deployment to practical matters – is, rather, merely that the *Zeitgeist* of academic fashion is presumed to have killed off this type of enterprise. The resultant neglect has often had reductionist consequences for what were fulsome non-reductionist concerns in past theory, whereas the dogmatic ethos of past institutional theology has happily largely gone. Philosophy of atheism has certainly been of profound value in routing faults and institutional corruption in Christianity as well as in other theocratic imperialisms. To conclude with this philosophy, however, that such coups show there to be no transcendent universal truth is merely to conflate atheistic psychology with ontology.

Generalisation in philosophy and science has not achieved the status that would be superior to conjectural knowledge, in the relevant sense. Is the idea of a true universal theory anachronistic? Current research in cosmology and astrophysics seems positively to embrace the prospect of constructing such a theory in future. Certainly, to realise such a hope would involve a tricky enterprise.

Furthermore the very complexity and use of chaos theory that such a project requires undermines the claim that poststructuralism has moved to a position of singular understanding that excludes universal truth. We still have to proceed piecemeal here because of our ignorance of the identity of the universe or multiverse. Nancy Cartwright (1999) has refined the notion of theory-nets. These are frameworks that are prior to theories, and so they do not privilege 'the theory' as the focal functioning feature of concepts. Rather, they utilise sets of theories. We can argue from this position that theories to be derived from the contents of other subjects are candidates to be incorporated into a new philosophy. To this we should add Ian Hacking's (2001) perspective, which reveals to what a large degree such moves, including scientific methods, are influenced by and are manifestations of 'social constructions', though he positions how a certain realist approach to science can be sustained by a refined understanding of what it is to be a social construction.

An unwanted consequence of privileging a particular academic ethos is a premature binary relation: one either is or is not a believer. Generally philosophers fall into one side of the binary relation: atheism. We should not allow the mood of transient culture, even if it lasts from the Enlightenment to poststructuralism, to pretend to be the grounds for deciding what is a question of serious ontology. Religion apart, God is a serious issue. Yet atheism has brought democracy and feminism to a Christian world that seemed only exceptionally to have desire for them. Nevertheless we should argue the merits of arrays of theistic ontologies, versus atheist ones, gathered in theory-nets. It is not that we should consign the critical insights and logic of philosophy to oblivion. Rather, we should preserve and develop critical techniques; yet we need to develop clearer accounts of how little we know in areas where we are bold.

In daily experience, the world is not composed of a group of departments, or faculties, or modules, or subjects that are not joined to others. As with a child learning joined-up writing, we have yet to learn how the disparate continuum that is the (multi) universe is cemented together. It was to some degree helpful of people like Hume to break it up in bits – because our pictures of it were cracked. Hume, terrific though some of his philosophy is, made the mistake of thinking that he had discovered the truth about how things are. As his letters show, he was very much a man of his economic and social times – indoctrinated by his desire to share the company, attentions, stockholdings and tastes of aristocratic Enlightenment.

With the emergence of modernism[4] in the nineteenth century, scientists often ignored the warnings of great creative thinkers in the humanities, not least those outside of philosophy. Baudelaire,[5] for example, produced a new account of ambiguity and argued that we have difference, not progress. Evidently there is much new technology of enormous value. This does not prove that theories of science are true; it only shows that such theories work. But philosophers generally enthusiastic with the new science, and neglecting to measure many of its ambiguities, sped on into the twentieth century and demolished many, admittedly grotesque, transcendental monstrosities. There have been exceptions, for example the philosopher David Stove. The book that occupied the last three years of his life is entitled *Darwinian Fairytales* (1995); he there points out that the four main principles of Darwin's conception are to be found in David Hume's *Dialogues* (1935: 172, 186, 200).

Although philosophy has constructed an array of helpful specific innovations, it has done nothing to solve or dispose of ancient philosophical problems. Its extra contribution, however, has been to proffer a reductionist mythology which has been obliquely presupposed as logical grounds for dismissing transcendental approaches to life. Russell came as a prophet with logic and empiricism, by use of highly technical systems that did not even solve paradox, and sprang on us basic problems of paradox that he could not solve; nor have others since.

Oddly, this contradictory basis was largely taken to show us that past metaphysics had been wrong about transcendence, and sometimes about the practical world. Actually Russell almost completely neglected the logic which could be candidate to prove these approaches of his modal logic.

In particular this is a strange omission in view of later developments in the second half of the twentieth century when possible world-semantics were harnessed to them. As Dummett (1993a: xvi) states: 'The advances in logic were due to the realisation that, for all modal logics, the semantic values of (closed) formulas should be taken not, as in the traditional manner, merely as truth-values in a system of many truth-values, but specifically as subsets of an underlying set.' Certainly, this development should be interpreted in its historical context. Even so, that an underlying basis has been exposed for what was taken to be a sort of bedrock foundation is of some moment in a culture whose disposition is to suggest that there is no underlying transcendent metaphysic, though of course I am not assuming that the latter should be based on that development. There is a comparable state of affairs in cosmology. As I argue in Gibson (2000: 149–51, 199–202) and in chapters 4 and 5 of the present book, the occurrence of underlying super manifolds in cosmology should query the assumption that we know what the physical foundation of the universe is.

Russell's books on transcendent matters and the practical life, impressive as their journalistic prowess and clarity are, are quite valueless as philosophy in even his own professional senses of logic, since in them he never employed the sort of logic on which he researched, and ceased to research. At the side of this type of situation many theologians have largely either cowered before the resultant myth, or they have produced compliant exercises in undue diligence to its spirit. Meanwhile philosophy moved on in some areas. It is becoming increasingly clear that, for example, Wittgenstein's research on logic before, during and after his *Tractatus*, and his debates with Frank Ramsey, have more than historical interest. While Russell was revising the second edition of his universalising machine the *Principia Mathematica* – replete with its inextirpable paradoxes, which are carefully imprisoned in somewhat ambiguous policies so that they seem to do little damage – Wittgenstein had embraced some of the problems that Russell did not relevantly face. For example, what is it to move or that one cannot move outside of finite calculations, while acknowledging that infinity invades the foundations of mathematics?[6] It is a part of this problem that we misunderstand our own history. For example, Wittgenstein is usually taken to have agreed that we construct, and do not discover, mathematics. But it may be that this former interpretation suffocates Wittgenstein's agreement with the role of counter-intuitive discovery in the pursuit of mathematics.[7] As we ascend the scale of generality in the universe, our inclination to confuse a thing with its opposite may increase. Likewise, an argument that God does not exist may drive into reverse over its own advocate.

Starting again

Originality is a function of a certain consequence of alienation. This function is used to remove alienation from ignorance. It involves, as noted above, a problem of recognition. It is not only that avoidance of crackpot strangeness[8] has made significant originality rare. The idea of God is just about as strange as you can get. So we have to go very carefully here, so as to avoid allowing the fashion of the times to coerce us into consensus, though avoiding consensus for no reason is obviously pointless. But philosophy has not yet developed to a stage when it can, without controversy and speculation, demote or promote the concept of God. Although empiricist trends tend to discard God, the concept of God is too counter-intuitive for philosophers yet to have tackled and resolved the requisite issues in logic and metaphysics. I suggest that we develop a counter-intuitive strategy: we treat philosophical matters outside of theology, and theistic matters within theology, as a continuum, and do not concern ourselves with the division of the subjects into the two disciplines that we find, for example, in universities. This continuum shares continuity with other subjects, as does philosophy. This is not to theologise philosophy; nor is it developing an apology for theism. Take it as any other philosopher's enterprise in research. So novel and exotic questions should be triggered by the continuum, and taken seriously: is God a virtual reality simulation? Is revelation a cosmological and not a religious topic? Why should not biblical semantics be a part of an analytical philosophy of language? Is typical contemporary theological language a redundant private language disproved by Wittgenstein?

As Rorty (1998) has supposed, we might reconfigure some history of ideas in ways unfamiliar to its custodians, though I do not here adopt Rorty's chosen path. Such reconfiguration could dispute some accounts of the New Testament, in contrast with some theology. Gibson (2000, 2001) develops a basis for applying logic to biblical semantics. Chapters 5 and 6 of the present book show how this sort of approach can be extended to assess issues concerning representation of divinity and transcendence. The result of this is to direct us to query the fracture of such early Christian features from theology, without wishing a return to the sort of former disputes about biblical theology.

Chapters 7 and 8 build upon these chapters by examining our sense of continuity concerning supervenience and mentality in modern and earlier contexts, including the New Testament. A recurrent conclusion is that originality and the semantics of rationality in the New Testament are relevant for metaphysical philosophy, not least in their relevance for issues of metaphysics in Christian theology. So it is good that philosophy should be untimely in its metaphysical quests, and in ways not concurrent with paradigmatic influences in philosophy. Philosophy should not be a service industry for the present; some writing is worthy for a future context as a way of contributing to the present.[9]

One neglected arena that was given attention by past theologians and ancient philosophers such as Plato concerned with topics of divinity is philosophy of mathematics and its relations to transcendence. As we shall see below, the increasing function of this subject in frontiers of logic, creativity, metaphysics and ethics is reason enough for attending to research in this discipline (though limited technical presentation will be used in this book). Pascal's mastery of mathematics led him, not least through correspondence with Fermat, to incorporate and contrast issues assessing philosophy of mathematics as they can be expressed in creative presentation in debate with topics in philosophical and devotional theology, as well as some ways in which these impinge on biblical and systematic theology.[10] Pascal began, and terminated, research when, it seems, he understood the epistemological significance of at least the result of Fermat's Last Theorem and other deep mathematical issues. Consequently, with such esoteric matters, we should not leave aside past counter-intuitive connections made between apparently disparate subjects. With our now having a number of extraordinary complex proofs of this type, which delineate our ignorance, *in the circumstance when we have knowledge* of something (as argued in chapters 4 and 5), humility, revision and fresh construction of our universe of discourses and of possible futures are urgent tasks.

Clearly, the ways forward for us are not to attempt regression to some mythical reconstruction of a past world that was far from utopian in insights, and is best left behind us. But it shows that we may be more cyclic than we tend to think, or that there are underlying typologies to truth, or that the past is not as different from our presents and futures as, for example, Rorty (1998) maintains. Constructing, as new, an explicitly transcendent philosophy for the third millennium, and by use of semantic analysis, is therefore a familiar and unfamiliar enterprise. Some strongly conservative theologians might consider the book too indulgent about new and ancient possibilities; and what one might call some *avant-garde* theologians may close their minds to a future that can re-compose a new past. Perhaps this is exactly the sort of counter-intuitive turbulence one needs to investigate the prospect of composing identities interpreting the unique claims of theology.

Even for those indisposed to view such a project with disinterest, there are healthy reasons for giving it attention even as a thought-experiment. Culture's consensus is not invariably a recognitional process for understanding. When it has discarded much or some of its past, it is worth assessing what strengths might have been ignored or misrepresented. This does not presuppose that the way forward to a theological future is solely through the past. The point is that, at this stage in evolutionary or devolutionary culture, we are insufficiently cognisant of what it is to have even the contingent conditions to achieve relevant deep knowledge and understanding. This is especially so in connection with culture's relations to science, to allow it that some past or present authority or spirit of change has demonstrated negatively the necessary or limiting properties of answers to fundamental questions. A subset of this domain is theology. Consequently it is a modal fallacy to infer generalised reductionism for theology from our grasp of current knowledge. This judgement stands independently of theology as a piece of philosophy. Philosophers themselves would do well not to use the amateur 'philosophies' of theologians, or their ecclesiastical presuppositions, neither their apologetic stances, as bases for dismissing the significant technical issues which arise most naturally in metaphysics of theology, just as we should criticise philosophical imperialisms.

Certainly, the world has achieved things that thankfully enable us to leave many past theological conceptions behind. No doubt, however, future knowledge has yet to incorporate missing components from the past. This should encourage philosophers to allow a wider remit regarding some theological questions than typically one finds in many research works.

We humans have a yet mysterious inability to assess the identities of difference. Might we claim all we need to do is connect it to the unknown? But the unknown is not an algorithmic function of the known. Consequently we tend to be insufficiently wary of a simple truth: the counter-intuitive identity of contingent inferences can produce a large-scale surprise from a known antecedent. That we can only derive a conclusion from premises is a trivial truth. Just what this entails is still largely a mystery. So hidden in the obvious is counter-intuitive disclosure or revelation.

Transcendence is partly a function of ignorance and/or unknown facts or state of affairs. Therefore, the conclusion that all transcendence is consequence of ignorance is false. In view of this, we would do well to attempt to allow for surprise in arenas where we do not allow or wish for surprise. In other subjects, vexed treatment or neglect has often attended possible and actual relations between creative originality and formal analysis. This book attempts to find a direction by which there can be a *rapprochement* between such creativity and formal issues. This does not have to (and does not) presuppose in the author a formalist or logicist belief for the solutions to problems. Rather, counter-intuitively, the reverse. This is exemplified in theories about the beginning of the universe: trace the universe back to its material commencement, and we have an original, creative singularity in which all forms of law collapse into infinity functions. On a reverse analogy of this scenario, deep in the current universe, and perhaps in our unconscious, is the unification of form with content.

This book is about grounds for transcendence. Since the usual traditional range of such investigations extends to rather more than a few million words, a book of a hundred and thirty thousand can only be offered as an aperitif. It is not composed, however, as an introductory sketch of such issues, but it is a working research on a central group of fundamental problems. The subject is theology while the operating focus deploys some original philosophy, logic and semantics. There is no reason why one should not produce original philosophy for theology, and philosophy that is intended as a contribution to change philosophy outside of theology. This is different from offering a philosophy whose standards or criteria are derived from within theology as a discipline. A philosopher who researches metaphysics and systematic theology can be likened to a micro-physicist who works on astrophysical cosmology. There is a lot of junk in his and other theories, as well as in space. There are territorial disputes, the quantifiable scales are different, while the principles are the same and may need to be revised.

Certain analytical philosophers, reflecting a confusion of borders with content, may claim that philosophers should not offer solutions to questions such as the meaning of life. Such philosophers may assume, wrongly, that logic is on their side, because traditionally it is strongly associated with that reductionist camp. Rather, the present book embodies a policy, and a subtext debate about this, which argues that logic and research can be compatriots of theology, though much theology turns out to be wrong.

Logicians themselves need to be aware that there is a problem if one adopts the assumption(s) that humans are always relevantly rational, or that we have an explanation of what this signifies. The philosophical logician Alex Oliver (1999: 269) has, with some effective proof, warned us that:

> Because we [philosophical logicians] have not yet reached a critical distance from our own logical practice, we fail to see it as a cultural artefact and instead view first-order logic (or its kin) as the hidden inner machinery of the natural languages we all speak.

At the side of the truth of these judgements, we note that Oliver properly employs logic to prove how this truth is reached, in the course of which he finds fallacy and misrepresentation in a variety of distinguished philosophers such as Russell.

On the one hand, logic has mythology in it. On the other hand, there is a use of true elements in it, which correspond to some, but not all, necessary and sufficient conditions for depicting the external world. One of our problems is to what extent, and how, this blend of logic as cultural artefact and logic as map of the external world obtains for transcendence and theology. This alternation is also relative to other subjects and their relevance for their polarisation. Thus chapter 7 below both re-assesses the susceptibility of logic as a tool to depict aspects of the resurrection, and investigates new possible ways of developing logic. It would be incorrect to conclude that this is because of a need for an arbitrary logic of the resurrection since it cannot bear the weight of formal logic, or that this spiritual topic is in a relation of irrelevance to logic. Rather, logic is still in its youth and has yet to be rendered context-independent in status. Conversely, the resurrection, if true, has an immortal ancestry-relation, even allowing for its proper contextualisation in historical circumstance, that many theologians oddly leave out of their studies. Even if all the resurrection claims were to be false, it is of significance for a philosopher to attempt to assess what it would be for it to be true, since this confronts us with deep problems of what we are, and what universalised possibility would be. Moreover, logic cannot extirpate paradox from its foundations, and the resurrection is said to be a manifestation of paradox. One does not need a universal family of paradoxes to recognise a common ground here.

It is the job of philosophers seriously to assess their various views, and ban premature dismissal, reduction or inflation of strange claims. Especially if they are counter-intuitive, we should be very alert to the possibility that it is the fashion of history, and not their internal properties, which has moulded our present. In such a scenario, the present should facilitate new futures, paradoxically as well, to retrieve new senses from the past for the future. Chapters 1 and 2 here attend to the ways in which normality is the seedbed of reason, as a proper subject for a generalised philosophy. This involves composing the philosophy of consciousness in the ways it concerns what is simplicity and the mind's relation to complexity, in connection with the history of consciousness. Some trends in the ancient world, which I suggest mirror the unconscious, are manifested in modern history. Consequently, some humanity has not come very far from its origins. With such imperious human consciousness still stillborn in its birth, philosophy has yet to recognise what it is to live.

Conversely, chapter 10 discovers that some ancient rationality in creative language and the consciousness it mirrors are very far from being primitive. It has often been assumed that the New Testament merely implements the usual or normative ways of reasoning in first-century religion and society. This neglects the potential for originality and individuality. For example, there is the unwarranted assumption that New Testament literature employs incomplete syllogisms, which in any case misconstrues Aristotle's concepts about the matter. We need entirely fresh investigation of how reason relates to the origins of Christianity.

This state of affairs is itself part of a larger problem, which chapter 10 targets. That is to say, what is the identity of original rationality as a feature of creative literature that transcends its origins?

Part II

Prognosis

1 Complexities of meaning

Simplicity versus complexity

True simplicity is wonderful, if true; devastating, if false. If it turns out that the identity of the universe and its relation to itself is complex in relevant domains, simplicity will have been a conceit, which amounts to propaganda. Simplification that is tied to transient fashions in culture can operate like a rationality of totalitarianism, while seeming to be pluralistic. The notion of transcendence has not fared well in this situation. Past overblown claims have brought discredit on some concepts in this sphere. There are opportunities within current research areas of philosophy, logic and literary linguistics by which to construct fresh approaches to transcendence – ones that have consequences for philosophy, and for areas of theology, even in such arenas as the concept of resurrection. Internal to such enterprises is the topic of complexity and the ways it functions.

The present book is not concerned with the traditional issues of the simplicity of God, as it is with the ways in which complexity is a property of justified knowledge, working scientific hypotheses, and the identities of artistic insight, in relation to discussion about God. I am not concerned in this book, however, with the usual philosophy/science-belief relations and confrontations with Christianity; or with methodology, but with actual analyses of specific issues: to construct possible solutions and ways forward in understanding representation of God in relation to metaphysics and language.

An aim of the book is to shift some goal posts, to challenge and bypass certain entrenched debates, to do metaphysics and philosophical linguistics in, and not just for, theology. The book's concern with simplicity and complexity is not one of exploring either the formal concepts or their application in theology and philosophical theology. Rather, the chapters are devoted to applied analyses of topics that have moulded some Christian theology, and to assessing how one might develop fresh insights into them with the application of philosophy and linguistics. The choices of subjects are intended to portray the wide range and applicability of the book's theses as a basis for more extensive future examinations.

The foregoing partly depends on what notion(s) of simplicity is posited, and what conception of meaning is presupposed. On the former, it is worth attending to what the main originator of simplicity, Ockham, actually argued, i.e., a contrary series of simplicity theories, rather than the later views attributed to him; hence chapter 2 below. Conversely, it will be suggested that at the deeper levels of epistemological significance – be it in relation to pure mathematics, logic, and the astrophysics of the early universe, creative aesthetics or ethics – truth is counter-intuitive. It will be claimed that this concurs with the fundamental truths of Christianity. For example, a suitable concept of Christ's resurrection is itself counter-intuitive to empirical and logic categories. Nevertheless chapter 4 proposes that it mirrors, at levels of qualitative infinity, resemblance to some creative and pure mathematical functions, without this type of parallel being inappropriately restrictive as to autonomy and quality of belief.

Counter-intuition 1

Some positions in theology are almost an embodiment of some scientific policies. If the policies are true and applicable, this is apt; yet the equation of theology with science may incorrectly conflate 'true' with 'works'; confusedly blend a normative edge of science without heeding esoteric and disruptive trends within standard science; and blur naive scientific realist modes of intuition with the counter-intuitive forms of relevance by which science often achieves new insights. So some reflections on properties of theory within advanced and newer science are appropriate as perspectives for assessing its boundaries with theology. Central to such a project is the variety of sense of proof. Proof and theology have at least one similarity; it is that in their deeper or more problematic areas, the function of intuition is unstable and risky which counters standard moves in judgement. These can be summed up as fibres of counter-intuition. Merely exhibiting comparable features does not unify counter-intuitions for philosophy, theology and for proof in some sciences. It will be suggested in the present book, however, that there are some aesthetically, epistemologically and logically connected aspects shared between theology and some properties of science, without at all wishing to conflate them. One of these aspects is that of counter-intuition.

With regard to the expression 'counter-intuition', it is relevant for the development of the book's strategy to focus provisionally on the idea of there being a notion of, or associated with, counter-intuition, and then offer some estimation of how this relates in contrast to some of Wittgenstein's comments on 'intuition'.

The expression 'counter-intuition' is a widely employed tag which, as far as the writer is aware, has not been explicitly the subject of published research work. This itself may be an interesting situation in a century of massive concern with theorisation.[1] The term may mark a variety of families of distinctions. It seems to range from 'surprise' to a necessary contradictory consequence that opposes a proposition one had previously judged certain. We will consider examples of this below, though Gödel's proofs about the non-provability of the foundations of arithmetic would be an instance of the latter type of counter-intuition.

Clearly, there is a question of whether or not such distinctions crafted in subjects different from theology do obtain for theology. Aspects of this will be examined below; yet *prima facie*, on a variety of theological approaches, knowledge of God is counter-intuitive either in principle or for a range of contexts. But perhaps some theological readers may be impatient with the appearance here of philosophy of mathematics (though no technical knowledge is required) in a study of theology. This issue will be attended to later, but some comment should be offered here: there are profound similarities in metaphysical areas of, say, ethics and philosophy of mathematics, as Colin McGinn (1997) and Bob Hale (1994) have argued. For example, both ethics and mathematics are outside of space–time, and yet have (by the exercise of will) a causal impact on physical states within space–times though they are themselves acausal. Obviously, such states of affairs themselves, on certain analyses of relevant contexts, have parallels with God. Within a perspective of Wittgenstein's priorities, it is noteworthy that, in his change of October 1929, he formulated aspects of the concept of different calculi, of the use of numbers and equations, which is part of a continuum with his project of language games. (This was a complex development, not only of historical interest, since it gets to the heart of fundamental and unresolved issues.) In this perspective philosophy of mathematics and 'ordinary language' games occupy related, or connectable, spaces. I argue that, as with many other considerations, this leads us to awareness that nonformal theological language, without any formal content, can be extremely exact, creative and logical; such a project, of course, will take some time to articulate. These remarks are solely for the purpose of attempting to sketch a rationale for relating formal matters outside of theology with those within theology though the present writer has no interest in 'formalising' or skewing theology as either a science or a theoretical formalist enterprise. If one were to choose a single factor from many at this stage in our discussion which points towards a reason and conceptual policy as to why one should *not* thereby be committed to the conclusion from the foregoing judgements, we should merely need to think about the role of creativity and approximation *within* mathematics, logic and science *where* they deal with the deep counter-intuitive frontiers which query, inform and redirect their presumed identities.

Philosophical theology has absorbed an inclination to model possibility on the analogy of rationality provided by interpretations in philosophy, logic and science. We may wish to debate this absorption by moving to the frontiers of new research in such spheres. Historically some of these are set in profound studies that can still inform us, while we may wish to transform them. There are what might be termed counterfeit or false counter-intuitions, and it is obviously a problem at the frontiers of analysis to separate some of these from what will turn out to be genuine insights. For example, although Mathieu Marion's (1998) splendid study of the finite in philosophy of mathematics does not have any explanation of what 'counter-intuition' is, he uses the term to criticise Whitehead's and Russell's formulation of the Axiom of Reducibility. Very crudely speaking, this axiom concerns the way in which aspects of propositions are universally related by the same explanations, so as to avoid vicious-circle fallacies that are a result of his theory of type. The aim was to achieve universality through reduction and simplicity. Marion (1998: 57) states of it: 'This axiom, needed in order to re-establish the standard interpretation, is counter-intuitive, and was considered by all as a blemish.'

If it is a blemish, then we have a case of counterfeit counter-intuition. Contrariwise, some ideas may appear to suffer from this counterfeit identity, yet on a certain interpretation; this identity may be bound up with the observer's inability to separate out a counterfeit form from the genuine thing. So, for example, Casimer Lewy's (1976: 108–9) claim that a debate fomenting at the same time around C. I. Lewis (1912), has a counter-intuitive identity. And we should note, again, that Lewy does not explain explicitly what he meant by 'counter-intuitive'. He argues: '[The] consequences of Lewis's definition have been called the "paradoxes of strict implication"; but they are only paradoxical, in the sense of being counter-intuitive, *only if* strict implication is identified with our pre-formal, intuitive concept of entailment.'

Now I am not concerned here with the merits and demerits of Lewy's general claims, but only with his use of the term 'counter-intuitive'. It is proper to observe that he of all people, obsessed as he was with definition or explanation of terms in what he wrote in his life, had little business passing over in silence his introduction of this mysterious term. Of course we all slip in this way, yet my interest here is with the connection of technical matters. Let us suppose that, whatever the status of Lewy's overall views on inference, he has a justifiable point here. Namely, that there is true counter-initiation that looks like paradox but is not. This has significant value for how we approach originality, dissent and deviation and, conversely, an all-too-plausible product of thinking that has presentational force yet is vacuous in significance. The balance between these two extremes is a mean not yet achieved in most educational policy, let alone in philosophy.

Lewy (1976: 85) explicitly argues that 'a concept is *not* a "recognitional capacity"'. If in any central sense this claim is true, when combined with Lewy's use (but not mention) of 'counter-intuitive' there emerges a fundamental problem whose proportions he did not consider. Allow me to make a general assertion on this basis: we often fail to recognise counter-intuitive truths because human consciousness is disposed in such a way as not readily to recognise such concepts. If this is a tendency of our human consciousness, then it also assists us to characterise how we produce counterfeits of counter-intuition. Presumably this situation could be a combined result of many factors. One could be an internal disposition to irrationality. Construed one way, this opposes Aristotle's view that we are rational animals. Aristotle's view does not square with my analysis of Hitler in Gibson (2000b). Someone may retort that Aristotle is right in principle but often wrong in practice. This is not much good for men who are walking around implementing Aristotle's doctrine that women are mutilated men; and less so for the female gender. I return to this issue in chapter 9.

If the trend of the foregoing is anywhere near the mark, it supports the contention in this book that one of the largest instances of counterfeit counter-intuition, for which we have no recognitional capacity, is the concept of simplicity. It will be claimed that things are complex, and only by a trick of suppressing complex premises – that all simplicity presupposes – can it seem to be the case that truth is simplicity. By applying the idea of a 'counterfeit' for simplicity, I do not intend to deny the value of utilising simplicity.

Nash 'simplicity'

McAleer (2001: 296) quotes John Nash's response to his enquiry about simplicity, in which Nash expresses appreciation of principles of simplicity, and Nash refers to his axioms for bargaining solutions as relevant examples of the simplicity in relation to these. Nash is also concerned in this context to warn of the 'the danger of "over-simplification"'. He concludes that: 'It is certainly true that simplicity has a major function but also it's difficult to think that a simple "rule of simplicity" can be given so that, by simply using that rule, it would be easy to produce good scientific research!' Given this observation, which I take to be correct, it eventually follows that there are degrees of simplicity that oppose simplicity as a singularity. Or it is the case that there is a singular parsimonious 'simplicity', a consequence of which is that an expression such as 'over-simplified' has to be converted into a binary sense of a false or inapplicable sense of simplicity. Or it obtains that correct statements, such as 'it is difficult to think that a simple "rule of simplicity" can be given so that, by simply using that rule', involve one having to conclude that there is no singular law-like principle internal to simplicity.

In a sense, then, simplicity or some versions of parsimony are perspectivally reductionist. They presuppose specificities whose sharp focus does not adjust relevantly from other levels, which are internal properties of the subject of simplification. For example, consider Nash equilibria – ideal situations where outcomes involve the players' strategies that are mutually cooperative, and the solutions are internal to the scope of the equilibrium points, in which each player utilises her maximal prospects in ideal games. Taken as an instance of simplicity, this form of the Nash equilibria omits to discern the difference between a reason and an incentive, as Paul Weirich (1998: 74–129) elegantly shows. This interpretation of the Nash equilibria needs a complexifying addition to isolate a property within the equilibria, which from the perspectival viewpoint of their simplifying functions is obscured, namely the distinct functions of a reason and an incentive.

This state of affairs points, with other appropriate evidence, towards a worry that I have been articulating in the present and other books, namely that complexity is the prior and fundamental substratum of logical identity and of the physical world, in contrast with simplicity, which at best is groupings of analytical schemata that mirror harmonies and mappings in the world's physical complexity. Within this type of scenario, there are simulations of such simplicities, which function only as approximations, and are often too easily taken to be ground for justified belief that simplicity is prior to complexity. If this conclusion is correct, and yet if it is resisted in parsimonious policy-making or application, there is a disposition in such agenda to up-grade and over-generalise the focus and scope of identity of scenarios for simplicity, according to which result there will be a consequent counterfeiting of simplicity. Since such counterfeiting is lodged as the focal point summarising complex functions, what is actually the justification yielded by complex theories and their data will be conflated as evidence for simplicity.

One reason for this confused state of affairs is that there are counter-intuitive asymmetries in new theories. This situation obtains in much of the insights conceived in Nash's theories. For example in his (1950) seminal paper, 'Non-cooperative games', he develops a 'dynamical' approach to the study of cooperative games based upon reduction to non-cooperative form. This latter form is postulated to have an infinity of pure strategies. As Nash (1951: 295) concludes: 'Thus the problem of analysing a cooperative game becomes the problem of obtaining a suitable, and convincing, non-cooperative model for the negotiation. The writer has, by such treatment, obtained values for all finite two-person cooperative games, and some special n-person games.' This amounts to a counter-intuitive stack of complex asymmetries within the sights of simplicity, not least between the relations of '*infinite* games' and '*finite* two-person games'. So, as I think Nash presupposes in his remarks, we need to look anew at the relations between complexity and simplicity.

Summarising the concept of simplicity in the present and my other studies in response to these problems, I conclude the following. Simplicity is a perceived midpoint between two functions of complexity. First, the (often suppressed) premise or presupposition of simplicity is complexity. Secondly, simplicity entails complexity, while complexity does not entail simplicity. That is to say, simplicity is a technique for being able to view complexity. When actual complexity is reduced by, say, Ockham's Razor, the simplicity logically depends on the complex antecedent that it summarises. So complexity is an actual property of the universe, depicted in language, while simplicity is a function of explanation.

Kolmogorov complexity

Research studies in simplicity, for example in the collection edited by Zellner *et al.* (2001), present us with evidence of real progress in this sphere. One of the studies in this collection – that by Vitanyi and Li (2001) – refines the notion of Kolmogorov complexity. That is, in the view of Kolmogorov (1965), simplicity is the shortest effective re-description of a sequence of regularities. Although Kolmogorov complexity does not presuppose regularity in the way Bayes's rule does, its reductionist thrust is viable within the limits that it compresses what is known. It is not a context-free principle for proving that complexity *per se* is simple.

Vitanyi and Li (2001) argue that they have shown that Kolmogorov complexity applies as a universal principle for single random predictions, and that each single property holds for all incompressible binary strings. As Aristotle proved in the 'Sea battle' argument, demonstrating that all propositions aimed at future contingencies are binary, and that each has a discrete solution, does not prove that we know the empirical reference and truth-value of all the propositions.

Vitanyi and Li (2001: 138) observe that Kolmogorov complexity is the length of the shortest binary programme from which the object can be effectively constructed, which they term *the algorithmic information content of the subject*. Yet in the domain with which we are concerned in the present book – qualitative domains – the sphere is at least partially non-algorithmic. This also applies to large domains of higher mathematics. For example, Diophantine equations admit of no algorithm determining whether or not a given equation is soluble in integers Z, a result which has been derived from Hilbert's tenth problem, as Skorobogatov (2001) notes.

It is interesting to consider how an algorithm of the future might be envisaged as a function of Kolmogorov complexity. Basically there could not be a Kolmogorov complexity function for the future. Conjecture apart, the future has no shortened length. The future cannot be qualitatively foreclosed. To those who are familiar with complexity, complexity will seem fairly straightforward. We are so entrenched in the myth of simplicity that we often misinterpret our own abilities to be complex, and construe them as simple. Consider the 'simple' old gardener who knows everything about growth. It is simply there, and obvious. The complex judgements, to him and others, are the very simplicity of nature, with all its complexities, variability, chaotic patterns and familiar cycles that never quite conform to the intellectual simplicity of the technical models.

Perhaps one of the most counter-intuitive areas of counterfeiting simplicity is the idea that Christian belief itself is simple. For example, the resurrection stands as an extraordinary contrast with any notion of simplicity and patterns in organic life. In chapter 7 it is contended that the concept of resurrection is a fertile ground for new theory in virtual reality, complexity theory, and counter-intuitive areas of logic (complementary to chapter 4), as well as creativity in cosmology and aesthetics (in keeping with chapter 5). An upshot of this is that the traditional opposition between faith and reason collapses. Counterfeit reductionist simplicity is what supports this opposition, not any New Testament or deep theology or philosophy. Even for the world-view internal to the Gospels, the narrative consciousness works so as to point up the irony of a narrative about unbelievers standing by while Christ raised the dead. We do not need scientific empiricism to inform us of the assumption that if you observe it happening, then this amounts to proof that it is true that it is happening.

For those who wish to metaphorise this language, or invent a new historical dress, there is still the internal voice of such an intertext contradicting the separation between faith and reason. In a total work of art, proof and reason are in unity. As the Jewish robot tailor said to Woody Allen, who asked for simple clothes, in *Sleeper*: 'For you, we got simplicity; we got complexity.' In history simplicity by sleight got the upper hand, no doubt partly because it is best for political control under totalitarianism without free speech. In the third millennium, things have got to be better, and different, to make the true connections.

I concur with the studies in Zellner *et al.* (2001): simplicity and complexity have not yet been finally identified or definitively connected. Although Wittgenstein did not explicitly analyse the expression 'counter-intuition', in the *Tractatus* he commenced what was to be a lifetime of examining related problems associated with use of its antithesis – intuition. In the *Tractatus* he asserted that:

> 6.233 The question whether intuition is needed for the solution of mathematical problems must be given the answer that in this case language itself provides the necessary intuition.

> 6.2331 The process of *calculating* serves to bring out that intuition. Calculation is not an experiment.

Even so, §6.2331 does not require that the non-experimental identity of calculation entails sufficient understanding of calculation so that no new knowledge can be produced by untried inferences.[2]

Wittgenstein knew that there are chronic limits to computable decidability and mechanical inference, and made contributions that were in advance of his time.[3] Although we may interrogate, and yet sympathise with Wittgenstein's criticism of Gödel's proofs, they strengthen Wittgenstein's criticism of our inability to prove certain things. According to Gödel, if axiomatic set theory is consistent, then there are theorems that cannot be proved; and there are no constructive procedures that could prove set theory to be consistent. In effect, his work shows that we cannot prove the foundations of arithmetic, and demonstrates that for some mathematics there is no answer that we could prove to be the answer. Whether or not this is true for God is a distinct issue, of course, since Gödel's theorems do not prove that certain mathematical theorems are inconsistent, only that we cannot achieve consistency by proof. He proved that there are statements that are true, yet which mathematicians cannot prove (given established senses of 'proof').

Sometimes this phrasing is absent, so that, actually or effectively, an expression such as 'mathematicians cannot prove' is replaced by 'cannot be proved in principle'. Nevertheless, Gödel's proofs entail, as at present understood, only the more modest anthropomorphically quantified approach to logical humility. It eventually follows from these points, and other premises developed below, that there can be true statements which we cannot, using established procedures, prove, but yet they are of a comparable order of precision to pure mathematics. We do not have to argue that theology is as precise as logic; we know that the two exercise different kinds of knowledge, which one should not confuse or conflate. Nevertheless, the present argument is that certain spheres of transcendent theology about God have such extreme and counter-intuitive types of precision. But because cosmology and mathematics have only recently moved into or begun to grasp the logical identities of relatable exotic domains, we are burdened with an undue history of contrast between theology and science. Nor, again, is this to export a mechanistic or universalised notion of science to theology. Rather, such claims derive from the current and ancient deeper, edges of progress in science and its theoretical formalisms.

Imagine Kant's view, that we have no knowledge of things as they are in themselves, applies to such theorems and proofs. It would follow that, within the sphere of 'things as they are in themselves', and what is thus beyond the scope of our current grasp of proofs, there could be another sort of proof or unrevisable knowledge of deeper mathematical truths. These proofs could be immune to the Gödel theorems of undecidability, discontinuous with present ways of grasping proofs. This has parallels with our knowledge of the earliest astrophysical cosmology and the deepest terrestrial physics, in the sense that the former violates many intuitions in the latter subject both quantitatively and qualitatively.

But such a Kant-like position in ignorance of a thing in itself, I shall argue, cannot be right, or at least not universally applicable to knowledge. Mathematical intuition is a special arena in which unexpected routes to surprising discoveries appear. For example, after centuries of disagreement and blind alleys, Andrew Wiles (1995) has proved Fermat's Last Theorem. It is interesting to assess some of the leading mathematicians' attitude to Fermat's theorem, before it was proved, as evidence of scant attention to the possibility of their scepticism about the prospect of a counter-intuitive shock to their intuitions. For example the distinguished mathematician A. V. Tolstikov (1989),[4] writing for professional mathematicians, stated that, 'An unhealthy interest in proving this theorem was stimulated at one time by a large international prize, which was abolished at the end of the First World War. It has been conjectured that there is no proof of Fermat's Last Theorem at all.' Given that the theorem has been proved, and without wishing to ascribe to Tolstikov the requirement that he should have been prescient, his censure and his unqualified report of an anonymous conjecture that there is no proof illustrate how one might fall on the wrong side of accurate intuition of a counter-intuitive matter. There is the further feature, not to be explored here, of why free enquiry into the unknown is being castigated as 'unhealthy', why it is not balanced by encouragement of healthy interest in proof, and to what extent such factors distract a thinker from positively assessing a counter-intuitive domain.

The theorem arises by considering the possibility that there is a generalisation to other powers of the proof for Pythagoras' theorem. Here one presupposes a principle of arithmetic computation by which a simple law of addition entails that if '$x^2 + y^2 = z^2$', then '$x^3 + y^3 = z^3$'. However, the latter consequence is false, according to Fermat's now proved Last Theorem. That is to say, there is no cubed solution in whole numbers. So here we have a hard, deep case of falsified mathematical intuition – one that derives, not from esoteric speculative calculus but from elementary algebra, though Wiles's proof is counter-intuitively complex, especially in the way in which it connects apparently unrelated mathematical domains together into one proof. Fermat's Last Theorem is of course only one of a large group of counter-intuitive sets of mathematical statements, which can be cited to broaden the sense of the thesis here being presented. It may be that, as with one paradox, we may eventually discover that counter-intuition has various different families, which may or may not be transitive in their relations to each other. But for the present let us assume that counter-intuition marks a concept that can be generalised over relevant cases of surprise in widely distinct subjects.

It eventually follows from this state of affairs that even if, as the *Tractatus* argues, the intuition needed for the solution of mathematical problems must be the necessary intuition internal to such language itself, then our grasp of professional calculative competence does not entail that we have knowledge of what it is to be the limits or relational identity of that language.

If the negation of this were true, then any mathematician who knows the two relevant mathematical principles in Fermat's Last Theorem would thereby know whether it is true; but none did. Consequently, counter-intuition, using this example, is that state of affairs in which in its strong form, a professional competence in a domain will permit the negation of the truth of the domain. No doubt there are many forms and grades of such counter-intuition.

If, then, we wish to make a Kantian move, and apprehend a barrier between the world of physics and the world in itself, we may find ourselves both too narrowly and too widely engaged with our modestly endowed minds. If we do not know how universally to generalise over the limits to logical thought, how can we mark the distinction using such limits? Conversely, many pieces of calculation in the astrophysics which are deployed to conjecture facets of the identity of the early universe, in pure mathematics, in microphysics, leak evidence of an overlap condition between finite and infinite quantities and qualities.[5]

One of Penrose's conclusions, refined in his above-mentioned publication, which is partially supported by Butterfield (1998), is the view that there is a non-algorithmic physics. This may or may not support the idea that consciousness itself has the same property of non-algorithmicity. But if even the former is true for, and in, some domains, then it would enable me to expand this conception of counter-intuition to include or map qualitatively similar states in the physical world. (A consequence of this may be that the truth of counter-intuition can show that physicalism is false.)

Although wishing to avoid fallacy by conflating one empirical form of infinity with a transcendental immaterial qualitative function, yet by the same token our intuition has no basis for determining that our rational intuition recognises or articulates an understanding of the counter-intuition required to calculate in this game. But the new frontiers of philosophy, cosmology and logic have far exceeded the strictures which theology incorrectly thought to impose on itself in the modernist reductionism over the last century. We should not retreat to a reactionary scenario. Rather, we need to reconsider whether or not modernism poured out the baby with the bath water, as a new universe of logical discourse supported by counter-intuitive empiricism emerges over the future's horizon.

Metaphysical meaning

To some extent, in the emergence of modernism and poststructuralism the identities and collisions between these two presupposed 'movements' have been smoothed away or been institutionally packaged in fashions which I suggest might not be ideal for progress in apprehending some of the deeper issues. There are too many for one book to serve them. The present work attends to typical issues so as to concentrate on matters of logic, theory of meaning, originality and transcendence. The focus on these has to do with some of the ways in which fresh research on philosophy could query and redirect substantive zones of discussion concerning the claims that belief in God has a new future at the frontiers of reasoning.

An upshot of the arguments in this book is that meaning and truth are unexpectedly realist. A corollary of this, however, is that the deeper, fundamental and universal domains of realism are also counter-intuitive. If the latter point is not understood as an internal property of realism, then it is easy to impoverish the scope and identity of realism by proffering some analogue that fails to do justice to the external and conceptual worlds. Part of this issue includes the recognition that relations between these two domains are themselves counterintuitive.

Although this book is not about Kant, it challenges a world-view that arose partly because of his influence.[6] I argue that we do not have to follow Kant, on one interpretation of him, in maintaining that physics can discover nothing about things as they are in themselves. Even if Kant were to be correct, we are still faced with a counter-intuitive body of knowledge that confutes a mechanically calculated presentation of what things are – even before we add 'in themselves'. We may perhaps come to agree that the universe is infinitely qualitatively complicated. It may be that this infinity has simplicity as an internal property of its generalisation; yet we will not be able to recognise it if our intuition is, in itself, tuned to – what seems to be the fallacious consequence – that all knowledge is itself composed of recognitional concepts. To discover what this may amount to even in outline, we shall need to reassess a variety of ways of looking at the past and our present, so as to defocus, and refocus, philosophy and philosophical theology, for the future.

Counter-intuitive pictures

Do humans have, internal to their perceptual apparatus, a disposition to recognise pictures of God? Well, let us adjust this to comprehend live metaphoric pictures of God in language. Or, perceive metaphoric portraits of God? On this approach, or a suitable variation of it in distinct time zones and geographies, is it an internal property of rationality that a 'normal' perceiving agent might be able to, or could, recognise such versions (interpretations of God, allowing for the separable problems of formulating an epistemology of believing)? Further, is the impact of environment and context a causal condition influencing (facilitating or blocking) such recognition? Are all these conditions basically equivalent in different eras of human history, for example in New Testament or poststructuralist times? If they are different, are they relevantly different enough to change the internal psychological conditions of what it is to recognise a 'picture' of God (in the foregoing senses)? These complex questions begin to introduce the difficulties of assessing whether or not having a concept of God is itself a recognition capacity. Certainly, in one frame of reference it is not: intentionality; but is such a restriction only a property of concepts 'of' God which are not really concepts *of* God? Clearly, this question itself presupposes a nest of other problems. A purpose in presenting this regress, albeit all too briefly, is to surround the question of 'What is an instance of relevant recognition?' (in relation to representing God) with a contextual perspective in which counter-intuition obtrudes at many points where at first one may think the terrain is firm and recognisable. Contrariwise, the main thrust of the present book is to develop the proposal that, if one suitably concentrates on some of these issues, we can establish the viability of claims that a transcendent God can be represented in our languages and semiotic strategies. A corollary of this is that some of the ancient ways of articulating narrative concepts of God in the New Testament God are susceptible of precise characterisation. These temporally remote and contemporary modes of representing God are not necessarily now incorrigible nor are they conceptually unlinkable to past concepts of mentality.

If, as argued in the present book, having a concept is not necessarily a recognitional capacity, it follows that we all may have missed what we deem 'the obvious'. From experience we sense that we know; however, with counter-intuitive recognition we may think that we have grounds to know, while we do not. Roughly summarised, in application to theism, this could be an invalid consequence of modernist theological reductionism, and its perception of science, which thereby has missed a complementarity that obtains between theology and the causes of such reductionism.

Many issues crowd around such misdirected influences. For example consider the foregoing in relation to the question: (A) Can we picture God?

Regarding (A), various postmodernisms may have drawn conclusions too quickly. Logicians do not yet have a full grasp of what it is universally to lay down logical criteria by which to answer the question: (B) Is it true that 'necessarily, whatever is drawn as a consequence must be contained in the antecedent premises'?

We do not have grounds for assuming the probity of such a 'law' for metaphysical inference; nor, consequently, do we have a clear idea of (B)'s operation as a taskmaster for theology, though some sense of metaphysical necessity is established (see for example Kripke, 1974, and Dummett, 1993: 331–48).

It is worth considering a piece of modernist history involving the conjunction of (A) and (B), in relation to what I have termed 'counter-intuition', though since the present book's priority is metaphysics, only select and angled attention will be given to logic. Is it true of Wittgenstein's picture theory of language that it has been demolished? Certainly, Wittgenstein considered that his theory as it stands in the *Tractatus* has problems, though there are recondite issues about its qualified or transformed appearance in Wittgenstein's (1998) *Philosophical Investigations*. We need fresh work on reason and imagination which could enable us to produce a new viable concept of a picture theory of language that will be of some merit in application to theology,[7] for example partly as implemented in chapter 6 below, on virtual reality metaphysics.

We will come to various issues embracing this question below. For the present it is worth concentrating on the idea of what a picture would be. This has interest both for a speculative or revisionary metaphysics of God, and for negative theology. The issue of how to interpret a picture in Wittgenstein concerns his crisis and change culminating in October 1929. Philosophy biography should not detain us here more than necessary, so I hope theological readers will allow this relevant digression into the recent history of philosophy. Hintikka (1994: 27) argues that it is not even a half-truth to maintain that Wittgenstein gave up the picture idea, since he was even more of a picture theorist in 1930 than in 1913–21, though obviously in a sense different from earlier. In 1930 the picture is variously a portrait, a genre picture or an incomplete picture. Importantly, this shift from a token picture involves the concepts of interpretation and typology. I suggest that this links up with the proposals in chapter 6 concerning virtual reality simulations. We should not fracture this relation with his earlier philosophy, however, since in 1913 Wittgenstein states that: 'We must be able to understand propositions [of] which we have never heard before. But every proposition is a new symbol. Hence we must have *general* indefinable symbols'.[8] This space for unprecedented newness, though it has a formalist purpose in the context quoted, is well within the limits of Wittgenstein's later *Philosophical Investigations*. Here in 1913, without presenting the point, Wittgenstein has paved the way for counter-intuition, since this property is precisely to do with the unfamiliar, the surprising use of expressions that we already (seemed) extensively to know.

The purpose in tracing Wittgenstein's work here, and pressing its implications beyond those which, perhaps or at least in extant published manuscripts, Wittgenstein did not work out, has very little to do with a Wittgensteinian pursuit. Rather, we are here concerned with the attempt to expose and isolate the identity of possibility in relation to metaphysical possibility in language. The foregoing considerations concur with the prospect of logical conditions for counter-intuitive knowledge of God. Humans are able to understand propositions of which, at some biographical stage, each person has never heard before, using familiar elements and new senses. These familiar elements, consequently, have (previous to such usage) been general indefinable symbols. In a sense, we have here primitive features for devising live metaphoric portraiture for narrative about God.

Hintikka (1994: 32) observes that in 1929 Wittgenstein envisaged systems of calculi to take over the role of the truth-function theory of the *Tractatus*, and these are the ancestor of the language-games of the *Philosophical Investigations*, though such calculi are not explicitly developed. Hintikka (1994: 35) notes that, in Wittgenstein's middle period, disenchantment with 'the logic of tautologies', as a mediator between elementary propositions and complex ones, reflects a hope that the solution would amount to a better account of the logic of complex propositions, which would do justice to his later insights into games and the way people mediate between language and world. As Hintikka (1994: 33) shows, Wittgenstein considered a phenomenological explanation of language to be impossible, and sought a 'physicalistic language' and 'physicalistic system', concerning which they can only be compared to physical reality.

Now a subject that was not addressed by either Wittgenstein or Hintikka, but which supports and can contribute difficulties to the above situation, is the cosmology of the early universe. Current researches lead one inexorably to the conclusion that the 'physical' is less easily contrasted with the *a priori* (theoretical system of calculi and empirical theories) and the physical world.[9] This problem is not a consequence of accepting the apparent success of Spinoza's sort of project concerning the mythical status of the *a priori*, concerning a debate that has surfaced in various forms in late twentieth-century French philosophy.[10] Rather, it has to do with current scientific viewpoints respecting physical states in the astrophysical cosmology of the earliest universe and related microphysical states, as for example Martin Rees (1997) explains the data. According to such scientific assessments, in the first few microseconds the universe's matter did not (and according to many, in its last phase will cease to) display compliance with the standard laws that are displayed by observations of most of the universe's history and in our present. This involves the scenario in which matter and space times collapse. Consequently, for these 'time-points' it is not possible to sustain an *a priori* contrast with experience. There are two prime reasons for this state of affairs. The first reason is that the contrast is not there. Secondly, there is no possibility for humans to experience it. The latter point is also true in the novel sense that the *a priori* distinction is a function of possibility arising out of material empiricism.

Explanation of these problems could take up the space of a book.[11] Suffice it here to conclude that one possible way of accounting for Wittgenstein's thesis in such a state of affairs is to retain its point, and conclude that the remaining phenomena are transcendent. If in this scenario we can conclude that there are physical states, then his thesis would be true, but infinitely expanded. If we take up Rees's (1997: 221–34; and 1999) astronomical view, that there are other universes – multiverses – that display different physics from ours, and apply this to Wittgenstein's physicalist thesis, then we will have an extraordinarily rich counter-intuitive exponential conception of his claim. That is, all such theories require that language in some sense correspond to reality. We could then fold this back on itself, in a manner reminiscent of making connections between different worlds in chaos theory.[12] That is to say, it is a subjunctive conditional possibility contingent on the present argument that the physical world is counter-intuitively complex, and thus attempts to find a correspondence of language to such a reality will be proportionately complex. We need not require the premise that another universe's (multiverse) physics have to be brought in here to support the contention. Rees (1997, 1999) points out that some of the exotic conditions at the beginning of our universe are still embedded deep down in the microphysics of our universe, though macrophysical laws are contrary to them. If we have a general correlate of this in the physical world, then, again, a physicalistic model of correspondence between our language and the external world could be immensely unexpected and complex, not to say equivocal. For example, in this context what would we do with Wittgenstein's (1998: 187) point in the *Philosophical Investigations*: 'A description is a representation of a distribution in space (in that of time, for instance)'.[13] This echoes Wittgenstein's concern with pictures as projections in space in the *Tractatus*.

We may wish to eliminate the idea of picturing the *negation of a picture*, which he there envisaged. With a scientific cosmology in the third millennium, in which there are problems of possible anti-matter in this universe or an anti-matter universe, with dark matter as invisible obverse of our observed physical universe, with dipoles that can be unified into monopole particles, we will have to be critically susceptible to counter-intuition. It is too easy to apprehend the foregoing quotation from Wittgenstein's *Philosophical Investigations* as the song of a drowning ghost (the *Tractatus*). Rather, it may be someone swimming in infinity, having sensed how there/here language corresponds to the physical world.

In such a perspective, we can draw the conclusion that (in a way Wittgenstein did not develop, or reach, but was on the track of) the idea of a picture theory of reality sensitive to the identities of the physical world, if cosmology is introduced, becomes feasible. It would be enormously complex and counter-intuitive. This type of point of reference is better for theology than a rough and ready everyday impression of science for a theory of how language counter-intuitively corresponds to the world of divinity.

2 Simple-minded philosophy

Myths of simplicity

The notion of something's being extraordinarily, or even infinitely counter-intuitively, complex cuts against the main thrust of many traditional approaches to understanding. Science tends to be conceived in terms of its championing investment in simplicity. Theology has inclined to engage with the divine virtue of parsimony. Non-intellectual culture seems to vaunt itself as the straight-forwardness of common sense. There are many competing notions of and assumptions about what is simplicity. Accordingly, with unconsciousness irony, simplicity assumes the identity of complexity. Here confusion is often vaunted as clarity, and clarity is conflated with simplicity. Corporate global mass media mainly thrive on often-facile dumbing-down – fed by profit-driven recipes. Political counterfeits of simplicity disguise complex muddles to gain election. Simplifying misrepresentation foments cultural turbulence. Results of this use of simplicity to trash the rich and muddled multiple identities of the world are to engender false consciousness a virtue. In such a state of affairs it should be obvious that clarity is not as simple as it may seem.

Against these disparate claims for simplicity, this book argues that the deeper foundations of personal life and the universe are counter-intuitive, complex and at variance with various forms of simplicity. To conceive and launch such a feature of what might be termed 'counter-intuitive metaphysics' as a function of transcendent theology, one should address and assess the identity and source of its antithesis – simplicity. This regresses to William of Ockham. It is not good enough to exchange established, and often somewhat over-polished, recipes that often pass for the concept of Ockham's Razor. Its extensive use in the sciences and humanities requires that we address the matter in some detail. This involves a battle with the history subsequent to Ockham, which has sometimes distorted memories of his philosophy and theology.

A philosophical biography of simplicity

Contextualisation of cultural ideas is a prerequisite for identifying unstable properties of those ideas. Particularly is this the case when later retrospectives mirror the exploitation of an earlier original thinker. This facet of analysis also obliquely illustrates how the present author wishes to integrate the importance of historical contextualisation and discontinuity with the present, as a qualifying function of his presupposition that there are (often counter-intuitive) continuities associating different time zones of history. The history of Ockham's intellectual biography is a stimulating example of the appropriation of history as a function of the later assumptions.[1] Ockham is purported to have conceived a simplicity, which I argue he never successfully composed. A case of imperialising the past so as to sustain a mythology for empirical science: science is simple, just like God. Well God is not so simple, this book contends. Although we all labour before a dark mirror when looking at the past, it is worth attempting a portrait of Ockham for present purposes by explicitly engaging with the role of the past – and present – in one's interpretation of Ockham.

Arriving at Oxford in 1309, the Franciscan Ockham was eventually perceived by the Chancellor of the university and secular theologian, John Lutterel, to have fallen from grace. This was partly because Ockham did not accept this Chancellor's own Thomistic doctrines. Lutterel was fighting a rather lonely rearguard defence of Aquinas, since Ockham's philosophy was pre-occupying most of the English scholars in his subject.[2] Ockham had studied under the previous Oxford Chancellor, Henry Harclay (who died in 1317),[3] and he had embraced the latter's criticism of John Duns Scotus on universals. In about 1315 we find Peter Aureoli developing similar criticism. Ockham was not, then, the only dissenting original thinker in a burgeoning trend of new reflection, which was stimulated in part by the unexpected revival, and modification, of concepts of supposition (denotation) theory. Scotus's work acted as both a major focus for and an influence upon scholars at Oxford. He had reformulated aspects of recently past scholarship in ways that attracted Ockham's debt, often through disagreement.

God was central to Ockham's philosophy. He was a theologian who did philosophy with a penchant for a certain brand of logic. Although his researches in logic are detailed and widespread, they are not a formal system in our modern sense. Ockham was more explicitly interested in formal questions of logic than Aquinas, yet his instinct and understanding fall short of Aquinas'.

Ockham's fundamental principle for God and logic is simplicity. This is not a project about presentation. (It is easy to think him ironic about simplicity when we view the often-torturous complexities of his logic, though his writings betray no sense of whimsicality. In fact there seems to be a marked absence of any sense of humour or irony in his sensibility.) His simplicity has its ideal in 'God': the unity, the necessity. 'Ockham's Razor' is a label for the philosophical counterpart of God: a principle to reduce, or keep, entities to a minimum. Just as the theologian views polytheism as a corruption threatening monotheism, so Ockham's philosophy treated the multiplication of species as a corrosive infecting our perception of world-structure that mirrored God. Ockham's programme relies on the reduction of ontological categories to just two, substance and quality – though he has no systematic logic worked out for implementing such a scheme.

Ockham produced an extensive formal philosophy. Yet, rather like Bertrand Russell, he did not integrate his formal interests with his dialectical (for example. ethical) writings. This perspective is only slightly misleading, since Ockham's dialectically presented political philosophy only obliquely embodies some of his other philosophical concerns. But Ockham sometimes makes an explicit, albeit unexpected, connection between the dialectic of *obligations* and the logic in his *Summa Logica*. For example, his philosophical logic there deals with the concept of 'consequence' and impossibility in its varying paradoxical forms under this general heading.

From a perspective within our own current world, Ockham might be described as carrying out a thought experiment, and in this respect it is interesting to compare his undeveloped interest to that of our contemporary Roy Sorensen.[4] Stump (1989) illuminates the way Ockham connects the topics of 'obligations' and 'insolubles'. 'Insolubles' were forms of conundrums or paradoxes, and this linking of the two topics together was usual in Ockham's lifetime. He attempted to show how impossible propositions might not, in disputations, obviously entail a contradiction. This pulls against his reductionism in ways that are not acknowledged in his theses on simplicity.

As Spade shows,[5] Ockham permits self-reference in his logic. Ockham's technique, modifying Walter Burley's, is to submerge the collisions in premises concerning relevance to yield a possible world which satisfies typical conditions of possibility, yet produces a state of affairs that unexpectedly reconfigures subjunctive conditional boundaries. This is not unlike Lewis's (1986) wider pluralising of worlds, increasing entities, not reducing them. Gensler (1996) has recently shown how one might discover such interconnections more secure than Ockham's. Ockham did not develop his work on obligations theory within his political philosophy. Yet it seems clear that he was implicitly injecting the results of research into his political and ethical theory, in the way he combines canon law, logic and case-precedent technique, for example in his *III Dialogus* (Ockham, 2002).

Research on logic readily inclines a philosopher to give attention to the mental bedrock that facilitates the use of logic, and the perceptual spheres that are its media of operation. Although Ockham was committed to Aristotle's maxim that 'man is a rational animal', he believed that this truth is often submerged by other psychological and dispositional tendencies, and certainly his political philosophy (see below) indicates that this is true of humanity. Unfortunately, Ockham's own stress on the roles of the mind and universals provoked him too readily to internalise the grounds of knowing. A contemporary of Ockham's, Durandus of Saint-Pourçain, stressed the person who observes − the agent, rather than the object known − as the ground for knowledge. Ockham was so impressed with this approach that with the aid of divine intervention he supposed that one might have an intuitive cognition of a non-existent thing. But in usual circumstances, 'intuitive cognition' for Ockham marks the knowledge of a present singular individual with properties.

This situation is partially causal and conjoins with one's simultaneous abstractive cognition of the individual with properties. Abstractive cognition of this state of affairs lays the perceptual and propositional mental grounds for repeating, and thus extending, the process and cognitions to like individuals. Memory is partly composed from such cognitions, and when there is a temporal lapse after intuitive cognition, there remains an imperfect intuitive cognition permitting the observer to infer the truth of the relevant past tense proposition representing a given experience (see Marenbon, 1987, 186). These distinctions were the subject of extreme technical debate, bound into the science of the times. Adam Wodeham (see Tachau, 1988, ch. 10) was inclined to follow John Duns Scotus and dispute Aureoli's view that intuitive cognition is understanding by means of which the individual is either present *or* appears to be. Wodeham nevertheless learnt from Aureoli that it would be possible for a perception to satisfy the same truth conditions if an absent entity were simulated, and so, on Ockham's hypothesis, delude the observer by causing intuitive cognition. This is quite a different problem, Ockham thought, from having intuitive cognition by means of miracle. It is interesting to consider how the science and technology of a period affect philosophical theorising: would televised individuals have been a convenient presence for Wodeham with which to challenge Ockham?

Difficulty in defining Ockham's philosophy

Controversy and misrepresentation attended Ockham's philosophy in his own time and later. Philosophers of today display some qualified parallels with Ockham's relation to his, not always intended, deconstruction of elements in medieval philosophical traditions. His philosophy contributed to the medieval 'new modernism'; this is a designation Stephen Nicholls employed to characterise French medieval cultural contexts (see Nicholls *et al.*, 1991). One might extend the depiction of this 'new modernism' to Ockham, and to others, by describing it as a claim to return to the past while reinventing it as a new future for, and to dispute with, the present. Typical of this is Ockham's break with the medieval world in his treatment of logical and metaphysical relations. As with post-Enlightenment French romantic modernists, however, Ockham wished to look back to past archetypes (such as Aristotle) that he moulded in his own image for the future.

Central to the assessment of Ockham is the problem of measuring our own sounding boards. In the late nineteenth century and in the twentieth, what can be termed modernist logic[6] and its philosophy of language are often pre-supposed by philosophers, in differing ways and sometimes indirectly by contrast, as the correct or true frequencies for observing the quite different universe of Ockham. These modernist logic developments stem principally from the nineteenth-century work of Frege (see Frege 1953, 1969, 1977), though there have been many developments since his last publication written in 1923.[7] Conversely sometimes there is a romantic disposition to give the privileged status to Ockham's logic as if it should remain unchallenged by our analytical philosophy's research and logic. This priority has not entirely escaped the epoch-making study by Marilyn McCord Adams,[8] to which the reader is referred as the principal research resource on Ockham. For example, Adams judges 'Peter Geach [to be one] who writes from a Fregean bias' (Adams, 1987: 393 and n. 34). Geach criticised Ockham's two-name theory of predication.[9] Adams does not attempt to prove the basis for her curt, partisan dismissal of Geach and Frege. The problem here is not a matter of local in-house debate. It is a dispute about the identity of logic. That is to say, to what extent should a logician's work be judged by timeless, absolute standards? To what extent must it be seen in the context of its times?

Some fresh general considerations expressed here requires more research, not least since the generality and boldness of Ockham's theories lay claim to answers outside his, and sometimes our, logical ken. But as we now attempt to look back at him, a straight contrast between, say, twentieth-century philosophical logic and Ockham's medieval world obscures, fails to account for, explore or sufficiently query, complex interconnections and differences between Ockham's own philosophical prehistory and our contemporary philosophy (cf. Rorty, 1984). Assuming that there is such a thing as logical truth, however, or if we presuppose that humans have made some progress in understanding logic, it would be surprising to conclude that Ockham's position did not need revision or development after over 600 years.

For Ockham, the expression of language that is the soul-home of concepts and utterance is in the mind – the mental language (peculiarly like, but not quite identical to Latin) – as Paul Spade (1988) points out. In Ockham the strongest version of meaning is an internal utterance within the mind. This mental model is accordingly psychologistic, and it is reductionist. Is the concept of a mental language that is not itself the intention with which one speaks credible? Could Ockham's philosophy benefit from modern work that argues that all natural languages can be treated as manifestations of underlying neurophysiological genetic syntaxes or semantics? Even were there to be an affirmative answer to this question, do we yet possess the, or most of the, formal elements which would constitute understanding of the logical ingredients of such a map? Does the Latin of Ockham display relativity that is in tension against this purported universality? Is it proper to employ our modern formal logic 'languages' to symbolise (and thus to interpret) Ockham's philosophical language and logic? Our contemporary logics are highly formalised and explicit, with their symbolically refined artificial functions and operators. These logic languages are partially alien to Ockham's philosophical language. For example, as Spade remarked Frege's *Sinn* (sense) without distortion cannot translate Ockham's *significatio* (signification).[10] This is not because of untranslatability, however: it is owing to their competing theses: Frege's is semantic logic, whereas Ockham's is based on mental understanding. The medieval Latin he used, a hybrid of oral and written forms evolved into a sort of formal – often obscure – 'technical dialect', falls far short of the explicit and technical symbolism of our own logics. So an upshot of these questions is another one: when a medievalist paraphrases philosophical Latin employing our logics, can synonymy be preserved between the medieval ambiguity and our contemporary often-complex razor-sharp logic?

Geach has demonstrated how well Buridan initiated the resolution of problems in 'quantification into opaque contexts' that are still partly intractable in our current philosophical research (see Geach, 1980: 161–3, then 129–38, 148). One of these topics is intentional identity, i.e. only seeming to refer to a referent by use of a quasi-name with intentional verbs, as in: 'I believe that I am referring to a square-circle drawn on the ground.' Could this sort of intentional approach unexpectedly be utilised to map Ockham's own thesis that there is a 'mental' language to which he only intentionally refers? Is the mental language a non-existent intentional identity falsely invoked by a quasi-name and quasi-language? Is it a conceptual fiction? Ockham's supposition theory is itself so subject to equivocation that confusion over intentional verbs cannot be clarified. Ockham posits (in his actual Latin analytical language) his alleged mental language as a vehicle by which to override and secure his logic and reference. If his (linguistic) analytical language in Latin is itself an intentional medium of expression, then he cannot actually succeed in referring to his ideal mental language since it would be an intentional fictive object. On this account, Ockham's mental language and its two class domains function solely as a myth: a complex abstract object of his imagination.

Perhaps we should look synchronically at differences within our own contemporary philosophical traditions and controversies to gain a clearer sense of the diachronic problem for us of identifying Ockham's philosophy. Difficulties of paraphrasing Ockham into modern philosophy are *not* like problems in (in the required sense, and to the relevant degree) unexpectedly new developments of our analytical philosophy. For example Russell's basic logic has been developed in directions of which, one would judge, he did not or would not approve. A case in point is David Lewis (1986); he is rather like an Ockham in reverse. Where Ockham wanted to reduce ontological plurality, Lewis went forth and multiplied. His theory is that we can 'invent' ontologies by making counterpart universes for other space–times. The universes he reproduces are modelled from our own indexicals of location (here/there), person (you/me), time (now/then), etc. that mirror our own world. I believe that Russell would have thought this sort of subjunctive conditional philosophising to be like confusing 'fairy tales' with real-life ontology.[11] But we can derive Lewis's logic from Russell's (and thus choose to ignore the latter's lifelong neglect of modal logic), even though some ingenuity is required. Yet we cannot derive Whitehead and Russell (1910) from Ockham's logic. This sort of enterprise, generalised, indicates that Ockham cannot consistently, in this arena, be paraphrased into modern analytical philosophy without inventing a logic and philosophy.[12] In any case, what it is to be a criterion of logical possibility, as a basis for refining or transforming a concept, is obviously not the criterion to assess what Ockham thought. Beyond this issue is another one: if one classifies logic as a subset of scientific knowledge, then one is committed to admitting some type of invariance to allow for the increasing explanatory power of theory. But this presupposes a questionable

form of individuation in the philosophy of history, and of originality. Can we
properly offer an intellectual biography of Ockham that in some way does not
consider non-scientific creative originality in Ockham's philosophy?[13] We may
wish to direct such queries to the ethical and political domains of Ockham. Yet
the interplay of logic as a discovery procedure for inference, and creative intuition, requires more attention in research, though it would take us too far to
investigate this axis for tracing Ockham's consciousness in his compositions.[14]

Impinging on attempts to access Ockham for us in our world-views is the
issue of the status of extending a concept beyond its framed origin. Using a
'function' to formulate predicate and quantifier logic (as Russell did, following
Frege, 1953) has revolutionised the identity of inferences involving generalisation. We should not underestimate the scope of this revolution, though
problems remain (see Smiley, 1982). The logical powers of the predicate calculus also enable sentence-forming operators ('and', 'or', 'if', etc.) and quantifiers
('some', 'all', 'the', 'few', 'scarcely') to be defined using logical predicates. This
calculus has many other transforming roles, which contrast with Ockham's
doctrine of terms.

These issues compound the fundamental problem of what it is for a modern
logical concept to be 'contained in Ockham's general premises'. Can there be a
relation of inference between Ockham's philosophy of logic and the achievements in logic research over 600 years later? When we consider our contemporary philosophical defence and criticism of Ockham, do they embody merely
the sort of narrow-mindedness Russell might have displayed towards Lewis, and
did show Ockham?[15] Consideration of such questions will contribute to our
assessing Ockham's modernity, limitations and potential more clearly, while
guarding against charges of anachronism or overestimation.

Ockham and reference

Names are fundamental for Ockham. Adams mentions that Ockham adopts the
traditional distinction (see Adams, 1987: 71), inspired by Aristotle's *On Interpretation*, that there are three kinds of names: spoken, written and mental.[16] Ockham
uses the word for 'name' that he employs to classify a subject *and* a predicate.
Yet they are functionally different. For Ockham, the proposition 'the *Titanic* is
wrecked' is composed of two names: one for the subject 'the *Titanic*'; and the
same 'name' for the quite differently functioning predicate 'wrecked'. Logic
should preserve differences of use in language; Ockham's naming strategy
destroys it: the subject and the predicate in the above proposition are actually
asymmetric in use. 'The *Titanic*' refers to an object. The predicate 'is wrecked' is
a state of affairs that is true *of* its subject (if or when true). Once wrecked, the
Titanic has the continentally necessary property of 'is wrecked'. This predicate is
a self-inhering term, though before striking the iceberg it was not even a property of the *Titanic*. The notion of identity is bound into 'the *Titanic*' in a way in
which it is not in 'is wrecked'. And using 'name' for both parts of the proposition 'The *Titanic* is wrecked' does not preserve that.

If, before the *Titanic* sank, someone called out and named: 'the *Titanic*!' it could logically yield the question: 'where?' and the answer: 'There!' But if someone called out: 'is wrecked', at most this peculiar response would attract the question: 'what is?' This latter question advertises the problem: with a predicate one does not know the identity of the thing of which the predicate is true (or false, as the case may be). Contrariwise, with the subject 'the *Titanic*', the identity of the subject referred to *is the* self-contained sense that is the use of the term.[17] This difference is fundamental in oral, written and the mental language accessible for us to test. Therefore it is basic to knowledge of Ockham's use of names to appreciate that his theory about 'name' is contradicted by the foregoing argument. His explanation does not work for linguistic use, and if a language were constructed according to his rules, we could not communicate when using a large portion of it (witness, 'I name this ship "is wrecked"').

Although he regarded Aristotle as his general inspiration, Ockham's application of names to propositions is quite contrary to Aristotle's concept of the asymmetry of subject and predicate in *On Interpretation*, as Geach (1980: 290–1)[18] observes. In claiming to retrieve Aristotle's teaching Ockham followed medieval contemporary tradition, which reinterpreted some aspects of Aristotle's later doctrine of terms. Ockham uses 'name' to represent two allegedly identical mental universals, which constitute a proposition: the subject and the predicate. These are often translated nowadays into the letter-names: 'N' and 'P'. For Ockham, there is here no naming difference between a subject and a predicate. But in the above work by Aristotle, the subject and predicate are asymmetrical in functions, even though in the *Prior Analytics* Aristotle later dropped the scheme in favour of a doctrine of terms. (Although Plato's *Sophist* was not available to Ockham, it is worth noting that those elements of Aristotle's asymmetry conception parallel distinctions in the *Sophist*, though for Plato the verb is classified in relation to its extension, whereas for Aristotle it is as a function in a statement. It is true that the distinction between name and predicate (or verb) in Aristotle is not as explicitly and exclusively defined as it is in our contemporary logic; but the central ingredients are there.) Now one would therefore think that Ockham was, in principle, in a position to choose to adopt the distinction of the functional asymmetry identities of logical subject and predicate, especially with his devotion to Aristotle. Yet he did not. Did it dawn on him that this asymmetry was in Aristotle, citing as he did from the same work in which this doctrine appears? It might be replied that since the doctrine of terms appears later in Aristotle, it is not surprising that Ockham, in any case, chose this instead of the concept of asymmetry between logical subject and predicate. Even so, for those who wish to 'modernise' Ockham's logic, or paraphrase it into our logics, Ockham's not choosing Aristotle's asymmetry distinction, fundamental to most modern logics, requires a judgement against Ockham's instinct. He did not here detect the deeper foundations of logic, as they have been developed long after Aristotle's, and then subsequent to his, lifetime.

For Frege, for Russell, and for most analytical philosophers, the predicate has no reference of its own because it is incomplete. It is like a function. On this interpretation, a predicate has to be linked to a logical name which refers. By the mediation of the logical subject the predicate is attached to the name that refers, and is thereby true (or false) of the name's referent; it has an ascriptive function so as to make its link with the referent. There are issues to be addressed in these areas, such as the need to concentrate on the role of quantified general terms, rather than Russell's own views of 'definite descriptions', and the effect it has had on interpretation of the predicate calculus. But, after all this is assessed, the difference between the enormous capabilities of the predicate calculus, as against the two-name theory with its supposition doctrine, is like contrasting alchemy with nuclear physics with regard to the transformation of metals.

Ockham had absorbed the common doctrine of terms (in which a proposition is made up of names). The enormous grip that this doctrine, together with supposition theory, had on Ockham, and much of the medieval world, is hardly to be explained by this, less than ideal, at points implausible, interpretation of Aristotle and its amalgam of supposition. Why did Ockham adopt this position? One answer, apart from it being a trend at the time, is that a doctrine of terms, or names, enables one to play more freely with imaginative possibility. A reason for this is that the doctrine of terms helps one evade the features of the actual relations required by language to represent the external world, while pretending a logical guarantee of true meaning. In other words, it is a covert theory of equivocation that subverts the relations between semantics, ontology and mental understanding.

Ockham's two-name theory is undermined by two other considerations that reflect thinking by Dummett (1991: 234, 294). The target of the two concepts is the relation of a predicate to the mental realm, as they go proxy for parts of the external world. Dummett's research has explored some hitherto ill-defined areas of reference. First, if predicates were to have the sort of name-reference Ockham ascribes to them and their mental and ontological counterparts, then to what does this commit Ockham? We would have to admit quantification over the *referents* of these predicates.[19] Ockham opposed Aquinas' view that 'matter, already understood under corporeality and dimensions, can be understood as distinct in different parts'.[20] For Ockham, the referents would need to be the indivisible essence or 'substance' that is prior to quantification. But second, even if quantification over predicate-referents were compatible with Ockham's philosophy, then this would commit him to an impossible position. That is to say, if we presuppose with Ockham that predicates refer as his subjects do – they cannot refer to a complete entity. For if a predicate refers, then its *referent* would have to be *incomplete*. That is to say 'is wrecked' is a semantic mirror of its ontology: there is no subject *in it* by which to refer to pick out this ontological subject. This is exactly the opposite of what Ockham needs. He requires a nominal universal in the mental realm to be referred to, which would have to be complete. Ockham could hardly allow an incomplete entity referred to by supposition. Ockham's theory of naming is rather like one's pointing to a shipwreck in thick fog, or down through deep water; the 'name' does not locate its own object, and it locates a wrong position because it has no knowledge of the effect of refraction on perception.

The conflation of subjects with predicates, we have seen above, is triggered by Ockham's use of a 'name' category for subject and for predicate. Ockham absorbed the common doctrine of terms. He and Walter Burley, with some differences, embraced the theory of supposition, which had been strangely restored from near-oblivion. Yet Aquinas, before Ockham, employed applicative quantifiers such as 'some', 'every', 'only' to explain that a predicate does not itself refer but it indicates a nature.[21]

Ockham attempted to avoid the problem, created through his failure to recognise the asymmetry of subject and predicate, by looking to his idea of mental language. Ockham viewed mental language as a phenomenon that mediated us directly to the world it represents. Shortcomings when trying to implement his two-name theory in oral and written language provoked him to download the elusive mental language.[22] How did Ockham suppose that the theory of supposition, linked to naming, connects with the mind? He supplied the connection through a theory of signification. An important study by Spade exposes aspects of the relation. Spade cites Buridan and Augustine to indicate concepts of signification, which were influential in Ockham's time (1975: 215). According to them, signification establishes the understanding of a thing, and that signs are causal lexemes that produce mental effects beyond the impression the thing makes on the senses. As Spade notes (1975: 218), the stress on mentality reflects, minus the sense-impression element, Aristotle's *On Interpretation* (I, 16a3f): 'Spoken words are the symbols of mental experience.' Stated very roughly, the later medieval trend is to treat supposition theory as a semantic hypothesis (proposing connections between a term's referring and its referent). In contrast, signification is an epistemological theory, concerned with understanding. The conjunction of these two approaches targets the conditions for knowing and learning in the medium of language. Ockham claimed to have direct knowledge of individuals. A term deployed in simple supposition in this perspective goes proxy for the concept to which it is subject. As Spade (1975: 222) explains, by contrast, Burley's view is that terms stand in simple supposition for what they signify. This involves a social view of language as a tool to communicate with others. Ockham proposed, in other contexts,[23] that there is a triangular relation in some acts of assent between mental language, spoken language and the referent. In these contexts he argued that the consequence of such a relation is that a person may know something that is the product of it (for example, that one entity is not another). Yet (to express it in a way Ockham does not) the person may not possess the recognitional capacity for having a concept of that concept. Ockham's main emphasis is on the grounds of a person's own knowledge, not social interaction, and on the causal efficacy of signification for mental states, together with the denial of natures.

From various twentieth-century philosophical standpoints, Ockham's causal theory of understanding is not well grounded in its own or our terms. Two of our contemporary views on the philosophy of mind are: first, that of the theory-theorists,[24] i.e. those who maintain that to speak of the mind at all we have (at least implicitly) to have a theory of it. The second view is that position held by the simulationists, i.e. those disposed to argue that we have no adequate theory of the mental.[25] In any case we simulate the mental states of others in our mental activity without presupposing a theory. Both could be partially integrated by utilising the function of 'implicit' in the theory-theory view. This could mark an innate mental capacity tantamount to a theory, along the lines of Fodor (1992), which is partially activated by a simulationist model. Each of these approaches is concerned with the role of collective social learning in the way Ockham was not, and as such they complement Burley's attitude.[26] As the simulationist Heal (1996) points out, justification or epistemic status is a holistic notion, and the notion of relevance is extraordinarily complex and undetermined. These points count against Ockham's signification. His signification is a semantics that naively causes mental language effects – or, more precisely, mental states (thoughts, etc.) cause linguistic (spoken, written) signification. Ockham had no grasp of the instantiation of relevance theory, complexity theory or simulation of others' states.

In relation to these issues, we now have fairly firm grounds for accepting the instability of linguistic signs, and their frequent indeterminacy relating to mental and oral uses. (This breakthrough was originally occasioned by Saussure's 1971 research into written Latin, discussed by Starobinski (1971); and work by Jakobson (1873, as well as Anscombe's (1957, 1981) rather different study on intention and mental causality in the contexts of their expression.) We also have Anscombe's (1975) study on the difficulties of classing the first person pronoun (in agreement with Kant). To this one can add, for example, Chomsky's more recent theories on indeterminacy in mind and orality in relation to the abstract identities of concrete entities. As Chomsky (1995: 21) remarks, 'the abstract character of London is crucial to its individuation'. These have generally been taken to fracture and dismantle the almost mechanistic symmetry that the Ockham scenario presupposes between spoken, written and mental terms. Even if there are criteria of identity appropriate to each, it does not follow that for each there is a fixed content to the criterion of identity, as Wittgenstein (1998: 20–110) suggested Moses' identity might be fixed in varying ways. One cannot sustain the view that there is a mapping criterion for which there is an equivalence of the relevant sort between Ockham's supposition in respect of spoken, written and mental terms. Ockham had a naive realist view about the way in which terms fix to referents.

Adams speaks of Ockham's view that the division between personal, material and simple supposition applies equally to spoken, written and mental terms.[27] This has been criticised by Spade (1988: xiii). He judged that it follows from Ockham's way of relating concept, thought, personal supposition and signification, that, with mental terms that may have personal or material supposition, we do not always know what we are asserting. Adams who supposes that has countered Spade's view states:

[T]he issue is not really whether or not one of our thoughts could be about something (in the sense of a term's standing for some particular) without our knowing it. Ockham allows that when I think 'Every man is an animal', the term 'man' supposits for lots of things without my knowing that it does, since I have no awareness of those particular men. Rather the question is whether on the above proposal anything would make it the case that the term was suppositing for these rather than those.

(Adams, 1987: 351, n. 104)

It is wrong to argue here that 'the term "man" supposits for lots of things without my knowing that it does, since I have no awareness of those particular men'. If a person knows the meaning of the term 'men', that person will know from experience and cognition that it is true or false that there are men. So at the very least, for those terms for which that person holds concepts which supposit in the singular and have (even conjecturally) more than one referent, it is not possible that 'the term "man" supposits for lots of things without [that person] knowing that it does.' This advertises the problem that, in Ockham, equivocation and ignorance are functions of his failure not to possess a viable theory of reference in his signification, but also of his system's inability to explain the complex presence and scope of relevance. His system does not explain introspection of pertinent contents in one's own consciousness. The presence of equivocation in Ockham's supposition and signification is mask for his failure to explain mental choice and the invasive role of complex relevance conditions in holding, knowing, as well as using concepts. A suppressed general premise behind Ockham's positions here is his misconception that if one conjoins the functioning mind to the world, then it will 'read off' the true interpretation of both regarding terms. Consequently, his need for equivocating between supposition and signification is hardly surprising in view of his principle of parsimony.

In practice, however, Ockham's procedure is sometimes the negation of simplicity, since he approaches a simple situation by multiplying entities. He invents mental classes to which the signifiers supposedly refer; people using language seem strangely unaware that these classes exist, however. Although someone might wish to notice here that Quine[28] appeals to Ockham's principle of parsimony for the mental realm, it is actually to dispose of precisely the dualism that Ockham championed, and Quine's move has the effect of blocking Ockham's argument for supposition, when he stated:

[I]t becomes a flagrant breach of . . . Ockham's maxim of parsimony to admit mind as a second substance at all . . . Better to drop the duplication and just recognise mental activity as part of the activity of the body.

In short, unusually for Quine, Quine's use is a sort of context-free employment of Ockham's Razor that does not comply with, and contradicts, the original contexts of Ockham's own (variant) uses of the principle of parsimony.

Accordingly this entrenched decontextualised usage of Ockham's Razor, even in philosophy, is one of the principal reasons for the present discussion. In this regard we should notice Herbert Simon's (2001: 35) disassociation of simplicity from parsimony when he plausibly maintains that in scientists' use of 'simplicity', thus-tagged, activities should be labelled as parsimony since parsimony 'is the ratio of the complexity of the data set to the complexity of the formula'.

For Ockham, 'Socrates is a man' is an instance of a categorical proposition. But Ockham has no general account of what it is to be a proposition. Following Ockham, Marilyn Adams paraphrases this sort of proposition as: 'N is P if and only if N has P-ness or P-ness inheres in N'.[29] This contravenes Ockham's Razor, since it multiplies entities for 'N is P' (and the technique requires increasingly complex *ad hoc* devices). The paraphrase mediates on behalf of 'N is P', intervening allegedly to make explicit the mental-language contract with the simple statement. This is at the centre of the two-class theory. In Ockham's two-name theory 'man' is a mental sign, a nominal or conceptualist-nominalist supposition that inheres not only in Socrates but also in other male humans. So, in the term 'man' employed of Socrates, it also 'denotes' all humans.

Aquinas would have had none of this,[30] since he did not allow that a general term, such as 'nature', had direct reference, for it is true of individuals – ascribed, not referring to an identity. The appeal to 'P-ness' invents a class that is not derivable from P, without the addition of a new entity: abstractions of the mind. Since 'Socrates' is symmetric in logical form to 'man' (in 'N is Socrates'), we should be able to redistribute its 'Socrates-ness' over other men. Obviously Ockham wanted to construe 'Socrates' as a uniquely suppositing term, with 'is a man' differently represented as a class name term. Yet he classifies them as names, which Adams formalises identically. So here their representation in logic is uniform. But their interpretation as to function is distinct; that is inconsistent. We should here insist on that to which Ockham commits himself. Symmetry of syntactic normalisation (the predicate has a unitary symbol, 'P', as has the subject) is the identity of its entities. No doubt we will be told Ockham did not intend this by his depicting the predicate-name as a complete entity. Quite so; but that is the problem: intentionality. Intentions do not rule words.

Resurrected Ockham

Can the two-name theory of Ockham be salvaged? It appears not. But imagine Ockham reading the foregoing with the foresight of (and disagreements in) our contemporary analytical philosophy. Were such an Ockham to have been available now, he might respond:

> I see the explanatory power of a logical singular term that presupposes a criterion of identity. It strikes a fundamental distinction with the logical predicate that I did not understand; and I admit that it is more accurate to represent the predicate as a function, asymmetric in role to the logical subject. Despite these concessions, it seems that their scopes have been

overstated. Your predicate calculus is correct, and my formalism crude, and I consider that supposition might be replaced with the following strategy, which I think achieves the same results. I restore something parallel with my two-name theory as follows, using your philosophical logic.

I want to disturb your confidence by exposing some weaknesses in twentieth-century analytical philosophy and logic, to make space for my own use of your distinctions. First, Frege used the analogy of a logical name to craft part of his concept of a logical predicate. And I understand that this analogy collapsed in a messy way (see Dummett, 1981). I can reconstruct my two names by taking the analogy, though I am unclear whether or not I was incorrect in degree or type to use the 'term' name of the predicate. Second, your contemporary philosophers when pushed have some difficulty making *definitively* explicit what they mean by 'referring'. There is the 'point-ing' origin of the word for 'reference' (German *Bedeutung*) in Frege.[31] Many twentieth-century philosophers sympathetic to Frege do not seem able pre-cisely to inform me what 'referring' semantically is, except to say that it is what a singular term does: it picks out a single referent, by acting to im-plement one of the subject's criteria of identity. Well, I wish to come back to this concession of ignorance. Why can this singular ability be achieved *only* by your logical *name*? I agree that my use of 'name' was itself foggy, but I was aiming at a label for a particular, not the narrower sense later ascribed to me. I am willing to drop, for my predicates, what you term 'referring', and Geach's analyses have convinced me that supposition theory is best eliminated completely, including from logically proper names. But I would like to conclude, with Recanati (1993: 401), that the differences between indexicals and proper names are largely pragmatic.

Now here is my original move. You have developed logic of indexicals: ('here', 'there', 'me', 'you', 'past', 'present' (David Lewis builds a whole uni-verse from them)). But I understand that you have a problem with the first person pronoun 'I'. Logicians often deem that the first-person 'I' can be replaced by the person's proper name. But of course that will not do, it fails some truth-conditions, including the third-person proper name contexts when you substitute it with a proper name. And if Kant and Anscombe (1975) are right to affirm that 'I' does not refer, we have an indexical par-ticular. It is more like a unique (categorial) predicate. It picks out a person in a particular context. Now why may I not generalise this over large sets of indexicals? I can paraphrase my predicate-name scheme into an indexical programme. If I may borrow an expression from Heal, this procedure can be called 'indexical predication'.[32] I appreciate that this leads to complex semantic analysis, and a proposal to analyse propositions according to a deep structure, which I cannot describe within my own terms. But for any abstract form such as 'the property of whiteness' there is a paraphrase back to the surface form, e.g. 'The donkey is white'.[33] So a two-name theory can be replaced with something that is almost parallel, yet it satisfies the notion of asymmetry between the subject and predicate.

Although we had no refined quantifier logic in the medieval world that treated quantifiers as predicates in the manner of Frege, I see no reason why indexical predication cannot be extended to general terms and variables. As for the mental language, I shall have to exchange it for the Fregean metalanguage according to which object languages are its manifestation. All this does not augur well for my principle of parsimony, but I may have to resort to the larger questions of cosmology to re-state it.

It would be invidious to reply at length to this revival of Ockham's exhumed and transformed philosophy. Even if one were to grant all his other modifications, one has to object that he is not able to tackle the central, and fatal, fault, namely that predicates are not proper names. For example, it is now proved by Denyer's (1998) argument that, at the very most (and perhaps not even that) *only* verbs and logical predicates which are intransitive, could be names. I refer readers to the foregoing study. A language without transitive verbs may suit some purpose, but it is not one for humans.

This may in fact indicate that if Ockham was on the track of anything, he may have left a trace of an investigation appropriate to depict a language of artificial intelligence, which cannot benefit from absorption by learning or translation of human language using transitive verbs. As such, one may seriously suggest that his logic, if it has a use, would be a device to map some features of the consciousness of a lower mammal. So his logic is unexpectedly reductionist. Consequently, Ockham's Razor, when historically situated in its contexts, is not a suitable model of human or divine simplicity, except for those strange contexts, perhaps typically those of false consciousness induced by, for example, certain dumbing-down forms of mass media in which humans are reduced in their operational capacities.

Ockham's Razors

We are now in a position to consider the complicated issue of what has, with some optimistic singularity, been designated as 'Ockham's Razor'. But the real-life Ockham was quite a different entity. When Ockham was a young man, his fellow Franciscan Roger Bacon (1220–92) had only recently died. Ockham's Razor (as his principle of parsimony was later to be termed) is to some degree a reaction against Bacon's theory of the multiplication of species. Bacon broke with other perspectivists (though their influence was less pervasive than Aristotle's theory of knowledge)[34] to argue that, for example, light multiplies in time, though this thesis was not, in his view, a matter of observation (see Tachau, 1988: 16–26).

Bacon's notion of multiplication of entities has some concurrence in a modern logician such as Arthur Prior, with Prior's counter-maxim: *Entia non sunt subtrahenda praeter necessitatem*: Entities should not be subtracted unless it is necessary (see Prior, 1976: 31). Later in Bacon's career (*On Signs*, 1267, and his final work, the *Compendium of Theology*, 1292), he began to restore and re-state aspects of the confused doctrines of *supposition*, while intending to remove some of its confusions, rejecting the notion of univocal supposition. It was left to the young Ockham to mull over the relation of his aversion to Bacon's multiplication sum, and his attraction to Bacon's late change of heart on supposition.

Ockham was averse to Platonism, and conceived Aristotle as a champion of this dislike. Everything in the world was singular, and there was no principle of individuation. Real universals do not exist. Ockham believed that the grammar of propositions might bewitch us into thinking that their complexity mirrored structures in the world, but below this semantic surface the universe's ontology has a proclivity for singularity, and so does our mental structure. He was convinced that we must therefore reduce the number of entities appropriate to these circumstances. Semantic expressions can be universal, as can mental concepts. Ockham's synthesis of these hypotheses comprised an original, not to say problematic, equation of semantics and ontology, not least when Ockham conferred his unexpected gaze on a similar tradition or the fragmentarily parallel views of his peers. In practice 'the' parsimonious Razor, which is the emblem of the perceived influence of Ockham, is often applied piecemeal, and episodically, by his successors, which in effect falsifies it as a universal principle. There was also contemporary opposition from writers such as Walter Chatton (2002), who asserted a rule contravening Ockham's: 'If three things are not sufficient to verify an affirmative proposition about things, a fourth must be added, and so on.'[35]

Ockham's Razor simplifies the quite various attempts by Ockham to formulate a principle of parsimony. This state of affairs could be evidence that Ockham did not succeed in specifying the vaunted singular Razor. The popularising aphorism, 'do not multiply entities beyond necessity', does not occur in Ockham. It arises from a number of sources, mediated, for example, by the editor John Ponce of Cork, in a 1639 note added to Duns Scotus.[36] This aphorism is usually taken to echo the spirit of Ockham's ontology, however. In the form just presented, one might be excused for giving it short shrift, by remarking that the only entity that exists by necessity is God, so according to this maxim nothing else exists. Therefore is it not false? But the Razor is resonant with Aristotle's maxim, according to which a single means, rather than nature and transcendent power, favour plurality.[37] In this form Aristotle has no use for 'necessity', though his 'plurality' is akin to one of Ockham's versions: 'Plurality is not to be assumed without necessity.'[38] Quite what 'necessity' has supposedly to entail according to Ockham is not, by him, definitively or consistently specified, though he does seem aware of some of the variety of different modal necessities.

Perhaps, intuitively sensitive to some counter-intuitive modal complexities, Ockham in some contexts excises 'necessity' and, for example, introduces us instead to: 'No plurality is to be assumed except it be proved by reason, experience or infallible authority.'[39] Ockham's Razor's use of 'proved by experience' conflates practical reason with logical theory (as a logical axiom). In the required sense, logical necessity is not derivable from experience. It is a category-error for one to take in this type of rule, 'experience' as a criterion for logical uses of 'plurality' (elsewhere in Ockham guaranteed by 'necessity').

Possibly such blemishes kept Ockham on the move (consciously or otherwise) to attempt other formulae to meet his taste for restricting plurality, or possibly they reflect his confusion, despite his central logical motivation, i.e. his wish to follow a law of non-contradiction. Ockham does not prove his principle of parsimony. This inclination is compatible with an anti-realist position and with the admission of truth-conditions for a minimal set of statements, which serve as the core for a theory of meaning (see Dummett, 1977; and also Gunson, 1998: 19–51). But there is a problem with this approach and the various forms of Ockham's principle of parsimony. As Wright (1980) argues in the context of late twentieth-century anti-realist versus realist debates, there is no way anyone could possibly arrive at a conception of what it is for a verification-transcendent state of affairs to be true as a result of training in the use of language. Ockham did not leave us with one principle. The plural occurrence of his parsimony (bearing in mind that Simon (2001) shows a difference between parsimony and simplicity) itself reduces to a contradiction of the principle. And even if we allow this to pass by, it follows that we have no consistent criterion by which to identify the form or test the purported existence of the Razor, and so on.

Marilyn Adams claims that the principles Ockham states as versions of the Razor are 'in the first instance, methodological principles, and it is not obvious how they are related to truth or probability' (Adams, 1987: 157). It is not formally evident what a 'methodological principle' is here. Anyway many cases of Ockham's use of philosophical or logical terms in his formulations of the principle might be drawn upon to illustrate that Ockham is not, in the first instance, expressing what would normally be considered to be methodological principles. Let us consider the foregoing employment of 'assumed without necessity' in the form (also quoted by Adams): 'plurality is not to be assumed without necessity'. This version seems to presuppose the negation of Adams's view, since its terms are those employed in Ockham's discussion of logic to express logic, in the first instance, not those of method or the logic of method. There are problems in mapping Razor terminology on to our modern logics. For example, 'assumed without necessity' is rooted in the term for 'possibility', in its use here. Generally in medieval uses it has something to do with modally positing (what we would term) a propositional function, while it does not fully comply with this latter type of modern usage.[40] If one were to attempt an equation of it with terms in the extant versions of our predicate calculus, it tends towards a premise, while also partially contributing a function independently of that, of sharing a property of a presupposition, together with a weakened sense of the 'assertion' sign.[41] In other words, there is a breakdown in an attempt to fit it uniformly and broadly, or narrowly, into the concepts attending our standard logical terminology. Nevertheless, this version of Ockham's Razor is no mere 'methodological principle', since it displaces space in logic otherwise occupied by different axioms and makes claims on the domain of logic and its putative ontology. If we draw on the traditions of *ponendi* on which Ockham rests, and then attempt a partial alignment with our logics, we meet a complex hybrid of assumption, premise, assertion and presupposition, bound into the conditional negation of 'necessity', generalisation ('plurality'), and axiom, applied with some confusion extensionally to ontology. It is thus apparent that Ockham is talking big potatoes for logic, not the small potatoes of methodological principles. He is proposing logic for ontology, not devising methodological principles, and is asserting reductionist logic rules of quantification, not methodological principles.

One of the difficulties in aligning Ockham's use of 'assumption' and other logical terms, including those in his Razor versions, is that in typical cases he accepts generalised logical laws, while he deems that they have exceptions in theology (for example, in his view of the Trinity). His belief was that arguments of given general logical forms of syllogism are universally valid when applied to all matters in the world. The same logical forms are invalid, however, if applied to the Trinity, or need to be so interpreted through a nominalist or conceptualist supposition theory that they cannot 'properly' be so applied. As Geach[42] makes clear, Ockham was confused about the relation of inference to ontology, and muddled about logical relations between first and second intention terms in logic. I leave aside here, as far as is practicable, other issues of 'nominalism' and doctrine, so as to isolate difficulties in his philosophy of logic. These exceptions are also ones often anticipated and rejected by, for example, Aquinas. So it is not self-evident that Ockham theologically needed to contravene the scope of logical laws, while it is clear that he held such collisions of his interpretations between logic and theology as a matter of sincere conviction. Consequently a reader of Ockham has to face a problem in Ockham's examination of the Trinity. Where one might hope for a resolution of tension in the use of assumption and Razor, there at the centre of the theological conception most important to him, Ockham admits that he has exceptions to logic.

Unfortunately this is not a deployment of methodological principle. Clearly it is a contradictory exception involving accepting true premises that imply false conclusions, which therefore disprove his inferences, the Razor rule, or his theological interpretation. This follows from Ockham's own rule of non-contradiction. It was an embarrassment to Ockham that Chatton employed the law of non-contradiction to demonstrate the (alleged) truth of the anti-Razor by considering the multiple components that constitute causal relations in an action (for example, wood burning) (see Maurer, 1984: 469f.). Ockham attempts to head off a possible accusation of heresy by limiting the scope of his logic and introducing a nominal or conceptualist interpretation of abstract nouns into incarnation theology. So at this juncture he opts for semantic speculation to warrant rigging his logic, which is itself a violation of his 'necessity' and adoption of a law of non-contradiction.

Ockham's attempted justification of his failure to apply the Razor in some doctrinal contexts appears in his extended version of the Razor: 'No plurality is to be assumed unless it can be proved by some infallible authority', in which, in addition to his appeal to Scripture, he adds: 'certain sayings of the saints and the determinations of the Church'.[43] As Adams acknowledges: 'Ockham always allows the claims of reason and experience to be defeated by contrary pro-nouncements of the Church, which should lead 'every thought captive'.[44] But Ockham does not feel obliged to take the further step of embracing the fully general theory of which such ecclesiastical determinations are instances. Although he prizes generality as a desirable feature in theories, he is more com-mitted to the maxim: a theory-maker should not multiply miracles, i.e. theses contrary to reason and experience, beyond necessity.[45] There are deep fractures in these viewpoints. First, there is no logical or philosophical necessity at all to accept pronouncements of an institution, especially if they are contrary to reason.

Second, there is a suppressed contrariety in his employment of the foregoing quotation 'every thought captive'. Ockham himself distinguishes between the authority of Scripture, which is infallible, and the authority of the Church that can on occasions – according to him – be wrong. But the quotation about 'every thought captive' comes from the New Testament (2 Corinthians 10: 5; cf. Eph-esians 4: 8, and Deuteronomy 21: 10), not from the Church's pronouncements (which are clearly distinct from the New Testament in this context, on his own interpretation). It is wrong, then, on Ockham's own terms, to use this quotation form as infallible authority, to underwrite the authority of an external institu-tion, which, he agrees, can be wrong in its judgements. Ockham deployed that guarantee to prevent allowing his Razor its full generality.

It is tragic, in the perspective of the medieval contemporary opposition to Ockham, to observe this internal inconsistency in Ockham's philosophy. A sincere believer is painfully doing what he takes to be his best, as he sees it, to pacify antagonistic inconsistent Church authorities by attempting artificially to manufacture agreement with them, when neither logic nor his Razor demands it. Clearly we should position all this with problems any thinker has when living in a quasi-totalitarian regime in which the threat against life is not uncommon, as a device for achieving conformity in belief. In contrast, Ockham's campaign, in the last 20 years of his life, to convict the Pope of heresy manifests a certain resilience and independence of mind.

We stand outside the limitations of Ockham's own life situation (but, as he would have done, have difficulty in standing outside our own) and are aware of the influence of our own times on our comprehension of Ockham. Nevertheless, could we attempt some damage-limitation or reconstruction of the fragments of Ockham's philosophy criticised above? First, he could have dropped his nomi-nalist analysis and reinterpretation of the Trinity. Second, one might argue irrespective of his *presentation* of the Razor's exceptions, that Ockham should accept (what we would now term) deviant logics as having equal status to the bivalent one, and allow him subjunctive conditional certainty in a plural world. This of course would not leave him happy, since it would entail that his options are only possibly true. Third, someone could designate the Trinitarian doctrine itself as incorrect, and so the false conclusions thereby implied by the true antecedents simply identify a route on which Ockham did not continue (or of which he was not aware). This issue might be expressed as follows: in the foregoing discussion we have seen that Ockham used the Bible to develop some of his positions (as he did more extensively in his political philosophy, as the section below shows). Almost none of the defining terms of the Trinity occur in the Bible (nor do synonyms of them). So Ockham could have redefined the incarnation so as to avoid the troublesome terms that he judged require a restriction in the scope of his logic. Unfortunately, incarnation terminology in the Bible is not nominalist-conceptualist, and the propositions there do not fit the two-name theory.

Fourth, one might utilise Alfieri's (1989) research, and propose that a post-structuralist estimation of Ockham's Razor removes the need for the type of logical consistency that Ockham sought in formal theory. Fifth, one could transform hints in Ockham, and argue that his unconscious is ahead of his formal consciousness. Maybe the solution to his formal logic problems is to dump his formal programme, and accept that, underneath his apparently logical inferences, at the cross-roads the collision occurs between inference using the Razor and the incarnation. The answer to some of Ockham's problems could be to metaphorise, as a 'game', areas of his whole logic. Although of course Wittgenstein did not suggest this type of enterprise,[46] it might be envisaged as a possible upshot of his analyses of what it is to 'follow a rule' in his *Philosophical Investigations*.[47] Of course, this is revolutionary even by our contemporary standards. Sixth, an Ockhamist could attempt to circumvent the foregoing and other criticisms by adopting the sort of paraconsistent logic that Priest (1995)[48] devised, fragments of which occupied some medieval logicians. In a paraconsistent scenario, there are limits to cognition (in Ockham's case the Trinity), and there are semantic closures smaller than the set of all propositions, yet which facilitate access to transcendence in part using set-theoretic reductionism. Roughly speaking, the paraconsistent approach has the drawback that it requires propositions to be true and false. This would help support Ockham's treatment of the Trinity, while eliminating his law of non-contradiction. A reason for mentioning some of these ideas is to indicate that, taken together, Ockham's philosophy of logic and his philosophy amount to a partial hybrid of competing logics.

But brute forms of Ockham's Razor have been accepted and popular since his time, increasingly with the emergence of experimental science, though with exceptions. J. S. Mill is rightly regarded as a mediator of Ockham's logic from the medieval world to modern philosophy. Nevertheless, in respect of parsimony, Ockham's Razor appalled Mill. In 1865 Mill attacked Sir William Hamilton for his use of a version of the Razor.[49] Hamilton's own positions on logic were sometimes incompatible with Ockham's. He was moving towards a quantification theory that, if it had any relation to Ockham, was one of contrast,[50] in which there is a closer relation to Frege's quantificational logic than to the sort of Ockhamist logic that Mill (apart from the Razor) had espoused. Later, Russell's practice of eliminating, where possible, existential quantification, and Hans Reichenbach's concern with simplicity evinced in his idea of logical empiricism, as Sober (1975) notices, have similarities with some uses of Ockham's Razor, though neither philosopher is generally compatible with

Ockham. Dummett (1981: 38, 317) applies a restrained use of Ockham's Razor in mathematical theory, while he notes that denying a thought by the process of negation is intrinsically complex.

Anti-realism's true Razor?

The foregoing challenged Adams's claim that the various versions of Ockham's five Razors are, in the first instance, methodological principles, and it is not obvious how they are related to truth or probability. Surely it is, in relevant respects, clear how Ockham relates at least some of them to truth. Adams's view does not account for at least one version of Ockham's Razor, which she quotes: 'When a proposition comes out true for things, if two things suffice for its truth, it is superfluous to assume a third.'[51] The expression 'comes out true' (*verificatur*) and the term 'word' are related to truth explicitly, by being the purported measure for true propositions in a thesis canvassing for a reductionist use of numerical principles as the basis for an austere ontology regulating generalisation in logic. For Ockham, number relations are real. Such relational propositions have truth-conditions and substitution instances.

They accord with a rough correspondence theory (not as well developed as those of Paul of Venice, and adopted without Duns Scotus's full realism, while yet they are not mind-dependent). Of truth, Ockham states that, 'truth, i.e. the concept *truth*, in addition to the proposition it signifies, connotes that things are such in reality as they are conveyed to be by means of the proposition.'[52] Although Ockham's theses are distinct from the semantics of Tarski-Davidson (in which to give the truth-conditions is a way of giving the meaning of a sentence),[53] yet the various features of Ockham's 'correspondence' presuppositions partially parallel these modern authors, principally because of the way he is attracted to anti-realism.[54] Ockham's 'correspondence' position was pressed by his anti-realism, a view that had some similarity with Peter Aureoli and Henry Harclay's disposition to dismantle direct realism.

Marenbon's view appears to offer the most explanatory promise. Ockham's rejection of essential essence realism, together with his acceptance of truth-conditions for the semantics of the external world, implies that his adoption of a conceptual system for understanding the world in terms of species and genera is merely one possible system. Yet for his contemporary opponents it is a system that has to be used if one is to achieve a full understanding of reality. Any of these interpretations involve a use of truth which restores to it the role not accorded it by Adams's opinions that the above forms of the Razor are methodological and that it is not obvious how they are related to truth.[55] The Razor's purported theory-generating informativeness seems to be its merit. But on occasions the Razor is contradicted by the presence of informative complexity in a new more productive theory (as with fundamental physics and superstrings[56]), which is more informative than a previous simpler theory. Although scientists appeal to Ockham's Razor, their use of it often explicitly conflicts with Ockham's own express claim that it should only be employed outside the scope of observation statements,[57] which complies well with his desire to press demonstrative science into admission of uncertainty. Ockham was aiming at a reduction of individuation in ontology, and he denied that some relational states between propositions have to be distinct.[58] Ockham's use of a complex procedure using negation to achieve reduction of entities, is itself also a negation of parsimony, since its strategy is to acknowledge complex propositions while positing them as such, then negating them to achieve their elimination.[59]

In this perspective Ockham presupposes holistic metaphysical conjecture as epistemology, couched as semantic method. In a sense Ockham has chosen the least equable, and yet experimentally productive elements, of two opposed universes of discourse: ontology and holism, though in experimental science their admixture is used profitably. But, as Horst (1996: 365–70) argues in a perspective outside of Ockham studies (that of computational philosophical psychology), this approach to simplicity is in danger of over-stating and misleading about materialism in relation to ontology and psychology.

Ockham's desire to bring parsimony to ontology internalises a tension between realism and epistemology. If one conceives that necessity in reason is a criterion of identity for restricting ontological plurality, then ontological contingencies may be unwarrantably censored (and this can cut against empirical productivity, as much as it can against semantics). Ockham's way of meeting this tension is to internalise a version of anti-realism into his epistemological programme. But this 'anti-realism' is precariously positioned in relation to the traditions that he controverts, in particular if contrasted with twentieth-century opponents of realism. Ockham, after what appears to be an early position in which he agrees with Duns Scotus, attacks the latter's strong realism,[60] though concurring with him that real relations are mind-independent.[61] His aim is commendable, in his parsimonious wish to place limits on excessively strong claims about empiricism, and at a time when scientific mythology and ignorance falsely generalised local experience.

Future contingents

Looking from his present at the universe, Ockham was to some degree aware that we are observing its past. If psychoanalysis has any lesson to teach here (see Bowie, 1993: 38–46), it is that analysis of the future is intentional, and the future is a sort of metonymy for present concerns, as well as a series of codes for covert absorption and transference of our pasts. No doubt such matters can be overstated. But with Ockham and his contemporaries, the most obvious constituent in their talk of future contingents, only slightly off stage, is their personal interest in that future. The study of God's knowledge of the future is an understanding of how he deals with his people. The conditionality of present life requires guidance by instruction in the principles according to which God knows the future in relation to people in the present.

In practice, however, the scholarly debates about such topics were often highly abstract technical affairs, and even used to feed earthly vendettas, networking through generations. Boethius refined the conception which is followed by Peter the Lombard in his *Sentences*, that God is timeless and has present capacity to know from all eternity everything he knows in the present. Thomas Buckingham took up this thesis in his *On the Contingency of the Future, and Free Will*. His thesis was an attack on Thomas Bradwardine's *De causa Dei contra Pelagium* (*In God Defense, against Pelagius*). Bradwardine's view was that humanity exercised freedom to choose, or not, to obey God's will without the interference of preordination. As de la Torre (1987, ch. 5) has demonstrated, Buckingham carefully refrains from explaining that Bradwardine accepted that the First Cause regiments people, yet they are able to act freely in secondary cause contexts. For Bradwardine, God, from all eternity, chose freely from the array of future contingents. Such contingency (*contingentia ad utrumlibet*) applies also to humans in the secondary cause contexts.

A generation earlier Ockham had attempted to apply his sense of simplicity to reduce confusion. For him, duration was the foundation feature of time. God has knowledge of the future. Aristotle's *On Interpretation* troubled Ockham. In accordance with the standard medieval view, Ockham took Aristotle to have argued that singular propositions about future affairs are not, prior to the time of which they speak, true or false. Since for Ockham this violates the doctrine that all propositions are true or false (to cut a long story short), there must never have been future contingents, or they are illogical.[62]

Ockham, then, interprets Aristotle as maintaining that God is, in a special sense, possibly ignorant of a future contingent. A reason for this is that – expressed that way – it is not an epistemological existent. That is to say, the future does not exist. Thus future contingents do not instantiate, self-inhere, or obtain now for the future, since it is neither there nor here to refer to. But God's absolute power, for Ockham, alters this bald state of affairs. We should appreciate in this context that for Ockham logic is possibility for ontology as well as for propositions; this is partly why he was agreeable to limiting God's knowledge of future contingents: in a strict sense, they do not exist, do not supposit. Despite this, God's omnipotence infinitely empowers his intuition, and God is also able, as well as willing, to make and implement promises about the future,[63] which both inform his use of epistemological possibility and construct intuitive cognition.

3   Transcending cultural limits in logic

Beyond simple transcendence

The previous chapter left evidence to indicate that, not only with the medieval world of Ockham, but also concerning our own grasp of metaphysics, we are far from clear on the depth and identity of the universe and how to depict its identity. This is even before we move on to enquiring about transcendence beyond the universe and/or outside of the physical domain. Summarising a trend of the foregoing analysis, I conclude that the idea of simplicity being the logically prior epistemological and empirical states in the universe is false, and that the reverse is true: complexity is prior to simplicity. Consequently, simplicity is not the defining of universalised or generalised knowledge. Rather, at best it is a symptom of the strategy in scientific discovery, which is a pale shadow of its richer ontological and conceptual parents: the actual external world. An upshot of this is that simplicity should not be confused with clear-headedness.

It is commonplace to argue that there are limits to language, which prevent our expressing knowledge of God. We rightly learn metaphysical modesty by means of some philosophies that teach us that traditional transcendental theologies crash-land. The priority of this book is to argue that it is possible to compose new routes to transcendence which are immune to this grounding. The study draws attention to problems in philosophy of logic and its insights, proposing that they both, on suitable interpretation, lead to fresh possibilities in theology. It will be argued that some new interpretations of logical theory can be used to expound a fresh concept of transcendence, and the viability of the possibility of revelation. The position of this book opposes the view that theology has its own logic; nor does it countenance philosophers acting as processing emperors who decided who has. The present study argues that there are some difficulties with which logic itself is faced when attempting to generalise over its own identities and philosophy.

Why should we resort to logic to characterise claims of revelation? There is at least an implicit tendency in criticism of the *possibility* of revelation, for its opponents to deploy rationalities (at least) perceived to be derived from logic traditions and their cultural influence. The most explicit concepts of *possibility* one finds in philosophy of logic. Such notions of 'possibility' often directly structure our senses of the alleged 'limits' to language. Literary formations of 'possibility' even tend obliquely to be a product of, or trade on, or rest on a regress of influences which manifest reformulations of rationality that still adhere to what is taken to be 'logically possible'.[1] It should be clear that the history of logic is interpretation, and not always certain exposure, of what it is to be logic; this situation is independent of whether or not we judge logic to be invented (constructed) or discovered. Thus logic is, in terms of our perception of its forms, a set of policies of justification that are purported to be (and could be, or could contain) universal laws.

The scope of logic

It is customary for some scientists to deride philosophy as antique in relation to an account of the external world, to be replaced by empirical science. Moreover it is usual to discover in this experimental science a strong employment of basic logical laws. Experimental scientists are often rather too keen, at times, to insist on the empirical truth of unproved metaphysical principles, such as Ockham's Razor – the principle of simplicity over complexity.[2] A gathering of these sorts of examples enforces recognition that most principles of logic are antecedently presupposed by realist science. The logic of equations in experimental science also displays a share-investment in transcendental propositions: for example, the occurrence of functional transcendental language blows wormholes through such naked scientific imperialism. Consider the well-worn example of equations presupposing light to have contrary quantum and wave properties. Such equations for light amount to a moderate case of counter-intuition, by which, according to a principle of teleological charity, physicists assume that contrariety constituted by two differing systems linked to a single ontology will, at some future stage be harmonised. Perhaps science will extend its own contrary charity-policy to transcendence in theology. Since we are subjected to inconsistency in formal logic and theoretical languages in scientific realism, we should be wary of judging that a retreat from generalising or decision to live with contradiction is the sole prerogative of theology. Consequently neither of these options is a sufficient condition for theological reductionism.

Limits and transcendence

Certainly, we should not presuppose in the foregoing use of expressions like 'transcendence' that they are synonymous throughout distinct subjects. Nevertheless a strategy can be offered to deflect equivocation. Let us link transcendence to paradox as a device with which to tackle possible equivocation over allegedly different uses of 'transcendence'. It can be proved[3] that paradoxes have logical relations to each other, whether or not they all share essential properties. If, following classical bivalent logics, we assume that the consistent limits to expressibility are marked by the outer boundaries of paradoxes (i.e., the junctures beyond which we cannot speak), then transcendence is the other side, as mapped by those boundaries. Adopting as canonical some attitudes to logic, it could be objected that logic should not be deemed arbiter of what is expressible. This view can take at least two forms. One version interprets this arbiter as the claim that expressible possible semantics have to be housed within this logical syntax – an extreme opinion that few would follow. The second takes bivalent logic as the definition of what is (consistently) possible (extended modally to other domains). On this approach the arbiter has pinpointed what is possible, though it allows that other linguistic universes, such as literary creativity, are the vehicles to articulate what is possible. The exact connection between this formal logic (as a criterion of possibility) and narrative logics has not yet been formulated.

One problem here is that paradox fractures the judgement that logical possibility is the criterion of expressibility. The reason for this is that expressions in logic do not cease to function instantly when they derive paradox: they transcend the limits of their own boundaries by expressing sense when contradiction is entailed. Consequently we have the mysterious situation that, if logic is taken to be a criterion of possibility by which to measure the limits of expression, then this truth is true beyond the boundary it often allegedly demarcates. So the expression of a limit, in appropriate cases, is self-transcendent. If this is correct, then those who wish to argue a reductionist thesis[4] about transcendence are faced with a collapse of the concept of a limit to expression. This is because internal to this limit is the paradox whose expression includes expression on the outside of the boundary only within which expression is supposed to be possible.

The relation of transcendence to paradox is that the former tears through the boundary of formal consistent limit to the totality of expressions using semantic properties within that totality and applying some of them outside that limit. Aquinas'[5] desire to discover scientific natural analogies with transcendent expressions might be seen as having a formal support, transformation and extension in the perspective of the foregoing, leaving aside his use of physical theory.

Counter-intuition 2

If there is revelation, then it has counter-intuitive properties. I suggest that counter-intuition, since it is the stuff of which creativity is formed, codes our flight instructions. How can we craft a theologically fuelled version of counter-intuition? It is intriguing to examine some general features of the logic that has attracted the application of the term 'counter-intuition' to it, though as far as I know no sustained research on the term is available.[6] There are typical general negative uses, such as Williamson[7] displays:

> [I]t is counter-intuitive to suppose that making competent deductions from what one knows is not in general a way of extending one's knowledge.

But the phrase 'in general' is vague here: certain relevant expressions in a discourse expressing provability will eventually imply a contradiction. This is exemplified by Gödel's paradox, relating to the inability for the foundations of arithmetic to be proved. So Williamson's above use of 'counter-intuition', given the possible scope of 'in general', is in some cases false. Accordingly, a state of affairs that is canvassed as false may be true; this is counter-intuition. Here Williamson's negative use of 'counter-intuition' upon examination allows the notion from which it demurs. In Gibson (2000) I argue that modernism's assigned fate for the notion of revelation in relation to transcendence, is in general an instance of this sort of vagueness and ignorance about the logical and metaphysical status of transcendence.[8]

Lewy's[9] research on meaning and modality uses the expression 'counter-intuitive' informally to characterise deep unexpected consequences, in relations between entailment and strict implication. One of his proofs is that a contingent proposition can in certain contexts entail a necessary proposition, which of course when it was published violated the general consensus that this move was not logical. Although one has carefully to regiment such a doctrine, yet it can serve us here as a meta-logical axiom that inference from this universe to transcendental reference to God is not in itself inconsistent.

Paradox

Lewy[10] is characteristic, in his not defining the term 'counter-intuition', nor giving it explicit attention. Lewy first deploys 'counter-intuition' to depict the so-called 'Paradox of Analysis': i.e., that a given proposition (A) is identical with a given concept (B).[11] Lewy states of this identity that it 'is paradoxical, in the sense of being counter-intuitive'.[12] So here Lewy inter-connects the problems of recognition, of identity between a proposition and a concept, with paradox. 'Being counter-intuitive' is not paradoxical, but puzzling in a sense derivable from Hacking (1985): there can be an actual ambiguity in, say, a mathematical rule, with the consequence that a use of the rule may be unprecedented and expose a counter-intuitive proof of it that modifies the concept of proof presupposed by the rule.

In certain ways, issues of recognising revelation, of its identity in relation to propositional expression and its concepts, together with revelation's edging on the borders of paradox in the sense of being counter-intuitive functions, have parallels with the above features of Lewy's observations on meaning and inference. A conflict of propositions or expressions can generate paradox – a form usually taken to be an ineradicable inconsistency in logic. Paradox has been deemed a facet of revelation in the incarnation. Although paradox in logic and revelatory concepts may not be deductively identical, it is worth considering their relations.

A central hard case of counter-intuitive surprise is Russell's Paradox. Frege thought that he had a consistent logic of classes. Russell proved that Frege's own system entailed a contradiction, in particular at the level of the universal class. If each lower class is used to define the higher class containing it, the final universal class[13] is unlike the lower classes and the way they have been defined.

Thus this is a way of speaking of the limit of formal discourse (because we cannot generalise noncontextually over all language[14]). Since in a standard view of Classical logic contradictions entail everything, it might be too much to expect a unified theory. This type of situation is generally taken to typify central and extreme problems in paradox. Michael Potter (2000: 119–201) explains that Russell's and Wittgenstein's response about the form of a proposition in relation to Russell's Paradox very much concerns the possibility of expressibility or entailment of inexpressibility.

As we reflect on the possible relations between them in the perspective of the foregoing problems we might do well to consider Frege – the 'father of modern mathematical logic' also to be an instance of narrow presumption. For he was inattentive on occasions to the restriction placed on him by Russell's Paradox 20 years before he wrote, in 1923, that 'my account is not designed to square with ordinary linguistic usage, which is generally too vague and ambiguous for the purposes of logic'.[15] There are now developed logics of 'vagueness', exemplified, for example, by Williamson.[16] There can be a precise logic of what is vague, and the customary example of the definability of 'fog' is sufficient here to index that thesis. Williamson canvasses the thesis that vague is a function of (partial) ignorance. This concept fits in well with a notion of revelation that participates in human limitations.

Frege had previously stated that, 'metaphorical expressions, if used cautiously, may after all help towards an elucidation', though he does not offer this as a systematic concession towards linking formal with nonformal expressions. But unfortunately Frege and the tradition which he spawned do not usually explore the metaphoric foundations of his formal logic and their interconnections. A core of Frege's philosophy of language, which is expressed in his study 'Sense and reference',[17] is based on 'reference'. According to Dummett,[18] Frege used the term *Bedeutung* to cover three features: referring, the relation of reference, and referent. Dummett claims that Frege never confused these uses. Whatever the case, Frege here made live metaphors: at least two of the uses are metaphors of the remaining one.[19] It might be responded that one should not confuse the origin of a term metaphorised with its use, since logicians employ the literal sense (whatever that would be) of a term. But Frege has one term here – *Bedeutung* – and three uses in the term: 'referring' is a metonymy metaphor for the 'referent', while 'reference' is a live metaphor derived from the metonymy relation.

Paradox is an entailment of the classical logical calculus. Although logicians recognise this, everyday work on the internal properties of logic tends to omit the fact that paradox undermines and constantly fractures all logic based on this calculus. Paradox is held off-stage as an embarrassment to normal performance. Paradox is like a coiled spring held taut against its own natural forces. Although Russell's Paradox, the paradoxes of material implication, and others, are isolated from normal logic business in analytical philosophy, they are actually internal to the predicate calculus. They are entailed presuppositions (in Frege's sense of the term[20]) of what it is to be proposition, inference and generalisation of all logical uses within the system. An analogy may help: if on an occasion (say a desert) water saves an individual dying of thirst, and yet as a flood it drowns people, we do not suppose that the water in the two different uses is a physically different chemical medium.[21] Likewise with some uses of a proposition that sustain consistency, and a global use that engulfs them in paradox. Each use, though distinct in some respects, uses identical properties to all other propositions and their relations. Accordingly, paradox – a complex function of propositions within a logical system, assigned to the border of reason, and suppressed from contact with ordinary use – is, in relevant senses, a property of all uses of propositions in logic. The concept of a proposition is shared through consistent and paradoxical uses.

I suggest that another way of expressing this state of affairs is to identify the relation of paradox as a live metaphoric property of what it is to be a logical system. A consequence of this is for paradox to have a semantic contract with nonparadoxical uses. The deep structure of propositional usage is buoyant on the limits of language. Dig deep enough into use of language and one will tear through the paradoxes underlying it, to transcend the closure of language by local semantic fields.

Transcending logic

A symbolist contemporary of Frege faced up to challenging this, as then yet, future paradoxical upshot of logicism. This contemporary was Mallarmé. Presumably he was unread by Frege. Mallarmé re-focused his general picture of logic and the mathematics of numbers into the possibility of transcendence in poetry. Mallarmé's *Un Coup de Dés*[22] also had many other purposes, but, as Malcolm Bowie[23] discovered, Mallarmé engages the conundrum, 'A throw of the dice can never eliminate chance', as a means both to accept and to violate canons of logic and paradox. He accepts that we occupy a prison of language, while articulating our escape from it. Bowie states that, '*Un Coup de Dés* is a world of alternative logics. The rules of the games are both respected and infringed . . . the poet's language of axiomatic self-evidence and sequential argument is disrupted by a precarious language of feeling and surmise which is intent upon making the impossible come.'[24] Now this should not be treated as special pleading by a humanities specialist who has no support from the scientific side. The distinguished scientist John Holland (1998: 218–20) is concerned to expose relations between the two even in contexts of contrast. Among other devices he proposes the employment of a (complexity theory) game to flesh out the basis for further progress in this arena, which challenge I took up above (in chapter 1) and in various contexts below (variously in chapters 4 and 5, for example.)

Although poetry and logic are widely different genres, the impact of paradox on exposing the fiction of consistency in logic, and Mallarmé's Pythagorean preoccupation with number and logic, make this a confrontation that interrogates their partial alignment. In this equivocating alignment, we should also admit the equivocation over 'inference relation', 'entails paradox', 'entails everything', and what requires a proposition's both being true and false. Mallarmé, often engaging Platonic ontology, places paradoxical transcendence as a projection in the spatialisation of sense and syntax to explore the internal strains between sign, medium of signifiers, and the signified.[25] I should now like to detour through a formal arena, which I believe can be connected to the present literary concern.

Wittgenstein, Kant and Fermat

This project outlined above, and related to Mallarmé, is not unlike Wittgenstein's use of transcendence and projection in space in the *Tractatus*. A geometrical model imposed on space can be a model for semantic fields. This has an as yet undeveloped relation to the more exotic sphere in the proof of Fermat's Last Theorem. Here a vast counter-intuitive universe of discourse, with unexpected connections, is the complex geometrical model for a space and surfaces. If we assume such a model as one of the ranges of expressions for semantics, then the traditional limit associated with the limits to expression within and against the upper limits of language deforms into a near-infinite and qualitatively richer domain than, say, Kantian notions prescribe.

The general point of this amounts to saying that, with the solution to Fermat's Last Theorem, the criteria of analogy, interpretation and the implied new concepts of recognition of mathematical proof are extended beyond the limits of what was recognised and interpreted as the content and scope of mathematical proof. Using these states of affairs analogically (as specialists in mathematical proofs themselves have done), it follows that we may not safely adopt, as law, presuppositions of scientific and mathematical proof in a given historical context as *the* definition of what proof's range itself is, though there are impressive and profound uses of such proofs. Consequently, it is an insecure foundation to implement contemporary notions of established proof as analogies for the limits of proof or sensible rationality in metaphysics or theology. The example of Ayer's contradictory thesis on verification is only the most obvious example of this. I suggest that for those who ban transcendent metaphysics as an in principle provable presupposition have fallen into the trap of false foreclosure of the scope of rationality.

The proof of Fermat, produced by Andrew Wiles,[26] functions from the basis of the elementary arithmetical concept that: with the equation for Pythagoras' theorem of the form $a^2 + b^2 = c^2$, by adding the elementary principle of addition combined to the equation, it would by unrefined instinct seem to follow that there is a solution in whole numbers for $a^3 + b^3 + c^3$. But this turns out to be a false assumption, as Wiles proved. It requires extensive work to flesh out epistemological implications of such work; however, it seems fairly clear that one of them complements the concept that having a concept is not necessarily a recognitional capacity. That is to say, at one level, to know does not entail understanding (as with the presupposition that if one masters the square law, then the cube law, combined with a combinatory competence, can be implied and therefore its consequence understood). An understanding of some of the epistemological significance of Fermat's Last Theorem involves recognising the limit imposed on the generalisation of pertinent knowledge: knowledge leads to blocking further understanding (see chapter 2 above). The proof is especially about how hitherto unrecognised barriers obtain on attempts to infer further generalisation from a particular case. From Wiles's research, we can see that this epistemological and logical asymmetry is deep within the foundations of knowledge.

This has implications for Kant's assertion – on the present analysis the false view – that 'We have no insight whatsoever into the intrinsic nature of things' (*Critique*, A277/B333). One might succeed in contending that Fermat's and Wiles's proof(s) can be used to prove that Kant's claim applies to conceptual claims less ambitious than the intrinsic nature of things. If this is the case, then it generates a *reductio ad absurdum*. For we do have knowledge, sometimes by a showing of the proof of what is not the intrinsic nature of things, such as algebraic geometry in the sphere of the Last Theorem. Even so, Fermat's Last Theorem exposes an extraordinary indictment of our lack of true counter-intuitive instinct in calculative awareness about the deeper and complex sphere of truth. With an appropriate admixture, then, of good counter-intuitive showing in our imaginative use of proofs, humans can dig deep into the identities of the unknown, while coming up against proof that we do not understand much of these operations or their identities.

We can, speculatively turn this situation against the claim, in, and of, the Kantian presupposition, that some ignorance of insight into the intrinsic nature of things entails that we have no insight whatsoever into such things. If the foregoing is even roughly on the right track, Kant committed himself to various fallacies here (quantifier-shift, segmentation, modal and schematic fallacies[27]), while obviously his actual texts are more complex than that straight view suggests. Even so, from Fermat's Last Theorem, on the basis of this new proof by Wiles, it is possible to argue that Kant is wrong about intrinsic knowledge. I wish to maintain that we can have intrinsic knowledge of a state, intertwined with revisable knowledge of contiguous matters. Paradoxical knowledge is a property of primary empirical functions in the universe, and we have some certain knowledge of them, though it can violate our senses of known structures. This furnishes us with a complex premise by which we can reason that in principle there is no separate logical problem for maintaining that we can have a slice of knowledge of things in themselves as they are intrinsically, in association with our limits of language and epistemology.

In this perspective, inference and representation can, I suggest, in principle detect Kantian supersensibility of substances – on his view unknowable to us – even if not observed by us. On this view, it is not (as with Kant) only those causal powers that affect us perceptually and confer knowledge on us, though we are inert or unreceptive to knowledge of substance in itself. Rather, in counter-intuitive ways the two types of knowledge are empirically and thus ontologically bonded in informative ways such that knowledge of the way things are in themselves, in substances, leaked directly into conceptual accessibility. Moreover, as Rae Langton[28] has demonstrated, fresh analysis of Kant leads to the need for a reappraisal of his relation to realism. Gibson (2000) reasons that, if any of the standard scenarios derived from observational results on the cosmology of the earliest universe are correct in certain key issues, then we can have knowledge of things in themselves, because the deepest empirical identity of the universe is counter-intuitive, infinite, because the beginning of the universe is bonded into things in themselves in ways that qualitatively reveal infinity in substance in relevant ways to oppose Kant's restriction, significant of course though his engagement is. If we are to be capable of representing the actual metaphysical aspects of such phenomena, then we need to enfold visual, literary and musical art, as live metaphoric theoretical images and mappings, into the sphere of counter-intuitive knowledge of things as they are in themselves – exotic a prospect though this is. Cosmology's results already require scientists massively to enlarge their representative techniques. Some of these descriptive moves are directly involved in live metaphoric depiction at the theoretical level. Deep proofs not only open up the success and further applicability of a new logical formalism. They also show the poverty of descriptive limits. The third millennium will no doubt exhibit vast new ways of exploring such domains with the introduction of techniques from the humanities as a means to characterise physical phenomena in cosmology and other science. The role of originality in the physical beginning of the universe is only one such exotic instance of the failure of science adequately to represent an identity. Perhaps Pascal comprehended Fermat's perception of his Last Theorem in some of these ways; namely, knowledge led to a grasp of our impoverished understanding of it, and the need for a virtual infinity of descriptive powers to cope with the depth and potential of a piece of universal knowledge.

Mallarmé's game

Although Pascal is a universe of discourse away from Mallarmé, the mixture of concerns that Pascal depicts in his *Pensées* (those of formal probability theory transcribed into aphoristic philosophy) might well be a lesson to us as a way forward. We may view with philosophical and logical sympathy the proximity of some abstract philosophy and literary innovation for the future.

Mallarmé's confrontation of, and obsession with, Pythagoras was to conceive a way of showing that a perfect world of order could co-exist with, and be triggered so as to engage creatively with, a world of chaos. Subsequent to Mallarmé's scenario, notions of chaos have been much developed, though they are still sources of puzzle and disagreement. At the formal philosophical level, Peter Smith (1998: 168) has explained some limits in attempting to define chaos, and counsels us to put on one side the idea that definition is central to understanding chaos. His treatment of chaotic motion gives rise, among many other insights, to the suggestion that it is a bounded set in a finite region that folds back on itself. So in this state of affairs, although chaos is transcendent with respect to ordered systems, it is not a function of unbounded infinity or chance. A facet of Mallarmé's poetic stance well exemplifies such a situation, as one of Malcolm Bowie's conclusions about Mallarmé's transcendence suggests (here quoted at length):

> Mallarmé's reference to gaming has a special grimness about it. For dice-throwers are not seekers after transcendence . . . The final line of the poem [*Toute pensée émet un coup de dés*: 'Every thought manifests a throw of the dice'] shows that the poem is a model of the thought-process at large, and that, within the terms of this model, thought is inevitably pitched beyond itself and towards the unconditional act, the game without rules, which practical good sense condemns. Harmony prevails between the two maxims if they are removed from their context and considered together; they are the first and second stages of an elementary syllogism. But in their context they behave differently. For it is a main purpose of Mallarmé's volatile textures to give voice to the hidden motives or 'illocutionary forces' that the maxims themselves leave unspoken. The awaited third stage of the syllogism – 'that no thought will ever abolish chance' – must be the case yet cannot be granted. This, the logical outcome of Mallarmé's argument, has been shown throughout the poem to be a cause of alarm, a challenge, and a lure towards the acutest form of metaphysical risk.[29]

As with the late Wittgenstein, Mallarmé has called the bluff in games and found another scarcely expressible one: all is self-evident beyond rules, yet indefinable.

Graham Priest[30] offers paraconsistent analysis of the limits of language, according to which a given proposition can be true and false. I do not agree with this conception.[31] Yet Priest's remarks might be capable of being transformed into other logical theories. He proposes that if we draw a limit in logic, that drawing of the outer border has already presupposed and marked the boundary of the outsider – hence the domain beyond which we supposedly cannot go has been trespassed. The reason for this is that the outer border is a definition holding for the other side of the interface provided in marking of the boundaries of the finite. Priest has argued that such paradoxes entail that logical language breaks through into infinity (though he neither offers nor mentions a formulation of counter-intuition). He maintains that the internal collapse of classical systems itself entails a semantics of what stands on the transcendental other side, outside the limiting boundary within the classical calculus.[32] Priest concludes his study by affirming: 'Exploring the limit of thought has a curious Looking-Glass property, however. In exploring the limit, one perforce finds oneself on the other side.' His point here is that of the limits at the enclosure boundaries of inferential systems at which logical transcendence and the 'true infinite' commence.[33] He notes that Hegel states what Priest regards to be the same idea:

> great stress is laid on the limitations of thought, of reason, and so on, and it is asserted that the limitation *cannot* be transcended. To make such an

assertion is to be unaware that the very fact that something is determined as a limitation implies that the limitation is already transcended.[34]

He rounds off by quoting Wittgenstein in the *Tractatus*:

> in order to be able to draw a limit to thought, we should have to find both sides of that limit thinkable (i.e., we should have to be able to think what cannot be thought).

Priest adduces a twist to the notorious conclusion of Wittgenstein's *Tractatus* that, 'Whereof one cannot speak, thereof one has just contradicted oneself', though hopefully Priest is not here asserting that if one speaks one ceases to contradict oneself. Although Priest's logic position can be criticised,[35] this will not preoccupy us here.

As to empiricism and logic, it seems evident now in astrophysical research that those exotic states outside of even relativistic space–times correspond qualitatively in some way to exotic states deep in extant physical structures (black holes, quasars, super strings, etc). So we do not have empirical grounds for postulating in principle the need for contradiction (or contrariety) between finite and infinite states. Consequently, if we also gather together the foregoing considerations, we have no grounds for claiming that, entailed in knowledge of finite and transfinite states, is an ineradicable contradiction, as a criterion of reaching knowledge of some infinite states. Accordingly, on empirical and logical grounds Priest is incorrect. Instead, we have the prospect of fresh series of unparalleled developments on the basis of current cosmological and logical researches.

A thrust of the present study is to argue that many diverse communicative phenomena betray transcendent possibility when they prescribe limits to their expressive boundaries. One can defend such pluralism by maintaining that each of such varying approaches instantiates a value derivable from a more fundamental logic refracted by the ways in which Classical logic trespasses on the converse outside limits of Classical logical systems, while this does not imply that all deviant logics or narrative theories achieve this.

Metaphoric logic

One presupposition of this pluralism pertains to whether or how one can link up logic to natural languages. The languages of transcendence and revelation are typically metaphoric, and this situation is often contrasted with 'the' Classical logical calculus and logics of scientific languages.

Whitehead's and Russell's *Principia Mathematica* paraphrased its mathematical logic into the English language.[36] This exemplifies in the context of a hard case that natural language can act as a vehicle for matters normally outside its purview. (Russell's and Whitehead's monumental work is complex and oblique in its relation to natural languages; notoriously, however, this state of affairs is not solely a result of the appropriate complexity of the subject, but partly because of the authors' involuted and inelegant approach to proof.)

The solution presupposed in the present book, to one of the discontinuities between formal and informal languages, is to maintain that all such formal systems are closer to natural languages than some analytic philosophers usually suppose, because these systems are composed of (often disguised or neglected) live metaphors. A premise for this position rests on the strategy that formal logics are themselves systems of live metaphors (this term to be explained further below) whose metaphoricity is constantly obscured or reified.

On this approach the logic of paradox can be used to imply that formal systems have incorrectly isolated languages (which always have) multiple layers into 'literal' linear levels. This metaphoricity is smoothed away into suppressed premises (which generate paradoxes) or discarded – as with Frege's 'tone' (*Beleuchtung* and *Farbung*).[37] One might easily play Frege at his own game, for those who wish to retain his logic, by having a policy of formalising all tone (perhaps along the lines of tree hierarchies in mathematical logic).[38] For those who retort that natural languages are inconsistent to achieve this, one may respond:

First, the paradox-generating inconsistencies of formal logics have not been deemed a reason for resisting the application of normalisation to them, so what is good for the goose is good for the gander. Secondly, one can learn a lesson from John Dupré's view[39] that there is metaphysical disunity in the foundations of empirical science that resists unification. Philosophical logic is no less immune to plural tendencies, while its practitioners operate a principle of charity in assuming a formal canon of inference based on an over-determining recipe of what is a formal proposition, while consequently it massively under-determines the logical possibilities of live metaphor. It is not surprising in view of this that new results of inference are not infrequently counter-intuitive and violate formal intuitions though this is no warrant for accepting an opposing imperialism.

One can extend this by suggesting that metaphor is much more extensive in philosophy of logic than has generally been assumed. The value of a function is a metonymy metaphor of the function. The right-hand side of a tautology is often a live metaphor of the left. In a precise sense the truth-functional identity between, say, 'conjunction' and 'implication': $((P \wedge Q) = (P > Q))$ – rests on, what I would identify as – the calculable live metaphor relation between the proposition forming operators, just as two distinct photographs of an identical subject complement each other. In identity statements (such as '$(A \wedge B) = (C)$'), Tarski's way of aligning truth-conditions of propositions to represent (to be) their ontological correlates is a case of the metaphorisation of a relation which is of course usually called 'correspondence'. It is only by a complex negotiation – not always explicit in logic discussion – through metaphor, that formal language is said to correspond with an ontological state. We know that neither syntax nor semantics is symmetrical to the external world. To presuppose the opposite is to treat Frege's single term for a three-fold function of reference, that of *Beleuchtung*, as a live metaphor taken from 'pointing' – *deuten*. It is not a genetic fallacy to note that the notions of 'referring', the relation of 'reference', and the term 'referent' are live metaphors; the second and third successively metaphorise 'referring'.[40] My argument is counter-intuitive to the norm: live metaphor resides unsuspected in formal logic and in this state of affairs logic and natural languages go together rather more closely than analytical philosophers usually allow. Thus the canvassed gap between formal and creative possibilities, not only with regard to transcendent expression, can be closed in type.

Realistic propositions

Counter-intuition is a relation of consequence of those presuppositions that it superficially appears to violate, and generates new insight. John Milbank's[41] 'metanarrative realism' is an instance of this type of relation. As he notes, it is the domain that Frei and Lindbeck term 'narrative' – for identifying God and some of his relations to humans. Yet 'narrative' can be substituted by any communicating function; as Budd[42] argues, there is a single value manifesting itself through the arts as diverse as music and painterly relations, in addition to narrative states such as poetry and story as well as film (a topic to be developed below). Just what the specific identity of this 'value' is, and what its ramifications are, of course, is problematic. It seems that it may occupy a logical space of something like a super-manifold. In relation to music theory, a start has been made by such scholars as Borthwick (1995: 173–7) to show how music displays various logic forms, and he expresses an interest in its relation to cosmological theory, which theme is given some outline planning in Gibson (2000).

I should like to propose that one can construct logic of counter-intuition, and that this logic would have a mapping relation to a matching realism. Counter-intuitive functions would have an ontological mirror: counter-intuitive realism, with a surprising ontology, though morphology is not symmetrical to ontology. But just as film can be a live metaphor disclosing ontological states, so a counter-intuitive logic of revelation could disclose divine qualities. (I return to this topic below.) Since a proposition is a function of its relations, it should be clear that we could infer from the above that the identity of what it is to be a proposition can be counter-intuitive. That is to say, conceptions of a proposition can be problematic, and reverse formal perception of its possible identities.

It can be argued that a consequence of this is the following thesis: apparently nonformal creative language content in, for example, theology, can be counter-intuitively propositional, i.e. logical. An extension of this concept is that other expression in such fields may have an unexpected tautological relation to formal discourse. The previous remarks concerning Lewy's (1976) views are relevant to the notion of a proposition here: we are sometimes at least unclear about the relations between a proposition, its own relations to its expression, words and concept – and consequently, thereby, of these to other linguistic phenomena which use these elements.

Writers in the analytical philosophy mould within philosophy of religion customarily support the distinction of propositional, versus non-propositional, ideas of revelation, though of course it is clear that a non-propositional view of a revelation might itself be characterised in propositional form. Roger Forsman[43] makes valuable analyses in an attempt to collapse the traditional distinction between 'propositional' and 'non-propositional' views of revelation. I am arguing that the counter-intuitive features not only of transcendental language, but also of philosophy of logic, leave it unclear at times what the claims of 'proposition' and 'non-proposition' entail and whether or not they are exclusive disjunctive modes of expression.

On the basis of the present study, one may conclude that the relations between propositional and non-propositional expressions are counter-intuitive. If so, this situation implies that these counter-intuitive borders are not only a function of the marginal, the borderlands, of two disputed territories. Such counter-intuition is a consequence of the inner, deep identities at the centre and foundations of logic. This state of affairs is intimately connected with the way in which formal contradictions recur at the limit of expression of formal concepts as conceived by a variety of philosophers as a consequence of their systematic presuppositions.

This approach is no covert attempt to convert hitherto non-propositional discourse into analytic philosophy, though it draws on new research in that discipline to push its borders outwards and redefine them at points. A subset of this position is that analytic philosophy itself is an undecidable subject. Consequently its (often-contrary) internal identities should be in dispute more than usually in evidence. A corollary of this view is that some of these disputed identities will turn out to be counter-intuitive.

A relevant sphere of logic entailed by this state of affairs and the topic of this chapter is paradox, to which in the brief space available I now advert. Russell's Paradox, and the paradoxes of material implication, have shown that there is (either in principle or in the state of our ignorance) no consistent semantics for our classical logical calculi. Consequently, the logic of paradox, as well as the systems that entail them, includes live metaphoric expressions. This metaphoric status is obscured by suppression. The axioms of formal logic and the paradoxes which are their consequences are not allowed, in the required sense, to be properties of the allegedly 'literal' senses of the individual propositions with which they identify. But this isolationism is improper.

Wittgenstein's unpublished manuscript pages attest to a severe problem about what a proposition is in relation to strict finitism's inadequacy, when he (contrite in his acknowledgement of the distorting impact of the Frege–Russell view) said:

> It became clear of course that I didn't have a general concept of a proposition and of language . . . I had used a metaphor (of the projection method, etc.) but through the grammatical illusion of a *unitary concept* it didn't seem to be a metaphor.

One of my aims has been to absorb and articulate the force of Wittgenstein's recognition of one's using metaphor, together with his admission of the restrictions involved in traditional uses of 'proposition'. It would be presumptuous to suppose that had Wittgenstein lived to work for another 20 years of innovative research, he would have given equally transformational attention to his view of what it is to be a '*unitary concept*'. However, it appears that, if one introduces the notion of counter-intuition – as a motif to mirror the foregoing review of some developments in logic, proof and cosmology – then Wittgenstein's emphasis on surprise, the dawning of an aspect, and the bewitchment by form, assist one to assemble the foregoing into a new proposal. There is a prospect of a philosophy of a counter-intuitive unitary concept. (For one to air the possibility that such a move would flush out deeper continuities between Wittgenstein's earlier and later philosophies (as well as various others) in his vast output[44] is only a hunch. But the conjunction of many aspects of his *Tractatus* and the *Philosophical Investigations* often appears to be one of varying counter-intuitive continuities, rather than contradiction.) These remarks have nothing to do with a scribal, methodological concern with Wittgenstein's writings; the target is what the working philosopher was presupposing.

In some ways the foregoing, at the level of conceptual policy and its logics, sublimes the contrast between propositional philosophy and thus the grounds for its purported literary antithesis, by claiming to expose an underlying counter-intuitive domain, topologies and spiritualities, which, upon appropriate reconstruction, unify features of difference as functions of the actual identity of transcendence. In this perspective, the philosophy of revelation has an analogy in cosmology, creativity and logic. The conjunction of these three domains is found to have the internal property of counter-intuition.

Part III
Infinite metaphysics

4 Philosophy of mathematics, mathematical physics and creativity[1]

The rationality of originality

Literature is a pervasive domain,[2] one strand of which is semantic logic.[3] I propose that literary creativity contains super-condensed counter-intuitive rationality.[4] This interpolation of literary creativity into semantic logic is of course an intended challenge to our senses of relevance and relation. To get to the heart of some of the issues, we have to consider what it is to be a creative language. This discussion encompasses contemporary as well as ancient literature, and the status of the identity of distinctions that we employ to map literature. Clearly such classifying expressions as modernism or *modernité*[5] regress to major questions external to literature about the relations of history to literature. Within these relations are other patterns that are shared between distinct phenomena, such as features of rationality and generalisations.[6]

My argument is that creative natural language mirrors types of functions that occur in higher counter-intuitive formal languages, and the philosophy of mathematics. Such parallels are very far removed from elementary logic and its artificial systems. For those who balk at the thought of a parallel within natural languages and philosophy of mathematics, they might read Wittgenstein's (1998) *Philosophical Investigations*, §179–97, in which he addresses central problems of how to understand use in ordinary language by considering examples of arithmetic, algebra and mechanics. Wittgenstein's argument is that use in the two-formal and natural language domains satisfies some common criteria. The present chapter proposes that types of creative uses in both sorts of language have parallel properties. Colin McGinn (1984: 134) has criticised an interpretation applied to Wittgenstein, according to which 'the meaning of a word is progressively constituted or created by its use over time – determinate meaning is the final *result* of temporally extended use'. Originality is more unpredictable than that. Wittgenstein was concerned, however, with emphasising a particular type of constructivism in some of his work, whereas I will be attending to some parallels between natural languages and higher mathematics that are especially concerned with non-algorithmic, and sometimes undecidable, relations as well as with paradox.

The alignment of depicting ancient literary texts in the present chapter with philosophy of mathematics may be surprising to many. But it is not only for those interested in the latter topic. It is addressed to those concerned with literary creativity, as well as with the rationality of originality. I maintain that this involves researching a philosophy and logic for a theory of what it is to be creative literature, and what it is to be philosophy of mathematics.[7]

For those familiar with Wittgenstein's manuscripts[8] the massive presence of the concept of 'language game' will not surprise, though the extensive integration of natural language games with his research on philosophy of mathematics is less well known or explored. I argue that these relations are counter-intuitive, whether or not one agrees with Wittgenstein. A reason for attending to his research is that the depth and originality of his work constitute a fine sounding-board, even if one disagrees, though not always: Wittgenstein's friend and former student, Drury (1999) remarked: 'Wittgenstein had a great horror of what Schopenhauer once described as "professorial philosophy by philosophy professors"'. This is akin to Bernard Williams's (1998: 3) classification of Plato: 'It is a weakness of scholars who study philosophers to think that philosophers are just like scholars, and it is particularly a mistake in the case of Plato'. This may be the point of his aphorism of 1938: 'In philosophy the winner of the race is the one who can run most slowly. Or: the one who gets there last.'[9] This reference to *Ecclesiastes* is typical of an irony that is always a complex play that interprets its source.

Natural languages comprise those that are not symbolically abstract, and ancient languages are a subset of them, with biblical languages being a subset within this grouping. In Gibson (2001) these are viewed within a Near East, rather than theological, perspective. Each subset has it own territory, there are difficult problems of generalisation over these semantic fields, and their overlap conditions are not understood, though there is progress. Let us call the logic features of these languages, which can in principle[10] be classified together, 'domains'. Let us put aside, insofar as we can, traditional assumptions about the intrinsic alienation between nonformal and formal languages. Differences there certainly are; what they are and how to represent them is an entirely separate matter.

Original literature and logic

Central to the topic of literary sense are the issues of the relation of the formal to the nonformal in creative use within natural languages, and the topic of metaphor. Internal to all these problems is the function of literary creativity. It is to these that this chapter gives attention, but in its relation to logic and counter-intuition and in many respects, it is a new subject for philosophy.

Such semantics often house creative *singularities*, and as such counter-intuitive logic is a suitable mirroring structure to represent their semantic innovations. The concept of a singularity here is extremely important, as it pertains to counter-intuitive logic, whether it is in an ancient poem or in astrophysics. It is the epicentre of a collision between a law like expectation, and disconfirming original deviation.

It is worth selecting an example from within this zone of sensibilities to illustrate a general point. Features such as the ancient ironising of a literary tradition are central. It is too easy (falsely) to deem the collective tradition to be the author, and enforce an inaccurate death of an authorial voice, because our modern tradition of collective editorial processing is conflated with being the text, though this is not to dismiss ancient scribal editing. My point is that ancient and modern perceptual reading traditions are sometimes elided into being treated as the author. At this juncture literary creativity may be misrepresented, if we fail to notice the change of criteria between origination and institutional procession of the text. Clearly, many scribes wrote for their royal superiors or controlling audiences and conventions were merged with their identities. But beyond such tendencies there function narrative worlds that are against the grain of a committee or school harvesting indoctrination.

There is a constant tension between the tendency to assume an external metaphysical reality as a basis for a use of a rule in, or applied to, language, and the opposed desire for anarchy in judgement. This is also true for competing theories in higher mathematics[11] and linguistics. In stating this opposition it does not at all follow that metaphysics or anarchy as textual presuppositional should be banned. Instead, metaphysical and anarchistic assumptions should be traced, tracked and fitted.[12] Of themselves metaphysics and anarchy are parts of a healthy diet.

There are many plural language games. Quite possibly a conjunction of metaphysical *and* anarchistic presuppositions are functions of a text's own grammar. This amounts to a distinct question to the narrative's ultimate worldview. Evident though such a point is, we should make explicit the differences and *différance*, in principle and wherever possible in practice, between the cultural ethos in a text's theme, and our own. Attempts to isolate its logico-linguistic identities will assist in perceiving this division of labour, among many other benefits. Someone might compose logical poetry to argue anarchy, or an author might use inconsistent poetry that showed an ordered world (or *vice versa* in both cases) – witness Aragon's (1928) *Traité du style*, with his proclamation of surrealism without reason, but in which he employed inference. We should not impose a logical game that is at odds with the narrative. Unfortunately, this high ideal is something to which one might aspire, though not uniformly achieve it, while this is no reason to avoid the attempt.

Language games and philosophy of mathematics

Gibson (2001: 15, 207–8) shows that slips in philosophy of mind, to do with intuition and aspiration to generality, are often the causes of misrepresentation of a language-rule, where we construe the use of a language game as a model for ancient language. The constant concern in Gibson (2001) and in the present context is to discover what it is to be a use of a given language as a function of what it is to be language. Sure, the difference between ancient and modern languages is a propensity[13] of this issue. A presupposition of such a harness is to mirror the problems of the extent to which human consciousness under the rubric of the psychogenesis of language may have changed (or not) regarding mental causality, semantic universals (whatever those are) and the conditions of expression.

Accordingly, language 'game' is a technical term, though as is well known it is crafted from its natural language use in, for example, chess. We should be wary of innocent use of this comparison, however, not least since, for example, Wittgenstein's[14] employment of the expression. It will help to develop this notion to explain it as a live (not dead) metaphor, a theory of which is to be found in Gibson (1997, 2000), though Wittgenstein does not propose this idea. The point in this interpretation is that 'language game' is a fundamental function inherent to what it is to be human (or other) expression and communication. 'Game' is, in a technical sense, presuppositional semantics; it furnishes the criteria according to which sense is represented in signs to mediate facets of the world. This is an extremely close relation between semantics and 'game'. Our perceptual instability that obtains when we handle 'meaning' all too easily triggers misleading depiction.

What Hintikka (1998: 23) has entitled 'Janus-faced language games' – ones that are concerned with true/false bivalent logic games, displaying conformity to the law of excluded middle, and are directly involved in issues of empirical verification[15] – are only one group of a larger domain of games of logic(s). Other games, however, exhibit significant, sometimes hidden connections with and/or dependency upon concepts of truth, even where they dispute them. Formulations of relevance logics are instances of this situation. These presuppose semantics relative to a basis (such as juridical pragmatics, ideology, aesthetics, or formal logic). In this context we should allow space for the ways in which, as Tait (1996: 161), states, we should not identify computations with proofs. When we are aware of the force of this position, we will allow that there are unproved truths, and truths for which we have no consistency proofs. This applies especially to new work in astrophysical cosmology, and, not less, to deep problems in poetry which in some ways mirror some logical properties of exotic astrophysical cosmology. Consequently, unproved truths, precarious though it is unguardedly to assert them, may not be a function of ignorance, but of the qualitative depth and logical insight whose internal properties transcend proof as we grasp it. Here Wittgenstein's investigation of bewitched reliance on intuition competes with the state of affairs that he did not address: true counter-intuition.

A very low-level instance of this might be tone. Seemingly a rather too obvious example yet a basic one, of a phenomenon in the language game of which we still have limited comprehension is that of the proper name. Is the meaning of a logical proper name that of referring? Let us suppose it is, as Gibson (2001, ch. 3) argues. (Denyer (1998) has proven that some of the formal and natural language ramifications of the asymmetry of logical proper names as opposed to logical predicates are fundamental as Gibson (2001) supposed.) But is this 'referring' 'literal' (evidently 'literal' here is a somewhat obscure word to use, since may it be that no one has yet satisfactorily explained its use)? Well, obviously not literal in a German sense of Frege's use for *Bedeutung* (reference) – for example, a signpost pointing (*deuten*). So what is it?[16] Is this a live metaphor of pointing? Is it ostensive reference? What is *that*? And does it betray that, hidden in formal logic, is a use of live metaphor? Has metaphor been extirpated from it? Here the focal point of concern to isolate is that the presuppositional function within a proper name – regarding reference – is both elementary, and necessary for it to convey a referent's identity; yet it is a recondite matter to determine. There is scope for differing views here; Smiley (1982) has a fine analysis of some of the issues as they concern definite descriptions, or epithets; but such disagreement is not going to assist the cases discussed in Gibson (2001), since it attends to those examples which were confused in their own presuppositional representation of a use.

At the side of the issue of reference in proper names, and in contrast with the confused intentional attempt to ascribe reference (denotation) to a predicate that does not actually pick out, by itself, a referent, it is worth noting the valuable studies of indirect reference in Recanati (1993) and of indexicalisation in Heal (1997). Concerning the latter, Jane Heal has isolated some conditions for how indexicalisation would be so narrowly specifiable that a referent's identity is successfully picked out using a highly unusual group of indexical expressions. None of this is relevant to salvage the cases criticised in Gibson (2001). Gibson (1998) showed in a context different from Heal's, yet complementary to her contribution, how some medieval logic might be redeveloped so as to extend analysis of informal elements (formally called 'improper supposition').

Wittgenstein was mostly concerned with how abstract uses rely on, or should be tested by, actual practice. In his later philosophies[17] he *did* engage with the problem of relating logical form to use, with which he (differently) grappled very early on in his *Tractatus*. It is usually stated that after 1945 he ceased work on the philosophy of mathematics, but this may not be true.[18] For him such exploration of the link with natural language games is central. I shall claim below that the extreme form of this issue – of how infinity and expressions, which have been iterated as non-logical, occur in finite expressions – is relevant to the question of creative literary language and its possible logics. This relation of creativity to logic is an agenda to which Wittgenstein was deeply sensitive, though it was off-stage from most of his immediate analytical concerns, though aphorised in Wittgenstein (1998). I conjecture that, for him, it lay ahead as a project that he planned to meet head-on at a future stage, but his journey was cut short by cancer. He showed clear signs within this shortening span, of urgent premature foreclosure on undeveloped large-scale projects. The trap would be for us to indulge in secondary tidying-up of Wittgenstein's probing, in seeming faithfulness to some carefully calculated end game. He had hoped to take more crazy[19] unprecedented turns. So should we.

The functions of use, context and intertextual criteria have parallels in natural language and philosophy of mathematics. Wittgenstein's later writings contain explorations of language games that show he furnished grounds for replaced concepts of calculus in higher mathematics with notions of games. A reason for this is that some higher mathematics is undecidable. He knew that the denial of this would lead one to conflate proof with truth. This knowledge reflects the thesis that the representation of significance in the two mathematical and natural language domains share properties. He opposed the view that mathematics is experimental (and so is unlike empirical science), yet he propounded the concept that mathematics is constructed from practice. This narrow window that avoids the experimental, as opposed to grounding in empirical practice (in the sense that the latter is not revisable, while the former is), is itself a counter-intuitive position whose force is all-too-readily obscured. A crazy question, therefore: what would it be to have a game whose empirical practice was grounded in infinity functions in − or as the antecedent cause of − the Big Bang, of whose residue radio-astronomy has indirect surveyable evidence?

Games, constructivist mathematics and infinite play

The mastery of use in many mathematical senses typically tends to concern language which is not itself *original*, and which does not introduce original changes in use, while a user's standard employment may be premised on a presupposition of the semantic value which commenced its first game-play, at another previous diachronic or synchronic cultural point as an original function. Although there are extensive theories of standard linguistic usage as well as of deviance, there is little decisive theory concerning the theory or *logic of* creative literary originality. The concept of a language game as a construction, or a process involving construction, is an aid to contribute to the anatomy of originality. Frequently constructivism is taken to be the contrary of, say, a mathematical game interpreted as a discovery. But given that recognising a concept is not an internal property of its identity (see Lewy, 1976; Gibson, 1998, 2000), it follows that discovery and constructivism may be, at appropriate junctures, mutually compatible features and functions of our use of language games.

On this approach, specifically contextualised originality is an archetypal game with a localised function (perhaps with a greater than local value) of incommensurability that can be transformed (or transforms itself) into a commensurable relation with standard use, usually once it is absorbed into a conceptual idiolect and its semantic fields. This does not have to concur with Kuhn's (1999: 36) later work, according to which incommensurability is a relation between parts of language, though this later conception happens to complement the view in the present context. Note also the consistency of Kuhn's view with my presupposition (though distinct to his own ones) that there is a live metaphorical continuum between the logical games of natural as well as scientific languages, allowing for counter-intuitive[20] transitions which are themselves new bridging games. Moreno (1999) maintains that Kuhn's latest position on incommensurability does not require a plurality of inaccessible worlds (relevant in view of the later part of this chapter).

Nancy Cartwright (1999) has refined the notion of 'theory-nets', derived from earlier German structuralist uses. Theory-nets are encapsulating and sifting frameworks for isolating and regimenting plural sets of theories into a more generalised conceptual form than a theory. (She tackles links between physics and economics.) This is a valuable tool for multi-disciplinary scenarios. Although theory-nets are distinct to the foregoing perspective, they can be employed as a concept to position relations between different language games and their depiction.

I argue that literary originality is itself a game whose values transcend other literary (and/or non-literary) games while presupposing a range of the latter's assigned values to be transformed. Theory-nets may be used to focus this notion of transcendence. The original re-use of a game, or one of its subsets, has the property of at least local incommensurability. Theory-nets have the job of highlighting or assessing conjunctions of such games in theory itself. So we can deploy this state of affairs to model the object languages that deviate from a standard game play.

A semantic conjunction of two or more distinct texts is an intertext. An original text seems to be a type of extended unpredicted counter-intuitive metaphoric intertext. (There also appears to be a psychological presupposition shared between such texts, in the sense that to track an intertext presupposes or requires some features of mentality as antecedents of the conjunction. Of course this is entirely different from the claim which is *not* being made; that the semantic value which is the conjunction is the description which represents an intention so to communicate the intertextual relation, though this conjunction may sometimes coincide with an intention.) The point concerning a metaphoric intertext is relevant because originality is partly a function of deep intertextual dislocating relations, together with semantics that derive from a fractured tradition, mentality and literary futures. We have the task of making explicit the criteria of original creative narrative. A culture, which imposes interpretations that have smoothed over the discontinuities comprising originality, may confuse computability with suppression of the new. Parallels with philosophies of language and of mathematics are helpful illustrations in this multidimensional situation. From the standpoint of a mastery of the technique of certain large domains of particular finite computations, a use's reconfigurations are algorithmic in a bounded manner. We recall that an algorithm is a function of a calculus,[21] and the algorithm has the capacity to 'predict' or, in the above context, to retroject.

Wittgenstein's use of 'calculus' was a very narrowly circumscribed one, however. Many uses of this term, for example, in the case of 'genetic algorithms', have a very different extended live metaphoric sense compared to Wittgenstein's. For example, what Kallel and Naudts (1999) consider being a 'simple genetic algorithm' goes beyond the scope of his concept, not least since it is unsurveyable. The present study allows that such concepts are included in the field of calculi, but treats as significant the feature that they are unsurveyable. It appears that such a restriction, together with the function of longpath random statistical analyses, is evidence that such genetic evolutionary employment of 'algorithm' is a quantifiable live metaphor. So this type of domain amounts to an interesting formalism to use as a precedent for theory-net modelling of creative language. If Gibson (1997, 2000 and 2000a) is correct to generalise live metaphor as a device to depict central aspects of creative literature, then such a model will assist us to depict the identity of what it is to be creative language.

If we avoid constructivism, we can construe the mathematical calculation as discovery of a conclusion; G. H. Hardy (1941) takes this approach. Wittgenstein fiercely disputed Hardy's nonconstructivist pure mathematics theories, as is witnessed in his handwritten notes (Wittgenstein, 1941) in the margins to his copy of Hardy (1941: 29–30, 40–1, 117, 119, 198–9), while he had esteem for Hardy's ability and dedication to the infinite. As Nedo (1993: 61–71) records, a significant part of Wittgenstein's (1978) analysis of Hardy's views is missing from the *Remarks on the Foundations of Mathematics*.[22] This omitted discussion is central for recovery of his appreciation of Hardy, while articulating Wittgenstein's criticism of Hardy. My reason for bothering to present this history is to prepare the way for positioning and disputing Wittgenstein's insistence on strict finitism, while he allowed for a defence of our use of the infinity that was criticised by Hardy (1929). Marion (1998: 189–91) has already nicely reproduced and interpreted the relevant sequence, so I quote his helpful presentation here, opening first with a passage from *Zettel* (§273) where Wittgenstein (1981) refers to the following remark by Hardy:

> That 'the finite cannot understand the infinite' should surely be a theological and not a mathematical war-cry.
>
> (Hardy, 1929: 5)

Quoting it, Wittgenstein adds:

> True, the expression is inept. But what people are using it to try and say is: 'We mustn't have any juggling! How comes this leap from the finite to the infinite?' Nor is the expression all that nonsensical – only the 'finite' that can't conceive the infinite is not 'man' or 'our understanding' but the calculus. And *how* this conceives the 'infinite' is well worth an investigation.

Marion (1998: 189–91) observes:

> [Wittgenstein's] argument is, simply, that it is misleading to characterise the distinction between finite and infinite in terms of abilities of human beings *vis-à-vis* those of God. In fact, Wittgenstein would claim that this epistemological characterisation comes to mind when one is not making the proper 'grammatical' distinction between finite and infinite series . . . Wittgenstein claims in his own terms that 'the infinite has the property of a law' . . . of a 'possibility of the symbolism', that of the fact that sets no limits to its application . . . [He] 'insisted on not conceiving the infinite as a huge quantity'.

In pursuing Wittgenstein's invitation to investigate, we may note that it seems not anywhere to have been suggested that his position leaves it open to develop a concept of the infinite as a mapping function for a range of original uses in literary games. The expression 'infinite' carries with it a wide range of associations. There is a danger of equivocation; but there is also the prospect of a bootstrap theorem: of inference or attachment between different, separated senses. Crudely speaking, if a line goes off a graph, it goes to infinity. At the other end of the range there are concepts of actual infinity. In certain contexts some readers may prefer to eject the use of 'infinity' and replace it with some sense of 'sublime', 'transcendental', and this will be an agreeable practice, if such readers wish to make the necessary adjustment to the presentation, since this chapter amounts to the proposal of the basis for a new concept. I claim that there is a complex series of relations between these qualities that enables inference between them to be achieved, and presuppose this in the present remarks, while concentrating here on aspects of the role of infinity.

The following considerations are central to the new interpretations associated with the employment of 'infinity' here and elsewhere in the present narrative. These uses of 'infinity' will not be suitable or applicable to all literary uses. I programmatically project this type of 'infinity' as one that can be assigned to a domain, or an ideal, of great creative literature that satisfies this designation. Between this type and examples of literary creativity with less of a claim to be grouped as such, there will be a gradient, along which, in principle, varieties of literary creativity display. Given that it is qualitative infinity that occupies the highest ranking, it will nevertheless be inappropriate to follow the usual debates about what example of such art is 'the best'. The reason for this is that infinity is itself without quantifiable limits. So 'the best' is a misnomer. Nevertheless, surely the contrast in principle of a fundamental qualitative difference between, say, Shakespeare's *Hamlet* and a Barbara Cartland novel is entrenched in objectively true judgement. Contrariwise, we may wish to dismiss the allegation that differences between, for example, *Hamlet* and Emily Brontë's *Wuthering Heights* rest on the unquantifiable merit of the former, in contrast with the quantifiable demerits of the latter.[23]

Although admitting the current limitations of our grasp of such associations, let us, rather, explicitly notice some relevant restrictions in our knowledge of logic. First order logic is undecidable, and not all functions from a known function to a known function are themselves computable, so there are undecidable sentences in logic.[24] Consequently our knowledge of what it is to be a measurable function in logic is severely restricted. There are also paradoxical entailments. Now it may be difficult for someone like Russell to walk across the formal space between such logic and literary language; but that space is negotiable. We here have precedents, with relevance logic, of logic relative to a basis that is literary creativity. (I am also concerned to allow for undecidable expressions, and will sometimes not pursue this matter, reserving it for attention elsewhere,[25] and will leave them under the rubric of discussion about infinity though, of course these two groups need to be separated.)

Exploring new pasts with future possibility

For those disposed to extract from such matters the conclusion that 'anything' goes, while they dump logic and embrace transient novelty for assessing literature, it should also be recognised that the negation of 'anything goes' is entailed by this expression. Of course this *full* range is never practised.

In the ways we employ 'anything goes' it is often a prophylactic euphemism for its negation in some uses. There is a need for us to attempt to get clear what are the deeper divisions of identity between what is experimentation versus what is a counterfeit *and* unexplored possibilities. We need a new counter-intuitive renaissance (not counter-renaissance) of logic. We were too long complacent in the last century, often superficially basking in versions of modernism[26] which do not do justice to its origins or future.[27] In respect of the above topic, we have not yet identified *what it is to be* the border between such subjects in the game of language. Is language an invented construction, or a discovery? Is there original sense? Or is it a counterfeit perception of its own potential? Or is it a function of a game, or the game itself? Certainly, such questions are under-determined or over-determined, and press in bizarre directions. But they squeeze out into the open latent aspects of unresolved encounters with our ignorance.

Are counter-intuitive (i.e. creative) facets of European modernisms versions of what, in the appropriate senses, has had, or will have, other manifestations? Modern cultural forms can exemplify this for the present context, though the hypothesis seems to apply generally. A reason for this sketch is the ways in which literary imagination and logic participate in such a flow of cultural dispositions, in relation to the prospect of accessibility for mapping in semantics and logic in such domains.

For example, Gibson and O'Mahony (1995) interpret the final high phase of Sumerian Ur's literary tragic oeuvre as a *fin-de-siècle* modernism; and Gibson (2000, 2000a) develops parallels between the literary logic of nineteenth-century French *modernité* and Sumerian. In some historic typologies there will be catastrophe deformations, for example elements of extreme personality disorder modernism in European nationalism, and Sumerian iconoclasm (see Gibson, 2000b). I do not see that this is incompatible with a counter-intuitive unpredictable future for our literary cultures. We require a model for cultural continuities and differences, along the lines of non-algorithmic counter-intuitive grasp of originality, which privileges absence and presence as a function of cultural innovations.

Gibson (1997, 1998 and forthcoming a) argues that to have a concept in or of a language game is not itself a recognitional function of understanding it. In this respect, we are rather like the human who, say, thinking in sixteenth-century BC Cypro-Minoan Cyprus, did not have much of a clue that her sign system exhibited traceable associations with Luvian and Dravidian, despite her having a mastery and perhaps a concept of her system. Likewise, we do have a concept of her using the system, and do not have much of a clue how to understand it. But this also goes for unexpected chunks of our contemporary knowledge, especially where we think we are the ones who know.

The interpretation of a conjunction for modelling ancient comparative literature, poststructuralism, and true/false logics, is a fertile, largely unexplored domain, which has significant interest for research on literary creativity, and consequently its relevance for logic of literature. Certainly, there are many issues such as intentionality, of which we now have explicit knowledge; but this is not itself understanding, and we regularly proffer examples of the former as though they were the latter.

We counterfeit perceptions of identities.[28] This disposes us to counterfeit identities of games, and of our narratives going proxy *as a rule*. In this sense, I suggest 'counterfeit' here is an antonym of counter-intuition. One of the subsets of the counterfeit game, of rule following, is the coercion of research policies in directions that mirror the unconscious that implements such counterfeiting. In a culture where corporate copying of mediocrity and the erasure of individuality fallaciously attempts to ensure quality by a degrading of qualitative properties through misuse of a quantitative criterion, we would do well to interrogate the functionaries who promote intellectual counterfeiting as a rule of policy. As a resistance to these aliens, we should encourage anarchy and modesty.

New values of the constructivist game

The situation is similar in logic research generally; we are not very good at understanding. This even extends to complex algorithms and algorithm-like expression. So imagine how unreliable we are in our comprehension of *non*-algorithmic fields of expression. And our consciousness seems to be non-algorithmic. Despite this we have a capacity to recognise new uses, or at least ones that we have not seen before, on the basis of some prior knowledge of semantic types in usage. We see the developing recognition of the relevance of the algorithmic within the developing pattern of applied mathematics in ancient Sumer, *circa* 2100–1600 BC, concerning the emergence of quasi-algorithmic calculations, as Robson's (1999) study shows. Here Wittgenstein's concept of a calculus as a mastery of a technique tested in practice is particularly interesting, for if he is right to place a game as a means to index a quality of human consciousness, then we may assign his results as devices to map some features of the ancient Mesopotamian and related mentality, taking due care over quantification into opaque contexts and intentionality. Corporate media seem to be inducing a denuding of the individual so that the tedium of the low level algorithmic, and the ancient quasi-algorithmic appear to be types that all too easily can be used as live metaphors to represent contemporary anti-individualist influences. And this occurs in our epoch, when the emergence of the non-algorithmic holds counter-intuitive unpredictable prospects. This perspective on collective contemporary influence to induce stereotype mentality is appropriate as an important means to strike a contrast between compliance with a learnt technique and the philosophy of creativity.

The non-algorithmic sphere of usage predominates in creative expression. Using the interpretations developed in this chapter as a thought-bridge,[29] we can provisionally associate some results from the analysis of our mentality as a preliminary model to analyse the archaeology of mind, as Gibson (2000a) demonstrates, and which in the present context is presupposed as premise and qualification on my remarks.

Relevance logic can be used to map some of these types, as clarified by Smiley (1998) and Read (1988). This is where pragmatics comes in by the appeal to a basis that may or may not be explicitly internal to the language game. If this basis is expressed by semiotic phenomena external to the linguistic domain, then it helpfully demonstrates that part of the basis for logic in the semantic domain is in the external world. Gibson (2000) presents this as a virtual reality relation between language and world. As Hobson (1995) explains, Diderot's use of digression and tracing of submerged likenesses is somewhat similar to virtual reality simulation and probing for new possibilities. The external empirical domain differs from, yet in function has parallels with, the concept of reference and the relation of an expression in a literary text being 'true of', in the sense that there is no reason why a logical function has to be coded in or only in a written medium. In this respect, then, relevance logics are radical yet recognisable ways of showing that the external world manifests conditions that can be depicted in logic.

Since we have paradox and undecidable sentences within classical logic, these features can be mapped as they occur in the external world. This confirms the probity of seeing that a deductive logic of ancient or many other texts is a subset of a perhaps undecidable domain that mirrors the empirical world. It eventually follows from such considerations that the literary customs were incorrectly characterised as essentially infected with illogical properties by logic formalists such as Russell. Perhaps some of these are really complex counter-intuitive logical properties. If they display paradox, so does logic. That these may not be composed of the same family of paradoxes is no problem because many logicians dispute that paradoxes in logic comprise one family (see Sainsbury, 1995). In this way, we might consider formulating a counter-intuitive mimesis:[30] language is not a copying medium of course; but an imaginative virtual reality simulator with counter-intuitive, as well as bewitching, tendencies (Gibson 2000a applies this concept to the ancient Near East). Clearly creative literature is nonformal in style. Just what this amounts to in relation to being rational is a deep question.

The rules that may obtain for a mastery of techniques that implement knowledge of such logic would be extraordinarily complex. But this might be akin to the complexity of a 'simple'[31] profound obscure poem, such as Shakespeare's 'The phoenix and the turtle'. We should remember that we are in the early days of what is paradoxically called chaos theory.[32] This may relate to our ignorance of what a formal logic of simplicity is. It appears that at least some ancient literary texts display chaos and complexity functions.[33] So we should beware of presupposing that our contemporary perceptions of logic are entirely successful scanning devices capable of classifying contrasts between 'primitive' ancient texts as a function of discontinuity with modern logic. This is so because complexity is a prime characteristic of our world, whereas simplicity is often a successful working counterfeit of the former, with simplicity invisibly trading on complexity (often by use of an unacknowledged suppressed premise, as Gibson (1998) contends).

We might mix distinct doctrines of constructivism and realist nonconstructivist mathematics, without equivocation. Just as one can produce an anti-realist account of a realist world (in which truth-claims are still veridical candidates), so with the two constructivist and realist approaches, in selecting from among the many versions of both these opposed conceptions. This mirrors a doctrine I introduce for consideration. Namely, that the external universe is itself constructed of differing realities whose representation or depiction should embody its ontological asymmetries. Pertinent to our ignorance is the point that we may misread one strand of sense as another. For example we might confuse nonconstructivism with constructivism, when attempting to retrieve a writer's view. We find Juliet Floyd (2001) convincingly and elegantly arguing that Wittgenstein was not a mathematical constructivist, though for many years he has been read as if he were. Obviously this does not suppose that the material world is psychology or logic. Rather, its dispositional and other identities are various, and require a multiplicity of asymmetric theories. We may be confident, however, that discontinuities in games are transition capabilities between games. Wittgenstein thought along these lines as early as 1930–3, though the present framework is distinct to his. As G. E. Moore recalled, Wittgenstein (1994: 104) argued the following: although knowledge of all our games would not yield an understanding of one universal game, all the games have propensities for one to move from game to game. And frequently we are unaware of these transitivities in others and ourselves. For example, without embracing any of A. N. Whitehead's later process philosophy, in his conception of identity theory in his pure mathematics (Whitehead, 1898), we find that he already had a mathematical 'process' relational view of identity in his algebra and geometry. This deems a point in space to be a process with varying conditions, which is tantamount to perceptual projection.

Another type of unsystematic mixing in applied mathematics, and one that has regular use in applied mathematics, is the axiom of choice.[34] This axiom has successful uses in applied mathematics, yet it also provokes problems such as involving undecidable entailments, and in a functional theory-net it gathers and invents a 'unity' for disparate functions. A generous pluralist developing a constructability theory, such as Chihara (1998: 316), recognises that his theory will not enable him to assert the axiom of choice, though he does not consider this ground for rejecting the theory.

Such preferences will partly depend on whether or not one follows Plato in respect of the Forms. The present author does not, though a consequence of the present argument is that a new nonconstructivist theory of types is possible. It seems that mathematics and cosmology show us to be yet too early in the history of science to know what the metaphysics of the universe is. A problem for such Platonism is that the fine-tuning which the material structure of the universe manifests, so obviously manifests an explicit counter-intuitive fine-tuning satisfying a criterion identity from deeper levels. On this view there is no hidden form (in the relevant sense) in the microphysics and astrophysics: the form is in the universe, not hidden behind it, complex and counter-intuitive though a cosmology would have to be to encapsulate its identity. Of course this is not to dismiss or engage with the debates about a transcendent identity external to the universe.

Let us, then, provisionally concede constructivism to be true for only *some* domains, or set of levels of mathematical and natural languages. Yet we maintain the claim that infinity might also be a function of these domains in some counter-intuitive sense.[35] The logics of algorithms extended from calculus cover a wide domain of constructivism here, though there will be many conceptions of 'algorithm' presupposed for such usage, and it is a separate question of whether or not these are reducible to the one notion (as with 'paradox', we are unclear as to whether or not this tags a mutually related single family, or contrary ones).

If we apply the idea, that having a concept is not (or is not necessarily) a recognitional concept, to the philosophy of literary creativity and of mathematics, then we have to admit that in extant formulations of these subjects constructivist status is combined with nonconstructivist realism. So we should represent this state of affairs as components in a theory-net to structure what we know or can know of these domains. On this approach, for example, we may have to acknowledge that, at least for some higher domains involving counter-intuition, we tangle constructivism with the discovery of nonconstructivist insights. In using this term 'tangle' I have in mind, as an analogy, Freeman Dyson's (1985: 73) attempt mathematically to characterise the early states of the organic world.

Counter-intuitive constructivism, literary games and infinity

Although many features of mathematical philosophy are constructivist, they are non-algorithmically so. Some of these are counter-intuitive non-algorithmic functions that manifest the concepts of counter-intuitive, realist nonconstructivist characteristics in this domain. These two options scramble a corporate imposition of constructivist tradition on universes of meaning that disallows the division of spoils between rational two power-blocks. Let us designate the constructivist prospect α, and the second the counter-intuitive realist domain β, and in the case of β it is not algorithmically computable by mathematical means, though it can in principle be known.

Although the world may generally manifest binary states of affairs, it does not follow from this that binaries comply with history's leading institutionalised philosophical influences. Prado (2003) argues that Deleuze's constructivism has infinity as one of its properties. Deleuze would no doubt have objected to

Prado's interpretation of the former's compatibility with Wittgenstein, however. Other figures, such as Bouveresse (1987, 1997) have developed important interpretations along more standard lines. Deleuze and Guattari (1994) have no problem in claiming that infinity occurs in literature, though some may judge that this amounts to a reinstatement of the sublime. Sure, some analytical philosophers will suppose that this is because they did not understand what they claimed; but empirical protectionism is hardly courteous to eclectic originality, nor objective.

There is nothing in Wittgenstein's late writings which requires that we have to be able veridically to master all uses of games, especially so if the domain is taken to be outside of the concepts we have of rule-following, though Wittgenstein did not explicitly expound this possible move (cf. McGinn, 1984: 124). That is, Wittgenstein's presupposition is descriptive principle, not pejorative prescription. Wittgenstein contended that a practical mastery of a use is necessary for understanding a language game. Obviously, this does not at all entail that one has to have a verification of such a usage at all times. So we may not draw the inference from our inability logically to map all language in literary usage, that literary games are not logical rule-following functions. Even so, these functions would seem to be extraordinarily complex.

Gibson (1981, 2001)[36] referred to Hintikka's (1962) research, though the profound and influential joint work by M. and J. J. Hintikka (1986), which exposed a whole new perspective in Wittgenstein's development, was not yet written. Hintikka's (1998) quite different approach is committed to a fresh future and scope for analytical philosophy. Hintikka (1998) devises a new conditional constructivist first order logic in which the infinity of the universe of games can be expressed by using, among other things, the identity sign '=' as the only predicate (Hintikka, 1998: 187). Wittgenstein, however, disallowed identity from being incorporated into the foundations of mathematics. The present study allows space for some of Hintikka's views, while presupposing that the universe of signification is sufficiently and relativistically rich to permit different interpretations. Hinging these together is the thesis about relative identity.[37]

Hintikka (1998: 192) states that in his interpretation, 'all questions concerning such a mathematical theory can thus in principle be reduced to questions concerning the logical truths of second-order logic', and he maintains that this seems to apply to 'practically all mathematical theories and hence to mathematical propositions that can be formulated in them'. His proof maintains that the entire higher order logic can be reduced to a fragment[38] of second order logic, and consequently this theory is translatable into Hintikka's new first or-der logic and language that has a finite range. Although Hintikka (1998) has major similarities to Hilbert's (1922) combinatorial approach, as he states, Hintikka (1998: 199–200) investigates the problem involving infinitary combinatorics of the objects of mathematical enquiry. Hintikka (1998: 204) explains that in some sense we can have a universal logic, and it can formulate its own truth-conditions. If there can be a universal language, it has to be extended beyond what we have and instinctively anticipate from the history of logic and mathematics. So, from such a relativistic position of constructivism, we can embrace the view that counter-intuitive realism (albeit of an unusual sort) is true, and that language can embrace infinity, if Hintikka is correct, or some other interpretation holds, with the present chapter as a complementary possibility.

According to Wittgenstein, since we cannot complete an infinite sum, the infinite cannot be a quantitative calculation – cannot be a function of a surveyable calculus, *in our constructivist* comprehension of experience. He claimed that, consequently, the infinite is a quality (i.e., on this view, such activities as counting, relevant ordering, and ending a calculation cannot be performed). Although it is true that we cannot, ourselves, complete an infinite sum, yet if God exists, God has. If God does not exist, the empirical universe and its origins, or multiverse and its infinite ensemble of universes, may embody infinite qualitative phenomena of which we may have experience. On the two latter prospects such infinity may be intransigent to our logical scrutiny, though given the counter-intuitive identities of exotic empirical phenomena and the unpredictable forms which higher mathematics takes, we cannot be certain that infinity is intractable. With the former viewpoint that God exists, God could have manifested or mirrored such properties of infinity in a variety of ways (for which see Gibson, 2000).[39] On both scenarios, human imagination may yet strike, or may have struck, lucky, or not. If we follow Hintikka's (1998: 187) equations, the universe is infinite in logical terms. (Of course we need to bear in mind that this is not an empirical statement about the astrophysical universe but a mathematical domain, though the unexpected ways in which new discoveries in pure mathematics not infrequently reify into microphysical ontology should give us cause to explore counter-intuitive links between a model and empirical states.)

So the question arises, what is the infinite in relation to finite experience, and how might the infinite as quality obtrude on these current issues? There is only limited space to propose future routes here. I suggest that nonmathematical domains such as certain examples of literature, music and art are media that can mirror, tap into or display infinite qualities whether or not this was intended. We should not of course confuse 'unquantifiable' with 'infinite' here. I argue that there are cosmological, logical and aesthetic grounds to postulate an infinite complex domain.[40]

A significant example of such a counter-intuitive instability, which might be seminal for future insights, occurs in a joint observation by the mathematician Freeman Dyson and the musician/chemist Christopher Longuet-Higgins (cf. Freeman Dyson, 1985: 55–6). In a hypothesis about the origins of life, Freeman Dyson devises a model for the emergence of metabolism. The error-rate for the ordered state in this model has a function Δ whose value is extraordinarily narrow and precise.[41] As Freeman Dyson noted, Longuet-Higgins explained that the quantity Δ is also the fractional difference in pitch between a perfect fifth and an equi-tempered fifth. Freeman Dyson explained that on a logarithmic scale of pitch, a perfect fifth is $(\log - \log 2)$ and an equi-tempered fifth is seven semitones or $(7/12) \log 2$. This micro-tuning precision is a function of the equi-tempered scale's general functional felicity. It is important for the philosophical purpose of the present chapter that there are such counter-intuitive quantitative cross-links between distinct subjects, with, in the case of musical creativity, the functions of the numerical values having completely aesthetic functions.

The counter-intuitive mystery of emergent physics

The occurrence of these links in the deep structure of three dimensions is, I propose, analogous with the identities of M-structures in 11-dimensional space. This is a model of a transformed super string universe in which concepts display vibrational harmonies (cf. Witten, 2002). Following Witten's (1998: 1127) account, typical string effects – consequently on 11-dimensional supergravity theory – are proportional to a new constant α' (of the order of 10^{-32} cm), which determine string size, whereas traditionally quantum effects are proportional to the Planck constant h. The deformation of the string constant α' is largely dependent on understanding the deformation of h, though this is not mathematically resolved for more than two dimensions (see Witten, 1998). This scenario is a function of what are anticipated to be physically feasible prospects within M-theory. In mirror symmetry, two distinct space–times within a very narrow context of topology can be linked to a real classical topology. In M-theory when h and α' are non-zero, there is a matrix in which an unprecedented noncommutativity emerges, and new dualities.[42] So, with respect to the function of emergence theories in science, we have no veridical provable basis in theory or empiricism to reduce creativity to a self-contained identity.

Inflation used to be a matter of an effect subsequent to the Big Bang. As a result of M-theory we now have inflation scenarios of physics derived from and co-extensive with this universe that obtained shortly before the Big Bang (see for example, Kane 2000: 125–6). If this result turns out to be correct, then it prevents us from treating the Big Bang as the space–time point at which – irreducibly and internally self-caused – the physics of our universe began. In a multiverse scenario, there will have been and will be a virtually infinite number of universes. If the primary theory of our own universe turns out to be the same for all such universes, then the traditional question of the cause of this universe regresses to the question of: 'From where did the first universe come?' In this way, with the suitable larger scale framing, the traditional problem is not dismissable by the M-theory scenario. The main objection to this restoration is no doubt going to be that there is no original cause since in the multiverse we have an eternally recurrent series. Well, a few objections. First, we do not know for certain what the primary theory, or model that depicts the necessary conditions for our universe, is. But if its inner core has been discovered, it does not follow that this core obtains for another or all other universes, even if this seems an elegant idea. This situation blocks universal generalisation for other universes by any known M-theory interpretation, since it cannot guarantee that the primary theory is the same for physics for the multiverse. Secondly, if I may merely briefly summarise the objection, which can be read in some detail in my other research.[43] A pre-Big Bang primordial black hole is sometimes postulated as the antecedent for our and other universes. A typical figure presented for this is a density of the order of 10^{94} gm^{-3}. To say the least, this manifests an extraordinarily high probability that there is no empirical pathway of inference from a primary theory holding in our universe to another universe – so as to guarantee the occurrence of the same primary theory holding for it – where a state of affairs of the order of 10^{94} gm^{-3} stands between the universes. Whatever the case, it is evident that for the physical theorist or theist to exercise belief here involves counter-intuitive transcendence about creativity.

On the basis of locally quantifiable, yet non-algorithmic equations, whose universalised identities remain matters of coherent empirical yet transcendental projection, we could compose a fresh concept of which the following is a bare outline. For each or some sets of finite identities of a calculus and its empirical implementation, there is a counter-intuitive analogue that has numerical and/or logical counter-parts in this universe, whose *emergence* and forms are counter-intuitive consequences of a constructivist analysis, while yet they are nonconstructivist functions.

'Emergence' has counter-intuitive relations to complexity, reductionism and creativity. John Holland (1998) offers a fine account of some relations of complexity to emergence. Typically some system is presupposed within which emergence occurs, and this system is generated as a function of a model that guarantees the operation of laws. Unfortunately – in relation to the origin of emergence itself – this is a circular sequence in which the properties designated by 'system', 'model', the 'operation of laws', and 'reductionism', do not exist. That is to say, to resume and conclude the foregoing argument of chapter 1 (in the section 'Counter-intuitive pictures'), for emergence the quoted proposition in (B) needs to have 'necessarily' deleted, and also the remaining proposition is false:

(B) Is it true that: 'necessarily, whatever is drawn as a consequence must be contained in the antecedent premises'?

Characteristically, emergence is a function of operating systems, and accordingly emergence is not a function without a presupposed context. In the perspective of the origin of all systems, such creativity cannot appeal to emergence without assuming what is to be proved. This applies both to the logic of complex emergence, and to relevant presupposed ontologies. A function is a use in a state, for example in a game theory model, and for which ideally there will be a prediction about other future states. In relation to certain aspects of supersymmetry, however, postdictions are predictions that are already known, except that they have to be singular consequences of the state that is thus depicted as a determinative test of the relevant theory. Supersymmetry is a partially worked out new basis for physics, not a veridical theory, promising though it is. As Kane (2000) has elegantly shown, a new major primary theory is required to harness and adjust supersymmetry, string theory, and M-theory to facilitate a position even theoretically to formulate a basis for a theory of everything that covers physical phenomena, as conceived to obtain for our universe. For example Witten (2002) has demonstrated that (M-theory) supersymmetry is likely to be of central importance in cosmology, in connection with dark matter and related phenomena.[44] One cannot as yet correctly adopt the supersymmetric insight as an accurate framework for *assuming* or explaining the truth of emergence without circularity. If proof for supersymmetry comes to fruition, this will not ensure a foundation for emergence because supersymmetry has not thereby been guaranteed as the state prior to our universe's supersymmetry.

Furthermore the hidden or broken symmetry presumed to be a property of our supersymmetric physical world is itself a function of the sort of counter-intuitive state discussed in the present book and in Gibson (2000). This opens up the way to a model and associated states for a fresh objective realm within nature, while in some ways, as Edward Witten (2000: xii) states, 'Showing that nature is supersymmetric would change that [our basic way of thinking about space and time], by revealing a quantum measure of space and time, not measurable by ordinary numbers.' (See, for example, Beasley and Witten (2003).)

Retrojective functions of this state are both easier (regarding standard models of particle physics) and virtually impossible (respecting anomalous singularities) to predict. For all past functions of the states of the game it is in principle possible to retroject what they are. But this is not so for the emergence of the game – or all models. The reason is that *the emergence of emergence is not an internal property of a model in which emergence is a function*. We may wish to assign what have crudely been called 'the laws of chance' or 'the laws of complexity' to a conjectured state prior to the existence of the physical state configured by the model under question. But that simply will not do, and is a dogmatic policy, not a calculation.

So we cannot consistently or empirically adopt 'emergence' as a universal constant to explain cosmic origins; nor can we thus assume self-contained creativity, for the universe, in the relevant sense, is not the sum of its parts. Rather, its emergent origin is in excess of its parts. For a state of affairs that has no such relevant parts, but for which there is a sum – i.e., emergent creation or creativity – it is fallacious, and without empirical basis, to use emergence as a property to explains its origins.

One of the possibilities in the scenario of non-algorithmic qualitative emergence is that number, quantity and logic themselves have qualitative counter-parts in their deep structure. For example, let us suppose that in a continuum there is a *quantitative* use and a *qualitative* use. This has its counterpart in the relations between quantitative analysis and the qualitative analysis, which uses quantities. Scientists can implement either or both analyses using the same material, except that the qualitative analysis tackles unresolved, often larger-scale questions, starting with an unresolved problem. Here the context of quantitative, or qualitative, use makes different contributions to compose a term's semantic value, since a use is a function of its context.

Consider colour words as an example:[45] red is red, but there are different reds; and there are variously functions of distinct contexts that code red values appropriate to those contexts. 'Red' in infinity may resemble 'red' in a constructivist context, but these terms may be accorded partially different values suitable to their domains. This is comparable with Freeman Dyson's double use of Δ for a musical pitch, and for metabolism. The sense of 'context' here also has a counterpart in the use of π below. Namely, depending on how high up you are in the series of this irrational number, your context of asking a question about what numbers π function includes will differ proportionate to the contexts in which it is asked. Sure, the bridge from one to another is not a switch from quantity to quality. Nevertheless, it is a counter-intuitive parallel whose surprising identity is a function of two entirely different contexts and subjects. Another focal point of significance for this equation is that the music of use of Δ identifies a quantitative value whose use is to express an aesthetic qualitative function. I suggest that the conjunction of these two features provides a thought-bridge to secure a transition to the concept of a mathematical quantitative value whose correlate in, say, literature is a quality. Using this bridge, we can extend its scope to model certain domains of infinities.

We are awfully ignorant of these matters, but it is worth pressing fresh investigation of them. This may involve building on, or recomposing some extant philosophies of subjects. For example, concerning a topic for which there is not much space here to reflect further: is it possible that the 'natural' vehicles, or homes for the expression of infinite qualities, are not mathematics or logic, but the creative arts? Could it be that Wittgenstein's insight, that the infinite is a quality, is correct yet was ignored because the way he depicted the idea was inappropriately dove-tailed by him into a quite confused over-determined, and limited middle modernist context, which understandably displays over-reaction to embrace the fashionable finitism of the period?

Constructivist empiricism of the 1930s was heavily influenced by modernist culture, both for good and bad, as well as for reasons that are at the very least disputable. For example, Hilbert (1925), employing his prior mathematical analyses, insists on the actually quite ungrounded disputable claim that *reality* is finite. Well, this is not the empirical universe, about which one might reasonably maintain this. But is this *reality*? Hilbert (1926: 108) claims that nowhere is 'the infinite realised; it is neither present in nature nor admissible as a foundation in our rational thinking'. It is most peculiar for a finitist, who insists on the limited powers of constructivist mathematics, to assume that the word 'nature' is secure – like a Platonic form. Wittgenstein was averse to Gödel's treating some of the higher levels of mathematics as if they enjoyed a sort of baroque ontological condition something like a super-reality, and not their actual abstract conceptual 'existence'. We may agree to this without acceding to Hilbert's sterilising amputation. In Hilbert's cultural framework, we are not even sure that there is a nature for, let alone only one supervening description of, the external world. Finitism does not have a remit to go outside of experience. But there are many things that transcend experience, even in scientific laws. Furthermore, observational cosmology, provisional though it is, displays many probable instances of phenomena that do not comply with our experience of 'nature'.

Consequently, it is unsound to presuppose that a theory of metamathematics can rule out of court the possibility of empirical realism that contravenes modernist or poststructuralist constructivism. As Garver (1994) demonstrates, Wittgenstein himself crafted a new identity for natural history – not science – but he deployed the unfalsifiable elements of what it is to be human, to have consciousness, and to use human language. Wittgenstein's radical last twist in his new philosophy of certainty is to show that these embody a transcendental condition. That is some achievement for someone who has been called a constructivist.

It provokes the question, which I think Wittgenstein did not raise. How would one *start* an infinite calculation, anyway, let alone complete it? If it is the case that there are already transcendental functions in life, we have a precedent for lift-off: transcendence can be perceived by use of what we are. Certainly this will involve our use of approximations; but this does not commit us to using a means devoid of infinity. As Hardy (1910) long ago argued, refining the *Infinitarcalcul* of Paul du Bois-Reymond, we can apply the concept of an approximation to the increase of a function of infinity, and implement criteria that distinguish between legitimate and illegitimate forms of approximation, which treat known and unknown functions. This appears to be sensitive enough as an approach to be able to allow for indeterminacies of narrative. We might then use this as an analogy for semantic functions. I think that this could be adjusted so as to complement the ways in which Marian Hobson (1998) interprets Derrida's use of infinity. It also finds support, to some degree, from his exposition of Husserl's transcendental reductionism, distinct though these philosophies are, while one should see that qualitative infinities are thereby presupposed and/or inscribed in finite media.

Although Wittgenstein was a (particularly unusual type of) constructivist explaining a philosophy of how we do mathematics, he was a transcendentalist[46] concerning consciousness regarding understanding. For example, in *Philosophical Investigations*, §209, he stated: 'But then doesn't our understanding reach beyond all the examples?' In contrast, at §220: 'My symbolical expression [of the rule] was really a mythological description of the use of a rule.'[47] Admittedly he is employing the latter to force acknowledgement that the former is a bar against those who would derive infinite series from a calculus, and that use stands outside of calculative procedures, among other concerns. But I wish to ensure that we make explicit the presupposition and upshot of §209: consciousness is a function that is non-algorithmic, and it is transcendent over semantic randomness as well as the rule-following of an algorithmic calculus. These ingredients are functions of qualitative perceptions, and as such are necessary properties of creative expressions.

We would do well to be more cautious than Wittgenstein was about the relations of randomness, calculus and infinity. His position was an expected one in the context of his time; but in the light of current research on logical relations between these as exemplified in pure mathematics, fresh horizons enable concepts of proof to be extended. Woess's (2000: 230–42, 284–8) mathematical analysis of random walks on infinite graphs and groups, furnishes theorems in which a sequence can move to infinity, with a boundary that is a set of infinite *words*. (These include harmonic aspects that nicely complement, from another standpoint, Freeman Dyson's (1985) above comments on Δ.) Such advanced formalisms can replace the notions of projections in space that the *Tractatus* proposed; accordingly, extensive new abstract domains involving (say, Markovian) probability also have, in principle, quite practical types of intuitive virtual realisations or visualisations, such as knot theory, tree or cactus structures. Although this vastly transforms Wittgenstein's version of 'surveyability', there is a sense in which theoretically these are surveyable, and the prospect of some future generation applying them empirically is plausible. My point, then, is that very complex mathematics have counter-intuitive mappable similarities to creative art, and these unexpectedly contain the logical anatomies that can be used as mirrors for literary and, say, musical creativity. Evidently there will be problems of interpretation concerning how to apply these. Yet almost all significant analyses involve such problems, so this is no new difficulty. The difficulty is a function of the content, not of questionable theorisation.

The outer borderlands of the finite and the computational in mathematics, logic and some scientific theorising, have strayed into functioning with, or adopting, the infinite as quality (with conjectural equivocation which Wittgenstein, for reasons internal to a calculus, not creativity, castigated). Some of the overlap conditions here will be genuine, and await further exploration.[48] Certainly, there will be counterfeit, poor, secondary, as well as great, counter-intuitive, expressions of creativity. The present concern is the narrower focus of what it is to be the possibility that a logical representation of natural languages is to be had, in the current context of literary creativity. Again, this is not the mechanistic formalist project of incarcerating creatively subtle forms of life in crude traditional logic. Instead, it concerns non-algorithmic properties, and higher spheres of symbolic languages. These have already entered the realm of infinity and largely been found wanting in constructivist contexts, sometimes quite correctly, by the mathematical specialists who assess them.

This type of enterprise would therefore be a counter-intuitive sequel to the depiction of aesthetic infinities in, for example,[49] the Moslem refinement of Greek geometric infinite lattices, the mirrors of Dante, the patterning of Bach's music, Goethe's poetry, Escher's visualisation, and the like. It is not unusual for finitists with an interest in pure mathematics, nevertheless, to concede that it is possible to presuppose that the expression 'infinite' is understood. As the philosophers of mathematics Niebergall and Schirn (1996: 286) note, in one approach they characterise but do not choose to adopt: 'It is presupposed that the expression "infinite" is already understood, and a formal explication is regarded as unnecessary.' I am not advocating an approach on this basis, though it is worth adopting it as a way of *introducing* the semantic notion for analysis. Here of course we should discriminate between ideas showing infinity in contrast with qualitative infinity itself.

5 The quality of creative language

Logic of literary creativity and philosophy of mathematics

The foregoing constructivist realist outline can serve as a token of a type to prepare the way to develop a framework, and be incorporated into the idea of the theory-net outlined above, as a model for use in some logics of natural language. The foregoing route is helpful as a means to stimulate exploration and assessment of the relation of creativity to logic. Gibson (2001: 23) raised the concern with aesthetic innovative power as the issue of universals and uniqueness. Gibson (2001: 40) registered the importance of a grasp of the asymmetry of analytical and creative language. This contention does not imply that creative and logical elements of language in literary usage have to be separated in their narrative functions, though sometimes they are.

It requires that one should recognise creativity and logic to be related.[1] This has a parallel with Wittgenstein's own interlocutor, Sraffa (1960), whose stylistics in his economic theory is sometimes similar to Wittgenstein's. Sraffa's theory presents a model that is open, though logically closed. Sraffa's composition of new 'thought bridges' facilitates counter-intuitive possibilities.[2] A closed logical model might, nonetheless, be open to infinite possibilities. Inattention to aspects of the frontiers of logic and philosophy of mathematics, as well as misrepresentation of the identities of literary creativity, might all too easily allow the false argument to remain, that, since literariness is an informally expressed domain, it has no logical properties.

Frequently creativity is contrasted with formal and scientific subjects. There are evident, and sometimes hidden, differences between such disciplines, though the issues of relations between symmetry and asymmetry should be investigated more. Surface symmetry may obscure underlying asymmetry, and *vice versa*. One such feature has been introduced earlier: the contention of this chapter that creativity contains super-condensed logic. Now this is not to maintain that literary scholars should cower before logic or science in their search for models. It may be quite the reverse: now science is more reflective about its identities, it may be recognised that – all along – it is at least partially a metaphoric enterprise, with creative qualities. Historically of course this was certainly the case; but the idea that science had lift-off from humanities because it became something exclusively objective is facile, since it neglects to account for the role of metaphor and imagination *in the contents* of much scientific theory. Certainly, the metaphors in science and literature differ; this is not opposed by the present claims. They amount to the contention that the live metaphor status of scientific and literary languages facilitates cross-mapping by theory-nets (see Gibson, 2000).

Let us suppose, then, that we are dealing with a logical domain γ isolated by a theory-net with semantic fields γ and/or β. These were explained in a previous section as: the constructivist prospect α, and the counter-intuitive realist domain β. In the case of β it is not algorithmically computable by mathematical means, though it can in principle be known by some means. This tracking may be by another mathematical game, a distinct language game, including imagination.

Many people's views amount to the following: a reader or author in either field represented as α and γ would not necessarily have a comprehension of all the sense and logic of her field. Moreover, the question that would strike her (i.e., 'What is the sense of this narrative of which I have cognisance?') would have a complex relation to her ignorance, as well as knowledge, of the field. This presupposition would be different from that of someone who, outside of the field, and say with Platonic competence, asked the 'same' question. The question's presupposition would differ in each case.

Wittgenstein brings this out by discussing questions about π. Does it have certain numbers in a particular position? This depends on whether or not you assign a Platonist realm to it; if you have only reached thus far in generating its numerical sequence, so that you have not yet reached those numbers, you can consistently conclude that π does not have the requisite number property φ; and *vice versa*, if you are a finitist. Wittgenstein (1978: iv. 9) introduces the relation of a fiction narrative; let us deem this the field α. He states:

> But what are you saying if you say that one thing is clear – either one will come upon φ in the infinite expansion or one will not? . . . What if someone were to reply to a question, 'so far there is no such thing as an answer to this question'. So, for example, a poet might reply when asked whether the hero of his poem had a sister or not; when, i.e., he has not yet decided anything about it.

This comparison with philosophy of mathematics and fiction bears on the face of it the present project, though we need to be very cautious about how far and in what way we take it. As Wright (1980: 168) states, the suggestion in Wittgenstein's text is that, with fictional statements, we are ready to allow that matters are simply up to the author; and Wittgenstein seems to be exhorting us to view mathematical propositions in the same fashion. Explicitly expressed, some things are not decidable, even or especially when you are the author. This itself is the truth of the author's functioning relation to the narrative, and/or the narrative's semantic identity; but there is more. Wittgenstein was arguing that the same question is different depending on your assumptions about the identity of φ, and π, in relation to your presuppositions concerning α and β, including their own presuppositional functions. Nevertheless, there is such a thing as the measurement of just those identities of, say, φ, π and presuppositions concerning α and β. So the relativity of constructivism turns out not to be a brief to say whatever we want. The above quotation is Wittgenstein's attempt to expose the identity of the language game when we cease to be able to calculate. These logical states of affairs appropriately model some of the problems we have when assessing, for example, ancient Near East literatures. It helps to explain disagreement, and how to represent it in, and codes for, the authorial and writerly voices of these narratives.

Contradiction and counter-intuition

In contrast with this, however, there is the oft neglected or unexplained feature already introduced, that of counter-intuitive states. Counter-intuitive truth is readily uncomprehended or (dis)missed. Ignorance may be confused with knowledge, and *vice versa*. It is a peculiarly common perception among some analytical philosophers that somehow the 'school' is logically clean, while humanities' subjects, such as literary studies, are fraught with contradiction and ambiguity. Certainly, there is truth in this; yet just so with analytical philosophy: the difference tends to be that some committed philosophers in this school readily detect detritus in others, while neatly, with formal aplomb, sweeping some logical systems' contradictions under the carpet, to achieve symmetry that hides asymmetry.

Paradox was something Frege thought to be an illness in others, yet Russell found it a necessary property of Frege's logic. In that respect paradox is counter-intuitive. Whitehead and Russell (1910, and the 1927 revision) believed that they had salvaged the wrecked system from internal contradiction, though oil-spills from it proved the opposite. In something of a contrast, von Wright (1983) works to develop a new explanation preserving the conception of truth in classical logic, though with an unexpected extension of it to treat 'Janus' propositions. The Fregean myth still holds sway in many areas, overlain by his undoubtedly significant insights, some of which are applied in Gibson (1981, 2000, 2001) with qualification and modification.

In extreme contrast there are paraconsistent approaches, for example Priest (1995), referred to earlier, for which propositions are both true *and* false. Woods (2003) offers new research in this arena, and he has his own disputes with Priest.[3] I propose that the paraconsistent views should be interpreted as a model for a group of the mind's propensity for confusion, duplicity or schizophreniform[4] use of rationality. Generally speaking on my interpretation of Priest's (1995) and Woods's (2003) views, paraconsistent philosophy of logic is a mirror of many a corporate double-face, and qualitative devolution of human consciousness. In crude terms paraconsistency is the rationality of doublethink – not unlike the world of George Orwell's *1984*. Since literary creativity is a function of the mind, it seems that such logic could also be one of a range of formalisms that might map varieties of fictional narratives, as Woods (2003) does.

So there are counterfeit versions of counter-intuition, of which paraconsistency is one. The question presses here: in what sense is paradox internal to human consciousness? Is paradox an inextirpable property of being language, or of only a finite set of domains of language? My answer is the latter. Subsequent to my introduction of a conception of counter-intuition in Gibson (1997, 2000), which as far as I know was the first such formulation of the subject – in fact perhaps the first to view the term 'counter-intuition' as a term for which one should supply a conception – Woods (2003) published a range of comments on paraconsistent 'counter-intuitiveness'. He places these as components of his view that the basis of logic is paraconsistent; while my concept of counter-intuition positions truth as primary, and its examples are internal facets of creative understanding – both scientific and artistic.

Woods (2003: 239) is right to stress that there is a dilemma over constantive nihilism (nothing is true) and semantic promiscuity (everything is true). My view is that some things are true, which is the basis for dissolving the dilemma when we relate this to ontology. Empirical reality is its own law, and is not epistemically or logically dependent on theory, only insofar as the primary theory of the latter maps the former. Furthermore, at deeper levels the empirical domain is strongly counter-intuitive. So those who formulated nineteenth–twentieth-century logic were in no position to impose a definitive identity on what logic is, though they exposed some important insights.[5] Generalisation is not a matter of a mechanical decision procedure, use of which leads to paradox. Generalisation over sets should be regulated by ontology linked to inference. I maintain that generalisation is counter-intuitively transitive over sets, and we need a revolution in developing devices to recognise the primary theory for this counter-intuitive situation. For example, there is the issue of how this problem and its solution can be configured by attempting to expose some logic of pure mathematics. From a somewhat different angle, though with a view to this as one of their ends, chapters 3 and 4 and other parts of the present book introduce the following to the current concerns: M-theory (see Witten, 2002; Beasley and Witten, 2003); mirror symmetry in massive Frobenius manifolds (see Hertling, 2002); torsors and rational points (see Skorobogatov, 2001). In another case we might learn more from Wiles's proof of Fermat's Last Theorem, which integrated different sets with enormously distinct identities and sutured them together to create bridges to new generalisation and proofs. In this sphere the notion of a set is greater than the sum of its member sets.

We can employ these precedents to employ such mathematics as a model for logic, in conjunction with counter-intuitive ontology. In other words, this turns the logicist project on its head: there is no reduction of mathematics to logic. Rather, logic is derived from mathematics and singularities. Clearly this involves benefiting from what research logic has discovered for us thus far. It is evident, however, that these and other related domains are not paraconsistent. I have added the concept of live metaphor to these strategies, which I have included in explanation of what logic is, and accordingly it furnishes opportunity for a qualitative continuum between certain mathematics. In the light of such potential for logic, we have a deeply counter-intuitive universe of discourse. It has been said that there are no surprises in logic. Certainly this is so for the ideal observer, which person we cannot number among us – for such a person would understand what logic is. So the argument, relative to our knowledge, for no surprises, is viciously circular. Human consciousness is not tautologous with understanding, and we are not capable of surveying what is beyond our ken. So we are surprised by logic, especially as it goes deeper. I think that paraconsistency is an accurate map of parts of our ignorance and the world as will. But when it is promoted to being what logic is, it is a modal fallacy incorrectly and imperiously exploiting limits of contingent perception wrongly promoted to map what is beyond it.

As Woods (2003: 125–8) develops his view of paraconsistency, he concludes that it is an ineradicable feature of our intuitions. Woods (2003: 325–6) thinks that it is inescapable that we are accountable for as humans with Humean intuition. To me intuitively it seems extraordinary that this purported insight be inescapable, and stipulated as a criterion involved in deciding what logic is. Since it would need a book to explore this topic, it is convenient that someone else has contributed to showing that Hume, in addition to offering us important insights, is in relevant spheres, a shambles in respect of Bayesian use of probability, for which see Earman's (2002) important study.

Counter-intuition and linguistic cosmology

Thus far, there have been a number of uses of the term 'counter-intuition' in this chapter, and it is convenient at this stage to gather together the thesis associated with it, though a more extensive research study on the topic is to be published.[6] Whether or not we agree with Lewy's (1976) approach to the logic relations of entailment, strict implication and their paradoxes, it is clear that he exposed some puzzling phenomena. In particular, he expounded the idea that contingent relations that appear quite obvious and unproblematic actually entail paradoxes. As I mentioned previously, Lewy used the expression 'counter-intuitive' obliquely to label this state of affairs; yet he did not give any explanation of counter-intuition, and seemed quite unaware of the need even to comment on his use of the term.[7]

A trend of the foregoing is to argue that counter-intuition is a key game feature in invention, discovery and confusion. We need a new counter-intuitive Renaissance (not counter-Renaissance) of logic thinking, despite and in addition to the many insights already gained. This does not involve a diachronic regression, but a progression that employs counter-intuition as a functional disposition of being a creative language game.

In contrast, we should be wary of counterfeits of counter-intuition in science, just as we should be averse to counterfeits in literary, logical and linguistic conceptions that could displace and conflate actual counter-intuition. The fuzzy boundaries between radical as opposed to counterfeit outcomes of experimentation should not of course be a reason for censorship or conservatism in taste; conversely, neither should they be used to acclaim the absence of quality. The notion of 'counterfeit' here is not merely the idea that someone copies the expression of a counter-intuitive conception, with the intention of promoting it as the original thing of concept. Rather, 'counterfeit' marks that we all have dubious grasps of understanding, and this at times generates misunderstanding as a criterion of (purporting to have) knowledge. Consequently, we are prone to engender counterfeit perceptions of our own identities, as a function of rule following. This is partly to do with our limitations in not understanding relations between unity in and development of understanding.

There is a margin at which creativity, discovery or the construction of a calculation/concept is undetermined and in which they are genuinely uncertain about the identity of the language game, or a new use of one. The attempt to preserve a distinction between 'counter-intuition' and 'counterfeit' here is to avoid confusing the two; its purpose is not to censor or restrict. Regarding for example literary counter-intuitive creativities, the sense of what it is to be counterfeit is problematic. This is puzzling respecting ways that can stimulate progress in exploring just what it would be to decide between the counterfeiting of a Classic.[8] A strange case is Hitler's *Mein Kampf*,[9] which we could counter-pose against, say, Shakespeare's *Hamlet*. Concerning the latter, Christine Brooke-Rose (1999: 162) points out thinking of Frank Kermode's reading, and quotes him to the effect that re-reading Hamlet can stun, can be 'a bit of a revelation'.

The experience of *surprise* is perhaps a contingently necessary (but of course not sufficient) condition for one's first experience of understanding a facet of a counter-intuitive narrative. Contrariwise, if we adopt the analysis in Gibson (2000b, and forthcoming b), presumably in the case of *Mein Kampf*, for example in the case of a devoted reader in 1933 (perhaps Heidegger?), the claim of having a recognition of a counter-intuition in the narrative, or whatever term someone might employ to designate this discovery, would be a *counterfeit* experience of counter-intuitive reading.

There is an analogue of this state: a natural disposition for us to manufacture, encode and emulate false consciousness as the true. We should expect these features to recur in the external world. At the side of this narrowed situation, another generalised picture obtains but can only be alluded to here; Gibson (2000a) argues that it applies generally to humans. Although there is decisive evidence that logic based on truth versus false expressions is itself viable, there are two problematic consequences that follow from the conjunction of this with appropriate theses on human imagination and self-deception. First, because we have knowledge that there is such a phenomenon as true logic, it does not follow that we have *understanding* of it. Secondly, it follows from a conjunction of this point with the previous two that presupposed it, that the psychological identity of humans is rationally pluralistic. A consequence of this is that the psychodynamics of human logic deviate somewhat from binary logics of the external world, yet not binary imagination if we follow Mikhail Bakhtin's (1984)[10] poetics, though his usage is metaphorised in ways distinct to the present study. One should heed criticisms made by Gibson (2000a) about problems attaching to extant literary philosophies of time. Even so, there is need to allow for the role of the abnormal states assigned by astrophysicists to the non-Planckian early universe to be incorporated into such philosophies, rather than allow straight-forward physicalism to hold sway as universal law. Human mental creativity, and, for example, in particular, philosophical and literary creativities, may have much more potential for mapping virtually infinite sets of possibilities than a standard analytical philosophy of science might presume.

Deviant logics can be mapped by binary logics.[11] Consider when we have a narrative from a remote esoteric narrative world: let us say, the Sumerian Rebel Lands (ka-bala) tablets, of mythological monsters and geophysical cataclysms. Gibson (2000a) shows that we can in principle logically map expressions. Such a generalised picture has a variety of subsets. An unexpected one is that most or all of the alternative deviant logics (and others hitherto not devised) may, subject to relevant structural constraints, originality or productivity, fit some literary narrative semantics. This somewhat oddly confirms the probity of seeing that logic of texts is a subset of a larger perhaps undecidable mental domain in the empirical world. Consequently, it is counter-intuitively true that this involves games of logic, since logic includes undecidable sentences in its foundations.

Counter-intuition has originality as its core internal property. This seems to apply to a large set of literary domains that compose original meaning. The occurrence of counter-intuition marks the transition or transformation (perhaps a catastrophe theory transformation) from standard or normative rule-following to compose an original construction or discovery. Here the antecedent games-rules do not, prior to the counter-intuitive phase transition, have a predictive capacity, though retrospectively they may be viewed so as to source the counter-intuitive consequence.

A range of counter-intuitive states in literature display use of universal claims, and frequently these are totalised into possible worlds or transworld identities,[12] as with subjunctive conditional or fictional universes. I suggest that, for example, Martin Rees's (1999) multiverse scenario – that of the astrophysical possibility of a virtually infinite ensemble of actual universes – furnishes us with a possible empiricism for some literary worlds.

The motive here is that on such an approach there is a presupposed pro-grammatic potential for a formal and creative semantics to be cross-wired together. We should recognise the significance of parallel senses and ack-nowledge that their narrative universes include counter-intuitive properties internal to construction, invention or discovery in both spheres, as well as how these display the necessary conditions for what it is to be a language, and an original one. Central to these conceptions are use, function and context. The respective relations of these domains will vary, not only in the contrasts between mathematical and rational natural languages, but with literary subjects: so a Victorian realist novel may be exclusive of a poststructuralist novel by Christine Brooke-Rose. The question then arises as to whether or not the semantics of a culture are, or are not, discontinuous, even where they appear to be co-extensive.

But between such contrasts there are counter-intuitive continuities. Derrida's (1998) study on monolingualism refuses to condone the claim that even within 'one' language there *is one* language. He chooses the example of Franco-Maghrebian. Derrida's (1998: 7) two opposed propositions are: (1) We only ever speak one language. (2) We never speak only one language. The equivocation is a function of the truth of the two. Their interfaces are counter-intuitive and functional. Thus in the daily life of the possibility of pragmatic communication there is counter-intuition. Certainly, this conjunction jumps levels between different domains of language uses. We should here be attending to the ways in which language games cross-fertilise each other, and the resulting instability that is itself a source of creative potential in various ways.

Chapter 2 above and Gibson (1998) demonstrate that Ockham's Razor is false, employing Ockham's own six contrary versions of those doctrines to prove this. Moreover any such use of simplicity presupposes complexity. As Gibson (2000) proposes, the concept of a cosmological singularity displays an identity that could counter-intuitively displace and replace the idea of simplicity. Internal to a singularity's identity is a counter-intuitive state of affairs: infinity as a function of finitude, infinity in matter–energy density, and the infinite velocity of light. So that which should replace simplicity is the concept of a counter-intuitive singularity with creative properties of infinity. Paradox is a property of the conjunction of the beginning of the universe with its future, and origin, not least since the former is qualitatively and functionally discontinuous with the latter.

Internal to this situation, complexity and 'chaos' laws are functions of transcendence. So they are verification-transcendent, though still empirical, and thus are not in Wittgenstein's sense 'experimental'. Consequently they have the strange[13] position or status of something akin to the *a priori*, while they are onto-logical. This amounts to a counter-intuitive deformation of the *a priori* into a continuum with the empirical. In other words, physical laws in this perspective counter-intuitively mirror sense and consciousness. Sure, this is a model, and needs much amplification, and no doubt revision; yet it can be skewed as a theory-net to catch general features utilising the conception of counter-intuitive mimesis developed in Gibson (1997, 2000). There are different senses of 'infinity' involved here, though this issue cannot detain us here due to restrictions of space. It is worth, however, again drawing attention to the unexplored philosophical significance of Andrei Linde's, and Martin Rees's (1999) hypothesis of a multiverse – an infinite ensemble of universes, of which the theory of a cosmological singularity has the function of creating a new game: i.e., a universe.

The typology of this scenario has parallels with creativity in literary narratives. The normative or standard linguistic laws are deformed or deconstructed into a game of original creativity. New worlds are composed which derive from, yet are distinct to, the prior narrative universes, though consequences of them. Most of the processes involved in this creativity are observation-transcendent, though empirical, together with the other properties depicted in the foregoing. And paradox stands at the centre of many of the greatest creative compositions. It seems to be fundamental to recognise that this sort of creativity is condensed counter-intuitive order whose surface manifestation is 'chaos' (i.e., complexity and randomness). This is similar to some literary creativity. Comparison of the scientific with the literary is itself counter-intuitive. The extraordinary metaphysical contents in the mathematics of quantum cosmology, such as those developed, for example, in the theory of Hawking and Turok (1998) are speculative and well outside of the veridical science of terrestrial physics. As Gibson (2000) observes, scientists such as Dallaporta (1993) have themselves, using labels such as metaphysics, drawn attention to astrophysical cosmology's inability ever experimentally to test a range of astrophysical claims that are forever beyond the Planckian range (see Gibson, 2000). Although literature may generate more possible worlds than scientific cosmology, the foregoing and other publications attest to parallels. These should not be over-stated and are highly complex, with counter-intuitive asymmetries, though we are in the early stages of entirely fresh developments. The theory of live metaphor for such science[14] and for ancient literature does something to bridge the gaps and transitions between the two subjects. We should also recognise that the formal logics of such topics as inexact concepts and of modal fictionalism, though in their early stages[15] of investigation and with equally interesting competing alternatives, pose exciting possibilities.

A. W. Moore's (1990: 217) remark, in his study that advocates a constructivist approach to infinity, evokes a sense of paradox: language is flexible. Grammar can change . . . Meanwhile, even though we must regard it as a special kind of nonsense to say that the truly infinite exists, it remains the case that we are *shown* that it does.

This '*shown*' recalls Wittgenstein's *Tractatus*; so it is apt to quote a remark of his which Moore (1990: 139) cites: 'Imagine set theory's having been created by a satirist, as a kind of parody on mathematics.' So there is something that both is and is not nonsense? Perhaps this opposition conceals the presupposition that it is from the standpoint of the viewer that there is an opposition, not from the viewpoint of infinity (if there is such a propositional attitude). Might the foregoing analysis facilitate ways to accept and reverse Wittgenstein's view? Imagine, say, satire having been created by a mathematician, as a parody on literature!

For science there remain empirical unmapped domains beyond the stage, which, for example, mathematics and cosmology have reached. We are unclear what the divisions of labour are here between the unmapped and the unmeasureable or the unmeasured. Qualitative functions are internal aesthetic subjects that, at least hypothetically, involve qualitative infinities. It would be premature for scientists to conclude that future science is reducible to quantitative nonaesthetic description, since a link between aesthetics and the descriptive content of empirical science seems ineradicable. Although such relations will be uneven and often counter-intuitive, yet science and humanities have been constructed by functioning with such mixed properties. There is therefore a precedent for cross-connecting different domains that have asymmetric qualitative and quantitative properties.

A qualitative continuum and live metaphor

At the deeper qualitative levels, logical grammar characterises what it is to be language; these in turn mirror what it is to be. In this perspective I suggest that there is a counter-intuitive continuum between different universes of representation. This will be a live metaphoric use of 'continuum' in the light of Wittgenstein's criticisms and consequent adjustments to Cantor's continuum as assessed by the present interpretation, and for example Marion (1998, ch. 7). This sketch is very schematic since the continuum relates to vast areas outside the scope of this chapter, though the suggestions here are original. The theory of live metaphor presupposed is devised in Gibson (1997, 2000 and 2000a).

The purpose has a general and a narrow component. The general aim is part of a larger research programme developing a theory of logic of natural languages in relation to philosophy of mathematics. The narrower focus here is to implement the conjunction of continuum and live metaphor for games of significant creativity in natural languages, in part by appealing to the occurrence of counter-intuition, for example, when laws deform in the cosmological domain for the beginning of the universe. Such counter-intuitive states display use of generalised functions. These functions are, effectively, from the standpoint of standardised world types, positioned as possible worlds or transworld identities,[16] for example sometimes stylistically explicitly expressed along the lines of subjunctive conditional world models.

Typical current claims to understand the continuum hypothesis conclude that the continuum is undecidable, which is appropriate for the present purpose. If it turns out to be decidable, this will be extraordinarily counter-intuitively so, which will also explicitly exemplify the latter quality. The continuum in mathematics proposes continuity between all real number series, though in a finitist version such as Wittgenstein judged that we could not have nonconstructivist features such as irrational numbers. On an analogy with natural language usage, this is akin to standard usage. Conversely the irrational numbers such as π, and related phenomena, identify with the qualitative deviance of which creativity is made. I include, then, the irrational numbers into my live metaphoric concept of the continuum. So this marks the divide between the finitist that was Wittgenstein in his time, and the emerging nonconstructivist continuum here for literary and cosmological representation. It seems that Wittgenstein was divided over the philosophy of the language game in a constructivist mould, and the areas of literary and musical creativity, to which he never seemed to give philosophical attention in ways he did to everyday language usage. The present chapter's approach to meaning retrieves Wittgenstein's constructivist black hole event-horizon from its impending end, to transform it into a nonconstructivist continuum.

Of course it might reasonably be maintained that this goes outside of Wittgenstein's actual philosophy. I am only drawing attention to a deep tension, his desire to avoid overstating the scope of finitism, and absence of analytical exploration of creativity in his writings, while noting the anguished, albeit briefly marked, presence of intense concern about creativity in them. Occasionally, even so, he adverts to mystery in calculations beyond the ken of human wit, as is clear from the following astonishing remark, neglected by philosophers of mathematics, which occurs in Wittgenstein's *Culture and Value*, that properly stands alongside his writing on the philosophy of mathematics:

> Even to have expressed a false thought boldly and clearly is already to have gained a great deal. It's only by thinking even more crazily than philosophers do that you can solve their problems. Imagine someone *watching a pendulum and thinking: God makes it move like that. Well, isn't God equally free to act in accordance with a calculation?*
>
> Wittgenstein, 1980: 75 (my italics)

Wittgenstein's apparently general remark[17] alludes, I believe, to his disagreement with Brouwer, the constructivist, with whom nevertheless he had some agreement. Brouwer's pendulum number is a recursive notion, but it is not comparable in size to 0, from the domain of the reals (see Marion, 1998: 195–7). Wittgenstein wanted to reject the approach, partly because it did not specify quantity in relation to 0. Wittgenstein's (1979: 221) view was that irrational numbers are a process, not a result. So, for Wittgenstein, Brouwer is both weakening logic and limiting empiricism, for are there not mathematics in which 'God [is] equally free to act in accordance with a calculation'? We might add, against Wittgenstein, a further question: is there not a universe full of subtle empirical complex *states* that are not (in the relevant sense) processes, and which are transcendental – that are the mirrors for free calculation? Of course Wittgenstein has let his cat out of the private bag, by mentioning God. Given the analysis presented in this chapter, however, let us suppose that Wittgenstein might wish to reconsider his position in the light of developments yet future to his final reflections on the matter. Maybe we can establish with some certainty, at least in principle, the type of ontology that would avoid his strictures against Brouwer. This would enable us to move beyond both their respective constructivisms, into a super-quantum universe of irrational numbers in which laws deform, and divert Wittgenstein's natural history by showing others (in a multiverse), and transcendental number theory on the basis that π is not algebraic (see Baker, 1975).

Cantor proved the occurrence of transcendental numbers, and he did not use numbers to show this. In the free play of signification that is significant for a literary game of creativity, there are no numbers, and we are free to act in accordance with a calculation. I am here condensing an argument to the effect that Wittgenstein was, in the above quotation, asserting that there is a domain that is in accordance with a calculation; this is the negation of Brouwer's pendulum number. So we have here the basis for a counter-intuitive transcendental continuum that can in principle map a free logic in which we are free to act in accordance with a calculation. This conclusion, which I have derived from Wittgenstein's above quotation, seems to show that, in respect of a domain of such freedom and calculation, he was the negation of a constructvist, though this bounces against his view of a calculus elsewhere: maybe he was here adverting to a radical new, undeveloped concept.

Live metaphor has parallels with qualitative analysis in science. In some respects qualitative analysis in science employs live metaphoric. This state of affairs has an unexpected relation to the way Wittgenstein, in the above quotation, introduced causality into calculation, despite his ban on experiment from the realm of the calculus. Qualitative analysis in science has a nonquantative component in it. Since in its present state all science uses qualitative analysis, it seems that universalised nonconjectural science does not exist.

Qualitative analysis has a particular relation to constructivism. Constructivism typically proceeds with the structures of thought; yet Hintikka (1998) replaces this policy with things or objects. Is constructivism a more cautious approach to mathematical and linguistic truth? Not in a universe which has counter-intuition. Since constructivism and finitism tend to exercise themselves on the basis of past and current experience, this disposes them to be blind to counter-intuition that is typically an unpredicted or unpredictable propensity of usage. In the case of creative literature, especially newly composed narrative, this will be very much the case, though it applies to science as well. In short, counter-intuition is nonconstructivist. Accordingly, the conjunction of constructivism with counter-intuition will incline to a dispositional reductionism in respect of new thought, even though those who adopt constructivism will no doubt sometimes episodically override this disposition. I suggest therefore, that, from the standpoint of concepts of contemporary physics and cosmology, the fine-tuning structure of the empirical world and their endorsement of counter-intuitive properties in them, there is warrant for the notion of nonconstructivist discovery of counter-intuitive properties in the universe, and thus in working theories of it.

On the basis of the analogy between games in these subjects and in literary uses, the above analysis supports the thesis of *some* mapping parallels between philosophy of mathematics/cosmology and literature, in concepts of use. There will be all manner of dissimilarities; but hopefully these are qualified or some excluded by the present study, though much further work needs to be done to sustain cross-wiring presuppositions to represent partially parallel properties in different semiotic and functional domains. Within this approach, hitherto undeveloped analysis of counter-intuition is fundamental; frequently it has lain submerged unnoticed in apparently straightforward uses. Wittgenstein's terminology, which might be re-applied to this state of affairs, identified 'bewitched [natural] grammar'.

Counter-intuition is an internal property of a variety of disparate phenomena, and their characterisation, where they implement constructivism or discovery. Internal to this state of affairs are the basic properties of use, function and context. Distinct, though fundamental, are the external world as a benchmark and its relations to such phenomena. The relations of the representational functions to the world vary, not only as displayed in the contrasts between mathematical and natural languages, but as manifested in creative literary uses. In semantic fields, the disparity between the external world and its standardised versions itself comprises a semantic construct and function of the relation. Since points of difference, as well as connection, can, in principle, be employed to identify core components of any language-game's use, the contrasts and the disparities are not contrary to this chapter's aim. It is important not to misplace the contrast here. We are attending to the conditions for what it is to be a creative language's use. We are not investigating the contrasting parallels between the particular token manifestations of normal use, connected though these are as tokens that portray the types; nor is this to presuppose some absolute meta-language hovering under the fields.

Counter-intuition and surveyable sense

A problem we have with counter-intuition, and not a problem *in* it, is parallel with the way we naturally tend to think that our reading text is the correct interpretation we instinctively assume for it. The psychological foundations of such intentionality, presented as determinate assessment, are themselves an important issue, not to be pursued here; but we all tend to feel we are correct. This applies to our assumptions, designated by Aristotle, that we are rational animals. Aristotle's dictum is usually assumed as a function of our inclination to recognise our reasoning as logical. Conversely, our fundamental instability, self-satisfied composure, and slim grasp of rationality are not easily disturbed, at least to the degree relevant for justifying our reasoning. In other words, we rarely, if ever, counter-intuitively investigate our assumption that we recognise our grasp of rationality.

Let us consider a case in point, already discussed, and its *resumé*: Andrew Wiles proved Fermat's Last Theorem, after over 20 years of research.[18] The theorem arises by questioning the natural assumption that there is a generalisation to other higher powers (higher than x^2) of the proof for Pythagoras' theorem. Although this is an elementary truth, it also relates directly to issues of higher mathematics and infinity. Here one presupposes the uncontroversial principles of arithmetical computation by which a simple law of addition and multiplication entails that if '$x^2 + y^2 = z^2$', then '$x^3 + y^3 = z^3$'. However, the latter consequence '$x^3 + y^3 = z^3$' is false, according to Fermat's, now proved, Last Theorem. That is to say, there is no cubed solution in whole numbers. Here we have a hard, deep case of falsified mathematical intuition – one that derives, not from esoteric speculative calculus but from elementary arithmetic algebra, though Wiles's proof is counter-intuitively complex, especially in the way in which it connects apparently unrelated mathematical domains together into one proof. It is worth comparing and contrasting some distinguished mathematicians' intuition prior to the completion of Wiles's proof. Even shortly before the publication of Wiles's proof, for example, A. V. Tolstikov (1989),[19] writing for professional mathematicians, stated that, 'An unhealthy interest in proving this theorem was stimulated at one time by a large international prize. It has been conjectured that there is no proof of Fermat's Last Theorem at all.'

Wiles's proof discards, as incorrect, a whole complex tradition of intuition. This shows that many a grasp of the capacity to survey a narrative or a large range of proofs is itself faulty or limited in ways we do not acknowledge.

Wittgenstein had a profound grasp of the ways in which we are bewitched by grammar in natural languages and in mathematics (that are parallel with the foregoing attack on our ability to intuit). Yet he connected our capacity to master a technique of reading a text and of calculating with our alleged ability to *survey* them. I think that it follows from the above analysis of counter-intuition that he was, in principle, wrong to include surveyability as he did, though his idea happens to work for a large group of propositions. Yet he was inaccurate, it seems, in a complex way that presupposes deep insights into how the concept of surveyability falls short of success for some higher mathematics and for literary narratives.[20] In a fashion, Wittgenstein had given the game away, as it were, when he withdrew his support for his own *Tractatus* thesis that all logic is computable operation, while yet maintaining his thesis that truths can be shown. When he drew near to the end of his life in 1951, others were devising mathematical and logic games that went beyond his remit of computability and surveyability (as Hintikka, 1994 points out).

And in astrophysical cosmology the ground had already been prepared, soon to be confirmed by observations and also proof to demonstrate that observation of the early universe was impossible empirically, decisively to fault and block the universalised use of his assertion that all proofs had to be surveyable. This is akin to a consequence of Fermat's proof: although scholars had the seeming capacity to survey the Pythagorean language game (over-tuned up on some mathematicians' confidence in later technical refinements of it), yet a knowledge and mastery of following its rules through the domain of surveyable cases did not entail *understanding* the game. The game being played is for one to connive at the physics of the very first phase of the universe with unsurveyable mathematics. This involves new games that require bridges[21] to each other for which we have only speculative criteria. In such domains understanding that transcends empirically veridical game-play, by engaging with non-surveyable proofs, is counter-intuitive. We should notice that Wittgenstein would not have allowed that, once known, Fermat's proof would thereby have become surveyable. On his view knowledge did not itself have to entail surveyability. Wittgenstein, like the perhaps time-trapped physics engineer he had been at Manchester, really meant 'surveyability'.

Natural languages and surveyability

An epicentre of the issue in the foregoing section is the point that higher language games of mathematics, logic, the cosmology of the very early universe, *and* the language game of creative literature are non-surveyable, especially to finitists and constructivists. At the side of this there are complex senses, for which Wittgenstein did not seem to allow, where early observational cosmology has many a counter-intuitive relation to indirect surveyability. A number of these are results of prior conjecture using pure mathematics that are found to have a provisional and an empirical correlate in this early universe. Namely, ontology is a condensed or sublime product of theory. We have to go ever so carefully in this new arena, one that hardly existed in Wittgenstein's milieu. Such considerations support the thesis that the counter-intuitive relations between theory and practice in the science for the earliest universe have a resemblance to literature and literary assessment of it, in certain domains of language games.

Clearly, formal languages exhibit many discontinuities with natural languages. Mathematics and natural languages are different games. For Wittgenstein, mathematics is composed of rules that do not, in the relevant sense, have semantics (are not propositions), yet mathematics shares being a game with natural languages. Is not this contrast between mathematical language and natural language a counter-example to the parallel I have drawn, i.e., that there is a game that is the continuum between mathematical and natural languages? Only in a manner that is irrelevant to my thesis. Even so, for example note that both display a sense of indeterminate rule specification, including for mathematics the halting problem that cannot be solved on any Turing machine. This is exemplified by computers' inability to complete a check on the software of certain arbitrary programs. In a nutshell: teacher: 'Go away and subtract 2 from 10 as many times as you can, and see what you get.' The pupil's answer, later: 'I keep on getting 8, teacher.'[22] This is not to argue that, for example, arithmetic is relevantly parallel with natural language semantics, but that non-algorithmic higher mathematics and some peculiar spheres of algorithms are (I return to this issue in the next section). We still can have a parallel between surveyable calculations and natural languages at some suitable levels. Of course, science mixes the two domains in any case; so this can be a way of mapping a crossover, though for Wittgenstein mathematics is not experimental. There are many vexing issues here, for future investigation, which may result in positive, not negative, alignments between prediction and recognition. For example, what is the status of Martin Rees's (1999) view on the multiverse infinite ensemble of universes in relation to Wittgenstein's (1978: 281) question: 'How is it decided whether an infinite prediction [here, retrojection] makes sense? At any rate not by one's saying: "I am certain I mean something when I say . . .".'

Let us, however, re-assess and explore the continuities. Sure, these will be awfully complex and we will involve ourselves in muddles. Let us note that there are muddles in mathematics, logic, and not only literary study. Obviously these subjects do not thereby display the same types of fuzzy[23] issues. Rather, the different scientific and the literary fuzzy issues are being related by complex bridges. Although these fuzzy explanatory positions are frequently of a different order from literary problems, this point needs forcing home against the confidence of an inveterate believer in scientific systems.

Since it was mentioned above that we have a problem with the axiom of choice – for example, as Chihara (1998) explained – let us air the point as it obtains here. There is some very advanced applied mathematics, concerning which there is a dispute over whether or not one can prove a conclusion, without assuming an arbitrary axiom for which there is no proof. Instead, we can only guess, using elegance and a taste for assumptions, that an equation is solvable. What sometimes happens is that if the axiom of choice is appealed to in calculations, it facilitates the solution of the immediate problem, but then generates others further down the line. Consequently, questions arise: what status does such an axiom have in finitist-applied mathematics? Is some applied mathematics a patchwork-quilt of proof that unnecessarily includes subjective conjectures *ad hoc*, disguised as necessary conditions for proofs? The latter is certainly true for some areas, for example, concerning recurring properties in principal classes.[24] It seems that for at least some domains where the axiom of choice was taken to be required, it is not, and can if extreme inventiveness were produced, be replaced with a calculation. That mathematicians embody this situation is an objection to those who assign a single constructivist identity to mathematics.

The conjoined activities of calculating, proving and verifying are extraordinarily problematic. For many specific higher scientific domains, strictly, there is no non-probabilistic solution without excess in theory, experiment or observation. This is not to suppose, as has been shown in this chapter, that a gap-function here is all that stitches together a comparison with advanced science and creative literature, though it facilitates recognition of some similarities. Rather, the thesis starts with the view that twentieth-century mechanistic science has given way to, or has to allow fresh identities for, a plurality of scientific worlds. Just because a scientific theory works, it does not follow that it *is* true; and its detailed scope rarely is. This gap between theory and the external world, thus explained, is crucial for the identity and status of the scientific theory as it ascends to the higher orders. With the recognition that there are many live metaphors in abstract and descriptive scientific language, comes the implication that the gap between natural and creative languages is closing, or where distant has mirroring live metaphor parallels. Nevertheless, this chapter's argument does not require partial closure of the gap. It only needs the admission that the identity of the gap is not one of global discontinuity, and the knowledge that both sides of that gap share comparable properties – especially where science cannot fully compute, calculate, observe and verify all the contents of its semantics in theory. A refined sensibility will perhaps prefer a mirroring of comparable properties on both sides of the science/humanities gap. There are differences, but these often skewed similarities; there are similarities, yet these obscure differences shared between sciences that mirror those in literature and logic. One similarity between science and humanities is the function of creativity – traditionally understated in science, while forefronted in creative literature. Creativity appears to be *internal to* the identities, and not just mental *and emotional* origins of logic, mathematics and science in ways that even now are only unclearly exposed.

It is therefore of value and significance to measure the metaphoric distance between the two domains, as well as to find formulable criteria or tests with their application to, and in, the games of scientific logic, as well as their remote literary counterparts. It is wrong to suppose that logic cannot represent vagueness, indeterminacy, opacity and inconsistency.[25] To some degree this concerns what we take to be the relations between human consciousnesses and subjects whose job it is to measure or assess representation.

Non-algorithmic cosmology, non-surveyability and literariness

Penrose *et al.* (1997) have argued that consciousness is non-algorithmic. There are different senses associated with 'algorithm'. For Wittgenstein it had the sense of a calculus. It seems correct to follow Marion (1998: 164–8): Wittgenstein did not assent to the law of excluded middle (i.e., if 'yes' or 'no' does not answer the question, then nothing does). This was the case in his handling of π, as mentioned in a previous section. The question thus arises, what is the semantic identity of functions in this non-algorithmic game? I suggest that, since Wittgenstein cannot avail himself of the response that there is no propositional sense – because he tied this to surveyability and computability in the fashion of a calculus – we can restore the proposal that the non-algorithmic domain has parallels with semantics. Semantics is a function of consciousness, as is non-algorithmic mathematics. I do not stake the case on this similarity, however; yet there are comparable features even in the domain of computable mathematics. Wittgenstein insisted that mathematics has no subject matter, in the sense that it does not refer to anything; it is entire unto itself, unlike natural language. But this also strictly holds for fiction language, and in a special sense for parabolic and poetical language domains. These are similar to modal worlds outside of the ontological realm.

Wittgenstein's attitude to realism in the *Philosophical Investigations* is complex and awaits clarification in some respects. He opposed straightforward verification, while avoiding the type of view now canvassed as intuitionism; yet he was sympathetic to a peculiarly plain though deep concept of (what may be termed) counter-intuitive realism. I would like to connect this with the problem of how Wittgenstein or a scientist tuned to local experiments as the only strict science, might approach the problem of the non-surveyability of the Big Bang. And link this issue to the hypothesis that in mathematical physics the Big Bang's representation is non-algorithmic – not to say quite crazy. We can conclude that such mathematics yields a proof, if true, that there is such a thing as unique originality in mathematical and empirical language games. This would incorporate indeterminacy, non-lawlike consequences of rule following standard physics, and their surveyability, not least because of infinity states in the specification of this space–time point and its energies. They also manifest global complexity properties. These exotic states of affairs are parallel in these respects, if treated as live metaphors (which they are, even within the physics) with original literary creativity. An original semantic world is born from a discontinuity. The phenomenon is unsurveyable, as to computability; it is not a calculus, yet it is a new language game, and it is indeterminate. The semantic functions encode chance patterns, and complexity properties. In short, they are counterintuitive. If we follow Rees's (1999) multiverse, of an infinite ensemble of universes, we have a topology to model a literary topology for countless domains of sense. Certainly, this relation could run away out of control; but this does not itself generate snags, any more than fertile physical theories do.

Retrojecting from our epoch to the first timepoint of the collapse of the physical world deforms into an ontological state for which we do not have a criterion of how we would apply the law of excluded middle. This complies with Wittgenstein's view, if we construe him this way, namely that the law does not hold in principle for our concept of what would be surveyable, but in a way that is not helpful to his thesis, since for at least some domains cosmology uses mathematics that are calculable, yet not surveyable, and not (in the relevant sense) experimental. It establishes that his thesis to do with global surveyability for mathematics is false. I argue that, consequently and more generally, constructivism is inadequate to the task of mapping many of the uses of mathematics in these exotic areas of astrophysical cosmology (see Gibson, 2000). Yet we should be very reserved about dropping the idea that in principle the law of excluded middle does not hold in the foregoing cases, distinguishing this position from the viable notion that in a context of incomplete surveyability it may not hold true. A reason for this is Boolos's (1998: 406–10) last study that leaves us with formal grounds for maintaining it even in paradoxical contexts, and I add for non-Planckian ontologies. Boolos's argument includes the point that even when we oppose the law of excluded middle we presuppose it in proving this. These parallel situations we find in philosophies of fiction and transcendence, so such a view seems to stand for creative literature's possible worlds too.

Wittgenstein (1998) had, in the *Philosophical Investigations*, however, a profound grasp of the acuteness of the problem of standing outside of veridical principles, for example:

§352 Here it happens that our thinking plays us a queer trick. We want, that is, to quote the law of excluded middle and to say: 'In the decimal expansion of π either the group "777" occurs, or it does not – there is no third possibility.' That is to say: 'God sees – but we don't know.' But what does that mean? – We use a picture; the picture of a visible series which one person sees the whole of and another not. The law of excluded middle says here: It must either look like this, or like that. So it really – and this is a truism – says nothing at all, but gives us a picture. And the problem ought now to be: does reality accord with the picture or not? And this picture *seems* to determine what we have to do, what to look for, and how – but it does not do so, just because we do not know how it is to be applied. Here saying: 'There is no third possibility' or 'But there can't be a third possibility!' – expresses our inability to turn our eyes away from this picture: a picture that looks as if it must already contain both the problem and its solution, while all the time we *feel* that it is not so.

§353 Asking whether and how a proposition can be verified is only a particular way of asking 'How d'you mean?' The answer is a contribution to the grammar of the proposition.

If we apply §353 to the opening cosmological phase of the universe, we have a case of the third possibility in §352. At §365, Wittgenstein resumes the point:

§365 Do Adelheid and the Bishop play a real game of chess? – Of course. They are not merely pretending – which would also be possible as part of a play. – But, for example, the game has no beginning! – Of course it has; otherwise it would not be a game of chess.

The denial that the game has no beginning could mean this particular game, or the creation of the game itself. The latter option fits the beginning of cosmology's referent: the universe, though, conjecturally, with a Rees (1999) multiverse conception, there would be no beginning. Yet the multiverse would comply with being a game, which opposes Wittgenstein's limit to language. Here by a bizarre move, the cosmological game is not *a priori*, but is not observable, and is empirical, yet does not conform to any surveyable empirical experiment. So, contrariwise, it is *a priori* of a unique time – rather like imagination. This latter position comes near to Deleuze and Guattari's (1994) denial that there is an absolute difference between the *a priori* and the empirical (though their philosophy differs from Wittgenstein's). And indeed this 'experiment' is not repeatable, and so, in Wittgenstein's sense, it is not fully an experiment. These properties have unexpected parallels in literature, in the semantic contracts between mind, creativity, the composition of original expressions – which in a range of examples is a creative singularity. These can be combined with the gathering of similarities in literature assembled in other parts of this chapter.

A solution to some of the above disparities in Wittgenstein's conception, is to accept that he, and others such as Brouwer (1967), only succeed in addressing an artificially narrowed set of possibilities when deeming them 'the *a priori*', not all mathematical possibility grounded empirically. There is a third possibility. There are other sets of counter-intuitive *a priori*, which are skewed by original and counter-intuitive matter-energy conditions. These occur in relation to what are, in some puzzling *senses*, identified as infinities. In a specially qualified sense, Wittgenstein (1961) might, after all, have used the expression 'prove' instead of 'shown' in the *Tractatus*. But the cosmology rehearsed in the present chapter can be used to show Wittgenstein's restriction to be false, if one is making a strong empirical claim by asserting that: 'only connections that are subject to law are thinkable' (*Tractatus*, §6.361). Well, we have just been thinking about the total collapse of law, in a state of affairs in which there still is a counter-intuitive empirical domain.

It appears to follow from the foregoing that it is untrue to say: '*How* things are in the world is a matter of complete indifference for what is higher' (*Tractatus*, §6.432). Contrariwise, there is a cosmological conduit and continuum physically and conceptually between what there is and what there originally was. We achieve knowledge of this by utilising Wittgenstein's assertion that:

> Logic is not a body of doctrine, but a mirror-image of the world. Logic is transcendental.
>
> (*Tractatus*, §6.13)

Counter-intuitive logic, however, should be included in the scope of this remark. This involves paradoxes, but the cosmology is paradoxical. How might we resolve this problem? By recognising that the classical logic, and to some degree constructivism, is unable to cope with a range of counter-intuitive games. We need therefore to attend to new futures, and primordial pasts, to escape from the artificial limits of too wide a dependence on mastery of techniques and practice, and too narrow an awareness of counter-intuitive creative possibilities. There are however possible ways of mediating some such impasse, for example, G. H. von Wright (1996: 84–5). He suggested that we refine and extend the notion of truth and falsehood to include domains hitherto untreated by classical logic.

An upshot of the foregoing analysis is to pave the way for accepting that there can be an *a priori* logic of infinities mirrored in a medium in relation to an empirical world. Comparable considerations transformed for literary universes of significant original compositions lead to similar prospects for logics of their games. Indeed, such writers as Pynchon, in *Vineland*, have deconstructed the two domains of possibility into one transfinite literary possible world: the original fictional world satisfying different sets of material conditions from ours, whereas David Lewis (1986) has posited other counterpart worlds.

We should note that in the above quotation Wittgenstein (§352) wished to expose a feature which is shared by indexicality, the mathematical theory of π, and a perfect omniscient perception of God, and the notion of picturing these by a third way. Having suggested a schematic basis for doing this, we find ourselves beyond the scope of Wittgenstein's intention, reflected in *Tractatus* and *Remarks on the Foundations of Mathematics*, to identify the limit to language's capability to express significance, be it literary or mathematical.

It is worth highlighting that, and how, he was averse to reification of language, yet (hopefully without violating that principle) he grouped together amazingly various asymmetric phenomena. I do not find this a worry; only let us realise the explicit remit in it, which involves mapping and picturing common functions in widely different natural and mathematical language families. On my account, these are susceptible of expansion as complex live metaphor, for which see Gibson (1997, 2000 and 2000a). This presupposes an appeal to a *mapping* capability that is transcendent by supervening over *differentiable* fields. This approach, if combined with the foregoing developments, takes us beyond strict finitude, through and past conventionalist rules, to domains and *manifolds*[26] that use typologies of infinity and counter-intuitive physical states. Even if physics is constructivist, and if, only by means of a rough approximation, the Big Bang scenario, or something like it, were to be correct, this leads to the conclusion that when constructivism overlays contemporary cosmology, it has to implode into a nonconstructivist explanation of the universe. Given that Wittgenstein hinged and keyed his rules and pictures in the ways he did (as interpreted in the present context), his own constructivist conception, as a consequence of his own other nonconstructivist insights, concessions and subsequent developments, has to give way to this type of anti-constructivist conclusion.

A function of the foregoing situation is the point that having a *contingent grasp* of implication is not itself the *understanding* of that or any contingent grasp of implication. Wittgenstein's statement in his *Philosophical Investigations* (§352) 'God sees – but we don't know' is true (if God exists); yet a consequence of it is that the goal posts, of how much we see and how we see, can and do change. In current astrophysical cosmology, provisional though it is, the goal posts move in a nonsurveyable supermanifold respecting a number of domains, though in principle veridicality would obtain for relevant domains. For some domains, such as a primordial black hole, there is no possibility of surveyability. So *what it is to be a game* itself has evolved into a new narrative universe: from constructivism, into a constructivism that entails discovery and not only invention beyond our ken, which is non-finitist in its mathematical basis. In this perspective, constructivism, finitism and strict finitism, though accurate and appropriate for some domains of mathematics, are inoperable for large chunks of pure mathematics, and for much of the mathematical physics of astrophysical cosmology.

Consequently, we should not allow the concept of constructivism to regulate the thought-bridge concerning the limits of the game of language, upon which Wittgenstein insisted. Even so, his acute analysis of games facilitates for us a grasp of how to embark on a journey to a nonconstructivist progression through the thought-bridge. This enables us to develop a rich concept of the counter-intuitive identities of games. So stretching the limits of language beyond constructivism enables us to produce a counter-intuitive map that will be of value for the topography of possibility in literary creativity.

Logical pictures, live metaphor and infinity

Wittgenstein died before he could develop a conception of metaphor that would speak to this primordial, creative and *avant-garde* matter. The present perspective proposes how one might do this, and not necessarily in a Wittgensteinian way. Since other publications[27] have portrayed how this conception would go, it will not be enlarged upon here, save for a few comments. As with a televised, filmed or virtual reality simulation, live metaphor goes proxy for its subject by means of a relative identity equation, under *a* criterion or *some* criteria of identity. (Gibson

(2001) explains that it is also important to allow for differing criteria of application in these contexts.) We could have the value of, say, '3^2' as a live metaphor of the function 'x^2'. Consequently functions and value and their relations can be used to explore exotic informal structures. Just as mathematics is not reducible to logic, while logic can interpret mathematics, so it is with the application of logic to literature. Traditionally something very roughly like this conception would have been called 'mimesis'. Yet when it is transformed by counter-intuition, it takes on the aspect of a multidimensional live metaphorisation of mimesis, as Gibson (2000) interprets the matter. This deviation from plain realism gives an unexpected twist to mimesis: a concept of what I label 'counter-intuitive realism'. This reformulation of realisms, and anti-realisms, results partly from the increase in complex high knowledge. A reason for this is that an exponential enlargement of qualitative knowledge often generates resort to indirect methods of constructing, or discovering, further mastery of knowledge.[28]

The concept of a physically or qualitatively transcendent singularity eludes the net of finitist conventionalism. (Wittgenstein did not seem to examine the idea of an astrophysical 'singularity', let alone an aesthetic one.) I suggest that this type of singularity has internal properties whose representation is a montage of live metaphors. This has parallels with creativity expressed in language games. Such a claim rides on the back of the ways Wittgenstein sutured different language games from different subjects, if combined with the present arguments. This is an extremely specific, counter-intuitive and unstable window of opportunity for comparison, viewing across and beyond a thought-bridge. Prendergast (1986) has depicted a new sense of mimesis, as a cosmic nerve of instability attended by creativity. Gibson (2000 and 2001) expounds counter-intuitive mimesis as a function of catastrophe, and complexity theory: as with the mapping of a birth, a new criterion of identity is the consequence of the collision between the old and the new.

We cannot safely allow, of course, that we have logical omniscience in these domains. This leads to the need for what Hintikka (1998: 240) has called 'informational independence', and the idea that we have to take into account the knowledge of entities in contrast with knowledge of propositions. 'Forms of life' in Wittgenstein is an exemplar (the foregoing section employs the term 'manifold' which can be presupposed as a type for forms of life) internal to a given phenomenon, and necessary for its identity. These given features are those that are synthetically necessary, without which the forms of life are impossible (see Garver, 1996). Garver (1994) locates various senses of transcendence within Wittgenstein's approach. The arena for these games is natural history and its grammar. But if we introduce finitism as a limit on (Wittgenstein's sense for) natural history, its introduction is blocked by the foregoing study because of the identities of cosmology and unsurveyability.

What a computable finitist assessment of limits does not allow for, however, is the concept of live metaphoric grammar.[29] Without wishing to reverse into limited forms of this particular type of approach, it nevertheless exhibits some prospects. At the side of this hypothesis, and partially complementary to it, we might consider the conception of a live metaphor grammar (using the sort of criteria for semantics specified in Gibson (1997, 2000 and 2000a)). It is not that such a grammar is not logical. Rather, that it is non-algorithmic and live metaphoric. These characteristics can be integrated with the policy of surveyable sense. Such work also complements the conception of a finitist analysis that yields a characterisation which leaves it open that conceptual literary semantics thus depicted does not itself have to be finitist. That is, it can be a non-algorithmic discovery function. Obviously if the future of a grammar is unpredicted or unpredictable, this does not entail that it is thereby illogical. Non-surveyable phenomena may or may not be calculable logically.

Consequently, we can incorporate a surveyable application of language into natural history that is not itself predictable as to the semantic identity of its future. That is to say, it is just what one would wish for a grammar of literary creativity. The level at which it is surveyable depends on how one interprets the grammar relations to the unconsciousness, intentionality, and the efficacy of the expressible medium. These considerations divide, rule and dispute a finitist insistence on a natural history that imposes limits on creativity. Just because such matters are nonsurveyable and counter-intuitive, it does not entail that they are indeterministic. Even if they are, as we know from global use of indeterminacy in the Everett many-worlds universe, this does not have to eradicate causality from such a universe. On this analogy, indeterminacy plus causality is susceptible in principle of at least partial surveyability. So the tie-up of counter-intuition with nonsurveyability should leave space for a concept of partial counter-intuitive surveyability, for which Wittgenstein did not allow. This has relevance for reading a literary game. It would be invalid to attempt an inference from the presence of some indeterminacy of narrative to universalised deconstruction.

The reasons for such a state of affairs connect with other fundamental issues: one alternative is that the *game* consequent on natural history is implanted a long time after the start of the universe. This contingently is implied by description of its current state, and its retrojective features; but this would oppose what we know of astrophysics – that our physics has some significant qualitative relation to primordial astrophysics. Or, we have to admit that the start of the universe *and* whatever caused it are components of our natural history.[30] Wittgenstein bars the latter option with his constructivism, though the role of limited surveyability in observational cosmology supports this latter option. The indirect evidence from this observational knowledge, for the primordial deformation of the lawlike empirical conditions in our terrestrial physics, also opposes Wittgenstein's claim about the surveyability of mathematics involving with natural history. Furthermore, the role of origins in connection with surveyability and constructivism produces major difficulties for these approaches. For example, the emergence of human consciousness, and the regress to fundamental debates about the origins of the human unconsciousness, and its consequent relations to consciousness as it perceives and records natural history, all seem to raise intractable objections to surveyability as a generalised principle.[31] The nub of the problems amounts to the very indirect observational cosmology support for the function of infinities in the first few microseconds of the universe, whereas Wittgenstein did not allow for such an empirical possibility. I have been arguing that this possibility counter-intuitively mirrors the use of nonsurveyable phenomena in literature. The scope of 'nonsurveyable' here is the technical use of the expression within philosophy of mathematics, and its sense does not in principle remove the prospect of logical scrutiny from a nonsurveyable, nonconstructionist standpoint employing counter-intuitive strategies, which occur in the deeper identities of logics and creativity identities themselves.

So, without logical omniscience to choose otherwise, we have to engage with some notion of infinity, as a function of the empirical claims in cosmology – together with its uses in higher mathematics; presumably logical omniscience would entail that, in any case. Certainly some of these appeals to 'infinity' will turn out to be confused, and the large divergent uses of the word (what the relations of such conceptions of infinity have to a use of infinity that is alleged to obtain for God) involve different issues we need not consider here.

We should also allow that since having a concept does not itself entail a recognitional capacity for understanding it might be perceived as a matter of taste. That is to say, accepting that there are infinities; or that they are accessible; or that they are instantiated in a finite (for example, literary) medium – or the negation of one, some or all of these possibilities, is a function of our own relativity inaccurately projected as a property of an external phenomenon. We may wish, however, to avoid consequences of this. For example it is false to judge that the contents of a toilet are the same order as Mozart's counter-intuitive creativity. On the basis of such a constructivist binary rule, we might be committed to following it to the consequence that there is, unrecognised by us, an empirical foundation that obligates us to acknowledge the point that: knowledge of *différance* and making connections, entails qualitative distinctions that are unsurveyable whose manifestation is empirically demonstrable. This is a rule-following problem of a language game in respect of aesthetics, of which Wittgenstein, despite my criticism, had, in *other* domains, a profound mastery. Wittgenstein's (1977, §320) example of Charlemagne is relevant:

> Charlemagne certainly understood the principle of writing and still couldn't learn to write . . . But there are two cases of not-being-able-to-learn. In the one case we merely fail to acquire a certain competence, in the other we lack comprehension. We can *explain* a game to someone: He may understand this explanation, but not be able to learn the game, or he may be incapable of understanding my explanation of the game. But the opposite is conceivable as well.

Written a few months before his death, in his manuscript *Remarks on Colour*, this paves the way for extending the idea of a game in which we do not understand another's game though the latter game is susceptible of explanation. We might here adopt an approach presented by von Wright (1996) about colour and the representation of qualitative degrees of difference. He imagines that some alien 'tribes' differ in their way of cutting and pasting degrees of colours, by their mixing colour-matching degrees and overlaps such as bluish-green. This situation contrasts with our usage of natural single colouring nouns, since their standard of whether or not a colour term is true or false in its use differs from our own. We might generalise this to aesthetic and literary sensibilities: for some people Derrida is an alien, for others a new future, yet for others a tired recent past, and so on. There are borderline cases of this general situation, such as a bizarre episode in early Sumerian narrative (see Gibson, 2000a).

What is the game of this *disagreement?* Is it merely a function of our modern games? Does it presuppose qualia and rule following, which are distinct to those of our game-plays? No, in Wittgenstein's view. If this is the case, then our inability to assess certain domains in such ancient literary play (apart from the limits on our part to retroject to this epoch) is itself a firm indication of the superficiality of the mastery we have of our own perception of techniques of rule-following, and of our ignorance of the depth of the human game of language. In this sense, then, I here redeploy the problem von Wright (1996) composes for alien tribes, as a function of our own current incapacity to understand what we are, and how to recognise (as a function of understanding) what we know. When we read ancient literature we need new moves in the game of avoiding projecting onto texts our own collective autobiography, and unconscious. In short, in reading we enact the role of an intertext, instead of reading it. Short of revelation, of course, it is the fashion to assume that we cannot escape from this impasse. My view is that if this is true, it is contingently true; and so the possibility of a counter-intuitive route around misreading obtains. Underlying this situation is the state of affairs that it is not a mere matter of the inefficiency or intentionality of expression that causes the misreading. It is significantly part of the counter-intuitive identity of what it is to be creativity. The logic of (causality or disposition of) misreading, I venture to suppose, has been largely neglected as a contribution to current debates about the identities of literature. The foregoing point does not naively have to presuppose that the text has to have a single sense for the present argument to be correct. Rather, in the perspective of the present, this matter has to do with the density, richness and instability of a multiplicity of senses within and without a great creative narrative.

We could include in this scenario possible worlds implemented as functions of literary nuances, and, as Gibson, 2001: 99 supposed, we could introduce some multiple conclusion logics, with tree structures, to map levels of sense. I suggest that such devices can resolve some of Wittgenstein's worries in *Remarks on Colour*,[32] learning from the ways in which quantum cosmology and string theory (see Witten, 1998) can supply concepts of games with rules that seem to be alien-like. This shows that what might have been thought to be alien is an example of our ignorance about deeper layers of our own reality and creativity.

That is to say, literary sensibility is counter-intuitive. It was the Nobel physicist John Bell (1987: 194) who affirmed that possible worlds quantum mechanics in physics, 'are like literary fiction in that they are free inventions of the human mind'; my idea is that this applies even more appropriately to cosmology.[33]

Qualitative infinities

The purpose in stating this argument is that infinity is thereby a function within our experience, concerning which we have conjectural knowledge of some undecidable games that are evidently not surveyable though empirical. Since there are logics of undecidability, we should not be averse in principle to logics of literary creativity. This point is the commencement of the chain from literature's ship to the cosmological anchor.

Wittgenstein asserted that infinity is not a quantity, but a quality. But qualitative analysis, though different from infinity as a quality, does have a puzzling relation to quantitative computation, which is a complex multifarious one that I think bears on Wittgenstein's remark. Qualitative analysis in finitist contexts uses quantities. Wittgenstein wanted to bar quantitative infinity from his account of mathematics, principally because of his arguments for surveyability as a necessary condition. Yet we have seen that this is not a sustainable thesis, especially in the light of developments subsequent to his death. It was not that he opposed in principle the use of transcendence, for that is a subsumed component of his philosophy. He did not go to address how or what this infinity might be interpreted to be. The present chapter offers some considerations to enter this sphere.

There will be substructures and subsets to such qualitative infinity, especially when finite constructivist properties are a medium of expression. In proportion to the latter's intrusion on the former's function, there will be asymmetric results. This is the multifarious domain that concerns those who might inaccurately scan the foregoing as a commitment to a uniform single grand unified theory that purports to identify all literary creativity with one quality. Not so. I have left it open that there may be entire domains of such literature that are untouched by these considerations, and by qualitative infinity. I may retire to any of a number of grounds to sustain this, including a scrambling version of internalist, externalist or plural presuppositions. A presupposition of this is the prospect for a theory of logic according to which all logics tend to implement a psychogenetic function of their inventors: there is a mirroring or causal relation between the logics composed by human mentality and the identities of human consciousness. This does not entail that for each type of logic, this does not have to correspond to its inventor's mental typology. These theses could then be introduced to model widely divergent varieties of creative imagination. Within this perspective, and also the foregoing sections of the present chapter, we might envisage a qualitative infinity in literature enwrapping a constructivist expression vaunting itself as absolute truth. For example, in a great work of literature a quotation might be taken from one of the imbecile influential politicians, and be ironised as a beautiful intertextual function, with the effect that a member of the classical academy of taste would judge the resulting work to be that of genius. Although Wittgenstein did not discuss such a thesis, he nevertheless had things to argue that should be borne in mind here, and as Schefold (1989: 333) states, these bear the impress of Sraffa's[34] economising influence: 'The bourgeois position of the contradiction or its position in the bourgeois world: that is the philosophical problem' (Wittgenstein, 1975: 69).

Gathering together the spread of considerations advanced in the foregoing sections, there are at least precedents for linking quality with quantity. Certainly there are many senses to these terms; it is feasible to pick out a schematics, however, for a continuous chain from the foregoing interpretation. I am arguing that finite semantics can house qualitative functions that are not finite, and by a counter-intuitive game dodge the finitist limitations placed on the possibility of expression of the infinite. This is not intended as a mystical proposal, and it allows that, as with logic, claims might be false. Someone may wish to maintain that all such claims are false. On my interpretation, however, a programmatic block on the idea of creative discovery of the infinite does not locate this falsehood. A reason is that qualitatively infinite creativity is possible by use of finite language. In this sense the results of mentality that are accurately to be called creativity presuppose a state of affairs: that creativity is condensed rationality. This rationality will certainly be of a type that is counter-intuitive, and thus is not a recipe for a conservative or reactionary agenda.

A qualitative analysis concerns an overall trend relevant to generalising over a quantitatively described domain. Cosmology is a handy example here, since a large domain of qualitative analysis is not just a larger-scale generalisation of quantitative analysis. The former is not reducible to the latter, though there is an informative transformation between the two. So it is with literary analysis. The subject of economics, and in particular prediction (for which see Gibson, 2000) is also pertinent, though the relations of this subject to literary analysis also involve counter-intuitive jumps. On certain economic questions one might use qualitative analysis in an externalist way. That is to say, a logic of preference for a certain state of affairs concerning an individual's rights with reference, for example, to preference or even distribution in relation to needs, or an internalist one to satisfy an individual's intentionalist taste. Often the two are combined. These options are comparable to how widely different groups of readers approach literature. We should map the individual's internalist perceptions, in the case of, for example, a reader who supposes that there is no realist or constant academy of objective aesthetic values, while leaving room for presenting the readerly taste with a Platonic agenda. But we should note that each presupposes sometimes hidden elements of the other. For example, Amartya Sen (1995: 19–31) identifies in some theory a lack of recognition that '*purely* internal consistency' entails relations to external properties, in making choice functions that presuppose motivations that entail external features.

So for example – to extend the application of this point, if an analogy can hold here between some economics and literary investigation, we will need to be sensitive to causal relations between internal and external reasons. One characteristic that masks the point that the internal entails external relations, is – somewhat oddly – the way some philosophy assumes that implicit connections are directly transparent. From such an imperious seeming vantage point it is all-too-easy to adopt the position that we survey what we know with a clarity which presupposes that we typically always pick out relations between the external and the internal. Supposedly, on this view, the trained rational mind is not easily misled as generally to miss important features, and 'consequently' we are supposed invariably to detect, for example, the borderline between the intentionalist and the intention with which we speak about, observe, believe in states of affairs, etc. Conversely this – not infrequently misleading – near-ideal observational position renders us dispositionally blind to recognising some relevant actual connection between the internal and the external entailments or weaker implications, of which the case Sen (1995) documents is an instance. Bourdieu (2000: 9–11) tracks the social counterpart of this epistemological fabric, and draws attention to Pascal's almost parallel viewpoint, in which Pascal expressed the idea that:

> Custom is the source of our strongest and most believed proofs. It inclines the automaton, which pursues the mind without its thinking about the matter.
>
> (Pascal, *Pensées*, §252)

Well, someone might wish to charge Pascal of employing 'without its thinking about the matter' as too strong, for people do think about such a matter. But this would be blithely to underestimate Pascal's point, which has to do with the intentionality we naturally articulate to dispose of actually 'thinking about the matter' so that we replace 'thinking' with its plausible counterfeit, which simulates so well as an automaton to obscure the external reality.

In our local natural history we master a finitist, strict finitist or constructivist practice; yet it presupposes some properties of infinity, just as a finite series has within it an infinite series of reconfigurations. For the present purpose, the idea that infinity is incomputable – is non-algorithmic in a range of ways – matches a literary aesthetic function. Namely, great creative literature is in some respects undecidable, at least by standard techniques of measurement. Let us suppose that this is due, not to incomplete or inappropriate means of computation, but to the fact that such an aesthetic function just is uncomputable. Now this can be constructed so as to have the strange, and apparently mischievous, implication that it is not a finitist function. It could follow from this consequence that aesthetic functions of this type thereby either are, or have family resemblances with, qualitative infinities. At this juncture, the division of analysis splits. For, on the one hand, it utilises a route using the notion of undecidability. And, on the other hand, we can introduce the theme of counter-intuition, devised in the above analysis, to conclude, nevertheless, that it is counter-intuitively decidable, perhaps enhancing the conclusion in suitable contexts (or degrading it, depending on your poison) with paradox. If this approach is viable, it will, to fit a wide range of contexts, expand into a complexity theory with a large range of different manifestations. The scenario will also mirror precisely a presupposition implemented in the foregoing.

The division of logical labour and the mixing of disparate logics in aesthetic creativity refract collusion between theories projecting the earliest state of the universe with its partially uncomputable super-physics that contravene standard microphysics, though they may be said theoretically to share a continuum. It seems to me that this stitching together, of two different (transcendent and normalised) narrative universes is what Wittgenstein would have needed to restore aspects of his *Tractatus* (§6) and create a counter-intuitive continuity of it with his *Philosophical Investigations*.[35] The outcome would of course be a transformation. It is in this sense that the present chapter opened with the question about literary creativity as a super-condensed counter-intuitive rationality. This does not include Gödel's assumption that such rational realms are a type of super-reality, though such a view is not ruled out by the theory.

There are self-evidently many realms that one would have to investigate further as well as with regard to their involvement with literary creativity, if one were to achieve balance in respect of a logic of creativity. For example, in what ways has music language-like functions in games of sound that are nonlinguistic, while resembling signification of the emotions? Jonathan Miller[36] has suggested that the multidimensional sculpted cornices, with their complex topological surfaces, are nearer the mark as a basis for modelling music 'language' – i.e. a physical analogue for aesthetic audio properties. If this were to be true, then the multidimensional topologies for a universe's structure in relation to its space, matter and energy could be brought to use as the beginnings of a formal model, not least with string theory of knots (see Witten, 1998, 2002, and Gibson, 2000). It would then be valuable to assess how such a model of music could enhance concepts of literary rhythm and orality that contribute to what is literature.[37] (The section 'Realistic propositions' at the end of chapter 3 develops an aspect of this point.)

Creative literature is a counter-intuitive mixture and consequence of standardised usage and the deviating original language game. In view of the foregoing thoughts, a significant question for investigation arises: what happens when ancient writers, without science, without modernist eurocentric logic, yet with unusual creativity exercise their minds and unconscious to compose a conjunction of games that speak to the meaning of life? In talking about ancient literature, focusing on those exotic instances of literature collectively entitled 'the Bible' frames our attempts to trace and track its identities in the widest possible ways. Literary analysis of the Bible is well advanced, while the study of its logic is not. This literature is a subset of the larger semantic domain of what it is to be literature (for which see Gibson, forthcoming b). So the present chapter covers only one narrow sphere of its narrative world, while situating relevant issues for ancient literature in the priority of a logic of literature. This type of engagement with literature is significant for topics in other subjects such as philosophy of mathematics and cosmology, among others, partly because of the counter-intuitive identities of literature that push, not just against but also beyond the limits of a given contemporary language game. So this is itself a manifestation of deep instability, termed in the foregoing counter-intuition. Such logic of literary creativity is often the antithesis of the academic tradition that guards it. In the perspective of the foregoing analysis, Wittgenstein's (1961) notorious remark is not a truism, but a counter-intuitive and elusive insight, which transcends the limits of his atomic language in the *Tractatus* not only pervading his early philosophy but standing beyond the frontier he reached just prior to his death:

> In fact, all the propositions of our everyday language, just as they stand, are in perfect logical order.
>
> (*Tractatus*, §5.5563)

Nevertheless what it is to be 'everyday language' is obscure – not in a negative sense. A reason for this is that such language is a resource for possibility and virtuality, which is not apparent from its daily usage.

This resource in language, of possibility and virtuality, is an antecedent that in conjunction with other features yields creative singularities. This represents a literary subset of a general state of affairs that recurs in artistic and material universes. Namely, creativity is the conjunction of counter-intuitive states with originality, which gives birth to a singularity. This characterisation applies equally, though of course differently, to the emergence of the universe and of great artistic composition. Applied to artistic endeavour, this amounts operationally to such a creative work being the conjunction of counter-intuition with original use of skills that internalises surprise or the sublime to craft a new identity. A consequence of this proposal is that, in relation to the foregoing quotations from the *Tractatus*, the elements of new counter-intuitive identities reside latent in the conjunction of 'everyday language' with 'perfect logical order'. The surprise of the new in great art is thus a perfectly logical affair. It is just that it is counter-intuitive, since creative singularities emerge replete with qualitative infinities, which are internal defining properties of creative identities. In such ways infinity is a live metaphoric function of finite – counter-intuitive – series. Accordingly, construction and discovery in perception are two sides of the same coin, not competing alternatives. The problem is that the toss of the coin has traditionally been argued in three dimensions, or two in the case of sentences. Rather, a toss of the coin – a throw of the dice – emerges and operates in knotted space, one with many more dimensions than the deconstructing gambler imagines. Consequently, a symbolic sign of great creativity is that it eliminates the chance it employs to compose an original identity.

6   Virtual reality metaphysics

Logic of metaphoric film

Stanley Cavell's (1979: 158) work on the philosophy of film states that:

> It is particularly worth cautioning against useless simplicity about this [i.e., 'the knowledge of the unsayable is the study of what Wittgenstein means by physiognomy'] because Wittgenstein's discussion of interpretation has what looks like a ready-made application to our knowledge of the subjects of film.

Cavell (1979: 156) had just remarked that film 'escapes Aristotelian limits according to which the possible has to be made probable'. I wish to propose that this escape is also present in certain counter-intuitive complex transcendent concepts that mirror the remotest boundaries of actual states of affairs, one of which is the metaphysics of divine transcendence, a subset of which is revelation. It will be argued below that such phenomena can benefit in the way we attempt to depict them by employing film – in the sense of its being a subset of virtual reality simulation – as a version of extended live metaphor. Although the following concentrates on how live metaphor in language might be depicted as a vehicle for revelation and/or the expression of a transcendent metaphysics, its purpose is not to restrict the approach only to language as the medium for expressions of such realms. Rather, here language is taken to be a complex live metaphor of which linguistic expression is but one of many domains of semiotic function; others include music, dramatic contexts, etc. In a more extended scenario, a human's life, and certainly the incarnation, is presupposed here as a, or the, totalised group implementing these expressions.

Logical possibilities

As to relation between the possible and the probable and their visualisation, twentieth-century theology was adversely affected by analytical philosophy. This has often been by indirect osmosis by theologians, and only occasionally by direct incursion. How should we begin to measure, assess, dispute and re-interpret such a multifarious situation, as a contribution to ways forward for future theism? We could attend to the issue of how to represent human consciousness in its relations to possibility and actuality.

One way of approaching this is to consider aspects of metaphoric visualisation in theology and philosophy, as properties of imagination and realist science, together with pertinent connections between them. Such a project and projection needs to include formal matters, but I hope that theological readers will hold on and not be put off, since it is for their relevance to theology that they are included. Paul Finney's (1994) work, on the expression of problems of expressing the invisible God in art by very early Christians, warns us that modernist literalising interpretation of their writings is unwarranted; or at least it misrepresents their subtle awareness of the possibility of depicting revelation of God in visible forms while not violating their own castigation of iconic idolatry. The present proposal of a virtual reality use of live metaphor is part of an argument to suggest that some of the earliest Christian writings, principally in the New Testament (for which see chapters 7, 8 and 10), are logically refined and creatively explosive original means of expressing the invisible powers of divinity by visible metaphor.

This route itself can be construed as a dispute with, for example, the sort of innovation that John Duns Scotus introduced into philosophical theology. His views produced a split in interpretation of being, as Pickstock (1997) has argued, not unlike an introduction of virtual reality as a category of being. In terms of the present approach, however, Duns Scotus's perception imposes a counterfeit version of reality on this issue.[1] Accurately understood, for the present purposes, the introduction of virtual reality is a possible universe of discourse, and not an ontological referring function. Rather, it is a semiotic medium for representing ontological states. The incarnation might itself be interpreted as the instantiation of a virtual reality: 'the Word made flesh'. But it involves false equivocation to convert this mystery into it only having the status of virtual reality, since this confuses a domain of possibility with an ontological referent. In the case where an ontological referent – say, the subject of the incarnation himself – is a perfect and unique realisation of a concept (for example, 'the word'), this is an ontological referent and thereby a newly created one. It is not itself an abstract world having the form of an ontology; again, it is a fresh ontological category of referent.

Although the present concept is very different from Kendall Walton's (1990: 65) approach, there is some common ground. For example Walton states: 'The idea that the spectator [of film] imagines seeing things which he also imagines to be unseen introduces no special difficulties, and constitutes no reason to reject the imaging seeing hypothesis.' Certainly, my present attempt to construe this sort of relation in the arena of depiction of immaterial properties of an invisible God is distinct to Walton's view; yet I take it that relating invisible and visible features in this technological sphere facilitates a precedent, by live metaphor, which can be reconstructed for the transcendent exotic scenario, as I shall argue below.

Looking back over the past century, as a path to progress for the future, we should reflect on how theology sits with logic and logic itself requires assessment. We should not be content with a derivative popularised and thus anaemic vision of logic; nor ought we to be saddled with overt technicalities of the type that render even philosophical reflection dull. Typically philosophical logicians say that we need a recursive principle that will scan counterfactuals as true for a modal world (cf. Evans, 1982). But this is a strong requirement, even for non-theological formal states of affairs. Conversely, we need to allow for the thesis that, as Penrose *et al.* (1997) argue it, understanding itself, and even consciousness, can be, or are, non-algorithmic.[2] You will recall that an algorithm is a theorem that encapsulates in its logical form the slogan that a given array of possible permutations only has a certain permissible and possible form of expression; so it has a predictive value. If understanding is a computable function, then the rationality of which it is itself a function can be said to be assessable by algorithmic computations. Negatively used, such legislation eliminates certain possibilities that violate or are not accounted for by the algorithmic function.

The supposedly exhaustive scope of programmatic inference – of which traditionally algorithms are an instance – is a product of the earlier overly mechanistic notion of proof procedure. This tendency is institutionalised in Whitehead's and Russell's (1910) *Principia Mathematica*. The then yet-future metaphysics of Whitehead's process theology has a still partially unexplored relation to his philosophy of pure mathematics. In the light of researches in logic, it has been obvious for some time that very little in the way of treating advanced issues can be resolved by such mechanical decision procedures. Further, such procedures sometimes conceal or articulate a suppressed internal speculative metaphysics of their own that was conflated with their logic and taken to be internal to its power.

For example, in Whitehead (1898), as Quine (1941: 128) noted, '=' expresses a relation which falls short of identity, and Whitehead and Russell (1910) did not realise that in their interpretation of identity theory they confused quantification with attribution. This led at least Whitehead to assume that strict identity was not internal to identity. Such a position weakened the sense of identity so that later he might confuse a process with identity. Nevertheless, there are deep issues in which metaphysic and identity interlock. We could assume the afore-mentioned confusion to be solved, or at least explicitly exposed and/or theory formulated for it, by deploying Geach's (1980) relative identity theory. The conception of identity in the present book is reminiscent of Geach's view, though it goes in directions not investigated by him, and counter-intuitively extended later in this book. Even so, Whitehead's (1898) work has some fine exploratory remarks about proof, which acknowledge the role of metaphysical interpretation that logic needs and presupposes (for example, a point is a process). Just because some of his interpretations of logic led to process theology should not obscure that he was somewhat more flexible and sensitive than Russell in some of his approaches to logic.

So one is not objecting to recognising links between logic, mathematics and metaphysics. Rather, we need to appreciate that there is a link and of what kind it is; yet such links can be counter-intuitive when dealing with exotic or elusive subjects. We should recognise that we are only, even now as we commence the third millennium, at the borders looking beyond our elementary limits to the central territories where solutions to such problems, if any, lie. Many twentieth-century philosophers have tended to assume, because of quite significant formal breakthroughs, that, contrariwise, the main problems have just been resolved. Paradoxically, the author of Russell's Paradox (roughly, that the set of all sets is not a member of itself and yet is) had already portrayed for us the depth of our ignorance. Yet he helped spawn a formal system that seems to discard the force of this situation, and thus stood as a misleading ideal for the twentieth century. Consequently, the theological reductionist programmes which tacitly or explicitly ride on many of the twentieth-century scientific or philosophical polemics, which presuppose the prohibition in principle of transcendence, have no remit to ban transcendent theology, though obviously, as with any subject, there are incoherent articulations of it.

If Penrose's type of theory (that understanding is non-algorithmic, or even has roughly similar properties), or any other comparable claim, is correct, then such negative philosophical legislation applied to theology is mere imperialism, even at the level of philosophy of logics. Accordingly, the generalisation that the component of transcendence in theology is untenable has had an illicit and too lengthy shelf life. Certainly, recognising this situation does not warrant the revival of a range of the reactionary and philosophically grotesque past versions of philosophical theologies and theologies of revelation. Nevertheless, the logically crude articulation of past scenarios is not invariably a measure of their (alleged) internal confusion. This popularity partially stems from the early twentieth-century modernist success of empirical science that Russell, among others, championed. The notion of a mechanical decision procedure that complies with or manifests conformity to a classical predicate calculus is at least not evidently true, and may be inconsistent.

Without going into a lengthy detour, it is worth considering, as an example (of the need for us to be wary of drawing quick conclusions about the 'nature' of science or logic) the thesis that even within Russell and Whitehead's logic research there is ambivalence, ambiguity and obscurity. There is also metaphysical potential, sometimes by misappropriation, in such states that do not comply with the narrow purist or mechanist views of mathematics, logic or science which Whitehead and Russell variously ascribed to their work. Certainly, more recent perceptions of their work by eminent logicians such as Quine (1941) and Shoesmith and Smiley (1978) take it as evident that these earlier pioneers did not have a correct view of their own work in crucial areas, though one would not thereby wish to belittle its significance. It is worth attempting to cast some new light on the case of Whitehead in relation to the foregoing. This is not because the present book includes any agreement with Whitehead's process theology. Rather, it argues that Whitehead's theology is a consequence of his interpretation of logical theory, in which he conflated his interpretation with the theory. Of course, one might respond trivially that it is obvious that his logic is intertwined in his later metaphysical work. But my point is somewhat different: Whitehead's now largely neglected 1898 study on algebra[3] contains metaphysics disguised as logic in its treatment of mathematics which are precursors of his process theology. If one considers Whitehead's theology to be wrong, another way of expressing this is to say that submerged in his logic are mistakes that facilitated his metaphysics. Clearly, he excavated some valuable insights in logic; the chances are, however, that if the logic is faulty, then metaphysical concepts built on it will embody this.

Even so, there is a mid-position in the relation between logic and metaphysics. This does not necessarily have to be a mean between two points, but there can be a counter-intuitive discontinuity in a worthy attempt to determine the identity of a solution. This formulation, together with the foregoing chapter, comprises an extended set of premises for the following.

Film metaphysics in language

We could notice how virtual reality simulations could be deployed as a logical figure to represent features of the external empirical world. This delivers an electronic shock to vivify the imagination of those who find the foregoing at variance with a theology borne from the assumption that scientific empiricism and logic have removed the power circuits from any powerful transcendent theology. Such a perspective extends well outside of the priorities of the present work, the theory of which has been harnessed elsewhere.[4] It is appropriate, however, to develop here the filmic aspect of such virtual reality theory as a live metaphor for transcendence. Film is the interpretation of performance, as with revelatory transcendence. Although Hans Urs von Balthasar has his own particular dramaturgical use of divine performance concepts, which is not being drawn upon here, his work is nevertheless illustrative of the metaphoric potential of performance art as a conceptual tool presupposed by the present book. I wish to argue that, just as in the *Tractatus* Wittgenstein took the live metaphor (by another name) – based on the analogy of an empirical external world drawn in parallel with spatial projection in geometry – as foils for a bivalent realist model for the logic of a proposition, so one can revolutionise the potential for visualising abstract models of the external world by devising interpretations of film as a logical typology for representing transcendent empirical subjects and properties.

Prior to presenting some philosophy with which to structure this notion, it is helpful to enter the field of film theory and its relation to select ways in which film theory has adapted aspects of psychoanalytic theory to prioritise certain perceptual features of film. So, compare, at one set of levels, the concept of revelatory narrative with the logic of cinematic film as a subset of virtual reality simulation. No doubt there are parallels beyond the point that we do not fully understand either. 'Suture' is a psychoanalytic term derived from surgery that is applied to film. It indicates a dislocation where two different scenes are placed together to form continuity within the theme of a point about the film subject. Clearly, the dislocation both preserves and omits fragments of narrative space. In this way, the notion of suture (of distinct features stitched together) applied to creative narrative is formally related to Thom's (1989) dislocation in the morphogenesis of an existing system(s) or model into a new 'catastrophe transformation'.

The concept of film also dislocates the process of production that made the film: the studio or film-location is in a sense akin to the mental preconscious realm. It is off-stage, albeit causally antecedent to the film, while its function is mirrored in the performance. Although structuralist film theory analysis is now a piece of cultural history, the value of some of its insights can contribute to sensibility beyond poststructuralism. In such terms, for film representation, there is an absent set; the dislocation within the film and between its psychological productions is smoothed over by creativity. The film is an imaging of creative consciousness, revealing something absent from but present in the film. As Oudart (1977) stated it: 'The revelation of this absence is the key-moment in the fate of the image, since it introduces the image into the order of the signifier and cinema into the order of discourse.' Heath (1981) commented on this position by noting: 'What then operates, classically, is the effacement of the absence, the suturing of the discourse . . . by the re-appropriation of the absence within the film, a character in the film coming to take the place of the Absent One posed by the spectator; suture as "the abolition of the Absent One and its resurrection in some one".' The lure of theological terminology for Oudart and Heath in a non-religious technical approach to cinematic ideology is novel, though I suggest that as a complex live metaphor it can be used to enrich and enhance a philosophy of revelation, whether in nature or in narrative theology. Speech occurs in revelation and film. Visual functions in both can be treated as object language expressions, or, for example, as referential truth-values of an object language.

Imagination and logic

The proposal for a live metaphoric film logic of revelation is a corollary for another thesis I wish to suggest: bivalent *and* deviant logics have a psychogenesis and therefore a mapping power which can be used to characterise distinct states of affairs in the external world. The world displays differing logics. Each structure has its own logic, and this does not presuppose either that there is no supervening logic to generalise over them all, or that one could do; those questions amount to further enterprises.

At an impressionistic level we might sketch a scenario by which literary creativity manifests varying sorts of logical conditions (for which see Gibson, forthcoming b): Emily Brontë's (1847) work depicts this montage of life; Beckett's *Ill Seen Ill Said* (1982) reflects Hallden's (1949) and presages Hawking's (1983) blackhole formalisms; Euripides' *Bacchae* matches Shoesmith and Smiley's (1978) multiple-conclusion logic; in *Under Western Eyes*, Frege's Platonism is condensed into Conrad's Razumov; Wagner's operatic poetry mixes Whitehead's and Russell's *Principia* with intuitionism; and, to return to the screen, Bergman's films (not to exclude his plays, for example, his Strindberg cycle) caricature Wittgenstein's philosophy of mathematics.

The psychogenesis of logics fits existential requirements; but this is a matter of imaginative possibility, and not a stipulative condition advocating equal status for all logics. No consistent proof exists to show that bivalent or deviant logics should operate as the criterion of truth, however; yet a large class of deviant logics holds the position of 'true in a possible world' or 'possibly true', not our actual world. If truth is a function of the argument-place of a proposition – its presupposition – then the secondary modal position of truth in deviant logics is a false prescription for truth.

We can agree with Sutherland's (1984) warning about dangers of obsessively narrow formalisms for reason, argument and persuasion. At the side of this, we need fresh exploration of poetical language, in case we possess it with an un-reasonable absence of any logic. Respecting many counter-intuitive logic discoveries to test our notion of self-evident logical structure, we are relieved of formalist Russellian prejudice against the logical merit in some nonformal literary language uses.

'Tone' is one such category. Dummett (1981) deemed it a ragbag, even after dry-cleaning it. Why should tonal uses not signify logical use? On one approach we could use mathematical logic to erect a tree-like order of levels in a set of hierarchies to represent tonal properties. Sentences are linear. Meaning is not. Sense has three or more dimensions, as with a topology or a theatre. The levels of tone are stacked in levels of first, second and higher order logics. These include functions for relations encoded by tonal puns, and for mapping tonal relations between sense and referent.

In times of logical difficulty we might appeal to the idea of an advanced Turing machine to answer a query such as 'is A in x?', and so consult what Shoesmith and Smiley (1978) call, in the standard formal parlance, 'an oracle'. On this analogy, some esoteric mathematics could be a metaphor for revelation streaming in from infinity. This would cut short the searches for reductionist truth as an exhaustive product of a finite domain (for the logic of this position cf. Tennant, 1978). That is to say, there is a principle of excess in some narrative according to which it has elements that are more than the sum of its sources. Such an amalgam would allow for a religious writer's own imagination, and its engagement with what has traditionally (and I believe incorrectly) been deemed sense beyond the limits of language.

Representation and metalanguage

It has often been supposed that revelation is tantamount only to mythology, which is partly due to the notion that the latter concerns the apprehension of (some) truth as unity in a possible world – deriving of course from Classical antecedents. Landy (1983) is right to criticise Aristotle for confining organic unity to mythos, however. He adds that 'the necessary ambiguity [of poetical work] means that the poetic unity does not imply a single truth or meaning'. If Landy intends it that a poem is not a linear string of singular statements of predicate calculus, his judgement is true. Yet 'single truth' oddly hypostatises what a refined logic need not slash to death with Ockham's presumptuous Razor(s). The above proposals for pluralist recognition in application of logics to texts, and especially the development of logical tone, dissolve the allegation of 'necessary ambiguity' as a poetic *necessity*.

A scholar who offered insights into visual arts and aesthetics – Lyotard (1984) – counselled us to drop the idea of metalanguage: there is no location for a truth-functional argument-place; there is no room, he assumed, for a stipulative formal language about creative language. But, against this, the following bivalent primitive schemata give grounds for showing that metalanguage does expose actual patterns in usage, along the analogy of filmic reproduction, which as chapter 8 below shows also has precise parallels in, for example, ancient Hebrew and Greek literature that presuppose notions of revelatory manifestation:

(1) n has the same F as y in P.
(2) The ultimate referent of y is n's referent.
(3) n has a set of properties not shared by y.

Here y simulates n's identity; the truth-value n might be a personal identity, or anything that satisfies a criterion of identity. God would be a value of n, in revelation; y would be the agent of revelation, where Fs would be replicated properties, with P the event or a propositional ascription of revelation.

Such formalism can entertain the question of how the foregoing type of concept applies to 'the Word made flesh'. Since chapters 4 to 7 explore some of the background to this arena, we confine ourselves here to noticing that, first, we can have a plural set instead of n, with n and m standing for parents of a y. Secondly, this is the logic for a genetic live metaphor which has a parallel in John's Gospel; for example, family resemblances: 'he who has seen me has seen the Father' (14: 9). Obviously, (1) to (3) above can be generalised in standard ways (with a relative identity theory, or Kripke's causal naming) to enrich and widen the application. Anscombe's (1981a) intentional identity would preclude confusion in principle respecting falsehood, where there is no dependency-relation of y on n, or where reproduction became indeterminate – in which case there would be no revelation, unless indeterminacy were that revelation.

Misperception of counter-intuitive realism in revelation, I believe, induces a false charge of narrative indeterminacy. And reader-competence is not solely a causal relation – especially in contexts of dissent. In a perceptive study, whose overall position would not concur with the present views, D. Z. Phillips (1982) nevertheless has forced Bergman's film reductionism to exemplify how beliefs such as revelation 'become impossible for people' (although he does not tackle the problem of justifying his prescriptive use of the intentional modality 'impossible for'). Yet the foregoing shows that the logic of film is not itself reductionist; it is co-extensive with revelatory logic at significant points. Alter's (1984) comments on Fowles's *Daniel Martin* (1977) illustrate the juncture for disanalogy between narrative and film (a film writer has to return to novel writing to expedite some metaphysical aspiration in *Daniel Martin*), which leaves place for the semantic superiority of revelatory language over film and revelatory event at the level of an ideology of communication. One might suggest that film has succeeded the novel as the dominant mimetic art form in this era. The structure of mimesis is shared in some ways by film and revelatory narrative. My view is that ancient creativity, in what was taken to be revelation, is, in a live metaphoric sense (to be explained in subsequent chapters), a primordial functioning of a performance semiotics, of which film, its narrative and virtual reality representation are our contemporary counterparts of ancient media.

The expression 'live metaphor' marks a distinction in metaphor theory, in contrast with dead metaphor, which requires further attention. It has varying amplitudes that are shared through film and mimesis in, for example, ancient narrative. Modifying Cohen's (1993) view of metaphor, for live metaphor, we can envisage live metaphor to be the consequence of adding, negating or deleting semantic presuppositions. This formal pattern has three-dimensional plus counterparts in performance. For example, take a bearskin, and place Aristophanes' maiden in it: the word 'bear' still has a descriptive role, but some coding has been excised – it has no ursine intestines, though it now 'has' human ones irrelevant to its identity; and it has gathered a new ontology. Similar alterations attend a statue or film of a bear (in accordance with (1) to (3) above).[5] We can connect this to White's (1982) version of analogical predication, in which he uses Aquinas and Kant, turned on its head. Namely, that we have, deeply set into what it is to be human language, a set of object languages whose metalanguage, within Christian theological presuppositions, is God's.

We can preserve a realist view of language with metaphor – even in scientific usage; one could adopt, for example, empty singular terms with negative free logic (cf. Smiley, 1982), which would sensibly comply with *new* interpretations of the logics of the predicate calculus. Within formal language live metaphor is also in evidence: I argue in subsequent chapters that a function's value, or any token instance, is a live metaphor of the function. Although this view will be developed in later chapters, it is worth pinpointing its central idea, and one that concurs with the filmic live metaphor here, as follows: entertain the notion that 'colour' is a type, of which any given token colour, say, red, is a value of the function. We can recognise the red as a live metaphor of 'colour', in the sense that there is an overlap of meaning between 'colour' and 'red', though the latter is partially distinct, just as x^2 could be regarded as having an overlap of meaning with, say, 3^2. On this approach a live metaphor could be identified along the same lines: the token 'red' is a live metaphor of the type 'colour'. This can be extended infinitely in certain respects, and we might regrade and mix examples of the distinction at any point. For example, we might say that the types 'blue' and 'red' combine to produce the token 'purple'; or, that these types are themselves live metaphors that mix to create the new live metaphor purple. Chapter 8 expands this conception and addresses it to the questions of representing God, and employs an abstract live metaphoric use of the live metaphor 'photograph'.

Realism, counter-intuitive proof and recognition

Central to such a conception is the view that mimesis can be transformed counter-intuitively as a device to represent transcendence. A presupposition of this position is one shared and refined by Christopher Prendergast (1986) in a French literary perspective: contemporary poststructuralist retrieval of mimesis involves recognition that mimesis is unstable and on the edge of normative sensibility when it is used for significant creative expression. I suggest that live metaphor in representation occupies this role. This, then, provokes an explicit presentation of humility, especially when dealing with theories of transcendence in science, theology or philosophy. We may not be in a position to legislate or even recognise what the limits of expressibility are. New complex tokens may not be recognised as a consequence of knowing a type. It is this situation that is part of the reason I give some attention to Fermat's Last Theorem – as an instance of this problem – in chapters 1 and 3 to 5 of this book. It is pertinent to isolate a facet of this matter for the present context. Wright (1980: 50), prior to the solution of Fermat's Last Theorem, explained how much of a problem the (then) unknown solution to it was:

> Our question then is whether an anti-realist is free to regard us as *recognising* new proofs. On the face of it he is not free so to regard new proofs, for our understanding of some unresolved mathematical statement is supposed precisely to *consist* in being able, ideally, to recognise a proof or disproof of it, should one be forthcoming . . . If someone claims to know under what circumstances a contingent statement would be justifiably assertable, we can reasonably press him for an exact account of what these would be. This is not, however, a reasonable demand in the case of a mathematical statement; we do not *have* a precise notion of what, for example, a proof of Fermat's Theorem, if there is one, will be like. If we did, we should know how to prove it.

I will not pursue the question here of the many ways in which mathematical statements contrast with rationality in philosophy and theology, though there are varieties of parallels when suitably qualified. Rather, for those who are committed to presuming that mathematics, and its uses in sciences, somehow make explicit and define the limits to expressibility are in trouble if they wish to claim that they have recognised these limits as prohibitions on the rationality of such discussion. Even with respect to contingent issues, realists, and especially anti-realists, cannot, in principle, recognise (or therefore prohibit) the probity of all unexpected or new statements of a significant class of large domains. Lewy (1976) and I variously argue that having a concept is not necessarily a recognitional capacity, even when we restrict ourselves to contingent inferences. So having a correct concept of inference is not itself the recognitional procedure for detecting all instances of true inferences. This seems true of theology as well, or even one might argue especially. But many theologians have appeared to give credence to the negation of this situation. In such circumstances it is too easy to dismiss what is not recognised by a mistaken assumption that one has recognised the internal demerits of a concept and its viability. Transcendence no doubt has its counterfeits. But the decision to dismantle its viability because of modernism, I am arguing, is a very bad mistake, at least in logic and domains of scientific and creative rationality.

I am not simply saying, however, that mathematics imposes on us a notion of rationality to which we should conform, not least because mathematics has an unclear and disputed relation to logic. The matter is complex and troublesome; it is also a scenario for transcendent optimism about infinity. Even so, for those who have retreated from transcendent theism because of the onslaught of (a very mechanistic and insensitive account of) positivist empiricism, or the like, the foregoing state of affairs can be used to prove that the assumption of defeat was false. To state the matter impressionistically: even for terrestrial science and pure mathematics it seems that the identities of proof do not involve a concept internal to mastery of it that we know in advance of a discovery what the rules or new concepts are of it which will comprise that proof. If we depict this in live metaphors and types, it is like knowing a type that is a live metaphor, and not knowing what the significance of the future new usage of the live metaphor, as it takes on a new value, will be. If this is true for secular knowledge, it is at the very least unsafe to rely on known mathematics and sciences as having supplied the necessary and sufficient conditions for either their own understanding or other subjects. Some (users of) trends in theology have become accustomed to acting in keeping with the negation of theologically transcendent states of affairs, however. We need a change of climate. Actually, really significant players in mathematics and sciences usually avoid this reductionist theological over-kill. Expressed another way, mimesis has an unknown future. It has an open future not closed by present cognisance, and the use of it to map theological transcendence in the past has been crudely under-assessed in some, particularly reductionist, positivist traditions. Conversely, as Roy Sorensen (1993: 157) has argued, in a profound study, decision theory in mathematics is pertinent to issues of infinity, and it has largely been driven in the past by a negative agenda. To this may be added a recipe for a fresh decision theory programme: with positive conceptual results, such as the solution to Fermat's Last Theorem, it is about time theologians and philosophers gave new attention to positive reconstruction of issues involving transcendence. Admittedly, the identities of rationalities in relation to mathematical proof and logic amount to a narrow diet. But oblique parasitic feeding on a deficient diet of negativity in this zone has led to unnecessary conceptual demise.

Mimesis, transcendence and cosmology

In view of the foregoing we may plausibly speculate that some scientific language is parallel with the use of mimesis in the humanities, to depict identities

as is narrative, in its usage of live metaphor in the foregoing schemata, which
you may recall is:

(1) n has the same F as y in P.
(2)   The ultimate referent of y is n's referent.
(3) n has a set of properties not shared by y.

Some scientific explanation and film representation go proxy for identities other
than themselves. Each satisfies criteria of identity for stipulation as to how to
represent by symbolic means the world outside of language.

Obviously, it is apparent that there are discontinuities in the sorts of realism
embodied in film, science and revelation, although Hesse's (1983) opinion
that: 'A great deal of scientific theorising, especially in cosmology, is not too
distant from the creation of science fiction' is rightly unsettling. I will argue that
there are reasons for such conceptual turbulence, which take us beyond Hesse's
criticism.

The accounts of ontology to be associated with realism are not self-evident,
and in Neil Tennant (1997) we find that anti-realism complies, sometimes surprisingly, with a wide range of irrealisms. ('Irrealism' is the term coined by
Bogossion (1989) to cover various blends and grades of anti-realism.) As Blackburn (1984) shows, there can be a multiplicity of true correspondence theories
of truth. Many logical and scientific discoveries have counter-intuitive structures; some results advertise a lawlike complexity which is so exact, yet is such a
violation of expected properties, that a deeply perplexing realism needs to be
developed, and one that will indeed *seem* incongruent, though it be a required
consequence of recent research in mathematics and cosmology.[6] It is in such
extreme phases that what might be termed counter-intuitive realism is manifest.
I wish to propose the concepts both that there is cosmological counter-intuitive
realism, and that it is comparable with revelation.

Jeffner (1972) argued that 'We can make truth-claims for problematic sentences and see them as statements, with a localisation in the real world.' In
Gibson (2000), and in the present book, I argue that this proposal can be generalised to the cosmological level. Current developments in cosmology now make
this a cosmological enterprise, linked to supergravity theory. Even in our
present world, there are many more than Einstein's four dimensions. With the
previous chapter's discussion on quantum cosmology, which reflects on supergravity and strange effects in M-theory based on eleven-plus dimensions,
counter-intuition is entrenched as a fundamental characteristic of the deeper
universe, which is in many ways discontinuous with how we naturally think.
The real world is unreal. As discussed above, had Pascal (*Pensées*, §252) lived to
see this situation, he would have appreciated that his contention that we have
automaton-like perceptual apparatus, which 'pursues the mind without its thinking about the matter as it is' applies to mark some local physicists' presuppositions when confronted with M-theory supersymmetry in Witten (2002). His way
of speaking now has the form not of an over-statement but of a very modest

way of pitching our modest limits in natural perceptual dispositions, which are not consonant with the depths of nature.

So our use of terms such as 'reality' and its varying ontological references correctly identify, or fail accurately to map, different levels. In other words, logic, epistemology and ontology are not only perceived by, but are also composed of complexity. So it is with transcendence and revelation. In keeping with this multiply sutured theme, the schemata above in (1) to (3) pick out features of the concept of relational states of reality in revelation *and* cosmology. For example, suppose that y in the schemata is Einstein's way of localising and mentioning n. Here n is a piece of space with gravitational and matter fields. But now we can go deeper in structure with n's referent in M-theory with Witten (2002). Regard n's referent as a small bit of that space specified in more detail, roughly, a flat-space slice with an underlying deep structure exhibiting a counter-intuitive family of properties F.[7] For example, the non-linear surface Einstein level y images n, and n has a deeper level reference to mirror symmetry that links two space–times (Witten, 1998: 1,128). At each stage the counter-intuitive nature proportionately increases. This is especially true in the early stages of the universe, but it is also true now. To be sure this is metatheory; yet it is not merely a model of language about language. It has empirical and ontological counterparts.

In cosmology the metatheory's immediate referent is a physical state. Einstein's y is a live metaphor of n, and n is a live metaphor for the minisuperspace. This is a form of cosmological, counter-intuitive mimesis. The logical structures, carefully interpreted, are a mirror of the empirical cosmological states. The present suggestion is that this has analogues in transcendence, not least since transcendence is a physical function in such astrophysical cosmologies. Although the senses of 'transcendence' here vary, yet there is no evidence that they are homonyms, though one should allow for distances between the concepts associated with the terms. There is no reason why an expanded form of the schemata (1) to (3) should not be able to represent some of the relevant overlaps between uses, to facilitate inferences linking and mapping the differences.

Typically, progress in cosmology unpacks stacks of counter-intuitive layers deep in the universe's history. This is not mere historicist emphasis. Rather, the structure of this realism is still a viable account of what the universe is (within the current states of working theory as live metaphor for justified knowledge), not only in exotic states such as black holes, since large areas of space and possibly all matter at the microphysical level mimic aspects of these exotic states.

We should not let pass unnoticed the ways in which this analysis to some degree differs from, for example, Hesse's (1983) proposed opposition between, for instance, Newton's and quantum physical approaches, as though the former is to be discarded while only the latter is admissible, with anti-realism to be the consequence of this opposition. At some levels maybe the opposition is right; but at others, as argued above, this tension is incorrect, and this recognition can lead to counter-intuitive realism. For example, it was noticed in the foregoing that Euclidean geometry inhabits part of Hawking's cosmology. This is indeed a simplified form of full superspace; yet this does not leave it without a realist ontological value in superspace function. The Euclidean role functions as part of the action, anti-realist. With regard to Newtonian realism, for example, in major research Saslaw (1985) employs a wholly Newtonian approach to develop the gravitational physics and history of the universe; this displays Newton's basic laws of nature as one set of levels in universal realism which still hold true, refined though they need to be for relativistic use.

Clearly, Newton opted for strong laws and initial conditions together with causality; while some of his distinctions, such as 'motion', are both live metaphors and empirical functions. Suitably modified, these have a resemblance to poststructuralist science in which metaphor and realism are conjoined features, even though Newton's physics and theories in quantum physics also operate with divergent concepts. Hawking's and Luttrell's (1984) concern with the initial conditions of the universe reflects this sort of blend.[8] In their attention to empirical observation, though deriving from a physicist's concept of 'many worlds' (Everett's (1973) deterministic quantum mechanical universal wave), one can readily identify a parallel with the Newtonian realist enterprise, adjectival though it is to quantum cosmology. On the basis of these relations, some of the metaphysical priorities in Newton's physics have their analogue in the counter-intuitive realism of quantum cosmology.

The idea here is that where various systems of physics overlap, complement each other, and variously improve upon one another in focus, yet when all such systems are successful working theories, then we have something live metaphorically akin to narrative spaces and narrative superspaces whose dislocations and conjunctions are evidence not only of provisionality, but also of explanatory richness and density manifesting creativity. The sum of such connections, and differences, is a function of transcendence. This itself is reminiscent of theology, and what could be regarded as quantum theology. Such a quantum cosmology is not completely regulated by indeterminacy. Rather, from the foregoing, its internal properties, on the analogy of cosmological physics, manifest transcendence, creativity and counter-intuitive originality. All these properties can be represented in premises that constitute an inference for finite material and temporal origins from infinite functions. These complex relations occupy both geometrical and spatial topologies in terms of being representational typologies. As such they satisfy the schemata (1) to (3) above.

It has been proposed elsewhere (Gibson, 1981) that some topology in cosmology can be used to map areas of semantics in certain creative language. So, for example, take (1) to be a criterion of identity, and F is a categorial predicate (cf. Dummett, 1981). F marks the satisfaction of a criterion of identity where the referent of n is God. y represents any point in the universe that disposes the function of a categorial predicate (it may indeed stand for the whole universe). Take F, in a superspace during the Big Bang – to symbolise some infinity functions. For example, going backward in time, astrophysical theory predicts a runaway effect for the speed of light by which its velocity becomes infinite (other such effects occur, such as infinite energy density). Assuming that the theory can be taken to be true at this scenario, I suggest that infinity is a categorial function of a categorial predicate that can identify a property of God's creativity.

This type of concept is presupposed as part of a battery of premises in philosophical cosmology, which I have no space to advance in detail.[9] For example, assuming a primordial black hole 10^{97} stronger than a 'normal' black hole forming the antecedent end – prior to the Big Bang – these are grounds to block the empirical possibility that our universe and universals emerged without infinite creativity functions overriding and suturing the dislocation before and after the singularity. The reason for this is entropy. Even if something came out of a cosmic primordial blackhole, there is a 10^{30} greater chance that a permanent chaotic quantum cloud would be the result, not the universe.

Responding to this, one might assert that cosmology is not secure enough to speak on such matters. Contrariwise, note that equivocation attends non-theistic attempts to infer the universe from nothing. The argument by Vilenken (1986) typically has to assume that 'nothing' is 'a state with no classical space–time'. Contrariwise, nothing is not a *state*, nor is it any space–time. *That* the universe exists is what is in empirical need of explanation. Evidently, for example, a consequence of research by Witten (2002), is that we should discover string and knot tessellation within such a vacuum, not nothing.

Sublime creativity and universals

I maintain that literary creativity in a well-formed concept of revelation would reflect the same sort of cosmological structure, as expressed in (1) to (3), though of course these are schemata that need to be extended. For Aristotle, 'poetry' was the mimesis of universality in the particular. This is tantamount to a corollary of condensing counter-intuitive realism in a live metaphorical (mini) superspace.

Gerald Else's (1957) view was that Aristotle's luminous sense is making something in which universals come to expression, 'for whom creation means *discovery*, the uncovering of a true relation' (my italics). Hutton (1982) draws attention to Aristotle's explanation of experience as the possession of universals (in the *Posterior Analytics*). The *Poetics* pronounces the familiar statement: 'Poetry, therefore, is a more philosophical and a higher thing than history.' It is often noticed that Aristotle must be placing 'poetry' higher in generality because he elsewhere regards history as not entirely absent of philosophical sensibility.

We need to tune this philosophical poetry into key. In the *Poetics*, chapter 9 especially, we find Aristotle employing logic terminology that cannot be consigned entirely to the *Rhetoric*: words like 'possibility', 'necessity', 'If/then', 'probability', etc. If Lear (1980) finds Aristotle dealing with metalogical issues in the *Posterior Analytics*, though dressed in syllogistic discussion, we can similarly detect trace of Aristotle's aiming for a philosophical logic of creative narrative in the *Poetics*. But if Gulley's (1979) opinion is right – that Aristotle designates what is plausible and not what is true as the making of a universal – then we have radically to reorientate and dispute with Aristotle on this score. Aristotle takes this view because he recognises fiction to be false. The foregoing proposal – that we can see deviant logics as the topology for fiction genres – can be applied now. Fiction can be surrounded (as a complex quotation) by bivalent logic in narrative discourse. The contrast and contact between bivalence and deviance complements and directs attention to what is true, correctly used. In this context, since deviance and plausibility are logically (modally) secondary, they give way to bivalence. Here we can displace Aristotle's plausibility priority. This state of affairs will not often be evident in narratives because it is true of the domains which are increasingly counter-intuitive in realism, the perception of which should incorporate a philosophy of perception which integrates concepts of joy and pain.

Lyotard (1984) reasoned that the postmodern condition renders the sublime inexpressible more sharply than previously. But should materialist deviance govern the boundary principles of an individual's condition? The *avant-garde* has to invest in dislocation from a deviant 'realism'. So it is no more a problem for those who wish to adopt revelation. Consequently, in revelation there resides in counter-intuitive realism the true *avant-garde*, and yet in the world the criteria of plausibility subvert the culture of truth when creativity is absent. Sutherland's (1984a) criterion 1 (i.e., 'Any successful revision of the content of religious belief must be undertaken in the context of European culture as a whole') is deployed by Sutherland as interrogating the presuppositions of that culture (and one could assume others). To this we can add that creativity in genius is the making of universals from the materials of such culture where the product is not the sum of its antecedents.

For these reasons the present arguments sustain the idea that in revelatory terms, infinity's counter-intuitive realism is ontological, distributed and immersed in minisuperspace through individual internal states, narrative and event. In discussion with me, James Ross[10] raised the following objection, and offered no criticism to the following reply. Ross observed that revelation would involve an infinite regress because of which even God could not (so nor could an agent of revelation) add knowledge from infinity to human knowledge. The method of the objection is that for each bit of newly revealed knowledge, one needs a fresh additional set of axioms with which to enlarge the set of human languages. Yet to warrant this conjunction of revelation with interpretation one could require a further set of axioms, etc., ad infinitum.

My response was and is that the similarity between this objection and Cantor's theory of transfinite well orderings facilitates the removal of the problem. That is to say, the objection only applies to attempts to ascend the series, not descend a series. And revelation just is a top-down typology, not bottom-up. Clearly interpretation is required and may be taxing. But this issue is distinct from the content of knowledge itself originating from an infinity-source or top-down sequence. Certainly someone is going to object, in any case, that we do not have any such accessibility to the effect of revelation. Although this can be countered, the argument here is a different one: what in principle would logic or metaphysics of knowledge of God have to satisfy? So, if a set of propositions starts out from the top of a series, i.e. at some infinity, then an inferential descent is certain without an infinite regress being a consequence.

In view of the reference to the *Posterior Analytics* above, it is interesting to relate Cantor's insights to what Lear (1980) has proved to be Aristotle's attempts to understand metalanguage and infinity. Cantor articulated the idea that a series is infinite in one direction while finite in the other. The infinite regress is a difficulty only if one intends, as it were, ascending to infinity. Predications tumble down a series, however, without their thereby generating an infinite regress, if the starting-point is infinity. This closure condition can be formalised and refined by Neumann's and Mirimanoff's *Fundierung-axiom*,[11] which has to do with this sort of behaviour for the descent of a series from infinity – and Prior and Fine (1977) improved and expanded the axiom for propositions. This sort of infinity has semantics, and therefore infinity has a semantic analogue. So it is in principle false to conclude that expressibility in semantics has to be finite, that is in the sense of there being a finite set of expressions such as that imposed by Wittgenstein in the *Tractatus*.

It may eventually follow from this, I conjecture, that one could offer an inference proving that (in the relevant sense of possibility) we can do more than solely 'show' knowledge beyond our own-authored epistemological limits. From other directions, however, we renegotiate the limits to propositional sense that has sometimes been assigned to the *Tractatus*. James Conant has convincingly argued that we should revisit the scholarly attempts to assess the 'sense' of the 'limits of language' in the *Tractatus*. One of Conant's (2000: 197) closing points is: 'The illusion that the *Tractatus* seeks to explode, above all, is that we can run up against the limits of language.' The position maintained in Gibson 2000, and here, is that the role of counter-intuition in logic and language implies that logic, thus far developed, cannot accurately elucidate what it is to be this limit. This is not only because, as Frege truly noticed, there are things we cannot define in a formal system. Rather, we have massively over-estimated the progress of our ability to track criteria of the limit to language; especially so, with recent developments concerning ways in which infinity and pure mathematics impinge on issues of constructivism, and discovery. Certainly, we betray our limitations. This has much to do with our assent to the spirit of an age, and, in a post-structuralist world, the ways in which finitism is made to service the taste for autonomy from transcendence.

The foregoing argues that qualities from infinity are nested in superspace in the universe. I have also proposed that this state has its counterpart in aesthetics. We can variously interpret this state of affairs as functions of divine properties in experience and nature. Since the infinity conditions that caused the universe are properties of its later history, Cantor's transfinite series are functions of the later history of the universe as well as its origin. But the strong form of Cantor's infinity relations enters into the spirit of such predications as revelation. What we deem instances of revelation will clearly depend on further disputable presuppositions. My task is not to identify these here. Rather, the foregoing is an attempt to disturb those who have assumed with too little warrant that the notion of any revelation is necessarily intellectually crude, and without subtle depth. Some will reply that, in any case this is irrelevant to the actual world, since it is the state of our most recent evolution to have discovered that the presuppositions are themselves vacuous. So, the argument runs, there is no point in attending to the degree, if any, to which humanist modernisms incorrectly depicted such claims. But future possibility is a function of contemporary mores that map the past, which are variously peculiar, unpredictable and at times entirely obvious.

This approach to conceptualising revelatory narrative is counter-intuitive of all narrative creativity in an extended sense of 'counter-intuition' (for example as applied to the solution of Fermat's Last Theorem) explored in the present book. A reason for this is that counter-intuition facilitates exploration of the prospects of composing a semantic topology to depict the conditions for manifesting a metaphysical epitome of God, i.e. the subject that comprises the set of all universals.

Part IV
Real-world solutions

7   Some resurrection logic

Reductionism in ignorance

In view of the previous chapters we are warranted in re-assessing a fashion to reduce the number of transcendent metaphysical entities. This reductionism shrinks what is deemed to be the scope of the real world. The use of 'real-world solutions' as a title for this part of the book challenges solutions dismissed by reductionist approaches to metaphysics. The aim here is not to wallow in over-inflated reactionary ontologies. Rather, it supposes the reader may be able to question fundamental assumptions whose status needs to be interrogated in the light of the fragility of the fashion that discards them, not least when illuminated by new universal perspectives in cosmology, logic and aesthetics, which have been presented and developed in the foregoing chapters.

Whether or not complexity has the form of simplicity in its deep structure, Arthur Prior's (1968) opinion that complexity may be primary serves to allow one use of the possibility that the newly discovered forms of complexity (and order in chaos theory[1]) require an increase in the number of transcendental states of affairs and their assessment.

Various traditions of Christianity lay claim, or are committed, to a strong presupposition of metaphysical transcendence and revelation. The central form this takes is in Christ, and the complex disputational history with which this subject is often clothed has left the beginning of the third millennium in a state of epistemic fatigue. The previous chapters argued for a foundation that has explicit and bold grounding in metaphysics, logic and semantics. A reason for this has been to challenge some modernist and postmodernist cultural histories, which are not infrequently incarcerated in normative structures, and sometimes presupposed as canonical by a variety of theologians. These tend to suppose that theological reductionism is a contingently necessary consequence of progress in philosophical, logic and metaphysical research. A fair estimation of the signifi-cance of a wide range of innovations and shifts in these subjects, I am arguing, readily facilitates the reverse conclusion. At the very least, the third millennium is witness to our profound ignorance about the identity of the universe and its deeper metaphysical relations, while the technical insights achieved in relevant subjects leave as an open probability the empirical possibility of the existence of an infinite empirical identity realised in an individual. Traditionally a theology of Christ proposes how this slot is to be filled. The most exotic region of this theology is that of the resurrection. Consequently, it is worth applying some of the foregoing analyses, their extension, and further proposals, to present a metaphysical picture that mirrors some of the concepts ascribed to this hardest of metaphysical cases, Christ's resurrection.

Even an atheist, who is interested in the formal limits to our knowledge of subjunctive conditionals, might profit from seeing how a unique set of conditions can produce a unique reversal in empirical possibility. For some, this will be science fiction; so it should be helpful for them to note that some cosmology has been so-called by critics, while yet some science fiction has a habit of becoming astrophysical science. For others, they will maintain that to use logic to launch the viability of a sensitive spiritual subject is an irrelevant collision of categories; but this presupposes what is not understood: the final relation of logic to aesthetics and spirituality. Just because over-sharpened crude logic has turned out to damage spiritual sensibility shows nothing of what relation true logic has to such a topic. Again, someone may wish to argue that logical possibility is not spiritual possibility. Certainly. But we have not shown that there is no known mapping relation by which we may infer a helpful route from one to the Other. Surely, if the objection is correct, then is it not contrary for one to have assumed in the first place that the logics of science and philosophy can require reductionism (leaving reactionary conservatism aside)? So, for as long as the interlocutor uses the criticism outside of the scope of reductionist context, it may be valid, if anodyne. And if one is not to commit oneself to an arbitrary set of infinite possibilities that facilitate everything, just what basis for possibility is the critic going to use?

What is possibility?

So perhaps such critics and we can, for differing reasons, agree that we can benefit from a fresh exploratory start. None of us has a full grasp of what possibility is and what is empirically possible; it is worth reflecting on how to gain insight into expanding our awareness of the scope of possibility. So this is evidently a good project quite independently of resurrection claims. If one believes that the resurrection is impossible, this chapter could be a means to challenge that presupposition. Should we not all accept that our grasp of what is possible is rather cloudy? I wish to argue that outside of religion (for example in physics and mathematics) the concept of possibility holds surprisingly extensive outer boundaries. Our capacity to imagine what is possible is limited by ignorance about the conditions that internally regulate it.

One of the major issues in attempting to construct a model or typology of possibility concerning the resurrection is to allow for the disputed historical identities of the Gospels, while positioning these in relation to the pertinent sublime properties that are asserted by them. There is no space here to become preoccupied with narrative exegesis of religious texts. So let us adopt the salient points in Luke's Gospel, as a presupposional candidate for what it is to be the resurrection.[2]

This study proposes a new approach to the logic of the resurrection, which as far as I know has not been suggested before. It is a philosophy and logic chapter, not a theological study; nor is it only a philosophy of religion study. Nevertheless this indirect route to a theological issue is intended to contribute directly to the interpretation of the concept of resurrection. So this chapter is not a study in method; it is concerned with logic, and the logic of content. The chapter amounts to an argument that we are committed to the inference that there is logic of the concept of the resurrection, irrespective of whether you are Christian or atheist. In view of the book's audience, technical matters in logic have not been presented, though drawn upon in presenting original proposals. So as to achieve generality that will apply to some different theologies and philosophical tastes, I have to some degree avoided commitment to specific interpretations in these areas wherever I could. In some cases this neutrality also side-steps the suggestions, to be argued elsewhere, that some alternative version of a doctrine is required.

Both atheists and believers talk about the resurrection in such a way as to require or presuppose some mastery of it as a concept; yet for both groupings there is a fundamental clash over its identity and status, with these disagreements extending to internecine dispute between many believers. Such conflict involves the question of whether or not logic can be used to identify and solve issues. We need to be modest here.

As Gisela Striker (1998) notices, Aristotle acknowledged that we could not formulate every valid deductive argument as a syllogism in the narrow technical sense. There are disputes as to what the identity of logic is, and the author could not hope to attend to many of the issues involved within the present volume's priority, though some attempt can be made to contribute to discussion. It is a surprise to some to discover that Aristotle never defined implication. Implication is central to logic, yet there are sorts of implication (such as legal inference) which are not deductive logic.

Some people still think, incorrectly, that all logic is or is reducible to syllogism; but this is false. Syllogism,[3] for instance, cannot directly represent predicates, and it cannot explain the identity of quantification. Large domains of logic are very different from syllogism, and the syllogism even on its own terms can be a dangerous tool, as we see from 'All men are mortal; Jesus is a man; therefore he is mortal.' The tense logic needed here, such as that devised by Arthur Prior (1968),[4] was only recently developed; there was no function in syllogistic logic to resolve such falsehoods. Sure, one can always fiddle an explanation of how to patch up such errors; but logic is supposed to be the science of universal implication, not an *ad hoc* amateur accident ward for the seeming cure of mistakes. Give the wrong treatment, and disease will eventually terminate the subject. Although basic principles of logic are clear, there is scope for development. So for example, Aristotle's clarity concerning the, then, limits of rhetoric theory (which has little to do with what passes for rhetoric in some recent literary studies) left philosophers without a capacity much to advance the subject. Research in formal logic over the last 150 years, however, provided insights that yield new pathways. This is partly why research on rhetoric is ripe for new advances, in particular concerning the relevance of content, as with Burnyeat's (1994) and Smiley and Priest's (1995) pioneering studies. Michael Dummett (1993) has argued that some issues in logic are much deeper and more unexpected than philosophers assume them to be; Bernard Williams (1998) maintained that the future identity of philosophy is not obvious. I suggest that the conjunction of these two views implies that the identities of certain relevant areas of logic are counter-intuitive. So logic and new possibilities are more unexpected in identity than we may suppose, though the fundamental elements are determined.

Some atheists have said not only that the resurrection did not happen but also that it is impossible. One does not have to assume that it is impossible, to point out that such people do not have a logical explanation of what the logic is that expresses this assertion. It should be clear that 'impossible' is different from and stronger than 'false'. I hope that atheists note the fundamental difference. It seems that such opinions merely reflect a suppressed premise that somehow science has banned the empirical veracity of the resurrection, though what the scope of 'empirical' is in applied science is entirely unclear at some of its frontiers, as we shall see.

Certainly, David Hume (1935: 110, n. 15) does allege that the concept of an invisible supernatural agent interfering with natural laws is inconsistent with those laws. So God is invisible, yet he manifests his likeness in visible agents. Hume's presupposition, concerning what it is to be an 'invisible supernatural agent', is confused, and anachronistically idealised. Attention to research on the role of the earliest Christians in art representation of God shows that, as Finney (1994) illustrates, and chapters 5, 6 and 8 of the present book argue. In these chapters, the function of live metaphor which I have attempted to expose seriously undermines a literalistic reading of various narrative presenting God which polarises the depiction of invisibility as an exclusive binary option over and against visibility. 'Visibility' is obviously a function relative to a viewpoint, not absolute in relation to everything. Presumably God can see himself, in an appropriate value of 'see'. Although analogies are themselves live metaphoric extensions which should not be confused with other domains, yet it is instructive to note that black holes are invisible (to us), yet are observable by techniques which employ wavelengths other than those that are not satisfied by the criteria for 'invisible' in the foregoing statement that black holes are invisible. Clearly, for qualitative reasons it is problematic to apply this sort of distinction to God's invisibility; however, it does make a distinction about the relativity of invisibility.

Paul Finney's (1994: 291) study reasons that 'The portrayal of early Christianity as a religion on principle hostile to the pictorial arts rests I believe on several misleading assumptions, the most egregious being a literalistic reading of selected passages within early Christian apologetic literature.'

Empirical possibility and belief

Let us now return to my above claim that David Hume (1935, 110 n. 15) is incorrect to maintain that the concept of an invisible supernatural agent interfering with natural laws is inconsistent with those laws, concerning what it is to be an 'invisible supernatural agent'.

Hume's position is contradictory, for the following reasons. First, such laws do not prescribe contingent necessity, but describe contingency. Secondly, contingency does not have a universalised single identity. Rather, it has various complex counter-intuitive features, so we cannot – without contradiction – read off the version of contingency Hume requires. Such points show that Hume was a contrary imperialist in matters of logic; that is to say, he embodies the weakness that he assumed believers in miracles manifest. (It is important, in a perspective of positioning Hume in the history of philosophy, to note that the Scottish Enlightenment is largely composed of individuals who, while they were philosophically highly innovative, were institutionally and often socially highly conservative and traditionalist. Although they were involved in disputes, yet they nevertheless occupy a non-revolutionary collective position in a way in which their French counterparts did not. Typically French Enlightenment philosophers were outside of the established tradition and fighting it in a revolutionary framework. Although Hume was outside of the, for him, desirable stability of the senior university world, even so, he was, at times, a somewhat fawning part of a conservative social context.)

Thirdly, a point one can construct from, for example, Wright's work (1980: 322–4), where he argued that empirical science cannot be used to derive a global empirically based logic. We do not know enough about the universe, and we do not know what it would be to infer an *a priori* logic from experiment. Actually, many empiricists deny that empirical global truths are known *a priori*. So someone who bans the logical and/or empirical possibility of the resurrection reaches beyond one's ability to prove his position, and commits himself to universal metaphysical totalitarianism; yet, oddly, what he is presumably trying to preclude is a judgement about what the limit of possibility is. Merely because a sceptic employs negation to bar an assertion does *not* entail that he is not thereby committed to presupposing universal natures that he needs to ban something. In short, we know a lot less than Hume thought we do about what it is to be the relations between logic and the universe. Consequently, with chapters 1 to 6 and 8 as complex premises, insofar as we know anything in the domains of universality, the resurrection is an empirical logical possibility, and a miracle would not be a logical departure from any relevant empirical contingently necessary state or necessary truth of logic – insofar as we have any deep grasp on the latter.

Some Christians have alleged that the resurrection is not susceptible of logical scrutiny. But they do not offer a proof, or offer consistent philosophy of mind about 'faith' that supports this. If they had been present when Jesus purportedly raised people from the dead, even on the presupposition of the believing observers who were reportedly there present, they would have been involved in contradiction. For presumably being present at an actual resurrection amounts to some sort of proof of it, at least in the way sceptics demand it, thus (on the faith versus proof scenario) excluding the opposition between faith and proof. Yet some are reported to have believed as a result of miracles, not least those who are presented as the subjects thus resurrected. Consequently, either there is no conflict between faith and proof, or they occupy distinct epistemological domains. It is worth adverting to a neglected point in theological misappropriation of a relation between philosophy of mind and formal logic. Even though faith is a necessary condition of adopting the resurrection of Jesus, it does not follow that the resurrection is therefore nonlogical.[5] In principle, the two states are not exclusive or in competition. Faith is a mental state, whereas proof is a complex mental and/or compositional event or series of events; so they cannot compete for exactly the same logical space, since they occupy different functional and dynamical topologies.

Logic is purported to be a map of what is possible. What this amounts to is of course obvious, yet is a very recondite issue. Even so, let us suppose that, for one to have a mastery, in the pertinent specialities, of some basic necessary and sufficient, as well as counter-factual, conditions, to permit discussion of the topic, one should also be pleased to press deeper into unresolved issues.[6] It might be thought that a difficulty for logic is that the resurrection of Christ is unique. In contrast, some might say that logic includes a generalised function of what it is to be possibility, and its universally consistent applicability; therefore its uniqueness is a problem. The resurrection combines both features unexpectedly: it is supposed to be a universal function, and to be unique. (This is akin to the function of a proper name: it is like a universal, standing for a singular identity. In this respect some religious uses of 'Jesus' as a unique signifier for the bearer, who is raised by himself from the dead, coincide with the unique ontological universal.)

We have here an analogy between these aspects of the resurrection concept and the origin of the universe: the beginning of the universe is itself – for our physics and us. So we can hardly consistently object to the idea of the resurrection on the grounds that it is unique and 'violates' laws, because these two conditions are said to be the internal properties of cosmology's view of the commencement of our universe. There are various ways of characterising this state of affairs. One can, for example, envisage both the beginning of the universe and the resurrection as the creation of universals that are condensed and disclosed in a single act, which defies normal matter-energy conditions, with infinity functions (qualitatively differently) attendant on the two events. In technical respects we might interpret the resurrection in time-reverse to the beginning of the universe. The latter is said to emerge from infinity-conditions (such as infinite matter-energy density and superluminal velocity), whereas Gospel presuppositions of the resurrection mirror emergence from a finite bodily state into something logically paraphrasable into infinity-conditions. (Clearly the two uses of 'infinity' here are distinct; yet a suitable counter-intuitive concept of tautology and paraphrase would hinge the two together – using the relative identity thesis developed below.)

Therefore it is no surprise to discover that the topic of 'logic' mentioned in the title of this chapter is not *the* proof that there was a resurrection. It is the subject of what it is to be a minimal set of logical conditions that are internal to the concept of resurrection: is it possible on logical and empirical grounds?

Some people will regard it as invidious or unseemly that what for them is the prime spiritual life should be, so to speak, decomposed into an abstract universe to which it is alien. Although this feeling is one for which the author has sympathy, yet at least two points resist it as a general truth. First, the Gospels appear to reflect a practical form of life that is disposed to resort to any unharmful means to convey the value of the resurrection to those who are alien to its world. Secondly, it is not clear, I shall argue, what it is to make this envisaged division of labour between the spiritual and the secular unspiritual abstract empirical universe. Certainly, the Gospels do not contain such narrative discourse; but neither do they refer to televised masses by the Pope. I have not missed the relevant reply here, with this latter response. That is to say, what it is to be a logical internal property of the truth conditions of the empirical resurrection is presupposed as and in its narrative functions, and not explicitly stated in the Gospels.

An entailment of this situation, if the resurrection occurred, is that the empirical truth-conditions actually will be alien to our expectations because it was a unique event whose counter-factual conditions violate what it is to be the physical world. The interlocutor perhaps retorts: 'but this is beside the point, because the original objection itself presupposed a questionable recipe about ethical taste to do with the propriety and felicity of switching from spirituality to empirical states'. This retort itself presupposes what is questionable: how do you separate the two categories into exclusive divisions of labour and ontology? Were not these two properties – spirituality and empirical states – what would have to be united in one identity for the concept of the incarnation, and its resurrectional consequence, to have the truth-claim they do? In short, if ethics is appropriately co-extensive with aesthetics in a perfect empirical life, we may not allow a division of labour that puts asunder a multifarious perfect life and art form. As chapters 4 and 5 present the issue, in the perspective of the current research on M-theory and its mysterious matrices, which appear to be the strongest candidates for characterising the internal properties of fundamental physical matter, knowledge of the division between matter and its contrary violates many a standard test of what is it is to be physical. Such developments of supergravity have dissolved the schizoid division on which modernist destruction of strong transcendence was based.

Of course some side-step this debate by simply deleting ontology from theology. But this is itself simply a reactionary deployment of an authoritarian use of misused liberalism. Just because certain versions of claims to, for example, resurrection stem from traditional ill-informed dogmatism does not entail that all interpretations are false. Sometimes this type of 'demythologising' dogma is cast as liberation from a sense of the believer trapped in irrelevant forms of belief. Certainly we should not vindicate belief in many of the last vestiges of imperious and indolent forms with which deconstructing modernists are faced. But such well-founded criticism does not entail its advocates' alternative. The death of a tradition is not itself the death of the metaphysical grounds of belief. All too easily do we humans conflate the viability of criticism with our contemporary taste. It is possible that belief claims are false. It is possible that past history might have falsely been in the grip of mythological Christian belief about miracles. And it is certain that much theology of miracles was myth and muddle. Yet, just as the falsehood of alchemy does not entail that there is no thermonuclear transformation of metals in quasars or the like, so we should be wary of treating institutional influence in theology as a means to discredit in principle the possibility of miracle that it so feebly depicted in the rational sphere. If, after truly ascertaining that there is no such empirical possibility as miracle, all well and good; the nineteenth and twentieth centuries, however, did not have the credentials to execute such a task. We are not yet in that position from the standpoint of sufficiently advanced grasp of scientific theory and possibility, however. The spirit of an age may reverse over past custom, sometimes due to bad interpretation of custom. Yet, whether we are believer or atheist, we should avoid the fallacy of employing the accident of evolved conceptual consensus to imply the impossibility of an alternative reality. To appeal to Nietzsche to endow us with the knowledge of the impossibility of miracles is merely to fall into the error that he feared: Eurocentric conservative imperialism taken to be the process of truth.

Let us vary the figure from resurrection to soul: even though I do not believe in the immortality of the soul. Robert Solomon (2002: 139) writes in his otherwise subtle book *Spirituality for the Skeptic*, that: 'The most important reason to "believe" in the soul is not the possibility of life continuing after death but rather the possibility of an essential *transformation* in the self during life' (assuming that in his use of 'life' here he does not intend immortal life). Obviously Solomon may choose whatever belief and internal coherence he wishes. But it is false to suppose that his view is what ancient or traditional Christians believed about the post-death identity of and role for the soul intended, whether it is resurrection or disembodied existence. Solomon has here metaphorised ontology, and slipped the product back in to go proxy for the supposed identity of a conception depicting the soul. If an atheist wishes to do this, that is his affair. Even so, if such a reductionist view results from a desire to rid society of transcendental illusion, it seems odd to do it by imbibing the de-ontologised semantic dregs that have been castigated as defunct. The way his account conflicts with traditional Christian and some other transcendental beliefs is rather like if President Lincoln had taken up the campaign for the emancipation of slaves, and announced that in law he had freed all slaves, but only done so by supposing that they enjoy metaphoric freedom, without the need for its ontological counterpart with actual freedom.

It is important to be clear on this – dead – metaphorisation of ontology, not only especially with regard to the resurrection, but also on the role of accuracy in atheism. Any atheist is of course free to metaphorise or trade on whatever terms she may wish to modify. What she is not so free to avail herself is to conflate reductionism with past ontology in an established semantic field. The history of ideas is closely involved with the history of philosophy, and the future of philosophy is partly dependent on an accurate representation of past ideas. It is a failure in scholarly interpretation not to position a term's history alongside its associated ontology. It is also a muddle, as a consequence of this merger, to foist a metaphoric identity on the scope of the relevant term or related concept. If a humanist culture supplants (what is later taken to be) an over-inflated ontology, then there will no doubt be a period of slippage, equivocation and generation of fresh sense using old terminology. Contrariwise, what is not creditable, and is misleading, is a twenty-first-century equivocation subsequent to such a period, which utilises such overlaps as necessary conditions of inference, to argue that it is in principle a confusion to suppose that 'resurrection' has not be a metaphoric without a transcendent empirical ontology. It is obviously possible that one makes false claims about miraculous resurrection. But it is illicit to suppose that somehow space–time ontology prohibits it; and it is false to presuppose that metaphoric use of relevant terms exposes a reductionist sense internal to the semantics of resurrection.

Even so, I agree, we need a clearer grasp on what it is to be 'empirical'. No doubt the interlocutor could score a point about the resort to abstract analysis here; but substantive objections should be grounded in principle, not easily revisable presentation. (When speaking of 'abstract', it here carries the same type of sense as does Aristotle's 'logical'. This chapter's position is opposed to a doctrine of abstractionism,[7] in which some properties of a subject are arbitrarily used to depict all of it.) For example, a sunset can be exhaustively described using geophysics and astrophysics. An aesthete may complain that such representation omits the main ingredient. Quite so. If the point is to show, however, that a sunset actually could exist, and what the logical conditions are for it to display aesthetic properties, the resort to empirical explanation is appropriate. Just as it would be with a logical concept of the resurrection, for those who suppose that there could not have been a resurrection. This state of affairs similarly applies to the deconstructed theologian who has acquiesced in the (I wish to prove) false belief that even a counter-intuitive empirical resurrection is not possible. Surely such a theologian has confused illogical reductionism with creative progress? Nor can I be saddled with an inaccurate presumption of what is supposed to be the converse of this: proof for the logical status of a transcendent (I did not use 'transcendental') state of affairs is not a retro-chic theological anachronism. The concept of resurrection reflects an epistemology that displays properties of counter-intuitive creativity depicting a singularity whose strangeness has partial analogues in features of the counter-intuitive transcendent scientific physical states in cosmology and microphysics (as Gibson, 2000, argues).

Ontology and retro-chic theology

In a preface Wittgenstein (1975) said that if one were to write anything of general significance it would be against the spirit of the age. Rorty, conforming to such a spirit, has said that, effectively, all transcendental religious claims are myths that should be treated in a reductionist manner. So he insists that such beliefs should shrink to becoming a subset of the philosophy of mind. Whether or not the resurrection is true and (or) is logical, Rorty's policy exceeds our knowledge of the universe. Therefore, whether or not Rorty's or Hume's views are true or false, their unprovable status commits the user to holding a sort of anachronistic totalitarian mythology of reductionism. Oddly, this is exactly the type of imperious dogmatism that Hume was attempting to controvert. Hume's belief was that in relevant respects, we could not supervene over history with generalised truths; yet Rorty does. But the Hume/Rorty claim that there is no relevant general truth of history entails its contradictory. Since they assert that history has this non-general property, it follows that history has a general property. Therefore their views are false.

Fashions come and go. Some poststructuralist retro-chic theology presupposes that realism is too restrictive for freedom of thought. But this underestimates the counter-intuitive identities of realisms. In some mathematics of physical states there are an infinite number of functions. This is realism with an exponential power for surprise and creativity quite unaccounted for in the philosophically naive irrealism of a theology without transcendence external to the human experience. Some theologians are so uninformed about realism that they assume that once realism has been dropped, then consequently so has the possibility of truth claims in a philosophy of language for the external world. But this is a false position. As, for example, Neil Tennant (1997) has shown, very many anti-realist logics preserve truth claims, even without a correspondence theory of language. Further, it is customary for reductionist theologians to appeal to Nietzsche when disposing of a correspondence theory of language. It should come as a surprise, then, to consider John Richardson's (1996) specialist research on Nietzsche, which shows that Nietzsche himself sustained and refined a counter-intuitive version of correspondence theory in his philosophy. Consequently, conception of correspondences between language and the universe is a much deeper affair and counter-intuitively creative than one might have supposed from a straightforward use of logic in analytical philosophy.[8]

Conceptual strategy

With respect to knowledge of the relations of languages to the world, what one should want to discover is a philosophy of logic that at least explicitly isolates, in relation to possibility, what preconditions the most exotic conditions an original state of affairs would have to satisfy and internally manifest to be possible, and ideally in principle be veridical. The claims of the resurrection fall into this class.

It is worth warning ourselves that such an enterprise is counter-intuitive, not in the sense of being novel or bizarre, but with the sense and association of what surprises logicians themselves face when attempting to interrogate the edges of the universes of discourse and physical cosmology, as well as the limits of our formal capacities at these interfaces. On the basis of research elsewhere (Gibson, 2000 and the present book), I suggest three such domains for investigation and extension, each to be paraphrased by the use of the sort of logic that I have been devising or articulating:

(A) mathematical physics and observational astrophysics of the very early universe;
(B) philosophy of mathematics;
(C) aesthetic creativity.

The reason for (A) involves study of what we are able to assess as the largest scale and extremist form of what it is to be actual physics, so as to grasp what it would be to be a transcendent parameter either using counter-intuitive versions of (A) and by contrast would be an account of rationality that is transcendent and counter-intuitive states outside of its physical scope. Of course current research on such things as M-theory (see Witten, 2002) problematises what it is to be 'physical' and 'calculable', which are of benefit to the discussion that may accord modernist notions of 'material world' more determinative credibility than they deserve. With respect to (B), philosophy of mathematics has hardly given any attention to current frontier research on such issues as M-theory, but it is important to begin work on such areas, so the current study attends to the preliminary concerns in this sphere, as they pertain to metaphysics and transcendence. The result transforms the traditional topic of the philosophy of miracle and resurrection. For those whose taste is atheism, this current discussion is of particular moment, since it shows that we are not yet in a position to know what the identity and limits of 'physical property' are, and consequently we do not understand what the limits of abstraction are. Such analysis is especially significant for what an 'object' is in relation to extending or transforming the understanding and application of Cantorian set theory, for example as Kit Fine (2002: 192) has formulated the issue in the context of Hume's law. For those averse to examining such abstract topics in a resurrection scenario, whether they be believers or atheists, it is about time such carping ceased and new objective discussion was allowed free range. Why should not the two be counter-intuitively engaged to the varying benefit of each, even as a thought-experiment? One feature of this motivation is that the concept of a counter-intuitive singularity, which is both a function and violation of near-singularities (for example, a primordial black hole as the antecedent of a universe), is little understood, especially where its properties are re-deployed for constructing an even more extreme form model for singularities. As to how such precedents relate to the physical basis for aesthetic properties within such a model is as yet very little explored, and hence the presence of (C) above. But it is just within this type of logical region, where exotic precedents coincide, that fundamental research is needed, and in the case of cosmology is beginning to get under way. Future researches for modelling the birth of new universes, as well as the possibility of the resurrection, reside in these domains. Both sets of conceptual realms are suffused with live metaphoric language, which facilitates the application of the account of such language developed in the present book and Gibson (1987, 2000 and forthcoming a, b). This extension of aesthetic comparisons may seem to extend well beyond, for example, Donald MacKinnon's (1974) use of Cézanne's painting to depict a manifestation that is a token of another – theological – subject's virtual presence, devised by George Steiner (1989).

Mapping between subjects

So I propose that we can draw on three realms of theory to devise a representational model for the present approach by associating (A) to (C), which will also extend and generalise other researches:[9]

(A) a concept of live metaphor;[10]
(B) a theory of virtual reality reproduction;[11]
(C) a theory of a formal model and M-theory for live metaphor making.[12]

So the concept of mapping relations between three different subjects has three parallel processing models, to frame the logic of the resurrection. The status of the resulting representation is not intentionalist; that is to say it is extensionally concerned with what is true or false in the external world – whatever is the puzzling identity of this cosmos.

A recurrent symptom of culture is that a certain style of philosophy is assumed to be or deployed as almost a criterion for a worldview. So analytical philosophy is typically associated with atheism as if the latter were a consequence of a real grasp of the former. So it is with much French philosophy. It is an interesting strategy, practised in the current book, to employ aspects of such a style antithetically to its normative-tending deployment. This strategy is itself a lesson for those who do not recognise contingency where it resides. Here is it thus worthwhile noticing how some of the present theme can be cast in a facet of Derrida's philosophy. (I offer this as a token of appreciation of Derrida's courteous compliment to my work, rather than criticism, as well as respect for Marian Hobson's pioneering research.) The above sequence (A) to (C) can be construed in the following way, which also illuminates further potential for the sequence.

Marian Hobson (1990, 1998) has articulated some of Derrida's concerns about reproduction between texts on the formal analogy of a cellular telephone network (cf. Gibson, 2000). One can extend this to match features of (A) to (C), as a complex form of 'aRb', i.e., speaker A, to speaker A_1, etc. That is to say the same logical predicates can be reproduced in different subjects, and used to extend a language and its generalisation over new domains. Consequently, where there is identification of the reference, predicates attached to it can be used to simulate, relay and reproduce the same identity, which can be increased exponentially in principle to infinity.

I propose an outline for a transformed extension of this relational network, which builds on earlier parts of the present book, and involves extending the following theory as complex live metaphor – a term and procedure developed in the present book, as well as in Gibson (2000). This is not of course a general associative use of dead metaphor. This live metaphorisation is a way of depicting features of the specific aspects in the extension of scientific languages, as demonstrated in Gibson (2000: 97–163). I think that a variety of different strategies may also sustain such moves, and my own can be characterised from different specific theoretical viewpoints, by which to enrich its potential. For example the foregoing use of 'extension' could be viewed as a switch of expressions from one semantic field to another field that is truth-preserving; or, a function generating polysemy. Jackendorff's (2002: 359–60) important study takes a version of the latter, which involves the concept of parallel instantiations across semantic fields with underlying functions of a shared abstract schema.

From earlier in the present book I here re-introduce and extend the 11-dimensional framework that stimulates M-theory. In mathematical physics relevant solutions are only worked out in two dimensions. In certain respects the projected solutions involve an extension of the subjects of languages, some particular functions of which can be interpreted as a special form of extension of a concept by live metaphorisation. As chapter 5 argues, complexity and 'chaos' laws are functions of a special sort of transcendence, and as such they are verification-transcendent, though still empirical, and thus are not in Wittgenstein's sense 'experimental'. Consequently they have the strange position or status of something akin to the *a priori*, while they are ontological. To this I add a concept from chapter 4 – that in mirror symmetry two distinct space times, within a narrow context of topology, can be linked to a real classical topology. In M-theory when h and α' are non-zero, there is a matrix in which an unprecedented noncommutativity emerges. Such creativity can be physical, mathematical and aesthetic. The expression of meaning itself has a peculiar relation to the abstract in mentality and to the physical world, which complies well with the 'strange' properties articulated in such domains as M-theory. Such a proposal is exotic and incomplete. It has certain similarities to a thought-experiment; yet as Sorensen (1992) shows, some new physics has been discovered by thought-experiment, and it shares some simulation-conditions with virtual reality. A further way of extending this type of enterprise outside of logic, yet susceptible itself to logical representation, is the recent work on computer model simulation, for example, by Robert French (1996). There is difference and slippage between the two domains that are thus related, while in such cases as are discussed there are mappings that preserve qualified symmetries between properties in distinct subjects, in his computer model for analogy making.

The conceptual policy rationale for applying (A) to (C) by use of (A) to (C) to the resurrection, is partly because: (B) is the most extensive formalism which makes logical claims about the preconditions for ontology while not being physically ontological (this phrasing does not prejudge Platonism). (A) is the most exotic and extreme complex state over which science theorises for what it is to be a physical state in the universe. On suitable interpretations, (C) explores the creation of universals, or construction of a new world, of beauty in, or as, a state of affairs.

Is there only one logic?

Someone may wish not only to oppose the choice of (A) to (C), but also to object to the supposition that logic can sustain a claim that there is only one logic. On the former, a reason for this choice is that they constitute, in part, what it is to be universality and possibility, and I will show this to be so as the chapter develops. Concerning the latter, one does not need to sustain a claim that there is one logic to be warranted in employing inference and logical paraphrase to connect differing concepts or uses of logic and even fallacious reasoning.

For those who believe that not all things are black or white, that there are viable deviant logics, it is not obdurate of one to presuppose that there are logical mapping procedures to net and characterise deviation from logical standards. What one needs here is a group of logical principles of a relevant sort that range over thoughts and their media of communication. Let us suppose – concede – for the present that for each subject there is another logic, rather than a Russellian bivalent logic covering all subjects. But since each actually is a logic, and because logic has inference as an internal property of its identity, then it has to follow that each logic has a paraphrasing language extendible to and encapsulating other logics (which is not to claim that they are tautologous). Just as we can translate from one language to another though their semantic universals may differ,[13] so logics can communicate by translating their differing presuppositions. (Even if we follow a range of presentation of paraconsistent logic, we can treat all paradoxes as one family, and therefore enclose them under the logical paraphrase suggested above.[14] Although obviously in such a scenario concepts of validity, soundness and truth widely vary. Ways of devising paraphrasing routes can be produced to facilitate inferential links between distinct logics.)

Creation and resurrection

Attempts to connect two or more apparently unrelated subjects are sometimes a stimulus to infer new understanding. Thus local physics, which has no observational foundation for black holes, is connected to black hole astrophysics that contravene many subatomic laws. It may seem audacious, even so, to connect the resurrection with cosmology. Some physicists, whose experience is based in laboratory experiment and its theory, regard theories about the very early universe as verging on science fiction. Many scientists have come to realise, concerning science's history, however, that some fragments of science fiction have a habit of becoming science. Although this is not itself a foundation for suggesting that the resurrection could have a cosmological counterpart that is science fiction, yet there are some illuminating parallels.

Resurrection and the start of the universe

Gibson's (2000)[15] analysis of causality and originality is presupposed here as a premise in the argument. In some later work Stephen Hawking[16] presents a *volte-face* about the universe. According to him, it now is the only universe; time starts with its commencement, and the universe will probably eternally expand, whereas Linde and Rees's[17] idea is of an infinite ensemble of universes. Such disputes show that we are grossly ignorant about the cosmos. Those who wish to adopt science as a foundation for stipulating what is empirically possible would do well to suspend judgement for a long time, so as to see which way the universe goes. Since cosmology is to some degree often-speculative generalisation of experimental science, the domain of accepted concepts in cosmology is a form of sounding board for unexpected empirical possibility, as well as the conjectured future direction for some science. Hence, allowing for the foregoing qualifications, if we gather a cluster of premises from the agreement among cosmologists, we can proceed as they do with some astrophysical consequences.

If, as most cosmologists agree, the universe goes back to a Big Bang, General Relativity's laws entail their own collapse (in the theories by which astrophysicists attempt to retroject back to the initial conditions of the universe's origin). The reasons for this are, first, those matter–energy density conditions and the velocity of light all become infinite. Secondly, infinity is not a function of observation or closed calculation. Here follows a schema that outlines what creation is, in contrast with what making or production is, drawing on Geach's (1969) approach:

> (i) y has brought it about that (for some x [x is the Universe]) and it is false that for some x (y has brought it about that [x is the Universe]).

That is to say, creation has no material antecedent or no antecedent that is composed of the consequent. Also (i) creates a consequence that satisfies a criterion of identity in the antecedent, while also adding another criterion of identity in the consequence to mirror that antecedent, a situation which also manifests an asymmetry between antecedent and consequent. That is to say, here is a concept of what it is to be creation derived from what it is to be causality.[18]

Scientists as well as philosophers do not understand what happens when there is a discontinuity between systems (and this models a relation between there being no corresponding system prior to the Big Bang and whatever comprised its cause). The relation between the causal state of affairs before General

Relativity and after General Relativity is therefore logical. One of the features not to miss here is the function of logical metaphor within local science and its proportionately increasing extended usage, the higher up the scale of generality and causal originality one goes. The more exotic the science is, the more metaphoric its measuring language becomes.

The identity of such live metaphor language is as follows, with '$x = y$' respecting a set of propositional functions F that unpacks into 'x has the same property F as has y' where the class of Fs is:

(1) constructed from predicables applied to values of x and y in the object language.

(2) The referent of y is the simulated identity of x satisfying a relative identity criterion.

Therefore:

(3) There is a dependency relation of y upon x^r since y occurs with an array of Fs which is a replica of corresponding elements predicated of x^r.

(3) rests on the premise that:

(4) y is the counterpart or image of x's referent correctly arranged and articulated so that y goes proxy for x^r or reproduces the specified class of x's properties.

So:

(5) The identity relation '$x = y$', with '=' defined by a set of Fs occurring in the object languages, can quantify over a single identity.

Consequently, other subjects can thereby represent the referent's identity, and this includes, for example, a sibling's reproduction of its parents. (An exposition of this concept of live metaphor within the semantics of depicting 'God' relevant for Christology is developed in the next chapter.) In this situation live metaphor can be used to express true or false propositions whose referent is in the external world, and whose ontology strictly implies creation. These conditions relevantly coincide with the logic of the resurrection. The death of Christ is discontinuous with Christ's resurrection, while it requires a continuity of causality and identity between the two states (subjects), through a partial or relative identity to allow for qualitative change. Since such an equation involves qualitative changes that entail a change of ontology, it requires the blockage of material laws parallel (in time-reverse) to the emergence of the universe. These premises provide the entailment that the concept of the resurrection would have to be a creation. Stephen Hawking has developed a model for the origin of the universe employing primordial black holes in time-reverse. This model can be used as a live metaphor, by which to construct the relevant point of similarity: out of high entropy which renders empirically impossible the reversal of a physical state, or its removal, there is a formalism to explain the routing for transcendence out of that state into its negation.

The above approach could support a realist or an anti-realist view of meaning. The use of metaphor is definitely not the employment of figurative language to discard ontology of the external world for the subject of the resurrection. In fact, we have seen that the presence of metaphor in a theology of the resurrection is no reason for allowing the (false) implication that the referential subject of resurrection is itself (dead) metaphoric. Conversely, the often vaunted opposite of this position – that of a rather naive realist correspondence theory of analytical philosophy – is fundamentally inadequate to represent the counter-intuitive identities and ontology involved in the logic of the resurrection.

The conclusion of this matter is that creation is counter-intuitive, logical and metaphysical, as well as empirically realist. These properties are also those internal to the concept of the resurrection. In each case, the concept of a miracle is central as an internal property of each event.

Creative catastrophes

Using developments of Rene Thom's (1989) catastrophe mathematics, we should immediately be able to recognise that the foregoing cosmological model complements an issue in the philosophy of mathematics. Thom constructed catastrophe mathematics with an eye to the discontinuity and continuity between a foetus and the born child. Thom's theory was devised to range over inorganic and organic systems. The term 'catastrophe' is only a formal catastrophe: it engages the concept of transformation of one state to another. This change need not be destructive. Formulating morphogenesis for embryology, Thom (1989: 121) commences with the epigram: 'and the word was made flesh'. For him 'catastrophe' is a formal term for transformations to actual birth of a new system, which he implemented as a type for other subjects, generalising them to treat formal mathematical relations. He employed the idea of a surface, whose formal representation is a topology. This general modelling devise is also fundamental in mathematical cosmology.[19] The mathematical concept of a manifold is a logical type that is an undergirth prior to the most fundamental level of geometry, and it is thus more fundamental than geometries that map the external universe. It is supposed to be the bedrock concept under geometric and physical dimensions. At appropriate positions these manifolds are infinite dimensional manifold vectors.[20] According to Thom (1989: 7 where M is the space in which observable entities can occur (the Universe of part thereof)) it contains a given subset K. K is the catastrophe set. A vector field X historically defines the evolution of the system – its development on M. A representative state of affairs of the Universe of M is depicted by *m*. If *m* meets K – i.e., if there is a collision by K on *m* – then a discontinuity in the system M comes to exist.

This can be used to structure a feature of a concept about God's postulated foreknowledge of the resurrection. On a realist theory of meaning, it is possible in principle to predict the occurrence of this catastrophe, given the above parameters. (The symbol m here indicates the state of continuity prior to the eschaton, while K represents its inception.) The scope of the catastrophe is not limited to the normal space–time restrictions (indicated by a light cone or set of cones), due to the unique boundaries. 'K' is a term designating the whole series of Thom's catastrophe models.[21] Consequently, catastrophe mathematics presents a formalism that enables a new identity to emerge from another system while occupying a position of identification and difference in that state of affairs. This evidently complies with some conditions both for creation and for resurrection. So we can piggyback with this Thom formalism on both, and propose that it strengthens the use of their conjunction, to exemplify an extension of what is possible.

Mathematical truths and ethics

Colin McGinn (1997) has done some distinguished work exposing the unexpected logical similarities between mathematical truths and ethical statements.[22] In a certain sense, mathematical truths lie outside space–time as well as in it; so it is with ethics. A result of this situation is that strangely typical mathematical and ethical truth or functions are both acausal in relation to us. As Bob Hale (1994: 303) notes, they themselves have a lack of spatio-temporal connection to us, while their implementation is of enormous causal relevance to us – we calculate our physical activities by use of them. So is the case with ethical truths. An aspect that is shared through such similarities and contrasts here is that our logical beliefs need to account for this symmetry and asymmetry. Just as is the case with ethics: principle supervenes over actions without it causally dictating effects, while that principle has consequences for physical action.

It would be a misunderstanding of this drift of comparison to suggest that there is an homogeneity in all accounts of use between mathematics and ethics in their relations to reality. Following Wittgenstein (1969), it is helpful to see that concepts (not concept) of use reach through linguistic expressions beyond and against reductionism and a restricted notion of empiricism. I suggest that we may take up his view that usage is much more complex and unexpected than we tend to meet in typical extant theories, as a means of connecting ethics and mathematical expressions. What he does not develop, but is a counter-intuitive next stage in theoretical explanation, is this. At a level deeper than different theories of realism for mathematics and the solely experiential grounding of ethics, is a counter-intuitive realism that extends to match the most general truths of existence external to language, including infinity. In a special sense, I propose that this has some qualitative similarity to the state of language and ontology required representing reality external to language immediately prior to the beginning of the universe. At very recondite levels, it appears that that state of affairs was partially expressed in or as the universe.

Empirical beauty

Since ethical and aesthetic phenomena share the feature of being qualitative values, this overlap between them is felicitous for their joint extension to a logically well-formed concept of the resurrection. Mothersill (1984: 384) regards aesthetic functions to be susceptible of analysis as logical predicates, though she is driving the link with a neo-Kantian scheme. This approach can be readily transformed to the present conceptions without the Kantian assumptions.

It has always been a problem that Wittgenstein's[23] conception of a picture-language, as a model for logical propositions, seemed to collapse[24] when certain abstract notions triggered objections: for example, the idea of a negation of the picture is itself a picture. And what would that be? Elizabeth Anscombe (1971: 78) judged that the truth of the *Tractatus* theory – concerning negation and the picture theory of the 'significant proposition' – would be death to natural theology. I have avoided commitment to these areas, and offered different approaches, which are partly complemented by Hintikka's (1994) distinct researches.

Wittgenstein replaced the notion of simplicity in his earlier work with concepts of complexity and physicalistic correspondence with the external world, which involves a counter-intuitive view of complex abstract representation. Music is one instance of a quite distinct use of abstract values that can connect with representation. Malcolm Budd (1995; cf. also 2003) proposes that the use of 'value' in such cases can be properly extended as one function to link up with other spheres such as visual art. A picture can be abstract, and act as an analogue as a live metaphor for an abstract semiotic visual function in and as a propositional form. We might consider a picture theory of language by supplying it with, for example, abstract expressionism as a live metaphoric counterpart to illustrate the idea of a type by which to model abstract operators such as 'if'. Although we have no decision-procedure to generate theorems as to how we might master all such relations, this is not really an objection to the principle of constructing analogues of the visual, linguistic and logical, since very little of our advanced higher levels of logic can supply that requirement. Given Wittgenstein's own interest in the application of the concepts of propositional functions as projections in space and its geometry (including in the *Philosophical Investigations*, 1998: 187), there are reasons to extend the idea of a painterly abstraction to link with formal abstraction (as, for example, Russian futurists did), and thence to pure mathematics where visualisation of abstractions is itself an explanatory function. (These references to artistic abstraction are here obviously metaphoric uses of such works for illustrative purposes.) In other words, the media of representation encapsulate physical and aesthetic features that are ontologically intertwined and co-extensive in the external world.

Perhaps it is obvious that the origin of the universe is not only an empirical but also an aesthetic phenomenon; yet this latter identity has had little scientific or philosophical attention. So some remarks are required to propose that there is such a subject for serious research. Surely it is not mischievous to observe that, if a given set of equations describing the sunrise does not contain aesthetic variable and functions, then such equations are empirically incomplete as an account of that physical state of affairs? I wish to generalise that sunrise over the universe's origin. Science has yet to discover how such qualitative properties are housed in and derivable from material quantification. Some scientists employ aesthetic criteria in theory for devising practical discovery-procedure in empirical investigation (see Gibson 2000: 135–8). This importantly complies with the restricted functional scope of an equation's relation to the physical state it depicts. That is to say, for an aesthetic component to be internalised in, for example Hoffmann's (1990) chemical research, it has to be functionally efficacious.

As Wittgenstein noticed within his examination of what it is to follow a rule, our linguistic use tends to parade as if it just is what it represents, whereas such description is an under-determination of what it is to be the identity of the phenomenon depicted. So it is, even more so, with aesthetic properties within empirical states of affairs. When, as with the proposed conception of the resurrection, the aesthetic is a function of the complex identity of a unique empirical state of affairs, we should proceed with caution, since even for straightforward situations in cosmological physics we have little idea how to represent empirical phenomena, let alone transcendent exotic states. For example, Hawking and Turok (1998) maintain that specific astrophysical states have an infinite number of physical solutions internal to their empirical configuration. There is no way of our number crunching such data with calculation. It would seem, therefore, a suitable act of scientific humility to restrain scepticism about the possibility of there occurring transcendent empirical states whose purported characteristics include infinity, and the perfect bonding of aesthetic functions with empirical conditions. After all, the Big Bang scenario would be a 'unique' empirical state assessable to physical representation only by live metaphor analogy to terrestrial physics; even then only by defying the alleged limits to the matter-energy, density and velocity conditions in the latter physics.

We do not have to accede to Aristotle's formulation expressed cryptically in the *Poetics*, that creativity is the disclosure of universals. Yet this does establish an illuminating aesthetic precedent for the creation of aesthetic universals. The Big Bang scenario seems to entail that universal lawlike patterns, or their condensed physical antecedent theorem-like sources, were laid down instantaneously (or virtually instantaneously) in a space–time point millions of times smaller than the smallest subatomic particle. Clearly this is creativity of a very deep counter-intuitive order. At the very least, it appears that there is a strong relative-identity relation between different levels and our present asymmetric levels of energy, radiation and matter. Some cosmologists prefer to expound this original state of affairs as a singularity in which just one (currently unavailable) equation would map all the future diverging empirical functions. This sort of state of affairs therefore collapses the distinction between generality and token singularity: by uniting them. If one can replace Ockham's contradictory versions of the Razor of simplicity, it may be, as argued earlier in the present book,[25] that a suitably counter-intuitive form of simplicity, which presupposes condensed complexity, functions only at the universal level and in the singularity that resulted in the universe.

If facets of cosmology can correctly be compared to artistic creativity, it is revealing to present the concept of an artform typically as a token instance of creativity which, in being an expression of an interpretation, attempts to depict, by that token, a type of universality. In a certain sense, at least viewed Classically on a variety of interpretations,[26] singular creativity is a representation of sublime generality in the particular. That is to say, creativity is the condensation of the conjunction of a set of finite expressions in such a way as to comprise a conception that is more than the sum of their atomic parts. According to Aquinas' aesthetical theory, in particular if we follow Eco's (1988) splendid study, the beauty of a subject is to be identified with its perfection. As Eco (1988: 117) presents it: 'The glorified body will correspond to the degree of grace and glory in the mind', and Christ's transfigured body would be an infinitely enhanced version of this, 'for splendour flows from the soul into the glorified body'.

It is in this respect that Wittgenstein's *Tractatus* offered a basis, which if re-interpreted and redirected, can support the idea that the aesthetic and the mystical are logical transcendence of the calculable, but I argue by employment of the counter-intuitive use of the calculable. In this regard, I suggest that Wittgenstein need not (in our use of the context here) have made the distinction in the way he did between 'proving' and 'showing', because some formulations of the transcendent (in his terms the 'aesthetic' and the 'mystical') are achievable by counter-intuitive uses of logic, though this is not to assume that the same insight cannot be reached by other media such as music. Consequently, the relation between physical creation and the resurrection follows this route. The logic of resurrection counter-intuitively harnesses the logic of physical creation.

It is an obvious consequence of the previous paragraph that such considerations have analogues in the biography of a person who has been conceived as the manifestation of spiritual creativity. Logic is a mere shadow of substantive content in such contexts, but insofar as it can function, a logical account of such an individual would focus on the particular as a revelation of universality. Consequently the resurrection of such an individual would have a relative-identity relation to his origins and life.

It is fairly evident that the theme of the 'word made flesh' works with the sourcing of creation in speech and creative composition. This offers a metaphoric framework upon which the physical and aesthetic cosmologies have a mirroring function. One would not wish to overstate this sensitive analogy, since it could distract from the qualitative import of the point of Christ's personal identity. Nevertheless, there is a firm counterpart-pattern between the creation of the universe and the logic of the resurrection: the creation of universals from metaphysical antecedents to produce a unique singularity that manifests aesthetic functions.

Wittgenstein's pioneering researches constructed some links between ethics and aesthetics. If we follow him, to some unquantified degree, ethics and aesthetics, in a range of ways, compose a continuum; this should be qualified by our ignorance, however. Anscombe (1957) showed how some hitherto un-ravelled problems about the identity of mental states prevented us from doing much successful ethics without an account of mentality, one which we do not yet have.[27] Consequently, we have as yet too little idea of how ethics embraces aesthetics. But it seems that on the basis of their partial co-extensionality, both creation and the resurrection are instances of the (quite various) conjunctions of ethics and aesthetics in addition to other characteristics.

Thomas Aquinas developed the thesis that beauty and its forms have an ontological implementation, and this truth is at the heart of what it is to be cre-ation and creativity. Eco argues that Aquinas' system is incomplete, and Aquinas does not therefore finally achieve the purpose that he intended. (He suddenly left off writing. Did he recognise the absence of aesthetical values in his use of logic, and its consequences for transcendent reasoning?) Even if one is not a Thomist, one need not concur with all his views to admit some suitable version of this as a relevant feature of aesthetics. Within a scientific framework of Ockhamist rather than Thomist presuppositions, the above mentioned research of Raold Hoffmann[28] proposes that molecular aesthetics is realised in ontological properties manifested in the geometry and relativity of molecules in crystalline states. We might construct a theory for such phenomena conceiv-ing, not by use of 'distance' as a metaphor between cosmology and artistic creativity or its critical theory but as an internal attributive feature of empirical phenomena. If one can generalise such data and theory, possible on a range of approaches, then we would have an ontological status for beauty.

Hoffmann's belief is that the doctrine of parsimony – that of Ockham's Razor – would support this project, despite Ockham's many contradictory ver-sions of the Razor.[29] It appears that the only way of restating and sustaining Ockham's Razor is to apply it at the cosmological level, as a universal function obtaining when all physical phenomena are correctly represented by one equa-tion. This state of affairs coincides with being creation, and in this sense an ancient doctrine of God's simplicity matches the initial conditions of being cre-ation. These conditions seem also to map on to a concept of resurrection as aesthetic creation.

It is possible that, appropriately interpreted and developed, with respect to the above sort of theses proposed, the conjunction of the previous two paragraphs can be used to imply that mentality, beauty, ontology and ethics are logically and epistemologically related. We can employ this complex set of relations as a live metaphor to infer that these properties can be constituted in a single form. Con-strued in a certain way, this suggestion is a schema for a piece of creative art. Interpreted in personal terms, it is a presupposition for being a person. The con-junction of these two options would be a person who is art form.[30]

Ranging aesthetics

Lacoue-Labarthe (1994) has delineated a subtle theory of how literary creativity and music theory combine. The aesthetic variable and functions in each mirror comparable values. Although we can adapt such significant interpretations, we need much more. Perhaps a logical aphorism can further discussion here: if music is not a language, then language cannot express all that is fundamental in the universe. On this interpretation, which I wish to maintain, music shares some properties with natural, scientific and logical languages. Musical language resembles, or has an informative live metaphor relation to, cosmological aesthetic language. Just as a musical score codes properties that are disclosed in its performance, so details of the universe's meaning are displayed in the unfolding cosmological observations. Correctly understood at a number of levels, this involves the assignment of aesthetic properties to the universe. [31]

One feature of this conjunction is the use of pure mathematics to provide ontologies for the very early universe, as for example in Wada (1986). The familiar claim that mathematics contains beauty is apt here; the application of the Schrodinger equation to the Big Bang illustrates this type of beauty, as exemplified by the mathematician Boukricha (1985). Superstring theory is at the centre of such mathematics, and they are also fundamental to some physics of sound. Accordingly, creativity in music and creation in superphysics have qualitative relations. This conjunction can function as a bridge to infer some musical aesthetics, carried by the mathematics, both into creation itself, and also to any act of actual creation. Since the foregoing has offered grounds for treating resurrection as a function of creation, it eventually follows that this resurrection has deep aesthetic properties. In a precise sense, we may consider that the resurrection's logic manifests properties of aesthetic composition, assisted as this live metaphor is by the formal similarities between mathematical truths and ethical values.

Clearly, we should concur with Ernst Gombrich (1986: 119) to be wary of imposing Platonic metaphysics on stylised beauty; yet agree with Roger Penrose (1994) in his suggestion that basic features of mathematics such as an algorithm mirror a transcendental order and beauty. I should like to propose for consideration that some types of literary creativity, including some types of poetry, share features with logic, musical aesthetics and visual aesthetics. Such a scenario would carry us beyond the limits of a mechanistic model of logic into deep areas of counter-intuitive logics. I think that in the *Poetics* Aristotle was heading for a union of literary logic and formal logic, which he did not survive to produce. That is to say, the deeper one goes into the foundations of formal logic the more unstable are mechanical procedures of calculation and criteria of proof, and further discovery (not invention) needs to be an end for logical insight. At this stage formal logic starts giving way to something like formal poetry: creative formal compositions. The deeper one reaches into the identities of literary, visual and musical creative expression the more like logic they seem to be. So it seems that a candidate for new logic – that will be derivable from our current logics, but in a counter-intuitive way – is the deep structure of creative forms. Namely, one hopes that the conjunction of logic and aesthetic is achieved in the foundations of future research.

In terms of a personal identity, the conception of Christ would be a perfect realisation of the best unification of different qualities. Perhaps we have seen to some small degree that addressing the logic of the resurrection triggers such possibilities into explicit portrayal. But, surely, that is precisely what a logical resurrection itself would be – a new life discontinuous with the old yet preserving its criterion of identity?

Creating universal art in ontology

Historiographical accuracy is a component in assessing the identity of a traditional literary source. New Testament scholarship has been fulsome in its capacity to add to the perplexity of readers of the resurrection accounts. Many theologians deserve awards for the enthusiasm with which they have interwoven later cultures into the Gospels. It is not always obvious that the results of such interpretation have been to contribute to the actual exposure of the contents of the resurrection narratives. For a logician, it is not clear what burden of proof operates, rather than what is canvassed as evidence, in such scholarly insider dealing. So let us attempt to avoid engagement with such matters, while presupposing a summary-core of claims internal to the New Testament.

This is not an attempt to examine the purported relations, gap, conflict or correspondence between the records and the events. Rather, it is a brief selection of facets of New Testament presuppositions that appear to match the concepts proposed in the foregoing study. Since the present chapter is not a study of the philosophy of belief, nor is it a formulation of the criteria pertinent to designating the resurrection narratives as having invariant application outside of their temporal contexts, I do not offer, but am aware of, the appropriateness of devising criteria for matching the present study's results with ancient narratives. But readers might be wary, conversely, of manufacturing the *absence* of such criteria as an obstacle in principle to regarding the history allegedly referred to in the resurrection narratives as a relevant basis for the logic of resurrection.

According to the New Testament Jesus appeared to people after his resurrection, as did Lazarus. They are reported to have had bodies, and the compositional voice of the narrative does not offer any grounds for ironising or idiomatising such bodies to render them redundant or somehow nonfunctional after resurrection. Narratives such as Luke 24 and Hebrews 2 employ the third person in direct reflexive formations such as 'he himself' equivalent to the first person 'I', tied to bodily experience. On this analysis, if such narrative depiction of Jesus and its history are incorrect, then the literary basis for the resurrection would be false, and there would be no point in pursuing any belief with 'Christ' as the subject. Contrariwise, if such narrative sourcing of the resurrection is correct, then we are not free to add any other ontology than the actual historical one, even if the problem of exposing the identity of that history is obscure. To admit ontology for the bodily resurrection is not to have to adopt an identical qualitative state prior to the resurrection, since the resurrection codes into its theme a transformation of state. But just as there are exotic states within the current universe that defy the physics we know, so consequently we should allow the possibility of an exotic physical state hypothetically associated with Christ that would be contrary to terrestrial biophysics. A property of such astrophysical states is that an exotic violation of General Relativity can occur within our universe in the presence of Newtonian functions. Given the strangeness of M-theory discussed above, it is a feeble move to dismiss the notion of an immortalised body as contradictory. This serves as an analogy to argue that the mere fact of a bodily state that is qualitatively transformed, with presupposed immortal or infinite properties, is in principle a veridical physical state of affairs. Expressed plainly in New Testament presuppostional form: there are strong logical and empirical grounds for, and none against, a straightforward acceptance of the credibility of an immortalised person in a bodily state. A consequence of the foregoing is that the New Testament reconceives 'unity' in a new qualitative infinity beyound recurring singularities (see Milbank 2003: 102).

Conclusion

The foregoing analysis has offered a basis for proving that the subjects marked by 'I', together with its proper name antecedent in their uses in the resurrection narratives, satisfy the following considerations:

(A) Reproduction of a personal identity through a cosmological cataclysm.
(B) Achievement through an act of creation that has counter-intuitive universals internal to it and the identity of its subject.
(C) A subset of the necessary conditions of this creation includes transitivity between ethical, aesthetic and empirical functions qualitatively characterised by infinity-functions.
(D) A live metaphor relation to the initial conditions of time in the Big Bang scenario, on the assumption that it is itself a complex mathematical live metaphor.
(E) The origin of the universe has a relation of time-reverse and (allowing for qualitative differences) matter-energy symmetry to the resurrection.

The considerations (A) to (E), together with their detailed development in the foregoing, are consistent with the transformations summarised above in the narratives of the resurrection. These include the elements of discontinuity, creation, criteria of continuity and the sharing of causal relations between two different universal systems in transformation, are common to the resurrection and to the other cosmological functions documented (inclusive of the philosophical functions) above. Obviously, more detailed analysis of the mapping relations between these complex cosmological and spiritual typologies, as well as the theory of live metaphor that associates them, can be performed; but in principle, the present analysis has covered the grounds of proof. Therefore, this chapter proves the logical empirical possibility that Christ rose from the dead and, hopefully, rather more.

8   The semantic logic of 'God'

Exploratory presuppositions

The previous chapter's presentation of a logic of the resurrection also serves to justify raising queries about whether or not we should allow an ancient set of narratives to be logically and metaphysically isolated from more recent approaches to theory, in the sense that we all have a tendency to suppose – rightly at some levels – that progress has been made in the evolution of human consciousness and its effects. At some levels, however, the aesthetic problem of either cyclicity, or development of artistic endeavour over large diachronic slices of history, obtrudes onto assessment of an ancient literature that participates and contributes, even obliquely, to broadening and challenging human perception of the meaning of life. In a poststructuralist framework quite different from the present one, Richard Rorty[1] makes a helpful analysis pointing up the importance of grounding a research theory's measuring terms in the object language literature that it targets. This involves discovering how and to what degree the terms in the original literature can themselves be used to generate the theory and/or assess its functional viability within the original literature. This implements the approach that some applied linguistic analysis should be an internal component of a philosophy of language. Given the vexed history of the relations between the literatures that performed as the source of Christianity respecting the use of terms matched with 'God', it is a worthwhile exercise to implement this sort of proposal.

Although much valuable research has been done on the relations between concepts of God in theology and in the historical origins of them in the Jewish and Christian bibles, there is need for further and rather different investigations into these relations. How aspects of this which can lead to a new perspective are recognised by noting some of the foregoing concerns with the metaphysics of representation, semantics and logic of the incarnation, and thereafter pursue an analysis in an attempt to discover how the patterns examined in the previous chapters have a similarity to their historical origins.

The literary and cultural antecedents of New Testament use complexly impinge on the question of the perceived identity associated with and the semantic scope of terms for 'God' in the first century AD. So the present chapter is concerned with the functions of *'l[w]hym* in the Dead Sea Scrolls (DSS) and the Hebrew Bible, together with their relations to *theos*, *theoi*, *angelos* and *angeloi* in LXXs and NT quotations. This chapter follows from work for a philosophy of language with applied linguistics commenced in Gibson (1981, 1998). This chapter will propose analysing applied semantics by deploying logic theory of meaning, implementing my view that logic and semantics are species of live metaphor. The latter part of the chapter is concerned to implement this policy as a function to develop literary theory.

This study of the semantic logic of terms for 'God' is here situated for a typical purpose to introduce and connect a multidisciplinary scenario, whose applicability hopefully will be generalised by future research as a contribution to the questions of what it is to be language, and to be logic. There are obviously vexed problems disrupting attempts to connect the (often-imperialist) territories of literary theories and logics (in addition to the difficulties of generalising over competing options with each domain). The topic of intentionality is merely one cross-mapping possibility between the two disciplines that could facilitate conti-nental drift to complementary overlap, but without tectonic collision, in the examination of divine referring expressions. Roughly, intentionality is the pre-supposition implemented as a semantic value of a referring term such as *'lwhym* in its relation to its purported referent. The assessment of dead languages amounts to an extreme and problematic issue, not least because intentionality is a presupposition used in live native use of 'God', whereas live intuition is dis-placed by the modern linguist's own learnt instinct as a presupposition in frequency of, say, *'lwhym* in a DSS text.

Logic in early stages of development and self-assessment had long, often un-helpful, though now largely ignored, applications to the Bible (see G. R. Evans, 1985). Institutional imperialisms hold sway over areas of logic; yet the problems of logic are deeper and more unexpected than some philosophers typically expect. Perhaps consequently analytical philosophy's use of logic is typically taken to be alien to or in opposition to literary analysis, ecumenical though the latter is. It is a criterion of analytical philosophy that its fundamental axiom is: any analysis of thought must go through an examination of language – and in principle offer a plausible philosophy of language.[2] But a peculiar feature of almost all analytical philosophy is that generally there is no interest in analysis of a particular language, especially its literary uses, to contribute to the foregoing criterion. If it were the case that we have already reached a position to render such an analysis redundant, all well and good; but analytical philosophy is astro-nomically far from such a destination, together with disagreement as to what would count as the stipulation of what it is to be language, and its relations to natural languages.

In these respects unresolved areas of applied meaning-theory in the seman-tics of the DSS and the Bible impinge on partially unsolved issues in the logical theory of meaning. A selective conjunction of both can illuminate each. We are in fact unclear about what it is to be a relation between one actual language and a logical theory of meaning. As with all languages, we have no exhaustive decision-procedure for specifying the holistic structure of Hebrew. This is further complicated by the asymmetry between a live native-based analysis of language that we cannot perform for a dead language since, for the latter there is no corresponding function for native user-intuitions. A semantic theory for a dead language (even if it is only implicitly presupposed, or is a premise to which semiticists have to be committed as a function of their arguments) is accordingly an over-generalisation that goes beyond the hitherto explored data. The main task of applied semantics is to discover the means to infer symmetry between semantics usage and generalisation. Logic may both come to aid this programme, and yet reflect the same type of restriction by labouring under its own limits.

Concerning a logical theory of meaning, the conjunction of 'logic' with 'theory of meaning' sets in motion a concern with inference and generalisation applied to the project of defining what it is to be true – or false – interpretation. This latter feature is often misplaced. Dummett (1993: 130) strikes the right note: 'a complete thought is to be characterised as that which it makes sense to qualify as true or false'. Application of logic theory to the DSS and the Bible is not a programme whose minimal condition for success is for it to identify what is true (though once such a programme is realised, the criteria for such an interpretation will already have been supplied). In so far as logic has any success in isolating what it is to be language, it can be employed to interpret aspects of groups of linguistic features, whose representation is a matter of significance or dispute, though it is not a decision-procedure by which the logician can impose imperialism. As with any epistemological conception, including literary appreciation, we only expose those properties of language that our presuppositions attract, together with accidental discoveries or inventions of sense. We usually are too confident an assumption that our theories determine exactly what it is to be the subject they target. We too easily fail to notice excess space ignored by our perception since the latter is not a recognitional concept of what it is to be the object language of our analysis. (For example, the European anarchist anti-logic *avant-garde* in the 1918–30 period was anything but new and used logic, while Whitehead and Russell's *Principia* confused premises with assumptions. No doubt the present study will unconsciously furnish its own instances.)

In addition to the above scope that can be circumscribed by true/false logics, deviant logics can sometimes be applied to interpret linguistic phenomena. Many typical deviant logics can be derived indirectly from bivalent (true/false) logical calculi (see Haack, 1996), and thus be networked into a generalised framework. It would be an anachronistic misrepresentation of this type of project, however, to envisage that the application of logic to language, ancient or modern, is the mere formalisation of a narrative. The deeper and more significant logical issues for applied linguistics reside within the purview of philosophical logic or theory of meaning; namely, the attempts to dig out what it is to be a language, and how creative narrative challenges and disputes its own roles. In particular, for the present chapter's purposes, logic is not a methodological manifesto, and it will be brought in (largely informally) only where the main priority of investigating issues warrants it.

A way forward for both the construction of the linguistics of a given language, say Hebrew or Greek, and the scope of logic, for example concerning what is reference and function, is to align such concerns in study of a problematic core-term in a body of literature. To give full-throttle to such an investigation would be to choose two such sets of uses in two languages in which contentions of mirroring and collision of semantics values occur. The employment of terms translated 'God' in the DSS and the Bible facilitates a start for such an investigation.[3]

When angels go proxy for God

When Newsom (1985: 24) discussed Qumran angelology in the liturgical text 4QShirShabb, she observed that:

> Many occurrences of *'lwhym* in the Shirot are ambiguous and might refer either to God or to angels, though such expressions as *kwl 'lwhym* [4Q40: 1. i. 32, 32–3] and *mlk 'lwhym* [4Q400: 2. 5]unequivocally attest the use of *'lwhym* for the angels. A biblical basis for *'lwhym* = angels is provided by Psalm 8: 6; 82: 1, 6; 97: 8; 138: 1, etc.

Before proceeding to the task of semantic analysis, a note is appropriate on the orthography of MT *'lhym* in relation to DSS *'lwhym*. We do not know enough about this change or other replacements by *waw* in DSS to presuppose that the spelling switch here only has orthographic significance, though it might have. But we should allow the possibility that it could mark some unknown semantic tonal or lexical contribution. In any case, as Ulrich (1995: 109) points out, the orthography of a number of biblical books from Qumran is inconsistent. Just how or if these reflect any semantic function is unclear, concerning this current issue. In view of the role of *'lhym*, for example, to code judges in Exodus (21: 6), together with the import of earlier traditions of orthography at Qumran and their irregular yet (possibly uneven) mirroring of practices generally in Palestine, it is worth reproducing Ulrich's (1995: 116) observation on the relevant orthography of 4QpaleoExod^m: although it tends towards a fuller orthography, it remains in the moderate range, with *'lhym* spelled without *waw*. Newsom (1992: 41) points out that, for example, 4Q374 *l'lhym* occurs 41 times, with *l'lwhym* once. If we take the view that at least some of the paleo-Hebrew manuscripts predate Qumran (while agreeing to the possibility that paleo-Hebrew copying was practised there), as well as allowing for manuscripts with the Jewish script being copied in and away from Qumran, we need further analysis to reach a conclusion as to the identity of the presence or absence of *waw* in *'lhym*. Schuller (1992: 97) observes that in the non-canonical psalm in 4Q381: 15 employs *'lhy* even where the MT and others have YHWH. Qimron (1992: 366) judges that the MT probably did not influence the morphology of Hebrew. So the following remarks attempt to leave a space for the solution to this problem, and avoid tying the difference of form to its conclusions. Nevertheless it is clear from the use of *'lwhym* in 4QShirShabb that Newsom's claim is true for a possible equation between the term and 'angels'; but what this notion of identity ('=') is, is up for interrogation.

As it is expressed by her, Newsom's foregoing equation ''*lwhym* = angels' is an absolute identity relation between 'x = y'. But as it stands this allows no difference between the two terms, and unless Newsom was supposing that *'lwhym* is here only a term for 'angel', and not 'God', then we would be committed to an angel who irreducibly is God and nothing less than God, which seems not to be her point. Obviously, since she, rightly, asserts that *'lwhym* 'might refer to God or to angels', we should extirpate her infelicity in logic to accord with the spirit of her observation, to become: 'x = y respecting a function (or set of functions) F'. (This approach to identity is well developed by Geach (1980).) That is to say, since in her view (I think correctly) ''*lwhym* . . . might refer to God', it is more accurate to define the identity sign '=' – the equation – to be one of relative identity, i.e., any referent or subject going proxy for God who, or which, does so by satisfying or manifesting features ascribed to God. (As with predicate logic and natural languages, such an equation is applicable whether or not the resulting narrative ascriptions are true or false. So this schema is applicable to polemical contexts in DSS and MT, etc., where the term *'lwhym* is used of subjects who are denounced, and other intentional contexts.)

In the aforementioned quoted judgements Newsom supposes that the Hebrew 'refers' to either God or angels. Leaving aside, for the present, what is intended in her remarks by 'reference', we should query this disjunctive contrast between reference to 'God' or to 'angels' for *'lwhym*.[4] This referential alternation does not have to follow from the linguistic data, though sometimes it is applicable. The present chapter is concerned with those more problematic contexts where the disjunction does not apply. In these uses I shall argue that there is reference inclusive of God and angel in the semantic function of *'lwhym*. Such a proposal is separable from and not necessarily in conflict with the employment of *'lwhm* in for example 11QMelch, interpreted as applying to Melchizedek. It is not here an occasion to enter into, but to note as important, the complex interplay in the Qumran *Sabbath Shiroth* between the ideal transcendental angelic priestly typology, and Newsom (1985) has introduced us to important background for this issue. Possibly Melchizedek is identified as the priest in the Assembly of God at the consecration of the angelic priests (cf. Horton, 1976). Such contexts, implementing thematic interplay between transcendent and human references, appear to circumscribe, not dispute, the interaction of *'lhym* as a designator of transcendent and human agents.

No doubt there is vagueness in some uses of *'lwhym*; but such a judgement may too easily obscure a measurable, albeit dense, sense of *'lwhym* in groups of narratives. The expression *'lwhym is* not a term with an entirely singular sense; and I shall argue that the word is neither homonymic nor indeterminate. A plausible scenario for such a function of *'lwhym* would be (very roughly) an agent whose function is to go proxy for another bearer: for example, an angel standing for the intended (contextually relevant elements of) God's identity.

Although this is not entirely parallel with regard to the semantics of *ml'km* (messengers), yet there is some overlap with *'lhm* with the role of communicating something (from God, or whoever) and its related action. This contiguity of sense reflects similarity in some of their contexts. Schiffman (1989: 49–51) describes the presence of the *ml'kym* in lQSa, 'The rule of the congregation', which emphasises the bearers of *ml'kym* as present in the assembly. These are messengers from heaven who, according to Schiffman, are to stand alongside humans; and he notes Bokser's suggestion that they represent the divine presence. The uses of *'lwhym* pick out the aspects of the bearers that go proxy for God as qualitatively apt realisations of (pertinent features of) deity. Often narratives (such as 11QMelch) employ the term to remonstrate with those agents who have failed to manifest the *'lwhym* identity (or features of it), who, by dint of position or purported function, are bearers of this divine term.

Before discussing texts, it might assist to spell out some basic aspects of this agency proposal. The thesis I am advancing binds together the quite separable roles of depicting angel and God. In this perspective the function of *'lhym* is to mediate properties of the referent of a subject (usually God) through a mediating function (frequently, a transcendental angel, though sometimes a human). This view presupposes that what has often been thought to be ambiguity (and let us not confuse this term with 'vagueness', for which see Williamson, 1994) is a double-tier function within the expression *'lhym*. On this analysis, *'lwhym*'s sense is that of an agent(s) mediating another subject's intentions and/or likeness. (We should of course distinguish this use of 'intention' from 'intentional'. I am not entering into having to postulate the intention with which the author writes.) The point of the foregoing is that within the semantic field there is a functional use which maps *'lwhym* with an agency sense. This use of 'intention' is therefore an intertextual function. It is not here an equation between authorial voice and author, though this connection is not thus disbanded by this more modest applied linguistic priority. To be sure, one might propose that the unconscious (such as refined by Bouveresse (1995) assessing Wittgenstein and Freud, or with Bowie (1993) deconstructing Lacan, or an amalgam of the two) itself has an extended and metaphoric relation to intertextual relations within a semantic field, and retrieve some such notion of an intention of an author(s) mapped into a text, tantalisingly unstable though such a counter-intuitive conception would be (for which see Gibson (1998)). The complex conception of the expression of a communal intention in tradition, as a function of this type of theory, is clearly an important requirement for future research.

Referring to God

Given the formal arguments concerning 'reference'/'refers', here briefly summarised (for further discussion see Dummett, and Gibson[5]), we should employ the categories of reference for *'lwhym* indirectly and with caution. It seems clear that *'lwhym* is not a proper name: it is quantifiable by the article, and scope operators such as *kl*; it does not appear as a proper name for a group, but as a description. And there is within *'lwhym* the ossified plural form, still largely unexplained functionally, and possibly susceptible of being triggered into plural function by paronomasia. Such data require the notion of *'lwhym* ascribing its semantic properties in nominal form, identity or characteristics to God. That is to say, *'lwhym* does not of itself refer. Rather, it is true (or false) of its referent, in much the same way as a predicate is true of its subject. For a term such as *'lwhym* to have a reference, in Newsom's sort of use, tends to trigger or be read with the presupposition that of itself *'lwhym* rigidly designates by reference, a reference only proper to YHWH in MT. But even if these formal analyses were opposed, the thesis being advanced in this chapter still stands on a variety of other interpretations of the linguistic data.

When *'lwhym* is used of a transcendent Melchizedek in 11QMelch it evidently functions to pick out a single bearer. But the scroll requires *'lwhym* to be employed as a description covering a set of such subjects, not least because of its quotation of Psalm 82: 1 representing the assembly of such bearers. In the scroll the heavenly Melchizedek is an agent manifesting God's identity. The fact that the plural form is employed here, and of a singular, maps into usage a stress on *'lwhym* as a function which delineates qualities of a type, and not a proper name-like value.

The function of *'lwhym* neither mediates one person, nor yet allows one to deem other subjects within its scope as homonyms, and it ranges over a very large plural set. But *'lwhym* mediates the identity of God in such a way that God is presented in the first person, or the *'lwhym*'s acts are identified as God's, when the *'lwhym* are accepted as God-sent. As with a merger of televisions with their presenters, they broadcast subjects different from themselves, though their chosen subject imposes advertising constraints. Sanders[6] contributed to reformulating our relations to ancient Christian and Jewish traditions. Two of his points are relevant here. First, Sanders circumscribes the view that after the Babylonian exile Jewish texts tended to employ an intermediary to represent God, and he notes that this does not imply God's remoteness. Secondly, Sanders highlights the ideas that, for Palestinian Judaism, close reading of sacred writings brings the pious reader into God's presence. I wish to re-orientate these two points, and propose a general thesis: in appropriate uses, an intermediary *is* God's presence, under a relative identity notion of identity discussed above and below. Derrida's (1978) view of metaphysics is that it circumscribes the presence of a transcendental property, while he would dispute that any meaning can yield such support. For him, the claim of a presence entails the absence of the feature it linguistically proposes. With *'lhym*, albeit in a radically different world, they suture absence and presence, exemplifying *différance* and thus marking that the referent of, say, YHWH is both present in manifestation and is entirely Other.

A recent trend in Old Testament scholarship rightly emphasises the contrast in sacred biography between a biographic subject as opposed to the 'likeness' of the subject.[7] But some uses of *'lwhym* are part of a theme in which God's identity is mediated by an earthly or heavenly agent going proxy for God. Relative identity is shared between a subject and its representative, or that agent who goes proxy for the subject, or a facet of it, as with the angel reproducing aspects of God. Its internal logic is parallel, in relevant ways, with other relations such as father and son, or any relation in which two or more subjects share common properties or one comes to personify or go proxy for another. This will alleviate the problem of the plural, because part of the syntax of *'lwhym* being employed is a switch mechanism that multiply implements singular and/or plural bearers, because part of the semantics involves mediation of qualities between agent and final referent. Much of the terminology in the narrative fields of *'lhym* includes fellowship language (*'m*, Exodus 3: 12, etc). So the relational tonal semantics are not solely those of 'relation to', but 'relationship with' referring and referent, presence and believer/witness. Thus the deep structure of this feature is that the term, in a certain narrow sense, always is a potential function of a plural subject, going proxy for one (other) subject. The characterisation here is provisional and brief, to be filled out later.

If such a sketch is accurate, we need to re-organise the contrasts and assumed conflicts between singular God versus plural agents to which the term *'lwhym* applied. Angelic uses of this term do not compete with the prime sense of the God-referent to whom this term is finally applied. Agents have the term employed of them because their likeness functions, or is intended, to manifest God's identity. Perhaps to encapsulate the semantic relations here, the notion of a portrait is helpful: it both satisfies its own criterion of identity as an artwork, and in doing so it felicitously represents, with interpretation, the identity of that for which it goes proxy and accordingly to which it refers. The creative research of Macé (1993) complements this approach by composing an explanation of reproduction of personalised visual image in literary form employing abstract predicates in prose; he uses the figure of a camera to achieve this. Imaging and interpretation coincide to satisfy a criterion of identity here in which semantic indeterminacy can be so unified in creativity to comply with a consistent function: the role of the narrative and its characters going proxy for another identity, that of God. The sheer density of such a possibility, rather than indeterminacy, is a fecund source for breeding new types of representation.

'Gods' and God

We should not neglect John 10's *theoi* in Christological discussion:

(A) *Ego eipa theoi este* I said 'you are gods'.

The key logic in (A) is that of, roughly, an equation whose deep structure performs to bind plural subjects with a relative identity function: a 'set of x's = y' respecting F, where 'F' stands for a set of properties which can be used as a criterion of identity for the equation and/or for the subject.

This quotation from Psalm 82: 6 is blended into John's argument between Christ and the Jews about the question of his identity and relationship between father and son. Jesus is presented as claimant to be the Son of God (a phrase we do well to isolate from 'God the son', not only because of the plural form *bny 'lhym* in Psalm 82). Yet the narrative in which (A) is set presents the Jews as interpreters who take this passage to express a different claim, that of equality with God. The passage in John 10 ascribes to Jesus an argument that not only opposes but also is deployed to dispute this claim. The narrative takes Christ to cite (A) as a counterpoise to the allegation of his equality to God. Strangely, since he applies an expression – *theoi* – that enacts an overkill for the task, by applying some sense of divinity not to him, but figures lowlier than he – human judges; by inference – the very people whom he is castigating for sarcastically elevating him to equality with God. This reads if anything like an explicit rebuttal of attempts to attach a substance or absolute identity sense in the reference to God. The narrative pluralises – quantifies – semantics and existence to range over mortals. To be sure, there are a number of changes of sense and divergences between Psalm 82 and John 10; yet it should be noted that we cannot dismiss the foregoing by using the information that the Psalm is Hebrew while John is Greek, since the agency sense is not only constituted by the plural form: the case for agency resides in the narrative frame and rhetoricised functions of the virtual reality matching semantic fields of Psalm 82 and John 10.

The singular term for 'God' is central to Christology. The rarity of singular uses of *ho theos* applied to Christ in the New Testament comprises a position in such semantic fields which are fractured by many post-New Testament uses, though Augustine's almost totally neglected later more mature writings on the Trinity, not least in their uses of the Old Testament, raise fundamental questions which provoke directions for, and concerning what it is to be the status of what is now customarily termed a 'social model' in relational issues regarding 'God'.[8] Nevertheless in *de Trinitate* (Bk I.13), while quoting Psalm 82: 6, Augustine entirely ducks the use of it in John 10: 30, even though later citing the adjacent verse when he came to examine John 10: 30, 'I and my father are one', noting that it is plural not singular (instantiating so it seems, Tertullian's puzzling over why this 'one' is neuter). Controversially consequent on these critical perspectives, one can measure the employment of *ho theos* when applied to the son of God in Hebrews 1: 8, quoting Psalm 45: 7: 'Thy throne, O God.' If we take the approach supported by this type of translation, this quotation cannot of itself be taken to dislocate the agency sense of the *'lhym* origins of *ho theos*: it confirms it. The bearer of *'lhym* envisaged by the composer of Psalm 45 was hardly implementing a substance ontology, particularly since the plural form there applied to an earthly king and narrative functions reflect a contract with and further differentiation of the juridical use of *'lhym* (appropriate for a stylised Solomon) in Exodus 21: 6 of a singular subject. In Hebrews 1: 8, however, the second use of *ho theos* qualifies and functionally subordinates (by anointing) the bearer of the first term to this second. 'God, thy God', is a phrase consistent with the DSS and OT presupposition of non-singular use *'lhym* which is also in harmony with monotheistic representation of a singular referent (or set of relevant features of its identity). Within the perspective of this priority, uses of *'lhym* mediate a depiction of the referent of YHWH (or the final referent of *'lhym*) while also coding a representational function and discrete identity (or relevant set of properties) of the agent of the final referent of *'lhym*. The double use of *'lhym* or an agent manifesting the final deity referent is so sharp in Psalm 45 as to approach Socratic irony for those unaccustomed to the role of the discerning reader of agency: just before the agency use of *'lhym* in Psalm 45: 7, verse 3 tells us that God has blessed the king forever. In 4QBerakhot (4Q286–90), [*hw*]*d whdr* – 'glory and majesty', blesses the earthly king, integrating a quoting allusion to Psalm 45: 4 (see Nitzman (1994: 60), in such a way as to mirror Hebrews 1: 8's use of the agency theme in divine reference. The transfer of *hdr* to the king here generalises the scope of the *'lhym* agency use to the themes which implement it. In the Qumran Psalms scroll 11QPsa, after the last psalm, 150, *hdr* employed in the 'Hymn to the Creator' in a manner reminiscent of Ezekiel 43: 2 in ways which ascribe such divine qualities to the angels (cf. Weinfeld, 1995).

The utilisation of the OT semantic field and theme in Hebrews 1: 8 stands in unexpected but consistent relation to the other plural translation of *'lhym* as *angelous* in Hebrews 2: 7 which cites Psalm 8: 5. It seems naive to ascribe ignorance of this semantic state of affairs to the author on the grounds of a traditional polemical, citation-text mentality that handles programmatic material which, for him, is ossified with respect to agency functions, in particular in view of the rich array of targumic and multifarious Greek translational directions in which the linguistic material continued to develop before, as well as after, OT, and within the other DSS societal groupings, while not least throughout the NT era. There are also the complex unresolved states and relations of the DSS Psalms to the Masoretic Psalter (see Flint, 1994). Although DSS extant parts of Psalms 1–89 are more uniform than later ones, yet there is still ignorance concerning their roles and polemic identities. This cluster of problems is subject to more indeterminacy since we cannot yet adequately generalise over the textual family identities of the DSS, even concerning non-aligned textual elements (see Tov, 1995). These factors, together with the postulated pre-Qumran distinct sources for some of the texts deposited/discovered at Qumran (cf. Schiffman (1995) and the differences between the later fixed Psalter and the Qumran scrolls – generally uniform though such activity was – further disrupts a smoothing out of appeal to a fixed stylised use of 'proof-texts'. Given the foregoing, and the Hebrews' author's acquaintance with the Hebrew singular and plural agency functions of *'lhym* in Psalms 45 and 8, picked out by different Greek nouns, the agency schema of Hebrew DSS and OT is explicitly programmed into New Testament use. Such a distribution does not entail that a term is used with the same thesis in different semantic fields. But the situation as characterised above does place limits on theological conjecture, which exclude an absolute identity and/or substance conception within the New Testament.

Philosophy of live metaphor

This puzzle is enriched by the genetic metaphors of sonship in many DSS and MT contexts, of which Psalm 82 and John 10 are ironised exotic instances.

Some traditional theology presupposes that the shift from plural 'sons of God' to the singular 'son of God' is a difference of ontology, with a divine substance attached to the latter. John's Gospel offers no terminology to specify this, though John develops the theme of the only begotten son. Thomas's later affirmation of 'My lord and my God', in its use of 'God' does not ontologically go beyond the application of *'lwhym* in Psalm 45: 6, and does not quite concur with an LXX 'Lord God' matching of the latter phrase with YHWH in it. Obviously, even so, there is a special type of quality – not only degree of unique divine sonship – being advanced in John; but my point is that this is not crafted from uses of 'God' which involve an ontology of substance. Instead there appears to be a functional theme of agency with 'God', keyed by uses of translations of *'lhym*, which extends into a genetic metaphor of unique sonship. Clearly this sonship domain occupies various levels, from Psalm 82's plural 'sons of God' to Christ, the uniquely begotten one; this uniqueness is constituted by a sonship relationship for which there is no precedent in terms of it occurring earlier than the semantics it has in the New Testament. But the precedent of a typology for unique sonship appears to arise from the semantics of *'lhym* developed in MT and DSS, in which a criterion of identity for reproducing God through an agent is ontologically switched into the begettal of a son for God the father.

Melchizedek and God

Rowland (1982) has discussed how the use of Psalm 82 in the Melchizedek scroll has parallels with the *Testaments of Abraham*, and with the *Similitudes* concerning the heavenly court figure. Whether or not we are disposed to accept his dating of 50 AD for the Jewish texts, or wish to adopt an older date, his scrutiny of the background is valuable. Particularly is this the case if the DSS or parts of them were composed away from Qumran, or were combined with other narratives that led to their influencing the evolution of tradition in the DSS. The coincidence of Jewish texts and Gospel may be informative for their disputing against some commonly shared historical arenas.

The Melchizedek scroll does not of course cite Psalm 82: 6, though it employs verses 82: 1–2; but this gap of thematic development within Psalm 82 is partly overcome since 82: 6 utilises some terms and interrelations that are introduced in the opening of the Psalm. The appropriate lines of the scroll read:

> 9. *hw'h hqṣ/q lšnt hrṣwn lmlky ṣ[dq]l . . . [ ]*
> *wqdwšy 'l lmm[š]lt mspṭ k'sr ktwb*

> 10. *'lyw bšyry dwyd 'šr 'mr 'lwhym [n]ṣb b'[dt'l]*
> *bqwrb 'lwhym yšpwṭ w'lyw 'm[r']lyh*

> 11. *lmrwm šwbh 'l ydyn 'mym w'šr '[mr 'd mty t] spwṭw*
> *'wwl wpny rš' [y]m tś['w s]lh.*

9. He decreed the acceptable year for *Melchizedek* . . .
and the holy ones of God for judgement's rule;
as it is written

10. Concerning him in the songs of David, who said:
'lwhym standeth in the congregation of God; in
among 'lwhym, he judgeth. And concerning him, he saith:

11. Return thou on high. God shall judge the peoples;
and that he said: How long will ye judge unjustly,
and elevate the wicked's face? Selah.

The translation here italicises the Old Testament's quotations or allusions. Isaiah 61: 2 fragmentarily occurs in line 9's 'acceptable year'; line 10b cites Psalm 82: 1; lines 10b and 11a deploys parts of Psalm 7: 8–9, with Psalm 82: 2 enclosing the sequence in line 11b. The employment of some of these expressions, including 'Melchizedek', in New Testament contexts in addition to John, exemplified by Fitzmyer (1971) and Jonge (1965) and Woude's (1965) edition of the scroll, highlights some features shared between John's use of Greek and Semitic material and the Melchizedek scroll, even allowing for the differences of thesis and development reflected in both groups of literatures. When Hebrews 1: 8 states that 'the son' bears the title *ho theos*, this parallels the application of *'lwhym* in the rulership context to Melchizedek in line 10 of 11QMelch, which matches the above ingredients and narrative frame of Hebrews 1: 8 citing Psalm 45: 7:

(B) *ks'k 'lhym: ho thronos sou ho theos*

Emerton (1960) maintained that (A) above is associated with the use of *theoi* to represent angels. Yet 'associated' here, if true, has to include a contrast with 'angels' respecting (B) and (A), because of their subjects, though certainly the MT elsewhere has *'lhym* indicating angels, if one accepts the semantic primacy of senses in the LXX and NT Greek translations of the term. A generalised account needs to incorporate and explain why 'angels' appear to be susceptible of the same word as humans and the incarnation subject. As mentioned in the foregoing, there is the celebrated case in Psalm 8: 5:

(C) *wthsrhw m't m'lkym: elattosatosas auton brachu ti par angelous*

This quotation, taken up in Hebrews 2: 7, reflects a narrow translation tendency; it is also similar to Psalm 137: 1, *angelon*; and Psalm 97: 7, *angeloi*. In these LXX passages the translation is an agency-relation function, one that overlaps with those of (A) and (B). But (C) is more explicit and presents the angelic component value, while humans in (A) replace this angelic value yet the agency function is equivalent for (A), (B) and (C).

Is quantification divine?

It might be assumed that the rendering of *theos* is due to a liberalising tendency because of a partial ossification of the term in, for example, ritual or festal usage. But this sort of approach does not allow for Alexander's (1972: 64) view that, for example, Aquila's retention of the plural *theoi* in Genesis 6: 2 is due to the translator's attention to a functional requirement.

This nest of issues also obliquely engages the shift from plural to singular subject at the semantic level which is syntactically undifferentiated in the *'lhym* form. It is worth proposing here for consideration the idea that there is a live metaphoric or even idiomising contribution in *-ym*. The concept of metaphoricity ascribed to syntax is itself a vast subject for investigation.[9] This topic relates to the differentiation between the use of an expression in a narrative and the way in which it itself can be cross-referred to or mentioned, or in some way alluded to by other words, or functions within the narrative, in addition to its typical use. Quantification itself (for our purposes here, plural to singular shifts) to some degree seems to display counter-intuitive properties, and this can disrupt the semantic applicability of a formal syntactic paradigm. One unexpected feature of the proposed inter-relation between logic and language for the present purpose is the identity of predication.

In relation to this topic, whatever the eventual estimation assigned to the founder of modern logic, Frege,[10] his exposure of the predicative identity of quantification was the first such analysis. Informally expressed, we can interpret quantifiers like *kl*, *ym*, *hkl*, and some uses of *h-*, as predicative or ascriptive functions. A function is an incomplete expression that ascribes a property to a referent, mediating that function by its attachment to a subject term. In principle, this parallel with predication leads to analysis of relations between quantifiers and predicate expressions (fragments and complex groupings). The point of this conception for *'lhym* is that it furnishes a basis for identifying the functional inter-connection between a singular reference to God and the plural use of agent media (for example, *angeloi*, *theoi*). It seems clear that the main focus of such functional cross-connections, even thematically, is that the media of representation (angels, people, the incarnation) are presented to depict, manifest, reveal or embody the Other (subject). This coding of the transcendent God as present in a functional relationship with an agent of manifestation is a contrast that has some parallel with Derrida's (1978) use of *différance*. That transcendence is marked in language is itself a violation of the limits of finite language: what is coded to be present is marked for its referent as an absence. Without wishing to suppose that Qumran and MT readers were aware of this formulation, their concerns with the presence versus absence of divine features in the use of language is taken to be a function of revelation and immanence. It appears to be the case that the logical semantics of God in *'lhym*, as well as its then as yet future translational histories, is tantamount to a complex unconscious mirror of *'lhym*'s intertextual relations of its narrative fields contexts. The common MT conundrum of a formally plural *'lhym* with a singular subject, on this approach, may be a metaphorised use of the plural ending to code for its use as a term which presupposes a medium or media of manifestation whenever God is the topic of reference. This may be construed diachronically as literary and psycholinguistic presupposition of reference for *'lhym*, which is variant in different contexts yet has some residual invariance as to dual or multiple reference involving agency.

The previous paragraph has application to aspects of 11QMelch's use of Psalm 82: 1. The invariance of reference is reified, and plural/singular references maintained and extended in John 10: 33's use of Psalm 82: 6. *'lwhym* occurs in the singular and plural in 11QMelch, line 10, which quotes Psalm 82: 1. The plural formation corresponds to the plural *'lhym* employed in Psalm 82: 6, and which is cited in John 10: 33. So at this level the priorities of Psalm 82, 11QMelch and John's Gospel interlock and display a common element. John 10 develops a condemnation theme in which a failure by Christ's critics to manifest the agency function of *theoi* is central to the presupposition of reference in Psalm 82 and John 10. In 11QMelch (lines 9–10), as well as in Psalm 82 and John 10, the juridical role of divine agents is the theme's pivot; this appears to match the juridical semantic reference core of Exodus 21: 6's ascription of *'lhym to* juridical bearers. We may see this emphasis in 11QMelch, if we accept that 'Melchizedek' unexpectedly replaces 'YHWH' in the scroll's apparent quotation of Isaiah 61: 2 (cf. Fitzmyer, 1971: 262). Here Melchizedek's *'lwhym* function partially reproduces parallel functions of the Isaiah 'YHWH', though we need sharply to restrict and bind such quantification over the two subjects, though the intertextual relations between the passages overtly overlap. It is of course too easy to convert this into an equation in which the John 10 Christ shares the functions of the scroll's Melchizedek. (In addition to many other considerations, it is not obvious that we can consistently employ 'Qumran theology' to support the equation, since the scroll's composition may not have originated at Qumran.) Parallels of function contracted by *'lwhym* in this juridical role, combined with the indictment presented in 11QMelch, Psalm 82 and John 10 are by now evident, however.

A presupposition of the general trend of the foregoing paragraphs (for convenience) can be termed a *phanerosis* relation. Summarily, from a standpoint of outlining *'lhym*'s basic functions, it is that for a function to be one subject, entails that an internal property of this conception is for such a subject to satisfy a criterion of identity of another subject: (it is true or false) that *'lhym* (angels, people) manifest God's identity. Identity is itself a tricky notion. Although God may be simple and certainly singular, in MT and derivatively DSS, God's relations presupposed in semantics and mediation are complex, not to say perplexing. But we do not have to offer a final solution on these matters to establish that representation of theistic identity is various. A consequence of examining relevant features of these matters in the present chapter, as well as other studies (cf. Geach, 1980; Gibson, 1981), I believe, is that identity is relative. Namely, "'x = y" with regard to a function F' (where 'F' is a description or predicate-fragment). In the present context, the two (or more) such conjoined terms could be *'lhym* and YHWH (with the former instantiating an agency role such as that interpreted by *theoi* or *angeloi*, etc.). Wittgenstein's (1998; cf. Summerfield, 1996) pluralist approach to fixing the reference of a name enables us to show that a given use of *'lhym* satisfies at least two criteria. First, a reference to the deity is presupposed. Obviously if this reference is to an intended yet non-existent deity, there will be reference-failure; but the intentional semantics apes the securely referenced semantics to God, and so it has relevant functional parallels with true reference. The metaphoric extension of these type of schemata to non-monotheistic uses of *'lhym* and comparable Northwest Semitic theophanies may help to depict the conflation between proper names and descriptions of deities which is the subject of polemics in the MT. The mode of emphasis in 4QMysteries (Schiffman, 1995) may reflect a concern with such relations at Qumran. The very similarity of competing theological ontologies is armed by the use of 'God' termed of the same sort which, in the nature of the polemic, does not carry with it, in certain contexts, qualities which advertise the differences of predicated identity between conflicting theologies or gods.

Secondly, an entailment of this semantic value is that there is a presupposition of an agent as logical predicate[11] internal to *'lhym*. On this analysis, then, there are two referents, and two logical predicate-fragments to *'lhym*. Of referents: YHWH, and angelic medium; of functions, the semantic value assigned a divine property (crudely, *'lh*), and the plural logical predicate *-ym*. This division of labour, however, is partly a manner of speaking. There are no grounds for supposing that one should treat this as etymology or traditional plural syntax. The recent work of Chomsky (1995) would be a strategy for taking this topic further as a subset of a philosophy of language.

In traditional DSS, MT and Greek syntax conceptions, quantification is somewhat isolated in comparative terms from ascription of semantic values in predication. As far as the functions of these syntaxes go, clearly, they have significance for applied grammars, though one can also propose an extension of the critical work by Barr (1961) and Gibson (1981, 2000: 202–5, 250–2) in which institutionalised semantics (such as the, still recurrent, confusion of a word with a concept) is extended to the subject of syntax. The following comment could be read as a fragmentary scenario for such a project, though with a constructive aim. The issue of quantification, in particular quantification shifts from plural to singular, and *vice versa*, connects with whether or not *'lwhym*, in being a function of angelomorphic categories, can also, in the same narrative space–time field function, thereby refer to (or be presupposed to be true of) a singular referent. 'Mention' is that operation in which a linguistic item within the narrative is itself the referent of the term, which in this case is to strike a pun. Since 'mention' is a species of 'use' (i.e., a term's function in a narrative), it would be incorrect to suppose that in principle if there is paronomasia in a term's use, then we have to accept that the contribution expression's normal use is suspended or cancelled or inoperable. In other words, there is a routing within the narrative thematics and its use of semantic values to retain, as part of the use of a term that refers or is true (or false) of its referent, a semantic contract between the contents of paronomasia and the usual referring function. This impinges on the above suggestion that, without falling into a diachronic conflation, there is some degree of invariance prior to DSS in MT, carried into Qumran angelology and theistic representation, concerning the metaphorised plural ending and multiple reference and agency in *'lhym*.

Such distinctions appear to match some of the semantics in Genesis 1: 26–7. This passage, notoriously, displays an apparently plural use of *'lhym* ('Let us make'), prior to, and subsequent to, which the same form *'lhym* is qualified by singular syntax, and while narrating the same theme of plural action. The philosophy of action for this is a continuum between God and agents, satisfying a single criterion of identity. This is not to say, since the identity is relative to a function, that in there are no criteria differentiating media from the source of reference. There is evidence of similar shifts in quantification in an Ugaritic non-monotheistic semantic field that is noted in Gibson (1976: 281). This polemicised use seems to compete with competition in which disputes about the identity of reference engage with commonly shared frames of the form of reference. In the appropriate form, this implies that in the states of affairs in which there is ontological disagreement, there is in Semitic material the grounds for generalised dissent because there is a presupposed parallel use of reference and quantification.

The possibility of disagreement entails the precondition that there is a set of expressions that agree with a disputing culture, for dispute to have expression. Chomsky, of course, systematised the conjecture that universal syntax has a mirror universal semantics, though in later work he complexifies this approach in Chomsky (2001) by adding concepts of indeterminacy of consciousness. The status of this claim can be settled by examining reference-claims in counter-cultures to discover how quantification conjoins with reference to yield a generalised semantics. Study of DSS in conjunction with the Bible is a historically dense instance of such a collision and partial continuity. The trick is to estimate the scale of the crash and its survivors in references to God. So we are here concerned with the identity of what it is to be a criterion of the history of ideas, exemplified by the conjunction of philosophy of language and applied linguistics.

Identity of reference to God

Relevant logic features that the above has proposed of the applied semantics of reference in *'lhwym*, informally stated, are (where 'object language' is constituted by data from DSS, MT and NT[12]):

(1) x has the same property F as has y, where the class of Fs is constructed from predicables applied to values of x and y in the object language.

So, where "r" stands for referring in a subject, say 'x':

(2) What x^r has the referent of y in the object language?

(3) The referent of y is the simulated identity of x satisfying a relative identity criterion.

Therefore:

(4) There is a dependency relation of y upon x^r since y occurs with an array by which y is a replica of corresponding elements predicated of x^r.

(4) rests on the premise that:

(5) y is the linguistic counterpart or image of x's referent correctly arranged and articulated so that y goes proxy for x^r or reproduces the specified class of x's properties.

Consequently,

(6) The identity relation '$x = y$', with '=' defined by a set of Fs occurring in the object languages, can quantify over a single referent identity which is represented by plural referring functions.

(7) The use and mention of '$lwhym$ has a presupposition of agency as a function of its reference, and therefore it incorporates a logical syntax which can simultaneously refer two or more referents, with a semantic value ascribed to the final referent of the term.

Is philosophy of dead language possible?

Philosophers of logic have not yet fully explained what possibility is. This somewhat interferes with the question. It will not escape your notice that the Dead Sea Scrolls do not address this or consequent issues. Is the above question a subset of the query: 'Is a philosophy of literature possible?' (This question is tackled more extensively in Gibson, forthcoming a.)

Some views settled within analytical philosophy act as an imperialism that scorns literary theory and the prospect of placing it in some sort of conjunction with logic. The present writer is not a formalist who envisages a programme to mechanise creative literature. The frontiers of philosophical logic have, or should have, long since passed the site-debris of formalist excavations where there roamed such ghostly forms of simplifying Razors (see chapter 2). The future of logic seems to be like this: it is deeper and more complex than most have thought, like great creative Art: unexpected, counter-intuitive, and inimical to formal aesthetics. This itself approaches paradox, since logic is usually thought to be consistent generalised form with inference relations. But any predicate calculus worthy of the term entails paradoxes (cf. Sainsbury, 1991; Priest, 1995). So back to the blackboard. Perhaps DSS and biblical writers, unconscious of these matters, may better furnish us by their technical ignorance with uses in literature that more adequately furnish us with a path to knowledge. In other words, is literature a source for solving problems outside of itself; or, does one require solutions from outside of logic and/or philosophy so as to resolve the identity (identities) of logic?

Fragility and certainty combine to join logic and literature. To do logic is to solve everything else. The semantics of God occupy these positions, though we have to do with the absence of universality in literature's history. We have seen in earlier chapters the effects of the ways in which some standard logic systems generate propositions that entail paradox. After the First World War Wittgenstein began to explore, and in his crisis of 1929–30 determined a consequence of this state of affairs. In a sense we have only the barest glimpse of anything significant in logic or literature. A future renaissance would be founded on more generalised admission of this ignorance than is perhaps now possible within the confines of what is taken to be the theory of understanding.

I am here considering a novel approach to this issue: choose a dead language narrative; apply some logic to it, and find that such ancient usage is no less logical than our language. Furthermore, let us attend to problematic uses that involve a familiar range of substantive metaphysical problems. For example, the semantics of God in ancient literature inadvertently reverses over and trashes the assumption that natural language usage is untouched by distinctions known to our logics. To handle even straightforward purported expression of God presupposes a proposition about what it is to be language about God, which is a subset of a more general presupposed answer to questions about the identity of language. Such a strategy will also be of value to literary analysis or, say, to exploration of the Dead Sea Scrolls.

Gibson (forthcoming b) argues that relations within literary and culture theory are logically disturbed. This is not the place to rehearse a theory attempting to resolve conflicts between philosophy and literary theory, especially in the recondite sphere of dead languages, though it almost is. Summarising the concepts presented in Gibson (2000, 2000a, 2001), briefly and crudely outlined, the fundamental element for linking applied linguistics, literary theory and analytical philosophy (the last taken to include logic and philosophy of language) is as follows – and clearly, such a theory would have to be strong enough to operate as a generalisable explanation of language, and not be a hole-in-corner hypothesis for DSS phenomena: formal logic and philosophical logic are species of live metaphor. Literary usage is constituted by live metaphor. Reference itself is a form of live metaphor. Relations between logic and literary language are ones of live metaphor. Deep in literary usage, and deep within logic, there are logics unmapped by standard institutional traditions. A reason for this is that we are as yet in a primitive circumstance in researches into logic and literature (rather like medieval alchemists assuming that they discovered microphysics of metals).

As I have been arguing, a surface symptom of this state of affairs is the phenomenon of counter-intuition, according to which the contradictory or contrary of a statement proved by experts in the field is discovered to be true (Gödel's

Theorem is an instance of this, and Fermat's Last Theorem is a less obvious case). This is relevant to literature because counter-intuition is a function of creativity: disclosure, concealed in literary form. It is plausible to propose that in the *Poetics* Aristotle employed logical terms there, extended live metaphorically from his formal metalogical writings, because he judged that formal logic and creative literature are co-extendable species of metaphor. To be sure, just because Aristotle might have been correct on the proposal that logic applies to creative literature, and terminology for it, does not imply that the theses he attached to them are right. For example, as Green (1995: 37) notes, Luke's theology of God and the angels hardly allows Aristotle's distinction that privileges the action over the actor. A stronger concept dismantles Aristotle's thesis: a criterion of God's identity can be depicted by another identity (i.e. the latter can go proxy for the former), contra *Poetics* 6 and 9.

In the present analysis applied semantics and logic marry over the reference of a term. The earlier part of this chapter sketched how reference is a fundamental semantic value of DSS and MT. (If one disputes standard Frege reference theory, a complex theory of indexical predication might be constructed.[13]) I shall assume that we can, in principle, paraphrase one of these programmes into the other, in relevant reference uses, cumbersome though it would be; but I shall stick to what is better developed, that of reference theory, and propose that reference is a matter of live metaphor, with the semantics of theistic terms commonly manifesting these properties. Reference has three ingredients: referring, the relation of reference, and referent. Frege in fact used only one word for the three elements, as if he metaphorically extended the scope of the one, German, term, derived from *deuten* ('point'). These three features are thus metaphorically related. This metaphoricity may apply to other abstract terminology.[14] Paradox can be viewed as a device for proving that metaphor obtains in the contradictory propositions that comprise it, since they are not thereby manifestations of well-formed 'literal' sense. There are paradoxes pervading the large fields of meaning that comprises philosophy and literature. Whereas literature glories in them, analytical philosophy has swept them under the carpet – on which we frequently stand. Therefore it eventually follows that the conjunction of live metaphor in logic and the correct recognition of the qualifying implication of the presence of paradox, constructs a bridge between logic and literature. The logical semantics of God in DSS, MT and NT have already effectively portrayed this earlier in the chapter.

Metaphoric 'gods'

Live metaphor has not been given extensive attention, though the expression has some currency. 'Live metaphor' is the neglected sister of 'dead metaphor': '*root* of a tree' transmogrifies in death to: '*root* of a problem', a state of health distinct to live metaphor. A live metaphor goes proxy for some other subject or property by partially reproducing the other subject as a function of its semantic value, as with a photograph. This concurs with the frequently canvassed thesis that description of God is metaphorical, though this evident point should lead to the question of what metaphor is. Since definition is partly a disjunction of what it is not, it is embarrassing to recognise that no one has yet defined what 'literal' is. Yet, for example, Hanson (1992: 560) unquestioningly asserts that Symmachus' 'version [of Exodus 24: 10] confirms our impression that the Greek translators could accept the idea of seeing God in a vision rather than seeing him literally'. Again: 'it is possible therefore that [in Exodus 33: 11] the LXX's use of *enopios enopio* may be a slight modification of the literal Hebrew meaning' (560–1). But 'seeing him literally' and 'literal Hebrew meaning' are deconstructed by the asymmetries surrounding the presence and absence of a form of the Other in relation to a reproduction of that form, as the reader, I hope, has seen above. Consequently, I maintain that *'lhym* is a live metaphor, and argue that it participates in the construction of a live metaphoric thematic semantic field.

Since Aristotle's *Poetics* 21, the shifting sense of a term from one to another subject as the defining feature of dead metaphor has been given much attention. Black (1962, 1993) suggested an interaction between literal and metaphoric senses in which it is problematic to posit a straightforward regulative contrast between the two senses. There are many subspecies of metaphor. Dead metaphor has been the central target for such research. Conversely, uses of *'lwhym* satisfy requirements for being live metaphor. Live metaphor has received less sustained study. As mentioned earlier, Cohen (1993) develops a thesis on metaphor that can be applied to live metaphor, though he does not use the term. He contrasts an actual 'lion' with a 'stone lion'. The latter is a live metaphor, and it reifies the actual lion so as to reproduce a likeness, which therefore satisfies a criterion of identity for being a lion type, though it is not a lion. Cohen explains this as the preservation of presuppositions between actual and stone lion, together with deletion of some others (no actual fur, etc. in the case of the live metaphoric lion), and addition of others to preserve the similarity (stone legs with the live metaphor, to reproduce likeness). Here we have a semantic contract that complexly juggles with the replacement of tokens to preserve the representation of the identity of a subject. This parallels the ways in which *'lwhym* is a term that can be distributed over different media or agencies to manifest the final referent – God. The nearest state of affairs in modern experience which reflects the logic of *'lhym* agency is that of a photograph (as with Macé, 1993) or televised mediation of identities. Here a 'bearer' televised medium mediates a criterion of identity to convey a subject that it (as a construct of instrumentation) is not. DSS and biblical linguistic phenomena likewise encode visualisation in the semantics of *'lhwym*, not least in the use of angels to implement the epiphanies, for example in the use of Ezekiel 43: 2 in the Qumran Psalms Scroll. The most explicit case of this live metaphoric reproduction is when the identity of the angel is dispersed in emergence of the first person pronoun of YHWH to which *'lhym* is thematically joined.

The metaphoric roles of *'lhym* are variously specialised and internally differentiated. In 11QMelch line 9's purported use of Isaiah 61: 2, there 'Melchizedek' and 'YHWH' strike different semantic contracts since the former is a divine proxy for the latter subject, in which the proper name 'YHWH' refers to the *'lhym* (in line 10) who is, not an agent. This switchover is similar to the metonymy metaphor as a vehicle for personification, as advanced by Lakoff and Johnson (1981: 33–4), in which Melchizedek personifies YHWH.

In this personification by *'lhym* there is an enriching function because two subjects become tied together, as one mediates the other. Often a personifying metaphor may employ an identity relation figuratively, such as 'I wisdom dwell with prudence' in Proverbs 8: 12. Likewise, photographs personify subjects, rather like angelomorphic categories that personify YHWH. In this perspective *'lhym* are personifying live metaphors that go proxy for an intended divine personal identity.

A structural feature of the lines 10 and 11 in 11QMelch is that the *'lwhym* construed to be the singular, as a way of describing Melchizedek, refers to God's actions that his judging agent carries out (a point mentioned in 11a). This precisely is *'l* ('God's') judging as implemented by his *'lwhym*. But 11QMelch lines 10–11 give priority to the singular *'lhym* of line 10, a member of the earth-based *'lhym*; yet this singular *'lhym* (Melchizedek) is qualitatively distinct to them. As the contrast becomes crass, Melchizedek is instructed to return to heaven so that *'l* can judge these earthly *'lhym* judges employing his judge Melchizedek in heaven untouched by the sentences and yet be the advocate of them, with a transparent nuance on Psalm 110. The use of Psalm 82 in 11QMelch thus fairly matches the thematic rhetoric of the psalm, and the employment of it in John 10 conforms to the *'lhym*; as Carr (1981: 89–92) argues, this type of Melchizedek figure strongly connects with 1 Corinthians 15, where the judgement theme is developed. The condemned *'lwhym*, presumably alluded to in line 11 which quotes Psalm 82: 2, are judged defective because they do not embody the predicates which satisfy the criterion that encodes a reference to God via his agents in virtue of revealing God's judgements.

Exodus 3: 2–6 depicts an equation of identity between angel and God, but which commences with the term *ml'k*, and binds the first person pronoun of Yahweh with *'lhym* as medium of manifestation. Targum translation of Psalm 8: 5's *mml'ky'* embodies ancient interpreting acceptance on aspects of this relational schema, other cases occurring in Genesis 21: 17–9, 22: 17, 31: 11–13; Judges 6: 11–16. If the Genesis 1: 26–7 creation use of *'lhym*, as developed in the previous section, is accurately rendered, this relationally mirrors this schema with the plural pronoun complementing *'lhym* as a single term gathering both God and angels within its subject-scope, with Psalm 8: 5's allusion to creation. The likeness and image of God are replicated in the likeness and image of the agent-angels who replicate these functions in Adam, because the angels manifest the God whom they mirror. This type of semantic field and thematic interrelations between angelomorphic terminology and *'lhym* perform as a cross-fertilisation of agency between transcendent categories and created form.

So in the domain of the above contexts, *'lhym* is a live metaphor of a specialised sort. Again, rather like (if one may be forgiven the anachronism for purposes of illustration) televised or photographed reproduction of referent identities, *'lhym* offers a claim of simulation of the identity of a referent other than the medium itself, but in which the basic function of the medium is to be that identity. On this basis, *'lhym* is the literary tautology of visual reproduction, a sort of literary painterly poetics. In short *'lhym* is a live metaphor. Perhaps Caird (1980: 66) was tracking this feature when he wrote of double reference, or double derived reference. Current literary theory research particularly in French can be utilised to enhance the presentation of this visualisation in the literary (see Gibson 1998). The basic work stems from research on Mallarmé's *Un Coup de Dés*, its relation to symbolism, and projection of literary conceptions in narrative space and action, by Bowie (1978, 1993), Scott (1988), and Reynolds (1995). I suggest that one can paraphrase this live metaphorisation into a logical narrative metaphoric world by adapting some concerns in David Lewis's (1986) plurality of other worlds' thesis, as in chapter 5 above. (Clearly, this is not tantamount to accepting Lewis's ontology.) In this conception indexicality of pronoun and space–time are equatable, and co-extensive. Worlds can be reproduced in variant forms, and are accessible to each other by indexicalisation. Within the ancient purview of the above DSS and biblical narrative worlds of *'lhym*, such indexicalisation and matching of reified identities was the custom of the revelation of divine personal identity. Certainly, the theses in the ancient and modern world and their levels of formulation are fundamentally different. But the logic of live metaphor and reproduction of a world by indexicalisation have substantial parallels. Although the expression of live metaphor by use of modern electronic media is vastly different from ancient religious creativity, yet the functional core of such technology has externalised a similarity between it and an ancient dynamic of divine simulation of identity by *'lhym*. This is not because of any media connection between the two; it is because both implement the conditions of the concept of communication. It is the metaphoric logic of reproduction of identities, not the technical medium that carries and comprises the match between ancient and modern live metaphor.

In the later medieval European world many theologian-philosophers found it almost impossible adequately to get their heads around the reproduction of absent identities into spatially present agency, concerning intuitive cognition and imperfect intuitive cognition, for example that of Ockham. The fourteenth-century Aureoli was a disputed exception, arguing that intuitive cognition can be truly functioning if an individual only appears to be present, though is not.[15] Since we should be aware of the great gap between ancient and modern ways of perception, we may also take opportunity to recognise the various subtleties of the narrative fields of *'lhym* that long ago offered a conception of reproducing an absent identity in present function. This purview resolves a problem thrown up by a number of ways of attempting to represent the perceived tensions of *'lhym* and its counterpart *theoi* and some uses of *theos*. Fitzmyer (1971: 261) states that the word *'lhym* must refer to others than God, though he does not seem to want to exclude reference to God as well; yet he does not pursue the matter. In the light of the foregoing *'lhym* is a live metaphor with a capability within the one use in a narrative of multiple reference.[16]

Identity in Christology

John transforms the live metaphor typology, among other things, by stating: 'he that hath seen me hath seen the father; and how sayest thou then, Show us the father?' (14: 9). A presupposition of this identification partly derives from the polemics of John 10. The disputants misconstrue the force of the metaphoric referring function in *theos* with regard to agency: 'thou, being a man, makest thyself God' (10: 33). Their mythologisation of Christ's relational stance is fraught with a witless almost Neo-Platonic ontological litany of media mis-representation. They seem nearly to purvey the recurrent tendency to ossify the count noun *theos* into a proper name. Having undermined the interlocutors with the neuter 'I and my father are one [what]?' the Johanine narrator reports that the correct move is to instantiate the live metaphor of Psalm 82: 6, which triggers into ironic life their singular *theos*, bound by their referent God's first person pronoun, with the plural *theoi*, which effectively quantifies over the first person and deconstructs their singularity: 'I said Ye are gods? If he called them gods, unto whom the word of God came, and the Scripture cannot be broken; Say ye of him, whom the Father hath sanctified, and sent into the world, Thou blasphemest; because I said, I am the Son of God?' Here the metaphoric agency function of *theoi*, which embraces the scope of *'lhym*, is thrown down as a gauntlet to block the equality claim. Perhaps the role of Psalm 82: 6 here, and the way it acts as a deconstruction to fix the assertion of Christ being the son of God, requires attention different from some traditional treatment of John 10.

The live metaphoricity of *theoi* and its relation to 'father' constitutes a presupposition of inference to Christ as son of God, not the singular form *theos*. (*Monogenes theos*, the reading of the circa 200 AD Bodmer II papyrus, and the original hand of the Sinaiticus, are not problems on the present live metaphor interpretation of *theos/theoi*; improbable as the reading may be, it is sensitive to this function of live metaphor turned into the ontology of the father and the son.) The radical move, then, in terms of the antecedents of the multiple agency of the plural noun for God is that its semantic value has a new live metaphor ontology: the conjunction of God as father of his son. For the first time this transforms the interiority[17] of the communicative relational use of *'lhym* into relational familial ontology. That is to say, the presuppositional history of crucial uses of *'lhym* is deconstructed, condensed and transformed by the creation of a new live metaphor: the former live metaphor becomes the person of which it is now conceived of as the inexorable source.

In contrast, back down the road at Qumran, *'lhym* displayed a retreat in the adoration of the past *'lhym* as live metaphor for the mimesis of present perfect fantasy, without managing to go beyond reflections on the secrets of creation's parental relationships (4QMysteries[a], fragment 6.II). Qumran manuscripts show that the terminological semantics of *'lhym* preserved the letter of much of the MT semantic fields, but not the spirit of creativity in the live metaphor representation of God. The shift, from simulation of divine identity by a proxy presence, to the rebirth of the live metaphor as a vehicle for divine fatherhood and sonship, is a type of creative morphogenesis in which a counter-intuitive synecdoche is condensed from the live metaphor metonymy. Bowie (1993: 45) has offered a way of unlearning Lacan, as Lacan unlearned Freud, keeping in mind the absence from Freud of a conception of the future:

> One of the peculiar virtues of the Lacanian approach to theorising is that it does not require adherence to a stabilised and jealously safeguarded lexicon or conceptual arsenal. Lacan invites theorists of whatever persuasion to rediscover the pleasures, the mad exhilarations, of the future tense . . . 'The future' as Lacan describes it is a summons not to 'free' speculative play, but to inventiveness within an extirpable framework of constraints, just as the ripple and shimmer of his word-play . . . is propelled by a sense of paternal interdiction.

One of the tasks of literary theory here, as applied to the conjunction of Qumran and the New Testament (without assuming any exhaustive influence from the former to the latter), is to dislodge to the necessary degree the notion of community from theological apologetics. How do we explain that the original logic of, for example, John's literary creativity came to its future from a Freudian past that has the makings of community indoctrination that typically destroys the individual authorial voice? Accordingly, urgent tasks for DSS and biblical research are to separate ancient egoism from the communal subversion of originality; to examine what it is to be literary creativity, in addition to the function of communal tradition, as a path to construct a semantics of God.

As for the relations of logic, applied linguistics and literary theory which may service this complex conjunction of tradition with creativity, are we not now in a position to recognise, with Wittgenstein,[18] as against Frege (1969) that the distance separating what it is to be logic and literary originality is not as great as the latter?[19] The way, for example, in which Wittgenstein used dialogue, as exposed by Jane Heal (1995), to investigate issues in logic and language is a neglected counter-intuitive perspective by which, also, to comprehend some of the greatness of ancient literary creativity and its logics. The semantics of God is a suitably recondite challenge for such a perspective, which may yet throw light on the identity of language. We have seen that this identity relates to matters concerning not only reasoning but also mentality and concepts of personal identity. The next chapter examines these issues in relation to metaphysics and transcendence.

9 Modern philosophy and ancient consciousness

Philosophy of alternative cultures

Previous chapters have implicitly assumed the importance of further scrutiny of concepts of mentality and consciousness to issues discussed so far in this book. Contemporary research tends to explore these questions either in their present manifestations or in relation to a narrow specific range that is a result of past Eurocentric perspectives, such as drawing on the Classics or Greek culture. This continues to be of particular value; yet alternative ancient sources and worldviews have bearing on our contemporary concerns, and could make a considerable difference to how we shape fundamental questions and their answers. For example would an as-yet metaphysical philosophy of ancient consciousness based on, for example, Sumerian narratives result in a concept of the mind different from those that hold sway now? As Gibson (2000a) showed, a Freudian viewpoint is far from the complete picture of the Near Eastern world's concern with mentality and symbol. Beyond such issues of course is the question of whether or not such a topic as 'philosophy of mind' is just one philosophy that encapsulates what it is to be the mind, or if philosophy of 'mind' in different cultures will produce a plurality of philosophies. Even if the answer to such a query is in the negative, research investigating the impact of hitherto philosophically uninvestigated ancient data could affect the shape of certain issues, and give grounds for supposing that there are neglected ancient symbols contributing to the formation of the unconscious.

Is logic applicable to identity?

Is it possible to develop a philosophical logic, or philosophy, of culture that accurately generalises (supervenes) over ancient and modern cultures? Rorty (1979, 1997), for example, supposes that we cannot; this chapter argues that one can. The first person pronoun 'I' is a convenient starting-point. It is one of the most persistent occasions for the issue of supervenience, as well as a most elusive one. Does the first person pronoun have one or many identities? Should this question have different answers if applied to earlier historical periods?

Such an agenda presupposes a focus on fundamental questions of generalisability and identity, however. It is not uncommon for some people to assume that logic does not apply to some of the above topics. Nihilist subjectivity is one such example, which has found a natural home in some theologies. One does not have to suppose that an imperial view of logic holds for one to demonstrate that such a position is incoherent and misrepresents logic.

Even within the pluralist Dewy/James priorities of relativist pragmatism, a distinguished logician such as Isaac Levi (1997) insists that it is not possible for a person to hold a coherent grasp of a topic without relying on rational principle external to or independent of that topic. It seems, for example, that this policy has to supervene even over people who deny context-independent principles of rationality, for the reason that subjective argument does implement context-free (or context-eliminable) rationality even when a user purports to demur from it. But such considerations should be complemented by recognition (as Seigfried, 1996: 34–6 argues) that Descartes's separation-anxiety, that splits reason from emotion, underestimates the significance of pragmatic biological functions; it does not follow from this insight that an organic holistic framework has therefore isolated the role of reason, however.

Clearly, even someone who affirms that he 'does not believe that there is such an expression as his own true statement' ('there is no black and white') either has unwittingly acceded to a recognisable logical use of 'not', and therefore contradicted himself, or not succeeded in communicating to us the putative 'sense' of his mind. If the latter, he will have to explain to us his notion of affirmation and negation of which we are entirely ignorant. Even if the notion of truth is for him so weakened as to absorb an unstable sense of probability, he will have implemented the asymmetry between third and first person forms of expression (cf. Levi 1997: 37–40), because we are excluded from his alleged first person insight. This is not a problem of knowing his sense, and our disputing its coherence. It is the prior issue of his having no assumed internal comprehension of the notion that he claims to have expressed.

Of course one may wish to pass by in silence the question of whether or not we know of a logic that nets the law of what is possible. But let us suppose that, for some ontological and psychological human space–times, a law of contradiction is true. 'I am a woman' will attract dissent from my wife. Within this perspective the identity of 'am' necessarily is self-evident and incontrovertible, unless I am lying – which would be paradoxical in any case. (My overall strategy in this position is akin to what one may interpret as Aristotle's position in *De Interpretatione* concerning future contingents: not a law for all future tensed propositions; but a principle that, for a given proposition with which we are dealing, there is the entailment that it has a negation which one has to recognise in knowing its un-negated sense.)

There is absolute identity, i.e. one in which a substance or essence is presupposed when one identifies 'x is y' (Wiggins, 1980). In contrast, there is relative identity, in which one treats 'x is y' as a restricted identification in which a group of features F comprise the equation (Geach, 1980; cf. Lewis, 1991). In this chapter I will adopt the second, relative identity thesis. And we will still meet problems when we consider personal identity.

From the standpoint of epistemology, the generalised absolute identity relation, 'For all Proper Names there is an identically matching set of first person pronoun uses', or 'PN = I', is false or accidentally true, since they do not work for all PN contexts (e.g., sleeping, two-way amnesia); nor does the alleged third person replacement of the first person – the third person indirect reflexive – 'she herself' function to replace all first person uses. A singular occurrence of a relative identity, '"PN = I" with respect to a property (or properties) F', may appear less unsatisfactory. With respect to what property is it that such proper name semantics act as a substitute for the first person? This question bears on its face the absence of a strong enough claim to block the entailment that: if the PN indexes the personal identity of a bearer, then this identity is marked by the first person.

There are at least two reasons. First, at most only some properties of personal identity are shared through the equation. Secondly, there is no guarantee that these properties are necessary to the identity of the bearer. For example, 'Myra Hindley was known by Lord Longford and by Marcus Harvey' does not entail that they know, or agree on, the (or all the) necessary properties of her personal identity. Imagine three replies. Lord Longford: 'She is no longer the woman who killed those children.' The artist who portrayed her face, Marcus Harvey: 'I never met either of her.' Mother of a victim: 'My child has never been found; Myra Hindley killed her.'

Consequently, even if, or when, we possess criteria of identity for proper names, these are not tautologous with the corresponding criteria for what it is to be the (or a) bearer of the first person. And we should acknowledge our limitations in comprehending what it is to be a proper name in relation to such criteria. Gibson (2001) aims to explain how some criteria of logical proper names (partly based on the study by Dummett, 1981) comply with the senses of proper names in an array of natural language contexts in some ancient Near East languages. That investigation showed how features such as pun, idiom and epithets (definite descriptions) integrate with these logical explanations; but I did not reach a conclusion concerning the extent to which these logical criteria are stipulative for natural languages regarding proper names.

Bob Hale (1996) develops an analysis that attempts to refine and extend Dummett's criteria, constructed in combination with an interpretation of Aristotle's criterion that substance does not have a contrary. Hale's addition to research does not prove in principle that these criteria always expose what it is to be a proper name in all natural language uses. He measures degrees of difference between formal and natural uses, yet Hale further secures and extends the applicability of Dummett's thesis, while also outlining how it is that natural and formal categories contain complex divergence. So there is good and bad news: there is a set of logical criteria mirroring the complex conditions of convergence to, and departures from, decidability in natural language usage.

It eventually follows from these considerations that we cannot specify the referential identity of an inner sense for the first person pronoun. The main reason for this is that in typical logic the first person is supposedly a substitution-instance of the third person proper name class; but since there are complexities dependent on use within which there are sometimes undecidable variables, as well as intentionality, in employment of proper names, the significance of the first person cannot always be read off from its relation to its proper name. What largely gives the first person continuity with the sense of its proper name is that it is taken to refer. And we shall see reason to question this presupposition, and replace it with a weakened sense of 'identify'.

Knowledge of other minds

This mixture of knowledge and ignorance, which we manifest regarding logic of personal reference for proper names and the first person pronoun, has a corollary in the epistemology of mind. We need to take scepticism seriously; yet we do have knowledge. The matter of balance in apportioning these two opposed states is difficult and deep.

Edward Craig (1991) has argued that we do not have decisive reasons for universally assigning to each other understanding of the mental states of other people, in particular even in the situations of correctly having some knowledge and reasons for truly characterising such subjects, but he warns that we should be wary of taking this to imply that we always do have significant knowledge of inner states. We have some understanding of outer and inner states that comprise being human, while we do not have determinate conclusions about many unobservable inner states. Nevertheless consciousness seems to be a unique function. Obvious yet important is the feature that consciousness supervenes over other phenomena in a way in which they do not supervene over it. That we do not have perfect understanding of other minds is no evidence that we do not have knowledge of temporally separated aspects of the external world, since we have some capability of truly predicting and generalising propositions that are true. (For example, we can claim it to be true that there was mental activity in ancient Mesopotamia, on account of sites and their compositional tablets.)

These premises enable one to infer that the strong form of Rorty's (1979) mirror of nature, in conjunction with Rorty (1997), that we are frozen into the limits of our world, is false because we know general and specific truths outside of, and remote from, our experience. From this position it can also be argued that, if Rorty's view were to be true, it cannot be shown to be correct outside the present, since the present is its self-proclaimed prison. So it is internally inconsistent for Rorty to allege that one can thus supervene over a large domain external to the mirror of nature.

Speaking from the first person standpoint about other minds has some parallel with this series of contrasts and comparisons. We know elements of the past, just as we comprehend other speakers, though with some differences, including the state of affairs that the site-debris and compositional contents have parallels, to some degree, with a third person's utterances addressed to oneself. We may recognise statements that attest to multiple personalities expressed by individuals in the third person, yet not know how to define them or their interpersonal relationships.

Likewise we may know some of the sense of a given third millennium BC Sumerian tablet and its Syrian context, without understanding whether a Syrian composed it, though we know that he had a personal identity. Some distinctions between knowing and understanding are applicable here. The conditions that are satisfied for one to have cognisance of those propositions we know to be true, or to be true or false, of another mind, do not thereby entail that we have a grasp of even the conditions knowing of, or understanding, all or most of the implications which are internal to the sense of such propositions. I argue that, even so, by chess-like strategies, we can engage with our own and ancient empirical data so as to gain insights by a conjunction of one's own with other minds.

A first person account of oneself is in principle fraught with limitations, in addition to straightforward problems of self-deception of the sort documented by David Pears (1982). Sometimes this is because of a failure of deliberation in the activity of forming judgement (cf. Wilkerson, 1997: 127–9); in certain cases irrationality occurs when someone either rejects an external canon of reason or insists that his irrationality is logical. A basis for this limitation is mirrored in our incapacity to perceive and/or articulate an identical concept (or synonymous representation) of a given concept that we believe we hold. The mind could be a zone of the sublime or a Pandora's box. That is to say, having a concept does not entail having accurate representation of it as an internal property of our comprehension of it. We not only have incorrect concepts of a given concept that we articulate, we also do not readily deploy a perceptual facility to differentiate between series of weak and strong concepts (i.e., interpretations) internal to our grasp of a given concept, and their interrelated entailments as well as contingencies. This goes for knowing us as well as other people from their standpoint of the first person.

As Frege (1977) observed in one of his last journal articles, 'I have an idea of myself, but I am not identical with this idea.' (He unwittingly indirectly affords us evidence of the truth of his point because, despite his acute consciousness of the importance of truth in the function of judgement in what it is to be true thought, and how it pertains to judging the identity of the first person, in the same journal he also published a Pandora's box of obscene anti-Semitic thoughts.)

This state of affairs is further complicated by the often-intrusive roles of imagination and conjecture in one's attempts to construct concepts about one's own personal identity. In the state of affairs in which the foregoing is applied to our knowledge of other minds, and also to one's attempts to comprehend oneself, it is futile to anticipate a consequence, namely, that we have an understanding of the referent of others' or one's own first person(s), on the basis of partial success we have in having knowledge of others, and oneself.

Cogito ergo sum

Descartes is often thought to have avoided assumptions about the third person by his method of doubting in the first person. But his position collapses by means of an inadvertently self-imposed, albeit disguised, *reductio ad absurdum*.

Bernard Williams (1978: 72–101) faults both versions of Descartes's (1964) arguments for 'je pense, donc je suis' (of 1637) and 'cogito ergo sum' (of 1644) – 'I am thinking, therefore I am', as well as their empiricist or materialist antitheses in, for example, Lichtenberg and Mach. Such latter empiricist thought-event formulations, he argues, require 'the notion of objectively existing thought-events, and in supposing that it can start out merely from the idea of thoughts as experienced, and from that achieve the third-personal perspective which is necessary if this notion is to apply, it shares a basic error with Descartes. There is nothing in the pure Cartesian reflection to give us that perspective' (Williams 1978: 100).

To some extent, Descartes inadvertently concedes the grounds for this demolition. He agrees that the seeming inferential term 'therefore' does not function as a syllogistic consequence, since it would have to presuppose the universal generalisation for 'I', which is precisely what Descartes cannot allow in his project. Descartes was aware that he could not consistently presuppose a syllogistic law as a basis for his first person inferences, since the former assumes a general law of the form 'For all P, therefore Q', the function of which is exactly what Descartes had to avoid assuming because of his role for doubt in proving the project of pure enquiry from the first person without generalising it. In fact Descartes proclaimed the primitive undefinable nature of inference, but this was because he believed that when one perceives inferential relations these are self-evident because they are primitive. Gaukroger (1989) is convinced that strengths can be seen in Descartes's position if we frame it within what he argues to be Descartes's experimental problem-solving method. Of course, a problem with this is that since there are competing games and conflicting interpretations bred of experience, this group of ingredients hardly augurs well for Descartes's method of doubting when applied ecumenically to the experience of a disagreeable first person.

Descartes also wished to maintain that the inner self is not the immediate inference of the *Cogito*, but would be the product of other and further argumentation, thus leaving unstated and unproved what it would be to be the requisite first person subject and its instantiation. As Williams shows, any attempt to yield a substantial subject instead as a treatment of this defect contradicts Descartes's supposed elimination of the third person. We should also note that as part of this procedure Descartes has removed the human body as a means to determine the alleged referent of 'I' as the thing that thinks, despite his varying versions of the matter. Descartes does not explain why he has given the first person the prime position of being, and also placed causality on a par as an integrating function with the first person (cf. Jean-Luc Marion, 1998a), thus making it perplexing to isolate the first person as a functionally autonomous entity and one independent of assumptions.

Deleuze and Guattari (1994: 24–32) claimed that the *Cogito* demands only a prephilosophical understanding (p. 26), and thought that there 'is no point in wondering whether Descartes was right or wrong', maintaining that his subjective concept can only be a function of his plane. But Descartes judged that his

Cogito was true, and they proposed the principle for him that, 'A concept always has the truth that falls to it as a function of the conditions of its creation' (p. 27). From these points it follows that their strategy to construct a no-man's territory for Cartesian subjectivity implodes, valuable though their many insights are. Indeed later in this study, their statement, 'Can thought as such be the verb of an I?' (p. 27), which Deleuze and Guattari do not pursue in the book, if addressed, could lead to a profound conclusion, as I attempt to portray below.

The first person

We are left with a puzzle. The first person seems distinct to other pronouns and subject-markers in ways often different from relational contrasts between other pronouns and subjects. Yet we have no grounds in usage for assigning to the first person a capacity of itself in use to isolate some uniquely individual internal property of person identity or personal identity itself. Mellor (1991) and others have discussed the indexical characteristic of the first person, analogous with spatial expressions such as 'here'. One may argue that there are various differences between the two categories, however, though they are ones that do not block the way to use the spatio-temporal analogy for the first person. Indexical success in pinpointing a space–time location does not thereby contain all knowledge of what is or happens there. Likewise, this is the case with respect to the first person. The individual's body satisfies the spatio-time condition on which the first person is dependent; but it is a category error to implement this indexicality to be the first person, even for the most thoroughgoing, and naive, materialist. Geach (1971) has warned against confusing secondary parasitic uses of the first person associated with the body. Even where one has the same context in which relevant forms of propositions are replaced, there is a problem. For example, if (a) 'I am taller than you' were to imply (b) 'You are shorter than me' (cf. Smiley, 1982), presumably such as are Cartesian users of this inference are committed to the first subject having a shorter inner self than the latter. And in respect of (c) 'I do not know what I am thinking about my inner self', is evidently not tautologous with the same subject as (a), even if the bearer is the same subject.

Anscombe (1975) argued, in agreement with Kant, that the first person pronoun does not refer. I shall take this feature of her analysis as a point of demarcation. We have seen from a variety of angles that the first person both presupposes – and yet does not have the internal criterion of being – a third person, or proper name, sort of criterion of application. So it is functionally strongly different from the sense of a proper name. Descartes's own programme attempted to isolate the first person from the third person; yet he was logically driven back onto a third person knowledge. His conception is not susceptible of permitting the relevant symmetry between first and third persons.

I suggest that the solution to this is to recognise the first person to be logically a categorial predicate, which is a function of the referent of its subject or a logical categorial singular term. Being a logical predicate, it does not refer; but as a logical predicate which instantiates, by presupposing a criterion of identity, it picks out its referent, and without referring to it. The first person thus identifies its utterer as the subject and the context of expression as a criterion of its difference from a proper name. In a technical sense such a logical predicate functions as a definite description on a par with Frege's quantification theory, as well as Russellian descriptions, along the lines of 'There is an x, and x is F . . .' that of course do not refer; see the analysis by Smiley (1982), however. Heal (1997) has commenced work on developing a logic of indexical predication which does not require reference, yet which indexes a unique identity. This could be utilised to flesh out an outline for a framework for the first person. Such a conception articulates a parallel between the psychological and the semantic whose conjunction pinpoints the space–time position of the body and its interiority. Here the functional scope is narrowed so that it is coincident with the specificity of a proper name yet not by a referential means. If the first person does not refer, but it acts as a function to identify its unique membership of a singular class, it does not thereby isolate by reference any inner or immaterial sense of the referent of 'I', irrespective of whether or not there is such a phenomenon. That is to say, it predicatively goes no further than to signify that there is an identity (that identity marked by the logical proper name which it presupposes) unique to the source of the use of that first person.

On this approach, it could be, following Anscombe's view, that there actually is something mysterious about the ontology of the state picked out by the first person. Conversely, this is not a property that is identified by the first person function: that is not its work-schedule. The first person's singularity consists in marking the personal identity of its utterer from the unique functioning space–time position of authorial interiority, not in pin-pointing a mystical essence; nor indeed in self-evidently operating as a reductionist tag which functionally eliminates immateriality. A presupposition of the first person is the function consciousness. And the origin, as well as the identity, of consciousness is itself a mystery. In a certain sense, then, Descartes has an undetermined function made to operate as a known value in a proof. But a proof is not of this form. It would have been better to come clean: the ontology of the first person is too deep for present knowledge.

Neurophysiology of the person

Parfit (1984) has exposed some of the complexities that attend dualism as well as less than deeply rigorous exploration of its possible alternatives. In a sustained analysis Parfit (1984: 211) found that 'A person is an entity that is distinct from a brain and a body, and such a series of physical and mental events' is true, but so also is 'A person's existence just consists in the existence of a brain and body, and the occurrence of a series of interrelated physical and mental events.' I derive from Parfit a position about the role of the first person (and leave aside as secondary the definition of personal identity), by arguing that one's relations of psychological connectedness and psychological continuity, in their causal relations to the unity of a person's consciousness, produce an identity which is more than the sum of the parts – an individual. This concern with relatedness and properties manifests a principle of excess over a straight materialist or a physicalist's reductionist view of personal identity, though it does not entail Cartesian dualism. (With respect to immateriality, this is partly the result of an inference about the limits of materialism: since we are not clear what it is to be matter and its limits of generalisation, in view of our empirical restrictions to do with conjectural knowledge, we cannot define what it is to be 'immaterial'. It may simply be super-physics, beyond the ken of our current empirical experimentation – cf. Gibson, 2000.)

Research rehearsed in Damasio's (1994) review of neurophysiology and the identity of mentality complements the complex and restricted account, which is sketched in the foregoing. Damasio (1994: 245–6) likens our facility to reason to a drive that is operated similar to an empirical gained skill, but, therefore, one of which we are not, by dint of possessing it, its masters. This is similar to Wittgenstein's (1974) use of language-game patterns, conjoined with the uncertainty implemented as a function of rule following. Ebbs (1997) has shown to what surprising degree the first person is asymmetric to the third person in this latter regard, in such a way that it is problematic to generalise correctly over the mental realm for first person uses. Damasio (1994) argues that the functions of emotion causally impinge on and affect the functioning of reasoning and science. Since we are as yet ignorant of the criteria that operate in this domain, we cannot construct an accurate concept of the conjunction of emotion and inference in the role of specifying an individual's identity. My own arguments (Gibson, 1997, 1998) suggest that reason and emotion are two subsets of a shared identity, distributed over these intertwined domains, variable though their realisations are, sometimes with the borderlines between reason and emotion function manifesting partially merged identities. If this is the case, we require a live metaphor interaction theory to map relations between the two spheres, prior to, or in, the implementation of, discovering how to represent the identity of the functioning of the mental.

Such an outcome, I conjecture, will be a counter-intuitive conjunction of the sublime with materialism, which is reductionist in respect of neither. Therefore, the explanation of consciousness is outside parameters of empirical and theoretical controls. Consequently, it is not clear what we are, 'in the first person'. So we need to move provisionally and creatively. Possibly, if the identity of consciousness continues to elude empirical explanation (it has in evolution theory, as Andrew Huxley, 1982 claims), consciousness itself may be found to be a non-physicalist function, in much the same way as a portrait is not the identity of the colours and shapes that comprise it. In such a scenario, empirical science would need to relocate some of its criteria of identity.

Philosophy of sexual neurophysiology

Descartes's cavalier surgical removal of the body from the mind does not mirror the conclusions of typical current neurophysiological research. In view of

Descartes's own appeal to the science of his era, uninformed of some of it though he sometimes was, it is worth citing an influential scientist such as LeVay (1993). From this sort of study there emerge two ways of looking at the body and mind, which I shall not argue but take as professionally established hypotheses that should be taken into account in some form within philosophical discussion. The first is the idea of a continuum with differential and variegated ends to illustrate some contemporary researches on relations between the mind and body. In sum, we cannot unplug the mind from the body, whether or not immaterial personal identity or materialist reductionisms were to be the correct conception of the mind. Descartes (mis)led philosophers and some clinicians (on the latter cf. Hacking, 1995: 163–70) to split body and mind. Consequently, he divided the mind in itself from its contextualised identity. The result was an attenuated first person, desiring to multiply to compensate for the artificially enforced absence of relationship with the body. We should retain the secondary, bodily usage of the first person characterised earlier in this chapter, in which the body is the focus of the first person, as with other pronouns. So, there is the conjunction of the biological with the neurophysical in the perspective of: what is to be a person? To what degree does this attend to gender? Given the history of male dominance, the inversion of this in male embryological history assumes a comic priority: all men begin their embryological history as female, and only at a given stage does genetic information convert the male to a male gendered organism. It has been conjectured that this may have some psychological analogues in explaining male identity. Another thesis in LeVay's study worth mentioning here is that, whatever the identity of the human mind, the neurophysiological relationship of the brain and body and many of their typical causal relations to each other and the mind are not gendered in the way in which most typical uses of the first person pronoun divide their labour between male and female. That is to say, the LeVay survey of research concludes that, though male and female bodies are biologically gendered, the neurophysiology of the brain displays identical properties in typical male and female persons over about two-thirds of the brain's identity. This leaves one-third for gender differentiating elements. While this notion of proportionality is rudimentary, it seems to have the support of extensive research. If the distinction is sustained, and suitably tied to relations between mind/brain/body, it has some significance for some presuppositions associated with the indexing of the first person. On this approach, the first person is a function of space–time body contexts that are not primarily gendered. The overlap condition of a shared neurophysiology dissolves an attempted binary opposition in the psychologisation of sexuality, and reverses into being an individual.

Antecedents of Descartes

Current research on philosophy of mind has to revise the map alleging discontinuity between the post-Renaissance and medieval worlds. Confusions passed down the centuries seem to extend further back than Rorty (1979) maintains. It has been customary to discover Descartes as the inventor of the strong form of dualism that broke the link with medieval concepts of being human. This perspective sits oddly with the anticipation of Descartes's *Cogito* by Augustine in *De Civitate Dei* XI. 26 (for a review of some third person uses see Matthews, 1992). Augustine's 'I am deceived, therefore I think' has parallels in Descartes, since the latter included a large group of predicates as replacements for 'think' in the *Cogito*. Aquinas disputed aspects of the sort of position later embodied in Descartes. Pasnau (1997: 64–8, 193) plausibly argues that the medieval world was concerned with many of the same problems of mind and body as was Descartes, while he shows that Aquinas' rational soul is not identical to Descartes's immaterial mind. One can utilise Pasnau's (1997: 193) analysis to show that Aquinas would have concluded that Descartes's immateriality of cognition commits Descartes to assigning an angel's nature to the human mind (cf. Rogers, 1995: 209). Pasnau (1997) argues that Aquinas' concept of mental immateriality does not entail nonphysicality, while the mind is non-physical in the sense that the difference between the latter and the material is one of degree. In this Aquinas is in conflict with Descartes. So, though the questions and positions that Descartes embraces have medieval and patristic antecedents, the theses argued, for example, by Aquinas, fundamentally oppose Cartesian dualism.

The foregoing allusion to authorial classification of the first person paves the way to propose that some philosophical literary background of the medieval world is pertinent to the role of the first person and its generalisation as a figure in, for example, the development of French literature. Such illustration is clearly only a fragment of the type of work to be done, yet it will be supposed that it is typical, as well as introductory for certain Near East considerations to be introduced below.

As Catherine Pickstock (1997) demonstrated, in Descartes's concern with the *a priori*, with the univocal nature of being and its consequent susceptibility to comprehension, we have central ingredients developed by John Duns Scotus which also reflect medieval treatment of the certainty about perception of ontology. Descartes's aversion to multiplicity and emphasis on reductionism exposes him as an uneasy companion of Ockham's simplicity (the latter as discussed in chapter 2 above). Although Aquinas would have been averse to Ockham's programme for simplicity, he succeeds in integrating qualified functions for simplicity, which notion was later re-formulated and mangled by Ockham (though in respect of cognition Ockham was not always reductionist; cf. Pasnau, 1997: 61).

With this complex uneven background for the first person in the medieval world, the literary roles of the first person realign in conjunction with the emergence of, for example, French literature. The functions of the first person in the later medieval world assume a creative role for the birth of French literature. As Zink (1985: 16–18) expresses it, 'The emergence of French literature happens to coincide with the moment when art comes to the realisation that there is no other truth than that of subjectivity which is realised through art.' According to Zink, the thirteenth century recognises through subjective allegory that the interiority central to the subjectivity of the self is possible. The complexly ironed

Old French troubadour poetry that emerged positions the first person as the focal point of identification. Kay (1990: 49) demonstrates that the spatial roles of 'textual effects are arranged and organised around the first person position and that subjectivity is inseparable from rhetorical complexity' (cf. Spence, 1996: 15). As Pickstock (1997) argues, it is a characteristic of Descartes's programme around the *Cogito* that it is conceived in framed spatialisation, echoing a city motif, with the written signifying medium performing the prime function, rather than the mental. (From the standpoint of intuitionistic logics and paradoxes in standard logics, this spatialisation cannot bear the actual infinity loading which Descartes placed on it in his mental city, itself an echo of Augustine's *City of God*.) Such a pattern has clear debts to the above medieval revolution in evolving personal identity. I will briefly return to the medieval world below to add that to the obscure medieval conceptions, and we have to incorporate functions of grotesque and monstrous demonology in the medieval mental world of belief.

The imagination of the first person

A facet of this section can be summarised by stating that, in certain respects, the identification of what it is to be an individual – to be an account of personal identity – is a non-linear function or result of wider presuppositions reflected in, and as, facets of society under intentional descriptions. A person's identity and self-image of identity is usually considered in the context of its social and imaginative functioning. The logic of Frege also allows for this space and gap, as mentioned above (Frege, 1977), 'I have an idea of myself, but I am not identical with this idea.' Conceptions of personal identity disassociate with the role of the first person yet imaginatively conflate with it. We also found above that Parfit's (1984) analysis of connectedness and psychological continuity are central to grasping functions of individual identity and perceptions of an individual in the first person. These logical patterns can facilitate the extension of conceptions associated with a first person, and seem to warrant, as well as connect with, a projection of personal identity. It is a short but distinct step from this to generalise conceptions over groups of first person subjects, with the plural pronoun. Since people do not share personal identity, the obvious sense of 'we' is an externalised ascription of features that may condense into a singular will, purpose, conspiracy, or the like; but fall short of functionally warranting the pluralisation of the first person on the basis of singular identity. The conflation of two or more first person subjects into a plural pronoun is an opportunity for mythologisation of identity. Not only does some influential political ideology presuppose this myth as fact by reordering the priority of collectivity over singular personal identity; what has been labelled multiple personality reverses and internalises this trend as a mirror image of society. It is possible that the two states of affairs are causally related. In such circumstances, the first person implements a possible world(s) as if it were the actual one, usually with dire consequences.

Many hypotheses that have their birth in the conceptualisations of (normal or abnormal) personal identity can be, and have been, extended to cover collective social states involving groups of individuals. Such transformations are complicated by assumptions about both conscious and unconscious domains in the functions of (frequently suppressed) premises depicting personal identity. There is, for example, the emblem of a European collective unconscious, which no doubt Malcolm Bowie (1993) is correct to deconstruct. But such a perceived collective morass has its antecedents that derive from the ancient past. When one comes to what is currently taken to be the origin of philosophy in ancient Greece, research into history of philosophy deforms into the history of ideas. In an attempt to develop a transformative relation between the two spheres, it is worth attempting to conceive of how one can extend philosophical analysis to paraphrase some history of ideas so as to treat them philosophically.

Psychoanalysis of Sumerian gender?

It is relevant here to introduce a perspective developed elsewhere.[1] Obviously Freud was distortingly male-centred in his approach to the projection of gender conceptions in relation to women. Despite his obsession with actual archaeology, and his perceptions of it to be deployed as a psychoanalytical typology, his attention to ancient symbols as a font for mentality largely derives from no earlier period than Classical Greece, qualified slightly only by his paternalistic treatment of the Old Testament. Yet Sumerian and Akkadian divine and demonological typologies are replete, in some contexts, with resources comparably as rich in data for psychoanalysis as are much later epochs. Leick's (1994) pioneering study into sex and eroticism in Sumerian and Akkadian literature, though it does not explicitly address Freud, furnishes us with evidence that the periods of the third to the first millennium BC in Mesopotamia are a rich resource for the future. Leick (1994: 56) finds a link between common preoccupations of a female as love-object in Plato's *Symposium* – as interpreted by Lacan (1991: 44) – and the Sumerian goddess Inanna.

So interpretation of ancient public monumental, institutional records and cuneiform narrative ancient cultural phenomena is related to our contemporary psychoanalytical controversies. If logical clarity is concomitant of bold theorising here it will be recognised that central areas of analytical philosophy will have important insights for such controversies. For example, Wittgenstein's (1998) conclusion that public sense is a function of being human (the consequence of his attack on the private language argument) – is itself a component in a basis for identifying common properties in ancient psychological phenomena and our consciousness.[2]

For example, we should be aware of, and wary that, as Kearns (1997: 69, 70) remarks respectively of psychoanalysis's revision of Cartesian dualism, and of Lacan that, 'Obliquely, paradoxically, but most powerfully, psychoanalysis also resets the Cartesian mind/body split by creating a version of humanness that is at once all body and nobody'; and, 'Lacan's terms are almost paradoxically theistic, God cloaked in a prophylactic of mystery.' Kearns's reset Cartesianism is partially a transcendent function of the body in the history of ideas and of psychoanalysis in which body typology supervenes over time – typical of everybody, yet specific to no individual, though she is careful to resist notions of unrestricted generalisation.

At the side of this, and in focused senses internal to the perspective of Classical and Mesopotamian conceptual historiographies, we can detect a number of continuities and inversions in this sphere relevant for the next stage in the present chapter:

1   Freudian and Lacanian typologies, as well as Jung's, are in effect transcendent typologies which are sometimes operated with the same sort of patriarchal authority and identity as have properties of Descartes's and some facets of Mesopotamian theologies.
2   The twentieth-century AD psychoanalytical resetting of Cartesian dualism has an inverted analogue in Sumerian and Akkadian theistic typology: Mentality in its imaginative projection is condensed into the perceived divine body.
3   Descartes's immortal soul and its disembodied capability have not only an obvious parallel in Plato's *Phaedo*; the immortal soul has a significant matching in the semantic field of the Sumerian ZU.
4   In Sumerian and Akkadian mythology, the reunion of soul and body tended to be reserved for the god and divine kings rather than humans, in contrast with the Old Testament.

Multiple personality and personal trance

Psychiatry long ago moved on from Bleuler's (1908, 1924) inventive explanation of schizophrenia as an alternating personality and a doubling of consciousness. Ian Hacking (1995) has assessed the emergence of multiple personality, and opened up entirely new questions about our memory of the past in relation to science: new ways of forming and making questions are produced by new science and fresh conjectural knowledge. He observes that a new science can embody elements operating as a semantic contagion that generates invented memories. It would be too much to generalise this over all science, not least since Hacking is writing of multiple personality and the sciences of memory. But in the most general of sciences, together with some of the presuppositions of science in the twentieth century, cosmology has obliterated vast regions of the past. How our memories and the status of future science stand in relation to such elimination are not obviously always accurate in memory or prediction. Just as we recognise Hacking's account of the modern world generating and absorbing multiple personality, as well as the traditional formulations of schizophrenia as a split personality with all its inaccuracy, we are accordingly confronted with the function of history's maverick imagination in the ways in which it triggers collective influences and ideas.

A similar story can be told about the ancient Mesopotamian world. A further complication is that the history of ideas is an incomplete subject with tantalising parallels between Mesopotamia and Europe. Although the wheel was probably discovered in many places, it is not unlikely that recurrent psychological phenomena and their symbols have explanatory value for the representation of the human mind in disparate cultures and epochs. It would not be helpful to romanticise with an invented memory about the ancient past. But Hacking (1995: 139) observes from the data that symptoms of multiple personality evolve. There is a developing, and sometimes causally driven, influence from a society to mould the symptoms.

A central proposal of Hacking (1995: 142) is that the phenomenon of multiple personality, which may only seem to be recent, has a counterpart or some equivalent in the trance. I suggest that this state is a means to transfer portions of Hacking's thesis to ancient Mesopotamia, where the trance is a fundamental causal prototype state associated with humans. This is a vast and unexplored subject, and there is space here only for a few opening remarks reflecting ongoing research. The role of the first person in such contexts is metaphorised, though the entranced agent sometimes takes it to be actually the case that she/he hås multiple identities or some other identity. Trance, in ancient Mesopotamia in Sumerian, Akkadian and other Semitic traditions, is characteristic of possession states. These are typically induced by and are internal to, for example, incantation and ritualised magic spells, often institutionalised in the activities of the Maqlu – the witch (see Abusch, 1995). It should be realised that this includes a class of purportedly 'medical' or 'good' practitioners of the skill. To some degree, this class coincides with the position that psychoanalysts hold in twentieth-century AD modernism. The use of hypnosis in the ancient world in such circumstances has a parallel in some modern medicine, sensitive though our contemporary medics are to the contiguity of hypnosis to standard medical practice.

Female multiples

Hacking (1995) states that in the contemporary western world nine out of ten multiples (i.e., multiple personality subjects) are women. This situation is not of course taken to expose an essentialist peculiarity of being women. Conversely, as Rorty (see Balslev, 1991: 85–6) maintains, there is no feminist essentialism to counter traditional subversion of women. Rather, these histories of subverting women are in complex ways a mirror of how women were and are treated and characterised, the publication of which will contribute towards removing misrepresentation of what it is to be a woman. Many of the Mesopotamian contexts display a similar subversion of women. A facet of this concerns their subjection, and consequent susceptibility, to trance possession and incantation. Leick (1994: 204) notices that it is mostly women who are addressed by the institutionalised magic love incantations in second and first millennia Mesopotamia. Hacking (1995) has shown that the recurrence of multiple personality and its disproportionate attachment to women frequently originates with or occurs in an environment of child abuse. We can to a large degree only conjecture about the degree of subversion of women and child abuse there was in ancient Mesopotamia. Yet the signs are everywhere evident in the residue of ancient traces of life that these phenomena were awfully extensive and extreme. An outcome of such evidence would be to ascribe proportionately higher incidences of the multiple personalities and various other forms of imposition in, for example, Sumerian culture. The data seem to exemplify horrific states of affairs, including human sacrifice.

In other words, whereas modernism in twentieth-century Europe has an excess of entertainment media that indulge in grotesque subversion of woman, child and man, in ancient Mesopotamia virtual reality representation and ritualised enactment of perversion often had its corollary in widespread actual fulfilment abusing people. Given that our contemporary societies manifest extensive disorders that distort the personal identity, we may not be able to absorb the depth and amount of psychological trauma occurrent in ancient society that resulted from the practices advertised in Mesopotamian records and art, glorious though some of the ancient world's contrasting positive achievements were. In the light of such analysis as the foregoing, however, we have evidence to recognise that 'the glory that was such and such an ancient city' is an inept celebration that obscures an ancient city's functioning identity: a body politic to violate most of its populace's personal identity.

Projecting multiple personality on to deities

Investigation of Mesopotamian data yields clues and psychoanalytically charged evidence to enable us to retrieve a psychoanalytical interpretation that can be employed to infer grounds for a theoretically enriched, and not naive, view of ancient projection of extreme personality disorder symptoms. Obviously, we are not apprehending directly, even allowing for the role of the iconic deity and the narrative as imaginative sources of metaphorised and often collective as well as stylised products of actual mental phenomena. The analytical or aesthetic transfer from iconic or textually delineated face to mentality, is a tricky one. Yet the ancient, and sometimes attested, interplay between these spheres permits some inferences. It requires further study to examine the status of deities as counterparts of multiple personality, but some use of live metaphor would preserve the explanatory parallels, while allowing us to determine a separation of functions.

It is worth locating the role of the putative individual in some Mesopotamian mythology. The position of humans is roughly Aristotelian (of the *Poetics*) in which the person is subservient to the tragic action, while less privileged than in Greek drama. But the perceived deity has some similarity to Henry James's (1934) view, in which the foregoing relation is inverted and the action is subject to the deity. The conjunction of these two, I suggest, constructs a tragic trauma scenario. We could introduce Thom's (1989) catastrophe theory to structure aspects of this state of affairs. The collision of a supervening multiple personality deity with humans in Mesopotamian mythology mirrors memory of, and perhaps causally induced, trauma. Hacking (1995: 178–9) shows that some nineteenth-century doctors created conceptual space for the idea of multiplicity in relation to personality. We might extend and transform this in partial application to the Mesopotamian priestly activity and its implementation in the ritualisation of mythology, allowing for the feature of the priest as a functionary combining religious and medical roles. Clearly, there is a distinctive task yet to be performed here, of examining the criteria and measuring terminology in each of the ancient and modernist domains to assess the extent of matching. This could profit from Rorty's (1984) approach in which one would explain the philosophy of history within terms used by and internal to that history, in which, as Kermode (1985) states, the text is a world-system. To this it is important to add the role of visualisation as medium and causality. Hacking (1995: 137, 259) analyses this concerning our modern media, and ancient Mesopotamia's large-scale monumental art rehearses many of the cultic psychodramas (cf. Gibson, 2001). Such media are metonymy metaphors for the entranced first person's multiple personalities.

In ancient Mesopotamia and other countries the occurrence of animal deities and hybrids of human and animals is common. This appears to be evidence of projection connected with multiple personality. Hacking (1995: 279) reports the occurrence of humans with animal multiple personality states as a statistically small, and often repugnant, state of affairs. It seems that this statistic was reversed in the ancient Near East. Leick (1994) documents literatures that almost certainly had iconic implementations and ritual embodiments, in which human sexual parts are transmogrified into animals or animal members; other data attest to transvestites, hermaphrodite and gender-changes (Leick, 1994: 224). David Williams's (1996) substantial research into medieval literature and culture attaches to the foregoing distinctions. Some quite similar grotesque to Mesopotamia was occurrent in the medieval world, intimately bound into theology, worship and common imagination. Therefore, the equivalents in late twentieth-century AD societies of comparable phenomena are apparently a resurfacing of previous causal social dynamics.

Multiple personality deity

The two-faced Roman god Janus, engaging with puns on vaginal entrances, birth, and related characteristics in his narratology, is hardly irrelevant to such psychoanalysis. It is a puzzling matter, however, that with Freudian and Jungian psychologies not infrequently drawing on Classical Greek typologies, Greece itself has yielded no Janus-type deity. Schizophrenia is not multiple personality, though both states overlap regarding a few positive symptoms, and the multiple can exhibit schizophreniform features for short periods (cf. Hacking, 1995: 128–70). Janus seems to resemble this overlap, and his extreme personality functions seem to comprise a live metaphor for multiple personality.

As I explain in Gibson (2000a), Sumerians had a two-faced god named Usmu. He appears to be represented on the Adda cylinder seal BM89115, from the Agade period circa 2335–2155 BC. The seal displays the ancient mind's array of other cultic gods: Ea, over the stylised river; the winged goddess, most likely Inanna; Ninurta emerging from the flames. Porada (1980) proposed that this seal displays an architectural style resembling its large-scale counterparts that covered outer walls in major Sumerian cities in the third millennium BC. Kinnier Wilson (1979) explains the seal in conjunction with the Sumerian *Ki-bala* tablets, as a traumatic product of catastrophe mirroring seismic activity, to which Gibson (2000a) adds fresh analysis and interpretation. These texts also may use these motifs to allude to military crises (cf. Gibson and O'Mahony, 1995). Usmu/Umsu displayed the functions ascribed above to Janus, but also more specifically attended to birth and the destruction of the foetus. If we follow, Kinnier Wilson's (1979) interpretation of Usmu, we discover a world of abnormal psychology, with Usmu as a demon-god terrorising the pregnant woman, who contrariwise is supposed to be the guardian of the vaginal entrance. This is a function of Freud's Oedipal anxiety with a negative vengeance. The obstetric scalpel is replaced with the cult's sacrificial sword.

Usmu is only one among a pantheon of Freudian/Lacanian-like deities in ancient Sumerian and Akkadian theophanies. It is worth advancing the idea for consideration that much more recent resources of the human unconscious had some of these phenomena mediated to the mind. Direct mediation may be a problem for some such phenomena, though we cannot be sure of the ancient histories of transmission or the criteria for multiple independent inventions of parallel identities perhaps triggered by similar cultic mythologies. The relation between specificity and generality here devolves on the typologies we deem to concur with the mental causality of the unconscious, as opposed to (or in conjunction with) the controversial possibility of transmission down human generations within their unconscious. Certainly Skorupski (1976) has shown that transcultural influence through different media representing an event can preserve typologies even with varying depictions.[3] In such perspectives, it is hoped that the above exploration will contribute to answering some of the challenges raised by Colin Renfrew's (1982) *Towards an Archaeology of the Mind*.

The unconscious downloading ancient Sumer?

It is probable that the present study has offered sufficient evidence to expose a thesis about the unconscious. If the unconscious exists, it has a long history whose traumatic route can be traced to places like Sumer. If this involves some memory, even obliquely mediated by external phenomena and triggers, as well as our psychological dynamics, we should press on with much more research into this and other ancient pasts. A problem concerning the origination of such mediation or internal causal fixation, and/or transmission, of archetypes concerns the manner in which some of these ancient phenomena are much more explicit as data of public and conscious articulation in ancient Mesopotamia than typically they are in our contemporary world.

The parameters of ancient conscious mentality possessed content and external enactment that in the modern world we typically associate with the unconscious. But even recent aspects of modern conditions in consciousness mimic those of ancient Sumer. Is the evolution of consciousness verging towards devolution of the unconscious, with new forms of multiple personality mirroring this prospect? It could be that there was, in a place such as the ancient Near East, a large-scale case of collective ancient double amnesia: a traumatised collective consciousness slipped, under trance or anxiety, into becoming the unconscious.

Freud may not have regressed far enough back. The origin of consciousness in evolution has yet to be explained. Maybe the answer was mirrored in ancient Mesopotamia, or some such place, perhaps in stages. The evolution of the unconscious could be relatively recent. Perhaps in these origins there are relations of multiple personality, or schizophreniform functions, between the first person's unconscious and consciousness. To achieve explicit conceptions of these matters we need to keep in mind the formulation of two minimal conditions. First, we require an unequivocal grasp of what it is to be in the first person – a singular individual. Secondly, we need the minimal condition of a mastery of the threats of false consciousness. Descartes denied the first by reductionism, and unconsciously embraced the second without mastery but with his reductionism. Philosophy has usually been content to discover that the first person refers. Not only does it not, but this mistake distracts from the more significant tasks. That is to say, to identify the internal content of the referent of the first person (which is not marked by 'referring'); and to specify its relations to the unconscious in the perspective of its capacity to project its identities onto the external world.

10 Transcendent reason

Removing dogmatic assumptions

The previous chapter showed that reductionism and false consciousness threaten our attempts to recognise the past. A particular case of this is our retrieval of the identity of ancient sense. Prior to embarking on interpretation of how this relates to our grasp of matters that form the body of this chapter, it is important to retrace, reformulate and challenge a familiar, now largely eclipsed, version of an important issue. As with eclipses, we would do well not to expect the dark to be a persistent state.

Many a modernist division between the secular and the transcendent – between the physical and the immaterial – between sense and nonsense, has assumed that such a division is indisputable; has supposed that it is known; presumed that it is self-evident; has dogmatised that there is no transfer from outside of the normative culture into it. Even so, here 'outside' is a mythologising term. We are quite unclear what it would amount to so as to demonstrate that unique creativity in any social context is in relation to a person's creative contribution being more than the sum of her contemporaneous parts. As to where that element covered by 'more than the sum' comes from is currently anybody's guess. No doubt one guess is that it just is there; other familiar candidates are that the sublime arises from the ingredients. So it is often presupposed that: gone are the times when one could have sensibly supposed that something exists which is mysterious, transcendent, and destructive of cultured recognition of this division. An asserted consequence of this position is that all truth-claims are subservient to and arise from within human culture, the effect of which is to bar the propriety of the claim that some insight might derive, in whatever ways, from God.

Before moving on to address the central part of this chapter's topic, it is relevant to do by-pass surgery on a theological area, which has been taken as a ground for virtually prohibiting exploration of many versions – and in some theologians' treatment all possible forms – of transcendent expression. So let us now cast this type of problem in terms of a somewhat past, yet enormously influential, debate in biblical studies. In other words, any claims to transcendence in the world are subject to what is called the historico-critical method, according to which any violation of this division is an illicit move. For those happily situated outside, and in ignorance, of theological debate within biblical studies, 'the historico-critical method' may seem to be a mere phrase for a recipe. But for those trained within its aegis, in the nineteenth and twentieth centuries it had a ludic authorising role that vilified what seemed to be, and often were, over-inflated theses of transcendence and associated ontologies. 'The historico-critical method' – within biblical studies – was, and sometimes still is, taken to be the correct scientific method applied to ancient manuscripts and their 'histories'. It is fairly evident that this method is not what is taken to be the scientific method in techniques used by professional historians, and it largely stems from one strand of a nineteenth-century German tradition. Actually 'the historico-critical method' is a recipe to ban beliefs that transcend it. Certainly, if such beliefs are false, they should be discarded. But 'the historico-critical method' is an unjusti-fied recipe that presupposes as fact what at best is conjecture. The method is one of those familiar but unfortunate features of history: a fashion is so success-ful at a stage in history that it is almost taken to be what it is to be the identity of a subject. When history moves on to a fresh perspective, and proof emerges that the identity of this subject is quite other than that which the fashion ascribes it, the past fashion is not discounted from the subject, because it has become an internal property of the way the subject is perceived.

There are strange ambiguities in usage of 'the historico-critical method', which varies in the diverse traditions in theology. It is so much a chunk of the outdated, yet presupposed, dogma in some theological cultures that there is the assumption that we have moved on from such agenda, while to dispute the method has attracted the response within biblical studies that the distinction and its alleged consequence are self-evident. Contrariwise, if one were to adopt it as a principle, then it would prohibit counter-intuitive progress. We may wish to assign knowledge of the divine a special class beyond this accessible counter-intuitive knowledge. Yet that is not going to assist someone, on the historico-critical basis, to deny that we can have transcendent knowledge, of the relevant sort. Why? Because, in keeping with the hypothesis of denying special transcendent knowledge, one would have to be depending on the truth of this hypothesis to prove that there was a unique category outside of the hypothesis. So by *reductio ad absurdum* that method implodes. Moreover professional histori-ans do not, nor ever did, generally employ this historico-critical method. The historico-critical method is a marginal offshoot of nineteenth-century German studies, which theology variously adapted for its own polemical purposes. Without parallel in contemporary secular historical methodology, it became a rubric for a group of questionable recipes.

Even if one were to adopt the historico-critical method as a rule, much of twentieth-century theology did not take requisite account of a simple problem, which results in contradiction. Namely, if the historico-critical method and its later reformulations were to amount to a principle that thereby applied to all interpretation that is to be revised and deconstructed, then the historico-critical method has to be subject to this itself. Contrariwise if it is a partially applicable or revisable principle, then it is not an inviolable generalisation to which one can appeal to block the possibility of claims that violate it as a principle. This is parallel with the way in which A. J. Ayer's principle of verification contains the seeds of its own destruction.[1] So it is not surprising to recognise that theologians in the twentieth century who rejoiced in empirical science, as though it were logical positivism, should also have championed the mythic status of a principle that supposedly dismissed life that is not permitted by their principle of method.

This type of territory is worn and it needs fundamentally new investigation. The present chapter amounts to one detail in that direction, from the stand-points of the use of language and reason. Many modern scholarly attitudes to the New Testament comprise a special instance of this problem. Over the last 150 years the idea has been developed in biblical studies that premodern narra-tives are subservient to their original or first authentic social and conceptual contexts. Recent attention to literary creativity in the ancient biblical world has done something to sidetrack this policy. Nevertheless, much scholarly writing is evidence of a hangover from modernist presumptions about the conceptual restrictions attending New Testament writers. One does not have to wax Romantic or sublime to notice that creative products transcend the contexts of their birth. Somehow, a range of New Testament scholarship has appeared to neglect this point. No doubt it has something to do with aversion to, and demo-lition of, the anachronistic norms in conservative doctrines of revelation. Certainly we should not restore such muddled debates. But the deconstruction of their forms of argument is not equivalent to reducing the New Testament's identity to that of the culture in which it was conceived or to that of its first institutional contextualisation.

The foundations of the linguistics and logic that constituted the rational grounds and representation of this demythologisation are badly faulty, as some of the foregoing chapters have obliquely demonstrated. It remains to give explicit attention to a central zone of the reasoning that underpins the claim that the New Testament's rationality is that of certain parts of its originating culture(s). We shall see that many scholars have yet to uncover the logical identity of the New Testament. That is to say, rafts of consensus have floated the myth that most of the problem can be packaged and dismissed by what is actually a myth of its own. This frequently amounts to the mythologisation of Aristotle's logic, stitched-up as a faulty account of reason, which obscures the New Testament's use of reason.

In another respect, this study is concerned with relations between our contemporary research in philosophy of logic, the topic of original creativity in literary linguistics, how they impinge on Aristotle's connecting rhetoric with logic, and further work on the retrieval of his treatment of such matters. Such research strikes a contrast with some work on rhetoric, in particular some trends in New Testament scholarship (only the last part of the chapter will attend to this situation). If we wish to discover what, if any, engagement there was or could be between the New Testament and reasoning external to its purviews and worldviews, we need to develop fresh approaches as well as explore old ones. Cultural influences subsequent to the New Testament are, in a specific sense, irrelevant to its first-century meaning. An exception to this presumably is those who have attempted with some success to understand culture during or before the New Testament, and produced insight into those spheres and/or what it is to be a true expression.

A particular focus of concern here, then, is the identity of New Testament rationality in relation to its conceptual identity. The following analysis attends to one aspect of this, the relations between reason in Greek in and outside of the New Testament. A specific sphere in which these topics have important functions is the way the New Testament has tended to be made continuous with, and subservient recipient of, certain influences in Greek rationality. My argument maintains that there is no basis for this view, and that in any case it has been developed on the basis of inadequate accounts of Aristotle's writings. I argue that, as an upshot of this sort of study, we have yet to discover the identity of reasoning in the New Testament and consequently cannot concur with treatments that identify its logics with those cultures so far assumed to be its resource.

It seems almost too obvious to state that historical *ad hoc* selection of various bits of rhetoric theory, as though there were some rhetoric essence recurrent whenever the subject is treated, from any or all history will yield no theory true of any period or writer. An investigation of whether or not such metalanguage and object language universes are connectable, and the identity of their mapping relations, is only in earlier stages of research in logic. There are almost untouched, unanswered, recondite questions. For example, what are the relations between precision in great original music composition (supposing in some suitable sense that music has a linguistic syntax and semiotic system for emotions and aesthetics) and precision in logical form? Should we conclude that Mozart's *Figaro* is at least as precise in its own logical form as Russell's Paradox? Is there a logical rhetoric of music, according to which semantics is akin to *enthymeme*? We are some distance from tackling these questions, and a modest one will engage us here, in the hope of planning a future route.

It is apt to select a perspective struck by two of Wittgenstein's perspectives that are historical dipoles: philosophy as logic, and philosophy as grammar. He himself, unlike some of his followers, never seemed entirely to have polarised this relation, however. He used the notion of the bipolarity of a proposition.[2] Grammar and logic could elide into a conceptual monopole.[3] Within this focus, suitably extended logic entails grammar, and this implication, suitably routed, entails a programme of generalisation for a philosophy. The relations of logic to literary creativity are largely unmapped. One of its domains comprises the relations between following rules with counter-intuitive originality. Such a conjunction places deep questions against our grasp of what it is to be a rule, to the degree that we may not have a grasp of what it is to be a criterion for this notion of 'rule'.[4] The contention presupposed here is that great creative literature is logical and recognition of this state of affairs is achievable by structuring the ways in which rhetoric in prose, prose-poetry, and poetry manifest and are dependent upon logic for some of their persuasive power. This associates the concept of logic with what it is to be possibility.

Before proceeding to issues of rhetoric, let us reflect on elements for a logical foundation by which to develop a boundary (not an electrified perimeter fence) between logic and rhetoric. If such relations hold true, the principle of bivalence applies. Consequently such a philosophy as canvassed above would be true or false. Obviously it would be an advantage to know the further criteria according to which a philosophy is true. In Aristotle we have the founder of the sort of rhetorical theory from which in varying ways later rhetoric concepts derive. Many subsequent rhetoricians were either indebted to him or inferior in their insights, or dependent on the probity of his conceptions, even allowing for the obscurity, incompleteness or density of some of Aristotle's comments. Later accretions of rhetorical dogma have their place. Yet there is a need for rhetoricians to be informed more than they often are about current technical research in Aristotle's logical theory. The priority of the current analysis is not the important subject of historical development, but that of a philosophical logician more interested in current research concerning what it is to be rhetoric and its relations to logic, though one avoids being ahistorical. The philosophy of the emotions is significant in relation to rhetoric, though it will not be pursued here; yet it should be noticed that the type of expression 'I fear you' has a bivalent logical form, for example.

Aristotle is not only adding the logical component to the rhetorical skill of persuasion. As Schutrumpf[5] explains, Aristotle is critical of writers who privilege the skill, which plays on the emotions. Aristotle maintains[6] that, in the relevant sense, such use of the skill is unrelated to the truth of the subject; Plato makes the same criticism in the *Phaedrus* (267, c. 7), and Schutrumpf's view is that Aristotle's position on the emotions in rhetoric here is continuous with Plato. Aristotle is concerned both with the logical basis of rhetoric and with its contextualised natural history. Respecting the latter, the psychological character of decision-making in the light of the relativity of circumstance should be included and measured by logic in rhetoric.

Argumentum ad hominem

A response to, or misunderstanding of, the foregoing might be to argue the following inference:

> (α) Aristotle's Rhetoric takes *argumentum ad hominem*, gathering together the commonly held points of agreement evident upon reflection to rational animals.

Therefore:

> (β) Aristotle is not developing a deductive argument basis for rhetoric but proposing stylistics for assessing the presentation of (α).

Clearly (α) does not imply (β); nor has (β) internal properties of (α) that could imply (β). The present study will argue that (β) is false, though I presuppose that in some other sense Aristotle is concerned with style. One could, and should, simply remove or dissolve the problem composed in '(α) therefore (β)', by observing that Aristotle's use of evident truths common to rational people is a state of affairs to which he applies deduction of various types (not a metaphoric type of deduction). As Burnyeat (1994) observes, Aristotle's relaxed use of deduction is still deduction, and not a strategy to acquiesce in what by agreement incorrectly passes for reasoning at the hands of those who share such evident truths. His employment of signs does not sacrifice objective logical standards in the interests of achieving whimsical persuasion relative only to a recipient's subjective values. Rather, a major part of his contribution is to challenge just that conflation of the evident with *ad hominem* patterns of audience expectation. Clearly there is a central place in Aristotle's *Rhetoric* for Locke's (1996) view (expressed in his *An Essay Concerning Human Understanding*) of *argumentum ad hominem*, according to which a person is or people are faced with the consequences drawn from their own principles or concessions; but this position does not require that 'consequences' have not to be consequences.

If one excludes or ignores the role of logic within Aristotle's *Rhetoric*,[7] it is not possible to explain his early claim in the *Rhetoric* that '*enthymeme*s are the body of proof.' This expression, puzzling though it can be, identifies 'proof' as a criterion of *enthymeme*s. It hardly seems credible to reduce this to a subjective sense of persuasion.

Aristotle's dialectic, syllogistic and rhetoric

Aristotle treats these relations as a developing philosopher whose aim was to discover a universal framework for reason and knowledge, while attempting accurately to represent and integrate their differences. This presupposition should underpin attempts to focus him, while regulating it with our knowledge, and ignorance, of influences on Aristotle. But this is very different from the sort of movement, often only implicit to the users, which is explicitly sketched below. In some modern New Testament rhetorical studies the intrusion of scholarly imagination, and the implicit often unacknowledged or unconscious metaphoric extension of terminological metaphor in dialectical interaction, are self-authenticating processes, whereas in Aristotle, in the relevant contexts, such matters are assessed by deduction.

Aristotle probably had a qualified opposing reaction to the dominant function of Socratic dialogue, wary as he was of its potential, especially in the hands of philosophers less gifted than Plato, to attract ponderous and inconclusive examination of issues. Hintikka's[8] perspective on this sort of view (that of the problem-solving character of Aristotle's thought) is certainly important. He presents Aristotle's syllogistic, in part, as a product of his struggle with dialectic, in which there is some overlap in the problem-solving roles between the two.

Aristotle was sharply aware of some distinctions between validity in a syllogism and argumentative strength in dialectic; he allowed controlled interaction between the two domains without his always perfectly conceiving this relation. But he was sharply aware of many differences, such as the importance of context and smaller number of premises in rhetoric. Hintikka's view is that Aristotle took it that 'Logical inferences will then be those answers that are necessary *ad argumentum*',[9] and so including detection of fallacies. In this respect there can be a specific paraphrasing overlap between dialectic and deductive inference, distinct to inductive confirmation[10] since it is non-monotonic. One of the well-known gaps between Aristotle's dialectic and rhetoric is that the latter has an audience while the former has a responding participant. Aristotle is of course attentive to the condition that acts as a bridge between logical inference and rhetoric. With the latter as well as the former, assumptions and premises should be selected which are shared by all of the audience or for the most part in the universe of discourse, in a number of contexts precisely unlike dialectic.

If we are to focus on this bridge and its refinement or reconstruction, we should ask the question: What are the relations between rhetoric, logic and uses in ancient Greek natural language manuscripts? This multifarious question presupposes generalisation, which goes beyond our knowledge of its components; but it is possible to isolate some internal properties of its identities. These include elements of inference, form, necessity, relevance, content and originality.

Proof in logic for rhetoric

Notoriously, this concerns the relations of form to content, which returns us to the Wittgenstein polarity, its relations to metaphysics and what he termed 'natural history',[11] together with the role of the relevance of content to implication.[12] From what traces of Chrysippus we have, he deemed consequence necessary, but not formal; for Philo of Megara it was neither necessary nor formal.[13] Aristotle avoided defining implication, and concentrated on necessity with topic-neutral expressions so as to generalise over more subjects than he could have were he to have attended to the content of subjects. He conceived of formality by construction of topic-neutral inference patterns, and invented the notion of validity along these lines. This state of affairs demarcated content from logical form. The general result was a competition whose game-rules were roughly that if one selects form, then content is irrelevant and/or excluded and *vice versa*.

So what do we do? Research[14] leads to the conclusion that deeply set in or under the foundations of what it is to be true communication is a complementarity – a functional fusion between content and logic. Formulation of such a conjunction should be stipulated by criteria of relevance. This notion of 'fusion' will have to be counter-intuitive as, for example, the laws of physics are as they deform in creativity in the earliest phase of the universe,[15] and, for instance in the criteria of recognition for identifying systematic intertextual relations between apparently unconnected types.[16] Such an approach would have to incorporate the phenomenon of counter-intuition to isolate the unexpected from the incorrect. Gödel's Theorem is an instance of counter-intuition, namely where the negation or contrary of an expected inference is proved to be true. There are various classes of counter-intuition. I think that logical results such as these 'leak' facets of the deeper, still unexplored, foundations of logic, three of whose empirical mirrors are astrophysical cosmology of the earliest universe, music and art.[17] In this perspective, therefore, we are at an early stage of theory-construction in which the mysteries of future knowledge have been partially explored, and subtlety obscured, by the history of logic and rhetoric. In scenarios and research projects like these, it is confusing to assume or deem that pseudo-technical terms render and authorise ideas explicit, unless they are precisely related to standard concepts of measurement. This is where, for example, rhetoric and logic come to be of new value. Sure, there will be dispute and counter-intuitive instability in interpretative disputes; yet these should be distinct to theorisation, which runs like a possessed metaphor out of control. It is important to recognise and implement the perception that the mere occurrence of scholastic inventiveness is not progress; just as reading-off the sense of established standard expressions does not guarantee the truth of normative sense. So, while there are problems in logic research, and one needs moral counselling with creativity, the latter is fundamentally different from the production of arbitrary models by dint of authority or novelty.

Counter-intuitive solutions to paradox

At the side of this, a logician nevertheless should be embarrassed by her failure to make more of established foundations. Should philosophers be bolder than they tend to be? Are we too easily imprisoned in the spirit of the age? Could we not recognise the possibility that in part Russell's Paradox[18] arose because of the literary blindness and opposition to transcendent infinities in Frege and Russell? If so, this would be a substantive case of having a concept not being a recognitional capacity – that is to say, that generalised truth is counter-intuitive. An odd feature of this is that Whitehead's and Russell's *Principia* explains almost all of its mathematics in 'natural language', thus demonstrating the falsity of Russell's prejudice against the logical resources of natural language. So we have problems. Yet there is a way forward to conjoin logic with creative language.

The paradoxes of implication utilise formal validity and entail logical impossibility, since they require an impossible antecedent (or a true antecedent whose content is irrelevant to the entailed proposition) to imply a necessary consequence. A concept of implication based on content or relevance could avoid such a situation, however. It should be argued from this state of affairs (not that an ideal exposure of logic would contain paradoxes but) that:

(1) The paradoxes of implication are entailed by prior departure from some deeper logic.

If this point is not maintained (though in some philosophy of logic it is not), then the relevant alternatives are:

(2) A schizoid relation between form and content, which renders content irrelevant or detrimental to logical identity.

(3) An emphasis on relevance as the criterion of consequence, which excludes truth as a criterion of relevance and consequence.

I argue that (1) to (3) have to be deployed to imply that:

(4) There is universalisable logic, perhaps a single one, which matches validity to relevant content.

The history of logic furnishes us with many steps towards (4), though some current interests can distract one from finding the route to later stages in the journey previously taken seriously by Aristotle and others. Although reactionary perception should be avoided, loss of clarity by allowing rhetoric to dismantle the connection to logic is wrong.

A major programme of research for Aristotle's *Poetics* awaits the next step in the construction of a connection between logic and rhetoric. It is the investigation of what we can designate as the (quite unexplored) philosophical logic of creative language presupposed by the *Poetics*. Most of the logic terminology in Aristotle's *Prior Analytics* and the *Rhetoric* recur in the *Poetics*: these relations have not been subjected to extensive enquiry. Studies on the philosophy of emotion linking the *Poetics* and *Rhetoric* are important; yet there needs to be a new research project – what is the logic of the *Poetics*, and its relation to creativity? Clearly historical analysis has its part to play; though we here carry on with the urgent task within our cultural ethos. Internal to such research is the proposal that original creative literature, which may not comply with some formal canon of rhetoric, can be logical in ways that relate to a counter-intuitive concept of consequence, relevance and *enthymeme*. Some medieval and modern attention to formal validity deems that a contradiction entails any proposition. This has discredited mere form as a criterion of any significant explanatory power for logic.

Contrariwise, it is now open to assess how a live metaphor of logical form should incorporate creative use of language as a candidate for logic. This unexpectedly reverses up to, but not over, the later Wittgenstein, though with a thesis distinct, though complementary, to his. We should not under-estimate the concurrence of this approach with the early Wittgenstein's logic. In one of his notes he stated, 'The epistemological questions concerning the nature of judgement and belief cannot be solved without a correct apprehension of the form of the proposition.'[19] Since we do not have a perfect grasp of what it is to be a logical generalisation, we do not know, in the relevant sense, what it is to be the sense of 'proposition' as a generalised property. I believe that 'proposition' here can be proved to stand for any communicative expression conveying a thought.

The relevance of logical propositions

Part of the solution to this collection of problems rests on the significance of one's maintaining that content is irrelevant if and only if it does not belong to any concise subproof of such content. This concept of a subproof preserves[20] the features of proof for finite sequences in which abstract irrelevance and redundancy are distinct. Anderson's and Belnap's[21] relevance logic is not right since it presupposes that only if a propositional variable is shared by 'A' and 'B' is 'A → B' valid, especially in view of the incompleteness of relevance proof and semantics for first order logic. Lewy argued there to be a fundamental drawback of their work[22]: their relation of logical implication forbids suppression of premises and principles: there is no true entailment respecting the law of the disjunctive syllogism. If this is applied to the metalanguage relations of logic to *enthymeme*s, it blocks *enthymeme* omissions.

In this sense a concern with relevance does not necessarily have truth as an internal property, since (in the Anderson–Belnap thesis) a prior criterion does not permit *enthymeme*s. So if one slackens logic for relevance in the Anderson–Belnap mould, it backfires. Their approach prevents one from applying logical truth to a large class of discourse outside of the propositional calculus. The negation of their view therefore enables one to insist on truth as a precondition of developing a concept of consequence that treats necessity, formality and relevance. Consequently, a concern with truth is not a doctrinal requirement, but an internal property and precondition of a universalised explanation of inference in language. If the identity and role of such inference are clarified, then we will already have satisfied criteria for being a true concept of relevance conditions. So to isolate relevance as a competitor to Aristotle's own approach to inference splits what is properly fused together or associated in his concepts.

Outside of the (no doubt proper) pluralist ecumenical perspective assessing competing logics, much history of logic has confidently furnished us with a mangled account of some aspects of implication in ancient Greek logic, demarcated by the more reliable history by the Kneales.[23] Research has moved on since their contributions, with the pioneering researches by Lear,[24] Burnyeat,[25] Martin,[26] as well as Smiley,[27] and Geach[28] exposed how some untenable pseudo-Aristotelian doctrine is still conflated with Aristotle's own concepts. We should allow for the vast logic developments beyond the capacity of syllogism. The Greek συλλογισμος is not of course always identical in sense or scope to the Classical and subsequent use of the term 'syllogism.' He employed the term for other non-syllogistic deductions. These are sometimes ones that are too complex and/or cannot be represented by the syllogism. Aristotle's attention to deductive inference – as a presupposition of some rhetorical properties – is at the heart of his and our concern to expose what it is to be the identity of logic. On the one hand, we should be concerned with historical accuracy, attempting to retrieve the nearest to the true interpretation of what Aristotle wrote. On the other hand, a philosopher living now who wishes to understand what

Aristotle wrote, partial though its survival is, will also wish to explore the logical scope of Aristotle's own desire to render explicit what it is to be logic. A necessary internal property of this project is what it is to be possibility. An historicist emphasis which neglects Aristotle as a working philosophical logician, and which does not address and expand the abstract universe formulated by Aristotle's uncompleted research programme, will distort Aristotle's psychological autobiography.

Aristotle's conception of implication is self-evidently not explained solely in terms of his formal syllogistic theory. So, whatever scope one might deem syllogism to have, it says nothing about the limits of Aristotle's view of logical inference, quite apart from his approach to dialectic. But the deep range and instinct reflected in his logical theory are surprising. For example, Geach[29] has proved the truth of Aristotle's hunch, which the latter could not demonstrate to be formally true, that no modalisation of an invalid plain categorical syllogism is valid. Such syllogism is to be understood as existentially true (or false) of the universe of discourse. Insofar as this pertains to the present study, we should note, then, that the modal operator 'necessary' obtains for *de dicto* modal syllogisms.

Conversely, Geach[30] notices that Aristotle's doctrine of the asymmetry of the subject (ονοματα) and predicate (ρηματα) announced in Aristotle's *On Interpretation* was obscured by his later theory of terms (οροι) that his theory of syllogism implemented. Geach marks this theory of terms as 'bogus' because it blurs fundamental elements in thought and its expression, which involve and change the truth-conditions of expressions. This concept of terms imposed a notion of symmetry over the proposition, which discarded the internal structure and its asymmetry. The internal asymmetry of the proposition is indisputable,[31] though there are opposed theses about its significance. For example, Aristotle's choice to formalise a theory of deduction in the syllogism by use of the theory of terms, rather than all the insights he uses outside of syllogism, should be kept in mind when noticing that he sometimes implements the asymmetry of propositional contents thesis in his *Rhetoric*; these are placed in his deductive theory, however. In other words, on occasions he utilises logic more complex and subtle than his syllogistic theory absorbs or formalises in the *Rhetoric*. For those who puzzle as to why Aristotle should have proceeded to blur and discard his initial asymmetry of proposition thesis when engaging with the syllogism, there could be at least two, not necessarily exclusive, answers. First, Aristotle's grasp of the underlying theory of the syllogism is analogous with our modernist logic's conceptions of a computable function and proof-theoretic techniques.[32] In other words, Aristotle was concerned with the valid conditions for a metatheory of consequence, rather than a programme enabling one to formalise all statements occurrent in natural languages. Secondly, having discovered many of the necessary conditions for what it is to be logic, it is too much to expect that even Aristotle's resourceful originality would have proceeded to invent the requisite predicate logic from which to derive quantification and its modal calculi.

What stands theoretically and functionally between the theory of logical identity and rhetoric is the reasoning presupposed in rhetoricians' discussion of rhetoric. If this domain of discourse is not transparent, it will equivocate over the target subject. Such equivocation persists. Certainly, there are disagreements about the identity of rhetoric and questions within logic interpretation, which may impact on rhetoric with uncertain significance so as properly to attract dissenting opinion.

Yet there are neglected issues of potential ambiguity in syllogistic interpretation that can expose semantic indeterminacies in the syllogism that have family resemblances to equivocation in rhetoric. In certain respects this is a neglected area of research, which could reduce some actual and purported 'gaps' between the formal language of syllogism and use of natural languages in rhetoric. That is to say, the differences between syllogism and the use of deduction can be one of degree and not type. Sorensen[33] argues that the Barbara syllogism, 'All men are mortal; Socrates is a man; therefore Socrates is mortal' can be interpreted as invalid: we overlook the 'innocent' equivocation between the major premise's use of 'man' as an unmarked generic property, and the minor premise's shifted marked specific use of 'man'. If we were to switch these two uses around, as theoretically can be forced on us because the rules of validity do not mark the shift, then the syllogism would be invalid.[34] Sure, our intuitions about logical validity lead us to align the 'correct' interpretation with valid use of the terms. But the point is that if we are honest to the arbitrary 'fixing of the rules', we have here – internal to syllogistic theory – a semantic indeterminacy that preserves equivocation precisely where people assume that it is excluded. So we need logic of indeterminacy and vague predicates by which we identify these properties and how they pertain to determinate rule use. Haack[35] has already produced the basis for such an analysis that has yet to be deployed to such tasks.

This sort of problem is parallel with the informal mixture usually associated with some creative areas of rhetoric. Although the foregoing treats the issues as ones of equivocation, we could equally form a theory that would make explicit such phenomena and transcribe them as multiple levels of functions, more complex than Aristotle or many modern logicians allow.[36] Accordingly, we should regard with suspicion claims about semantic transparency and the total absence of equivocation in syllogistic deduction. Consequently, Aristotle's own recognition, that logic lies at the heart of rhetoric, has an unexpected corollary: standard interpretation of the valid rules of syllogistic are actually incomplete and allow or require some manipulation in some semantics of equivocation to preserve or interpret for validity. So the link between rhetoric and syllogistic is two-edged. This is not to be committed to the false consequence that unwitting intrinsically invalid equivocation, characterisable by fallacy, is co-extensive with the above situation.

As mentioned above, Lear's[37] view is that Aristotle's motive in developing syllogistic theory was metalogical: Aristotle was not claiming that all logical consequences could be formalised as a proof in syllogism. Rather, a direct deductive argument (for example, a triangle has interior angles equal to two right angles) can be recast as a series of syllogistic inferences. Hypothetical syllogisms can be formalisable in syllogistic only if they properly contain a direct syllogism.

Once we have retrieved or constructed an explanation of the deductive status of the *enthymeme*, we can relate this to our modern formal logic. Epstein argues that within the perspective of a formalised concept of relevance many classically valid arguments are enthymematic, i.e. suppressed implicit premises exist. For example when material implication produces consequences that act under a covering law for propositional contents with different and unrelated subject matter, there is a suppressed premise to do with a common function and presupposition of generalisation over consequence relations. In Smiley's[38] sense this is a theory of consequence relative to a context, content and its internal properties, which follows the sort of view Bolzano[39] proposed.

Enthymeme

Burnyeat[40] appears to have proved that the origin of the idea of the *enthymeme* being an incomplete syllogism comes, not from Aristotle, but from Cicero and his use of the third Stoic indemonstrable.[41] In *Prior Analytics* 2.27 the argument is that even if an *enthymeme* is completely furnished with what is absent, it still may be formally invalid. This contradicts the idea that an *enthymeme* is an incomplete syllogism whose validity is produced by adding missing premises. *Prior Analytics*[42] does indeed state that: 'a συλλογισμος is ατελη if it needs either one or more premises, which are indeed the necessary consequences of the terms set down, but have not been assumed in the propositions.' But it does not explain that this is an *enthymeme*.

We should leave aside so-called (actually quasi) Aristotelian and much traditional logic. Rather, let us enquire: is the *enthymeme* in Aristotle an abbreviated syllogism? Burnyeat[43] argues that it is not. Ross asserted that the point Aristotle mentions – the omission of a premise in speech – 'forms no part of his definition of the *enthymeme*'.[44] Typically if the *enthymeme* is applied to such a syllogism, it has to be the case that the omitted premise – one of two orders[45] – is presupposed by the user in the mind (εν θυμοι). Given the application of *enthymeme* to a temporally remote dead language text, how one would achieve the knowledge of a missing premise is often problematic. Such knowledge would, of course, rest on the assumption, which in that case would be questionable, that there ever was such a premise. This terrain is fertile territory for equivocation, which may disguise sterility.

Often premises are absent from the antecedents of consequents in syllogisms that are not *enthymeme*s. This point is extendible to deductive inference outside of syllogistic: sometimes here it is a matter of choices or subtlety as to which antecedent premises one may omit or has excluded. So it does not follow from someone arguing that a premise is omitted, that the logical remains are an *enthymeme*. Consequently, for those who have not implemented this distinction in their analysis of a narrative,[46] their assumption, that detection of a missing premise implies the presence of an *enthymeme*, is false. It equally could imply that non-syllogistic deductive inference, which is not an *enthymeme*, is present. A source for claiming that Aristotle advanced the 'incomplete syllogism' view of the sense of '*enthymeme*' is the Aldine of *Prior Analytics* 2.27 (70a10):

ἐνθύμημα μὲν οὖν ἐστι συλλογισμὸς ἀτελὴς ἐξ εἰκότων ἢ σημείων.[47]

An *enthymeme* is an incomplete syllogism from likelihoods or signs.

Burnyeat observes that there is clear evidence for the conclusion that ατελης in the manuscript was deleted and restored by scribal inference, and that it was based on an earlier use of the term in *PA*.[48] He points out that all other significant manuscripts omit ατελης, and there is a late arrival in 1597 of a gloss by Pacius, even though Pacius later volunteers the observation that other manuscripts, which he checked, did not have the term in them. The statement ἐνθύμημα μὲν οὖν ἐστι συλλογισμὸς ἐξ εἰκότων ἢ σημείων recurs in the *Rhetoric* three times;[49] it occurs without ἀτελὴς. This use of the statement, which does not draw attention to the absence of a premise by noting the imperfect statement of what is present in that statement, can be understood in at least two ways. First, it adverts to no other premises than what it states. Secondly, the statement stipulates an inference that is not identical to a perfect deductive syllogism, yet which is still a proof (πιστις) and which accordingly should be studied without reference to specifying an absent premise. Burnyeat[50] comments that none of the uses of '*enthymeme*' that precede Aristotle's pioneering technical definition(s), in Alcidamas and Isocrates invite one to provide expressions that the speaker left out of his speech. So the second option above complies with the prehistory of '*enthymeme*' and Aristotle's usage uninfected by a history of the future commentary after Aristotle. Burnyeat's argument here is that '*enthymeme*' is a kind of συλλογισμος – a proof. It is not a συλλογισμος of a kind.

In short, '*enthymeme*' is a deductive proof; it is not a defective proof, rendered imperfect by an absent premise. Nevertheless, of course, there are different strengths for the apodeixis and for syllogism. For example, one can infer another syllogism from a valid syllogism by strengthening the premises or weakening the conclusion.[51]

Aristotle's framework in the psychology of language for this proof is objectivist concerning the relation between speech and thought. The mental counterpart of the relevant *enthymeme* in speech is itself a piece of logic: the relevant aspects of thought are argued proof. This is rather like Frege's view that the status of a logical 'thought' is objective and parallel with its propositional expression. Burnyeat[52] notes that Philoponus derives the term ενθυμημα, not from εν θυμοι but from ενθυμεισθαι: 'It is called *enthymeme* because it leaves one premise for the mind to *think*.' Both the sourcing of the function here and the mode of expression leave aside the certain origin of an actual presupposed judgement in the author's origination. They re-position the function in mental activity, which need not be the author's, and present it in such a way as to allow that it might not even have been considered by the author. Instead, it could originate with a person reflecting on the narrative. That these matters are only possibilities does not weaken the conclusion that if such a derivation were correct then it does not have to follow, as it would in a syllogism, that a premise has to be missing.

How short is a chain of premises?

In the *Prior Analytics* an αποδειχις is a συλλογμος with antecedents and a consequence demonstrated as a necessary implication of those premises, of which a *reductio ad absurdum* can be an instance. Burnyeat[53] argues that the qualification τις after συλλογισμος complies with Aristotle's allowance that some such demonstrations function in a μαλκωτερον[54] fashion, a more relaxed συλλογιζονται in the *Rhetoric*.[55] Here, even so, the definition of ενθυμημα just is the same for συλλογισ–μος; ενθυμημα is not presented as an abbreviated or deformed subspecies of συλλογισμος. Someone might have expected that when the expression 'rhetorical syllogism' occurs in Aristotle's *Rhetoric* (1356b4–5),[56] it might be defined as a species of συλλογισμος. Not so: it is defined as συλλογισμος. We should again note that this term is often used with the sense 'deduction' and is not synonymous with 'syllogism'. Aristotle was not one to confuse the basic difference between the criteria of definition with an instance of an example thus defined, and even less with an extended or attenuated type of example.

Minimising the number of premises as a feature of *enthymeme* is contrary, since, for this to apply to a normal syllogism there would be just one premise for some *enthymemes*. In contrast two premises do not seem to be too lengthy a set for the audience to follow.[57] Aristotle does not make it a necessary condition for being an *enthymeme* that it has a premise missing from a syllogism. As Burnyeat points out, Aristotle himself explains the conversion from maxim to *enthymeme* using the example from Euripides' *Hecuba*:[58] '"There is no man who is truly free" which is a maxim, but with its continuation an *enthymeme*, "For he is either slave of wealth or chance".' Burnyeat points out that logically this sequence is complex. It possesses a disjunctive predicate, which syllogistic cannot represent – as with a number of other *enthymemes* in this section of the *Rhetoric*, though the use of deduction is quite evident. This reveals, of course, that Aristotle's συλλο–γισμος should not be restricted to, or have to include, 'syllogism', since it depicts deductive argument. So the determination of ενθυμημα is wider than syllogism, though not necessarily in the sense of being non-deductive. In particular, rather than being looser than syllogistic, rhetoric is at least in some contexts more logically complex. From the perspective of logical technicality and depth, rhetoric can make more stringent requirements than syllogistic.

'For the most part'

An *enthymeme* is a demonstration, from a large set of kinds in the *Prior Analytics*, which displays different levels of modalities. For all these variations the premises are sufficient to infer the conclusion. If we have a narrow view of the powers of a strict deductivist, Aristotle's 'for the most' could exclude deduction and include probability, though this would not reflect clear understanding. We should, of course, distinguish between: (a) what we think Aristotle actually wrote; (b) what it is possible to ascribe as the limit of its extended range of insight; and (c) how these two are affected by our contemporary researches into what it is to be logic and rhetoric. There is an esoteric and yet functional set of relations between the inner conditions that constitute what it is to be a statement and its functional relation to the logical theory, in the perspective of a statement's communicative use; but we do well to be wary here. Rules can indeed be presented as something underlying use in the sense of theoretical abstractions as properties external to the user's cognition. As Geach argues, however, abstractionism is wrong, though of course this is distinct to the limits of abstraction (see Fine, 2002).[59] So we need not attend to a schizoid division between use and grounds for use. Despite this, we need to allow that all theory is less than perfect. Accordingly, there will be an overlap and gap between actual use and its theoretical representation. Since there is also a gap between a user's cognition of what she states and her grasp of what it actually states, one should not be reductionist by imposing the hypothesis that the sense of the statement is what is agreed solely by consensus, nor merely what is 'evident'. And we should ascribe this awareness to Aristotle as a qualification on our sometimes too free use of his deductively determined framing of the evident truths, which he presupposes for rhetoric.

This situation also devolves on the psychodynamics of origination, as well as the degree to which the inscription of meaning in linguistic form acts as vehicle for types. Beyond the scope of current analysis is a dispute concerning a sort of complex general presupposition, which is as follows. If there are ontological universals, and these can be or are mapped by creative literature, then is such a generalised statement referring to, and true of, a slice of the universe, which contains (uses, presupposes, entails) internal properties of a truth-condition that applies to circumstances other than its token instances?

Plural generalisation of probability?

Although one should not argue that there is no probability in Aristotle's *Rhetoric*, yet its 'for the most part' quantification does not have to bear a probabilistic rendering, or an inductive one, for 'most' is a quantifier, and can be expressed using standard logic or Boolean algebra.[60] In other words 'for the most part' has quantification within deductive inference,[61] while Aristotle isolates dialectical from rhetorical argument (συλλογισμοι). Obviously, Aristotle's view is that probability can attach to ενθυμημα, for 'ενθυμημα is a *deduction* starting from probabilities or signs'[62] and this will affect its validity. Conversely, it would be a genetic fallacy to conflate 'starting from probabilities' with the subsequent 'deduction'.

What of Aristotle's claim that 'all our convictions come either through συλ–λογισμος or from επαγωγη' ('induction')?[63] We should note that Aristotle proceeds here by adding:

Now induction, or rather the deduction which springs out of induction, consists in deducing a relation between one extreme and the middle by means of the other extreme.

Moreover he volunteers the use of the expression 'it is necessary that' to represent relevant relations. So Aristotle's aim is not to achieve 'probable knowledge', but by use of επαγωγη ('induction') deriving deduction, to infer knowledge. This is akin to the use of 'true' in possible worlds or, in a different sense, a thesis associated with the expression 'possibly true'.[64] Aristotle is concerned to deduce knowledge employing induction as a start, not as a pervasive function of rhetoric. So this is not, in this perspective, information induced by statistical probability. The typical resulting inference relation in *enthymeme*s, in other words, is not inductive, but deductive, with its range limited by appropriate plural, not probabilistic, quantification. An undecided truth-value is not required to be a probability, and one may even take statements involving probability and present them in the form of deduction, as Levi demonstrates.[65]

Where knowledge is qualified 'for the most part' and likelihood in such contexts, it is knowledge whose quality is not uncertain, but whose quantification may have limiting boundaries that fall short of universalisation. This resists the idea that degrees of repute in evidence should be read as degrees of probability in our modern senses.[66] When writing of pregnancy here, it would have been bad taste to think that Aristotle was conceiving of a probabilistic partial degree of foetal existence, though he does write of invalid forms that are susceptible to refutation.

Inference in the Gospel of Mark

The position developed in the foregoing differs widely from the ways many theological rhetoricians analyse while attempting to discover rhetoric and *enthymeme* in the New Testament. Is it textually viable to apply a modern probability analysis construed as a New Testament *enthymeme*, which is taken to be the internal sense of part of Mark 3? Behind this approach and trend in biblical studies there tends to be the assumption that somehow someone has proved probability to be superseded by deduction as the identity of such narrative. Moreover it is often incorrectly supposed in these scenarios that probability is a more sensitive sphere within or as a tool for mapping literary sensibility. Certainly, if syllogism is used as the medium to provide this seeming inductive advantage, the latter can easily win. But the New Testament leans towards conditional deductive inference, and not syllogistic, nor Peircean implication. So the motivation, which interprets the *enthymeme* as an abbreviated syllogism with inductive inclinations for New Testament purposes, is suspect. In relevant contexts deductive reasoning is more accurate than induction. Thus if we discover that the New Testament skews sense away from the latter and embraces the former, this will oppose many a traditional desire to blunt New Testament narrative with the allegedly incomplete syllogistic *ad hominem* induction.

Such induction all too readily complies with the nineteenth–twentieth century theological fashion, which seeks a lower conceptual ceiling for New Testament rationality than sublime creativity might accord it. It accommodates neat recipes that comply with a policy to merge the origin of Christianity with the cultural customs of first century AD tradition. As with Shakespeare, however, a literary critic's too tight a grip on the antecedent conditions of emergence, which attend genius, is a death knell to that emergence. Therefore, in the relevant sense, the New Testament ought to be read as a transcendent violation of its time, and an opponent of those who read it to the contrary.

It may be stimulating to adopt a diachronically distinct and historically much later, for example poststructuralist rhetorical approach to the New Testament. This should not be confused with either assuming that it nets any of Aristotle's understanding of the *enthymeme*, nor with the supposition that it is applicable to the New Testament's linguistics. Therefore one should not infer from a blend of these options that Aristotle's syllogistic influence could be found in the New Testament in situations where scholars have imposed the probabilistic or reductive.

It is worthwhile for us to contrast the probabilistic type of *enthymeme* interpretation with the actual types of uses in a narrative such as Mark's Gospel. Mark 3: 24 employs the condition inference, 'For *if* a kingdom is divided against itself, that kingdom cannot stand'.[67] Surely this token instantiation is there to coerce the reader into taking it to be a generalisation? The implication relation in this statement is repeated in Mark 3 using 'household' and 'Satan' as a replacement for 'kingdom', thus entrenching other token uses to emphasise the inference as a generalisation. A presupposition of the conditional inference, of course, is that Jesus has been selected by the scribes to occupy the subject slot for the conditional statement. This deployment of the inference relation entails an extensive use of generalisation over differing types of contexts.

The logic of questions is still in its formal infancy, so we should approach the logic of interrogative irony[68] cautiously. Mark 3: 22 raises the question: 'How can Satan drive out Satan?' The function of the question is to posit it as an axiom, which is then used by conditional proof to convert it to a theorem. It presupposes logical functions concerning reference in relative identity, the law of non-contradiction, and predicate logic's negation. The succeeding statement, 'If a kingdom is divided against itself, that kingdom cannot stand', takes the question as a transformed axiom, and presupposes it to contain, as a premise for this inference, a generalisable rule of the consequence of contradiction, a rule which is taken to be transitive regarding subject. This implicitly presupposes a functioning scheme equivalent to metalanguage, by which token replacement of a type operates as an underlying function in the object language fused to the meta-language.

Evidently this logic is only a fragment of the literary senses in Mark 3; but it proffers a mirror to the presuppositions of the collective consciousness obtaining for both synchronic and diachronic axes.[69] For each the geography is important, since the narrative presents Jesus as preaching in the old territory of Baal Zebub. He had just commanded a sick man to take up his bed and walk and healed the blind. In the same territory, at the time of Mark, the ancient Phoenician archives available to Josephus, and previously to Nebuchadnezzar's scribes,[70] displayed the same liturgical myths, as had the Ugaritic Keret myth cycles of Baal. For example, 'he shall come down from the roofs . . . the sick man shall take up his bed . . . the blind shall be cured.'[71]

In Mark 3 the scribes attempt to identify Jesus as a function of their inter-textual history, so as to subvert his identity claims. So there is evident interplay of competing ontologies bound to different criteria of identity superimposed over 'Baalzeboul' and 'Satan'. Mark 3's usage of logic, episodically outlined above, is a structure for the narrative's conceptual dynamics. Within this per-spective, the reference of 'Satan' is tantamount to an argument-place that simultaneously slips its anchor and criterion of identity as the transcendent power figure. This reference of 'Satan' re-attaches, with another criterion of identity, to the (false) god motif of Baalzeboul, only to be deconstructed by Jesus' reasoning when he denudes Satan of Jesus' own interiority and Satan's external cultic geography. By these implications Mark entails that the criterion of identity for Satan is left for the original users – the scribes – to be the bearers of 'Satan'. Such linguistic phenomena are rich in logic. 'Satan' is parallel with the logical dangling pronouns[72] and variables that can take a range of values.

The status of reference and the criteria of identity are at the forefront of the use of 'Satan' here. Although reference and identity have varying explications in philosophy of logic, a core of features from a number of concepts has ready application to Mark's uses of 'Satan'. The tendency to the Phoenician spelling of Baalzeboul, which displaces the Hebrew ironising spelling of 2 Kings 2, com-plements the popular awareness contemporary to Mark of the older Canaanite backcloth against which Jesus taught, with the geography of Mark 2–3. I have mentioned this reference pattern albeit sketchily, as a complex function of the argument structure to make the point that the logic of Mark in these contexts is dense with subtle patterns and levels or multiple orders of use and mention.

Analytical philosophy has been very tardy in relation to such uses, which has contributed to its limitations. Logic is still in its provisional stages of develop-ment, while it has enormous potential. Syllogistic has no place in such an advanced literary space. Higher level predicate calculi and other mapping tech-niques are more suitable. One persistent feature is complex tonal pun, and research[73] has been done to introduce this to truth-functional logics, betraying Frege's[74] restriction of *Beleuchtung* and *Farbung* to non-logical domains.

So logical analysis should be sensitive to the thematic literary polemic; for war it is, against falsehood, in the narrator's hand. The foregoing example exemplifies the multi-layered functioning of the logic of polemical discourse. So we should be careful to avoid dividing the underlying functions of a narrative with its usage. Narrative is not a linear function; it is more like a multi-dimensional universe. Certainly, we should avoid incorrect formulations fusing surface structure with underlying functions. One of these would be to conflate Aristotle's rhetoric with the foregoing example from Mark, since the latter does not employ partial quantification and Mark employs a single statement in the role as a token for a universally quantified type.

False metaphor in some rhetorical scholarship

Perhaps we first should convince ourselves that we are capable of confusion. Although there are some questions as to what counts towards something being valid in deep areas of logic, such uses can only be fallaciously appealed to as a basis for the equality of opinions when fundamental categories of logic are violated. Prior to moving on to issues about logic and rhetoric, it will assist to give some types of examples.

Fallacy is a helpful technique with which to isolate problems of interpretation in rhetoric. 'Fallacy' is a metonymy metaphor. That is, mapping facility is not an exhaustive function of the subject that it represents. Explaining an undetected fallacious move in terms of fallacy confers a visibility on the unsuspected usage that was not even noticed to be a problem prior to such depiction. Confusion is alien to logic; and logical representation of confusion leaves out some of the qualitative disorder on which it operates. This recasting into logical form improves the unsuspecting user's formulation. I mention this because such improvement frequently obscures, from the unsuspecting user, the extent and extremity of the error that the fallacy displays, which needs further exposure in the unwitting metaphorical use of logic terminology. This way of posing the problem is itself unexpected to those whom it characterises. Of course someone may want to discount this context as an in-house irrelevant game. He may retort:

(1) Have any rules you want; anything goes.

Therefore rules are outlawed. Apart from reminding him that this itself is a use of the logic that he denies, we might respond, using his own criteria, paradoxically that:

(2) (1) entails the falsehood of (1).

Certainly, Mark's gospel has no possible place for the reception of (1).

Attempts to interpret logic need to be reducible to the theorems, axioms or presuppositions of inferences that constitute logic. Certainly the criteria for determining these properties may be recondite or problematic in certain respects, though the issues I address here are not substantively deflected by such difficulties. Quite apart from the issue of whether one invents or discovers further extensions for logic, classical and current logics have determinate identities which place what should be evident limits on a rhetorician's, linguist's and logician's imaginative contribution to extending or retrieving a hitherto unknown property of a logic's identity.[75]

It would not be a successful way of discounting the present points by suggesting that they merely fail to recognise conditions facilitating the extension of logic by foreclosing on the possibility of furnishing fresh results that are invisibly 'contained in the premises' of a pioneering inference. If such invisibility resists attempts to expose it as an actual property, then it has to be deemed at most a possible, not a bivalent actual, property. If this is the case, then modal logic will have to be brought to structure the premises and this downgraded version will have a straightforward logical form. But often assertions about a thing being contained in the premises remain just a foggy notion used to encourage imaginative prose ornamented with a few unmeasured logic terms (as in (1) above). This perhaps becomes a vogue because literary style is also a feature of rhetoric and the emotive psychology associated with it. Just as there has been false science and prescientific culture paraded as science, so there is some bad logic. There is a question of genuine uncertainty in deep waters as to what counts towards being a feature of logic; yet this is hardly ever a relevant cover for the fallacies characterised here.

So if one were to put the best spin on these mistakes, what is it to come to the nub of the point? Some rhetoricians (perhaps unwittingly) employ *metaphorical* uses of terms such as 'syllogism', 'implication' (and its tautologies), 'necessity', 'entailment' and '*enthymeme*', 'rule', 'law'. Criticism suggesting the inadvertent use of dead metaphor does not presuppose that logic does not contain metaphor. Rather, I have argued that logic, pure mathematics, and for example the languages of astrophysical cosmology, are an unusual species of live metaphor (and in a fundamentally different sense, creativity itself may also be anchored to one's capacity to compose live metaphors). This live metaphor is of course distinct to dead metaphor. One would be involved in committing modal segmentation and quantifier shift to purport that this technical use of live metaphor invariantly ranges over the domain of *ad hoc* dead metaphor fallacies.[76] In effect, the systematic development of such uses of logic terminology produces a hybrid pattern composed of words like 'premise' that are homonyms of the same logical grapheme 'premise.' A way of highlighting this situation is to articulate the suggestion developed in the present book, namely that values of functions are akin to live (not dead) metaphorisation – so function is live metaphorised from, say, 'x^2' to the live metaphor 'y^2'.

Consequently, among some New Testament rhetoricians' researches we discover something quite alien to Aristotle's own theory and practice, and one that is also inconsistent with uses of logic. Maybe an interlocutor retorts: 'so what? People merely use the idea in different ways later, and I for one follow that; so what's the problem?' The problem is that few philosophers subsequent to Aristotle, in the relevant periods in which the muddled view of *enthymeme* emerges, had as deep and clear a grasp of how logic should go as Aristotle did, and some of those philosophers who influenced Christian theology are among those who, to say the very least, are not renowned for their logical ability or depth, as opposed to mere programmatic technical competence in pushing around all-too-familiar moves. Certainly, Aristotle should not be treated as sacred canon, and there are differences of interpretation; but the range and identity of these have little to do with matching those who dismember his view of *enthymeme* with his insights. Self-evidently, the existence of an opinion about *enthymeme* and evidence of its influence are not proof of truth on the matter. Furthermore, it is often the later scholars ornamenting non-Aristotelian influences, and not so much these influences, who have triggered the chasm between Aristotle's conception and the idea, say, that *enthymeme* is a shortened syllogism. For example in New Testament studies it is not uncommon to come across a study in which a scholar selects a piece of narrative and presupposes that an *enthymeme* analysis is appropriate for it, though it does not occur in the narrative in the form of a syllogism. The narrative is then adjusted in its existing form by recasting it into something reminiscent of syllogism. Although this type of approach to narrative recurs in many scholastic contexts, as well as in the sphere of syllogism allegedly applicable to the New Testament, this style of interpretation finds a natural slot in allegedly isolating an *enthymeme*. In such cases it is the scholar who invents a syllogism and imposes it on to non-syllogistic fragments in the ancient narrative. It may not escape an impartial reader's notice that an efficient way of avoiding recognition that this is an inaccurate interpretation of the given passage is to have a handy thesis that something is missing from the narrative, which the scholar supplies, by alleging that it is warranted via an appeal to a device – the muddled *enthymeme*-as-syllogism claim – with the seeming support of Aristotle.

Such a procedure implements a number of fallacies.[77] First, a modal fallacy[78] of confusing a possible, yet not expressed, form with the actual use in the narrative under investigation. Secondly, a segmentation fallacy, that of recombining occurring expressions as semantic functions that they do not have in the target context; this is similar to the false hypostatisation in diachronic morphology, for example, in some Semitic studies.[79] Thirdly, genetic fallacies in retrojective form, of conflating a narrative effect with a purported original ground.[80] Since the literary effect in the narrative has been reformulated in a form that it does not have in use, such a fallacy conflates historical origin with logical nature, precisely in the way W. F. Albright did with his generalised approach to ancient language and logic.[81]

Some speculative rhetorical analysis displays a related confusion, that of merging logic and subjective use of mental experience. This is parallel with a pattern manifested in some Old Testament study.[82] On occasions such as the above type of scenario where a modal fallacy is a foundation for theorising, an implication fallacy[83] may be employed to achieve or justify an approach. To isolate fallacies as the above gives errors a certain retrospective clarity that was invisible to the unsuspecting user. This retrospection renders them evident in the way they were not in use – they are usually unconsciously disguised in obscure prose. So, for example, a scholar may argue that, though, or if an instance he or she is examining does not fit the usual logical or rhetorical canon, then the scholar assumes or asserts that he is using logic or a certain category of it; but this is a mistake about intentionality. That someone believes a statement obviously does not make it correct; this is as true for the mind as it is for logic.[84]

Whether or not we adopt Frege as the foundation to document the mistakes in this situation, or appeal to antirealist and irrealist logics such as those devised by Tennant[85] and Bogossian,[86] they all can be drawn on to sustain the foregoing sort of criticisms. A reason for this in such cases criticised is that there is sufficient relevant asymmetry between mentality and logic to map confusion between these two phenomena. There are many disagreements among logicians; but the foregoing types of fallacies do not even come near to nor are salvaged by logical disputes. Such cases exemplify Geach's[87] view that there is a general tendency to implant bad logic in didactic areas of some culture.

Conclusion

The significance of knowledge and the form of ignorance within the author's and the critic's uses of reason are important in assessing the functional capability of their compositions to bear logical analysis. Obviously, to some indeterminate degree, this is a problem contingent on the expressibility of the intention of the ancient author in linguistic form, and a matter regulated by the presuppositions of the scholar's analysis. The logical identity of a proposition and its use as a piece of reasoning involve a complex set of issues. Also, other uses, which are present in a narrative that make functional contributions to the context, can unwittingly be ignored. Logical analysis is not merely the task of abstracting out of a discourse the bits that seem promising as objects for transformation into inferential or syllogistic form. A discovery-procedure is just that; it should not be a circular antecedent assumption that what is presupposed is what is the narrative's identity.

Conversely, in a certain sense usage should not be transformed at all, but discovered preserved, in our attempts to recover the identity of the target narrative. To ignore this would be rather like a child who, coming upon the inference: '2 + 2 = 4 and possibly 3 extra', assumes that the extra ingredient was a sort of bonus that did not affect the sum. Certainly, this illustration is naive; but it is a simple form of complex muddles. In recondite areas of inference, it is rarely obvious to us that such errors are being committed – when they are. A true account of logic is a function of discovering the accurate relations for resolving when such slips are made.

Although philosophers and logicians diverge over the technical solutions and final form of the central problems, many applied strategies in rhetorical analysis have operated in ignorance of the type of insights unquestionably achieved, or offer contributions which could massively benefit from quite basic research on the philosophy of logic. Sometimes these are products of influences that intervene between our sources and ourselves. One major problem due for attention in the light of the present study, but beyond its scope, is the question of the relations between 'proof' (πιστις) and 'faith' (πιστις).[88] Are they homonyms or polysemes in New Testament usage?

Much of the New Testament world contests the cultures with which it battles. There is thus a danger of scholarly equivocation over such controversial writers by conflating the possible scope of social contacts within their world (but often not of theirs) as if they were conceptual influences. The routing of Greek rhetoric through Palestinian rabbinic Judaism would hardly be an attractive source to those writers whose reasoning disputes within a polemic to retrieve a vision of Old Testament fulfilment set against its perceived betrayal in Judaism. The occurrence of pseudo-Aristotelian rhetoric and Platonic forms in the Sanhedrin's stylistics[89] is evidence for a bifurcation between the authorial voices of such alienation for Mark, even before we see that this Gospel's reasoning and polemic introduces us to an original world of creativity and logic.

Leaving Romantic causality aside, this area needs quite fresh research: what are the psychodynamics of original causality concerning the embedding of controversial rationality in a new narrative? Here linguistics, literary theory and logic should be integrated in quests for answers. Within this priority is an abstract multiple query for applied narrative analysis: if there are universal necessary conditions of consequence expressible in a formal universe of discourse, and if Aristotle exposed properties of them, then would they appear manifested in some form in a diachronically unrelated narrative if that narrative succeeded in creatively expressing other universal qualities?

11 Conclusion

Some main traditions in modernist and poststructuralist culture, in particular philosophy and theology, have been parasitic on reductionism and empirical simplicity, not only of verificationism but also of some trends in applied sciences. Clear-headed consciousness is wonderful. In contrast, many notions of simplicity are contrary and complicated. Some scientists employ the term 'simplicity' to label their approaches, though as I noticed in chapter 2, Herbert Simon (2001: 35) plausibly explains that their activities should be labelled as parsimony since it 'is the ratio of the complexity of the data set to the complexity of the formula'. In any case a non-scientist would be baffled to be told to read and understand almost any example of significant scientific simplicity in its research form. So simplicity often marks a sometimes-useful myth that is replete with unstable contingencies. Life is more complicated than this myth. And simplicity belays the depth of both problems and opportunities. Concern with depth and theoretical felicity has exposed fresh prospects for transcendence, which makes reductionism and physicalism seem inept and over-generalised. The applied world of ethical problems exemplifies a complexity and need for pragmatic idealism, including a focus on the applied significance of abstract analysis of value and values as well as, for example, the qualitative functions of moral decency.

This book contributes a future Renaissance in this millennium, whose possibilities should not be conceived in terms of the past, nor should they be apprehended merely as a function of conceptual dumbing-down of a simplifying Razor. Such a critical perspective, this book has argued, has nothing to do with a crudely conservative theology, or with the untenable aspects of mythological medieval scholasticism, neither with what is now recognisable as a twentieth-century modernist mechanistic, reductionist stage in scientific development. One should perhaps look forward more, to a future counter-intuitive epoch, which by contrast would show up past modernisms as impoverished versions of what is possible and needed.

On the one hand, philosophy and theology should be bold enough to craft their criteria of identity in terms of its visionary historical origins – in ways it has not often done in the last 150 years. On the other hand, if culture is to benefit, often by healthy contrast from the articulations and insights of contemporary and future cultural influences, it will have to do better than the ways in which it typically managed its affairs in the twentieth century. Paradoxically, this involves locating innovative creativity in sciences and humanities at the deeper levels – levels that are themselves often at variance with the establishment in which they struggle for survival. Central to this is the judgement that the function of interpretation of the significance of such contributions is often not what normative culture makes of them. This extends to the merits of theory and complexity themselves, over and against practice. No doubt in these spheres there are redundant and less helpful approaches and emphases. Clearly, one should also aim for a balanced integration of conceptual and practical worlds. Reflection on the theoretical identity of ethical expressions can lead to assessment of pragmatic application. We have found, however, that those regulating or engaged with some extreme practical matters are not thereby necessarily people who have a clear grasp of that world. There is a proverb in which a discarded wise person – deemed irrelevant for normal purposes – is the one who has practical insight in a time of crisis when the city is attacked. This is almost a model of counsel for the corporate world which governments now take to be their ideal. Subsequent to true advice, truth is again forgotten.

It is the challenge to understand this sense of the irrelevant which is a central ingredient in one's being able to think relevantly about what is true. In this sense philosophy or theology are, or should be, especially counter-intuitive. The modern world's simple and confused complex concerns with materialism, whether it be science or consumer, which equates being a producer and consumer with being a thinker, should be in contrast to the elements by which truth has to judge what its criteria of recognition are. The previous chapter found that, submerged in the structure of rhetoric is no compromising, arbitrary shifting set of goal-posts to service relativism. Rather, good rhetoric identifies true relevance, which presupposes an objective basis of measurement; and rhetoric employs deduction, not subjective persuasion. The rhetoric of practical philosophy and theology should follow this direction so as to harness the qualitative properties of transcendence, since the foregoing discovered that metaphysical and transcendent functions underlie actual material, social and psychological worlds. Such functions contain transfinite and infinite values. And so theology's basis in the actual world and its affects can relevantly be transcendent instead of capitulated to reductionism.

That transcendence is counter-intuitive, that the latter is a central property of creativity, and reasons why materialist intuition would not have invariably detected those forms of life and interpretations irrelevant to its ethos. I conclude with this perspective because the world in which we live is prone to coerce us into confusing the muddled materialism of pragmatic utility with a true criterion for qualitative functions in education. But the point of life is beyond itself. So, transcendence should not be thought of as irrelevant to pragmatism.

It is somewhat paradoxical that the twentieth century's abuse of scientific modernist realism has illicitly furnished us in the twenty-first century with reductionism as a code to demolish transcendence. Contrariwise, as the foregoing argues, counter-intuitive functions internal to deeper domains of science do display sufficient conditions to attest to the universal pervasiveness of complex transcendence. Even so, philosophy is not simply divine; neither is God; nor is science. Philosophy will have to give fresh attention to the complexities of transcendence, and look for alternative futures.

Notes

Introduction

1 As far as I know, Gibson (1997) and Gibson (2000) were the first studies to address and formulate counter-intuition as an explicit conception, despite the regular use of the term.

2 Bogossian's (2002) research and other studies in Bermudez and Millar's (2002) collection reflect the type of positions that illuminatingly target pressing issues.

3 The collection of essays in Montefiore and Vines (1999) examines this type of situation.

4 Note that wherever 'modernism(s)' and similar forms are employed in the present book, the scope of Baudelaire's French *modernité* should be understood, as formulated in Kelley (1974) and Gibson (2000 and forthcoming b). For brief comments on reasons here, see the section below 'Exploring new pasts with future possibility', and note 45 to chapter 2, below.

5 See J. A. Hiddleston (1999).

6 See Marion's (1998) profound analysis of Wittgenstein and the foundations of mathematics.

7 See Floyd's (2001) view that Wittgenstein was not fully a constructivist.

8 For a further scrutiny of 'strangeness', as a Socratic feature, see Gibson (2000) and Gibson (forthcoming a and b).

9 We do not have to agree with Lacan's way of presenting this present tense use as a way of modifying the present as a supplement to Freud, though his theory may be an unstable way of evoking such a possibility. Cf. Bowie (1978).

10 See Gibson (2000: 82–3).

1 Complexities of meaning

1 For example, Lewy's (1976) one-sided research on inference, modality and meaning repeatedly uses the expression 'counter-intuition' to measure issues without ever mentioning what it means, though he gives detailed attention to just about all the other words involved. His research on this sort of topic began under Wittgenstein, and remained an obsession throughout his life, involving intractable disputes about definition with some of his colleagues, and Lewy (1976) was one of the few non-editorial works he composed in his lifetime. This footnote is not offered in a caring fashion to derogate someone who was obviously a distinguished scholar, and one of my former teachers, or to criticise his book which provides profound insights, some of which will be implemented below. Rather, this is to illustrate the potential in one's failure to recognise what one is arguing when using the term 'counter-intuition'; a point that no doubt applies to the present author.

2 Again, it is worth pointing out that I have no interest in the history of philosophy of

Wittgenstein, only insofar as it pertains to understanding philosophy. The above analysis does not attend to a group of relevant areas, dealt with in Marion (1998) and Gibson (2000a).

3 See for example Hintikka's (1994) observation that Wittgenstein's later work reflects or supports model semantics.

4 Tolstikov (1989); he notes that his study was written in 1984.

5 Cf. Penrose *et al.* (1997); Gibson (forthcoming a).

6 There are many different routes to sustain this point; see an alternative developed by Langton (1998).

7 This project will take a number of books to complete. It seems expedient to develop it in the context of investigations in a variety of topics, such as that of the present book, to articulate it in relation to other theories and applications.

8 See Wittgenstein (1996), *Notes on Logic* 201a–2 Recto, p. B4, p. 89 (second manuscript).

9 The extensive premises to argue this position are to be found in the author's *Divining Cosmology*, chapters 1–7.

10 For example, Deleuze and Guattari (1994).

11 For which see Gibson (2000).

12 See Smith's (1998) explanation of chaos theory.

13 Here Wittgenstein is examining the question, 'When do we say that any one is observing?'

2 Simple-minded philosophy

1 Ockham seems to have finished writing his non-political philosophy by 1324. He had lectured on the *Sentences* at Oxford between 1317 and 1319. The next compositions were his *Expositio aurea* (Golden Exposition, of Aristotle's logic) and the *Exposition of Aristotle 5 'Physics'* (Books I–IV); all these were written during 1321–3. In addition to these, by 1324 he had produced his *Summa Logicae*, the *Quodlibet*s, the remainder of the *Exposition of Aristotle's Physics* (Books V–VII) and his two treatises on quantity. As well as a *reportatio* of his Oxford Sentences commentary, Books I–JY, there is a revised version of his lectures on Book I, an *Ordinatio*, probably dating from 1319–24. With the implicit reference to and condemnation of Ockham as a heretic by Pope John (6 June 1328) in his bull *Quia quorunclam*, Ockham's work was disrupted. By 1334 Ockham commenced writing his, eventually very extensive, political philosophy, the first volume of which is *Opus nonaginta dierum* (*Work of Ninety Days*). Its extraordinary length and impartiality are amazing in view of his personal circumstances. Yet by late 1334 he had also composed and sent his *Epistola ad Fratres Minores* (*Letter to the Franciscans*), as well as having written I *Dialogus*, a very long neutral treatise on the concept of heresy and its application to papal authority, both now in English thanks to the fine editions of Stephen McGrade and John Kilcullen (see Ockham, 1992 and 1995). It may be that Ockham had intended to write more formal philosophy and logic; yet he was disillusioned with the projects when he was persecuted, and his later political and moral philosophy could be viewed, not as a long-planned addition to his overall philosophical position, but as a change of heart about what philosophy should be – a pragmatically based enterprise for abstract theory. As with other medieval scholars, we should reckon on our possessing less than Ockham's complete works. Non-extant writings and their detail, deemed to be obscure or of marginal significance, may not have been so regarded by Ockham or some of his contemporaries. It is possible that his lost writings, if rediscovered, would change topics in his philosophy. For example, Rega Wood draws attention to citations attributed to Ockham that do not occur anywhere in his extant writings (Wood, 1990: 30–1; cf. note 2 below). These appear in the sole extant copy of John of Reading's *Sentences*. This Reading, a Franciscan, typifies the lesser, yet ecclesiastically significant, type of figure who contributed to the

battleground of dispute with Ockham. By 1323 Reading, interestingly a former student of Lutterel's, was to be found as a consultant to the Pope at Avignon prior to Ockham's arrival. Reading disputed Ockham's view of intuitive cognition. He maintained that intuitive cognition of non-existents is possible. Although he was influenced by Duns Scotus, Reading here disagrees with him (see de la Torre, 1987: 166–74), and he bases his case on God's absolute power.

2 At least, those of which manuscripts are extant. See Courtenay (1992).
3 See Ockham (1967–88) *Ordinatio*, I, d. 2, q. 7.
4 Sorensen (1993).
5 Spade (1988: iv) explains how Thomas Bradwardine's research on insolubilia assisted him to craft a theory of signification that has correspondence theory properties.
6 I propose that 'modernist logic' be used to mark philosophical trends that run contemporarily with the familiar use of the term 'modernism' for a general cultural context. There is a need for research on cross-currents between these contexts and philosophy in nineteenth-century European modernisms.
7 See Frege's (1977: 21) study 'Compound logical thoughts'; cf. Dummett (1991a).
8 Adams's (1987: 388) two-volume work has only one brief reference to Frege, and four to Russell (pp. 136–7, 150, 536, 797).
9 Adams (1987) refers to the first edition (Ithaca, NY, 1962) of Geach's book. There have in fact been two editions of the book since 1962, the second in 1964, third in 1980. Adams was published in 1987. In his third edition, Geach (1980: 13), explains that he rewrote parts of the book, noting, 'The sections most affected by these changes are sections 32, 34, and 35. The only major change in chapter 3 is in section 36.' These include the main sections to which Adams refers. Adams (1987: 121, 388), having only one brief reference to Frege, offers no presentation or proof of what the 'Frege bias' is supposed to be.
10 See Spade (1975: 216), and the section below, 'Ockham on reference'.
11 Russell was unable to judge that work. Smiley (1982) assesses Russell on descriptions.
12 Adams (1987: 897–9) briefly refers to David Lewis in a 'taxonomical remark' on Ockham, noting his indexical theory of actuality. She observes that Ockham's uniform assumption that temporal indicators cannot be eliminated in favour of an eternal-present show that he was not an Indexicalist.
13 The relation between metaphoric language in scientific theory and logical space in philosophy is a facet of 'logic as a work of art'. A starting point for this new area of research is the use in Wittgenstein (1961) of a proposition as a projection in space, together with the role of space and geometry in Mallarmé (1914). For studies on this latter aspect, see Bowie (1978), Gibson (forthcoming b), Reynolds (1995), Scott (1988).
14 Bowie (1993: 37–42, 103–4, etc.) relates logic to creativity.
15 Someone might wish to adapt Ockham's theory of a 'mental language' by using the sort of innate syntaxes devised by Chomsky. Chomsky (1995) proposed a thesis that incorporates indeterminacy into his theories of mind, however. According to Chomsky, our ordinary uses, not some ideal language, are nested innately. This would be the opposite of what Ockham needs. Chomsky's generalisation of indeterminacy is also alien to Ockham, and it destabilises his nominal and causal relations. Offler (1990: 338 and note) has noted Russell's misinterpretation of Ockham.
16 Ockham (1967–88) *Summa Logicae* I, c. 1.
17 Dummett (1981: 59–62, etc.) offers relevant valuable analysis of proper names and other subject/predicate differences.
18 See Aristotle, *On Interpretation*, 1–3, 10, 11.
19 This argument follows Quine's work as presented by Dummett (1991a: 94, 234).
20 Aquinas, *Summa Theologiae*, I, q. 76, a. 6, ad 2. Cf. Adams (1987: 13–16, 679–997).
21 As Geach (1980): 201–2.
22 On links between these ideas of Ockham's and Wodeham and Rodington, see

Tachau (1988: 203–5). Walter Chatton (2002) attacked this aspect of Ockham's thought.

23 As White (1990), referring to Ockham (1967) *Quodlibet* III q. 8.

24 See Lewis (1966).

25 See Carruthers and Smith (1996).

26 Kripke's (1982) approach amplifies, in a different mould, social and causal roles, for which, if adjusted, one could develop further aspects of Burley's approach.

27 As Adams (1987: 329) states it.

28 See Quine (1987: 132).

29 Adams (1987: 378–87) mentions that Frege's use of 'is' could be brought into the semantic analysis; but Frege's approach to predication and the role of 'is' in such uses is the contrary of Ockham's.

30 Aquinas, *Summa*, Ia, q. 13, art. 12.

31 As Dummett noted, Frege employs this one German term with the three senses of 'referring', 'referent' and the relation of 'reference'. Dummett (1981) maintains that Frege does not confuse these separate uses. So do we here have one term, also containing two polysemes, or a metaphor?

32 Suggested by Jane Heal. This 'Ockham' reconstruction has nothing to do with Heal's theory and is not suggested by her.

33 A suggestion about paraphrasing (e.g. 'he's a right one') indexicality, not in a referential role, not in an Ockham context, and without my generalising thesis over whole general predicates comes from Heal (1997: 618–40).

34 See Marenbon (1987, 1990), for Bacon's Paris study and teaching of Aristotle.

35 See Walter Chatton, *Reportatio*, Paris, Bibliothèque Nationale, lat. 15887 I, d. 30, q. 1, a. 4.

36 Duns Scotus (1639: 723).

37 Aristotle, *On the Heavens* II, xii, 292a–b25.

38 Ockham (1967–88) *Ordinatio* I, d. 30, q. 2.

39 Ockham (1967–88), *Treatise on Quantity* II i, q. 1.

40 Aspects of this use of *ponenda* are not unlike a notion that Dummett (1981: 39) pointed out in Gentzen's use of 'suppose'. Gentzen formalised inference to allow for a use similar to natural language reasoning, 'Suppose that'. If contradictory inferences follow from that use, one can withdraw the premises that led to it. This complies well with Ockham's desire for non-contradiction.

41 See Haack's (1974) treatment of Frege's 'presupposition'. For scrutiny of assertion-sign, see Dummett (1981: 328–9).

42 Geach (1972: 288–301). Adams, 1987: 989–90 quotes Geach (1972: 296–7), concerning Ockham's use of *humanitas* and regarding Nestorianism. Although demurring from Geach's view, Adams never attempts to fault Geach's use of logic.

43 Ockham (1967–88), *Treatise on Quantity* I, q. 1.

44 Adams (1987: 1008–10). She is citing Ockham (1967–88), *Ordinatio* I, d. 2. q. 1.

45 Adams (1987: 1008–10) numbers this maxim 7.

46 White (1990) serves as a framework for this suggestion.

47 This critical type of point could be applied with profit to much of Ockham's logic. See Bogossian's (1989) assessment of this research.

48 Cf. Smiley and Priest's (1993) and Denyer's (1995) criticisms of Priest's views.

49 See J. S. Mill (1996: 418–19).

50 Geach (1980: 27) points out that the expressions 'quantify' and 'quantification' appear to derive from Hamilton.

51 Adams (1987: 156): 'Quando proposino verificatur pro rebus, Si duae res sufficiunt ad eius veritatem, superfluum est ponere tertiam.' Adams refers to its use in Ockham (1967–88) *Quodlibet* IV, q. 24.

52 Ockham (1967–88), *Quodlibet* VI, q. 29.

53 Davidson (1984: 24ff).

54 Boler (1982: 470). Spade (1975) suggests that Ockham might be committed to adopting a sophisticated coherence theory of truth. Coherence theory (inadvertently) allows internal contradictions: they only have to cohere internally.

55 A response to defend this use of 'methodological principle' might be envisaged. Does not Dummett, 1993: 164 employ the expression to describe an approach advocated by Wittgenstein (1998) and is not criticism of Adams's 'methodological principles' unwarranted? No, because Dummett is contrasting Frege's (and others') truth-conditional theory of meaning with Wittgenstein's methodological principle concerning *use*, whereas Ockham's 'Razors' use logical terms to govern logic and its ontology, in which Ockham proposed truth-conditional logic.

56 See Gross (1989), and resumption of this theme below in the section 'Anti-realism's true Razor?'

57 Ockham (1967–88), *Reportatio* II, q. 150.

58 Ockham (1967–88), *Ordinatio* I, d. 30, q. 1.

59 Cf. Horst, 1996: 365–70, from a perspective outside of Ockham studies.

60 See Ockham (1967–88) *Ordinatio* I, d. 30, q. 1, and *Quodlibet VI*, qq. 8–19, etc.

61 See Ockham (1967–88), *Ordinatio* I, d. 30, q. 1.

62 See Aristotle, *On Interpretation*, IX, 1–16, 18–25. Few modern interpreters would accept this view. Cf. Anscombe, 1981: 53. See also Milbank (1990) on Ockham's confusion in this case.

63 Ockham (1967–88), *On Predestination*, q. 1.

3 Transcending cultural limits in logic

1 For example, science fiction recombines logically possible alternative ways of reifying the laws of science to propound a future possible world, otherwise similar to our own. It is valuable to consider the ways in which Pynchon's novel technique is in some ways parallel with literary devices in the rationalities of medieval allegory, as exemplified by Madsen (1986).

2 Cf. Tachau (1988).

3 F. T. Ramsey argued that paradoxes are distinct in kind, though Russell disagreed. Sainsbury (1995: 133) points out that Graham Priest (see Priest, 1995) offers the best exposition of the case for a single family of paradoxes. Even if Ramsey were right, there is no objection in principle to proposing that the use of 'contradiction' in the various paradoxes can yield a sequence of inferences which hook up all paradoxes for the purpose of implying that 'transcendence' uses in the present context are transitive.

4 For example see 'Is Derrida a transcendental philosopher?', in Wood (1992: 235–46).

5 *In Librium Boethii de Trinitate quaestiones quinta et sexta* (Société Philosophique, E. Nauwelaerts, 1948).

6 Note Gibson (1987: 11–14), which briefly frames the relation between logic and metaphysics that complements the role of counter-intuition.

7 Williamson (1994: 220).

8 In employing this term 'modernism' I do so with the explanation of the term and its clearer source modernité in Gibson (forthcoming b).

9 Lewy (1976).

10 Those who experienced at first hand Lewy's almost obsessive, though sometimes justified, attention to hidden assumptions and terms untreated by explicit exhaustive formal scrutiny, will note his omission of discussion of 'counter-intuition' with surprise, appearing as it does in the short book over which he laboured for more than 32 years, at one point involving chronic terminal disputes with some of his faculty colleagues.

11 Lewy (1976: 69) is here representing the view that the proposition about a given thing is identical to the concept of being that given thing, which, with other matters that he is addressing, strictly implies a paradox, employing, for example, Quine's

manner of speaking that it is paradoxical to suppose that, e.g., 'the moon is round' entails that the English word 'round' is meaningful (in, W. V. O. Quine's review of E. J. Nelson, 'Contradiction and the presupposition of existence', *Journal of Symbolic Logic*, 12 (1947): 55; cf. Lewy (1976: 16–21).

12 *Ibid*, pp. 69–70. He notes that if one follows, e.g., Wittgenstein, in denying that the *word* standing for a subject should be sharply distinguished from the *expression* for it, then the Paradox of Analysis can be avoided, though Lewy proves this move to be inconsistent (*ibid.*, pp. 70–2).

13 i.e., the totality of all sets.

14 Cf. Sainsbury (1995: 129).

15 See Frege (1952).

16 Williamson (1994).

17 The year in which he also, in his unpublished diary, counselled that the Jews should be at least expelled from Germany; here obliquely showing that having a concept of logic is not a recognitional capacity for being logical in its criterion of application. It is instructive to see how some of Frege's formal insights have been reapplied by the logician Harry J. Gensler to the formal logic of practical ethics, since it makes explicit the sort of illogical blind side of Frege which implements the concept that having a concept is not in itself a recognitional capacity. The quotation is from Frege (1977).

18 Dummett (1981).

19 It might be that if the 'referring' sense is derived from ostensive reference – pointing – then all three are metaphoric uses.

20 See Haack (1974).

21 This supposes that the conditions are otherwise relevantly equal.

22 Mallarmé (1914).

23 Bowie (1978).

24 *Ibid.*, p. 124.

25 The research for these judgements is in *ibid.*, and it has been developed further variously by D. Scott (1988: 146) and D. Reynolds (1995).

26 Wiles (1995); see Singh (1997: 225–332).

27 On the schematic fallacy, see Smiley (1982: 117).

28 Langton (1998).

29 Mallarmé (1914).

30 G. Priest (1995, 1987); see Denyer's (1995) demolition of Priest's overall conception.

31 The reason for this is that his argument is demolished in Denyer (1995).

32 The present chapter is not the place to develop an assessment of Priest's own dialethic system of logic (which has gained little acceptance among logicians). My position is that his claims about transcending the limits of language can be derived from standard systems of logic and their paradoxes.

33 This is my summary formulation.

34 Priest cites from A. V. Miller's translation of Hegel's (1969) *Science of Logic*: 134.

35 Smiley and G. Priest (1993: 17–33).

36 The *Principia Mathematica* of A. N. Whitehead and B. Russell regularly confuses premises with assumptions. This indicates that having a concept of logic is not itself a remit for achieving perfect reasoning even when one assumes one has, which supports the argument that having a concept is not necessarily grasping an understanding of it. Thus the identity of logic and its permissible connection to theological epistemology is not to be contradicted by either logic or theology.

37 For a review of Frege's tone see Dummett (1981: chapter 2).

38 This could be implemented using non-Fregean logics, for example as pioneered by Shoesmith and Smiley (1978), though tone is not dealt with by them.

39 Dupré (1993).

40 In that order, since Frege is keen to show us that there is no route back from the referent to the referring.

41   Milbank (1990: 382–5).
42   Budd (2003).
43   Forsman (1992: chapter 3).
44   See for example Wittgenstein (1996) and Stern (1995).

4 Philosophy of mathematics, mathematical physics and creativity

1   In connection with the research that led to this chapter, for the use of library facilities I thank David McKitterick, Librarian of the Wren Library of Trinity College, Cambridge, for use of its facilities, and also in particular Jonathan Smith, the College archivist, for invaluable assistance over a number of years.
2   This use of the term 'domain' will be built upon throughout this chapter, and its sense should be culled from this range; additionally its sense will intersect to some extent with other terms, such as 'graph' and 'group' (as in Woess, 2000), 'field' and 'manifold' (as in Gibson, 2000), and projection in space, as in Wittgenstein's *Tractatus*, but with a different thesis associated with it.
3   Gibson (1981) did not give attention to the literary aspect of natural language. This chapter addresses that domain, but only as it relates to some issues in philosophy of mathematics that cast light on literary creativity (Gibson [forthcoming b] deals with philosophy of literature in detail). Such a relation is itself a neglected area in current logic research. The present chapter's investigation involves having to consider very general questions about creative language and its relation to logic, which address other subjects, associated with Gibson's (1981, 2001) arena, in order to permit further developments within the latter's scope. This is a component in building a new philosophy, as well as the logics of ancient narratives. My approach is that some theoretical philosophy is achievable by engaging with applied research, such as tackling ancient languages in a multidisciplinary engagement.
4   Gibson (forthcoming b), in particular chapter 3. To sustain the present view does not involve having to agree to a logicist foundation if one criticises some forms of probabilism as a basis for human rationality; nor does the promotion of a deductive role in rationality have to dispose of probabilism. Oakesford and Chater (1998) are of assistance in this arena, though they stress probabilistic models whereas the present chapter ploughs its own furrow in counter-intuitive deduction, though not to the exclusion of a relativist approach to include other concepts.
5   Williams's (2002) formulation of cultural genealogy develops a link between truthfulness within great creative literature as evidence of literary rationality.
6   See Gibson (1987).
7   Gibson (1981) attending to the application of logic to semantics, also lays a basis for, yet not articulated, the incorporation of this priority into the territory of the closely connected, but apparently distant, subject of the philosophy of mathematics, for example, G. H. Hardy and Hawking in Gibson (1981: 100 and 99 respectively).
8   This connection with mathematics was already present in Wittgenstein's *Tractatus*, for example, §6.2323 to §6.24; see in this relation Gibson (2001: 14).
9   'Im Rebbeb der Philosophie gewinnt, wer am langsamsten laufen kann oder: der, der das Ziel zuletzt erreicht'. From Wittgenstein (1980: 14); see Redpath (1990: 77) to whom I am grateful for discussion.
10   The phrase 'in principle' in the present study implements the idea that, even if current techniques of experimentation or calculation do not extend to support or prove a thesis, there are counter-intuitive approaches, new or neglected, that yield a basis for adopting an assertion as a possibility or probability of being true. This may involve theories about counter-intuitive realism, or the like, which recompose fresh domains of empirical possibility, sometimes based on new astrophysical cosmology of the early universe.

11 This reflects Wittgenstein's argued views; for example see Garver (1996) and Gerrard (1996).

12 I am using 'tracked', 'fitted' with the sense of Summerfield (1996) and 'traced' with Hobson (1998).

13 This propensity might variously be located as a function of influence external to language, or narrowed to a semantic field, though arguably the latter presupposes the former in a sense relevant to the functional scope.

14 Wittgenstein's philosophy of mathematics has of course been criticised. Although I have no interest in developing a defence of his views here, and will demur from aspects of his finitist approach in this chapter, it should be stated that much of this criticism was prior to the recent publication and availability of unpublished parts of his philosophy of mathematics research, and many have acknowledged that the ways his contributions were initially selected and omitted in early publications grossly misrepresented his argumentation. Since he was working at a deep level, there is a significant problem of misrepresentation. Marion (1998) should be read to correct and refine the debate. He points out that, for example, the criticisms by Dummett and Kreisel have got Wittgenstein wrong on a number of counts; furthermore, he documents how some of Kreisel's earlier criticisms were sometimes retracted or qualified, appearing in rather neglected later writings.

15 This term 'verification' should not here be confused with a logical positivist usage (also Wittgenstein 1922 does *not* use this term in his *Tractatus*). As Hintikka (1998) explains, there is an important ambiguity in the notion of verification.

16 Hale (1996) refines some of Dummett's work on proper names. The function of pun in Gibson (1981, 2001) is worth thinking about as a function of a given proper name's game-change. As Gibson (2001) chapter 3 explains, this is where, for example, the term marking the name's referring function activates a semantic subcontract that is a tone value, ossified in the morpheme. This pun in the proper name, derived only partly by conjunction with an associative semantics, performs like an idiom (for example, the proper name *yhwh* and Exodus 3: 12–15's assignment of temporal functions in it). Prior to the tonal play, *use* ignores the tone; mention of the term '*yhwh*' (or some subset of it) triggers the 'folk-etymology'. Sure, someone, wanting to be pedantic and wishing to extirpate any tone from logic (in the sense of Frege's *Beleuchtung* and *Färbung*) may want to treat this 'it' – this 'proper name tone' – as a homonym of the referring sense of the name, so that by interpretation within the Fregean significance of a 'pure' logical language, of which the logical proper name is an instance, seems not to be compromised. But on such an interpretation, logic still has to, and can, represent it that referring and tonal pun are functional partners, as Gibson (2001: chapter 3) shows. If the folk-etymology from a remote diachronic point is a function of the proper name pun, then this is evidence either that such a folk-etymology has already been internalised into the semantic field with the referring function, or that the pun itself contains a reference to such an external semantic source. Pun has logics of it own, and the semantic contracts between these and primary language functions are themselves game-plays, just as, for example, on Haack's (1974) analysis of deviant logics, they have a life of their own, yet are derivable from and co-operative with bivalent logic. In formal languages some sequences are logical but uncalculable, as is some literary sense. If we follow Derrida (1996) deconstruction is finite. I argue that it eventually follows from this that deconstruction is logical, and that non-algorithmic higher mathematics enables some writers to express some qualities of infinity.

17 I employ the plural 'philosophies', to indicate not only what have been called his early and his late philosophies, but also a range of other – transitional, intermediate, and varying in ways divergent from all these. The range of his work is yet fully to be explored in research; see for example, Bouveresse (1987) and Stern (1995). Although hitherto unpublished writings of Wittgenstein (1993, for example) have appeared,

there is more to come; and even where it is solely a matter of missing paragraphs edited out of manuscripts when earlier published, this is usually a topic of importance due to Wittgenstein's closely and counter-intuitive argumentation style.

18 In 1993 I discussed Wittgenstein's stay in 1948 at Rosro, County Mayo, Ireland, with Mr. Festy Mortimer. Mr. Mortimer was the cleaner of the house where Wittgenstein stayed; he specifically recalled having burnt – at Wittgenstein's request – a very large pile of used manuscript pages, many of which he said had mathematical writing on them. Since we know that Wittgenstein was working on manuscript vol. 137, Band R (see Nedo, 1993: 45), I suggest that in Rosro he was attempting further work on issues in the philosophy of mathematics. Judging by the remaining references to philosophy of mathematics in the *Investigations*, we should take these as evidence of lines of future research which he had hoped to explore.

19 On the philosophical use of this term see Wittgenstein (1980a: 75), and Gibson (2000, chapter 1).

20 See the section 'Counter-intuition' below for development of this term.

21 This echoes a feature of one of Wittgenstein's transitional views, as drawn attention to by Marion (1998: 3).

22 That is, all Wittgenstein's entries are missing from the published form, from 12.12 to 14.12 of his manuscript, vol. 126, pp. 116–33.

23 Perhaps some readers will dispute the above literary examples; and I may well be advised to choose rather better ones. Yet given that the examples used here have been deemed 'Classics', the disagreement itself somewhat draws attention to the truth of my contention.

24 See for example Boolos and Jeffrey (1989: 27–33; 112–20), with the example in mind of positive integers and computation by a Turing machine.

25 See Gibson (forthcoming a).

26 I include post-modernisms and poststructuralisms as subsets of this tag, since it is arguable that even with the latter they are functions of the parental Romanticism that bred modernisms. See Gibson (forthcoming b).

27 In a certain respect Baudelaire invented the central insights of 'modernism', though I agree with David Kelley who argued that the English use of the term 'modernism' is misleadingly disparate and hypostatised. The origin of the crafted counterpart term *modernité* in Baudelaire is as Kelley (1974) explained it; cf. Hiddleston (1999) and Kelley (1968, 1975).

28 An interesting example of this sort of situation is examined in Pearson (1998), which offers a fresh analysis of the Judaean desert refuge caves of the second Jewish revolt in the way it provokes a re-interpretation of Ezekiel 37, in contrast with the negative reworking of the Messiah of Ephraim story.

29 For Sraffa's 'thought-bridge', see Schefold (1989: 332) and the explanation in relation to the present chapter.

30 Although my thesis about mimesis is original, it has some sympathy with Proclus' view that rationalism or conceptualism is compatible with poetic mimesis and that the latter's function can represent the former (cf. Rangos, 1999).

31 This use of the term 'simple' amounts to a joke, for, as Gibson (1998) demonstrates, Ockham had a plural (sic) group of definitions of simplicity.

32 As often mentioned, 'chaos' theory is something of a misnomer; it has to do with complexities and randomness that are a product of small errors in initial specifications, also in the perspective of chance. See Smith (1998).

33 See Gibson (2001).

34 See how this axiom occurs in analysis of Zorn's lemma, mentioned below, chapter 6, note 24.

35 Such as developed in Hintikka (1998), though he does not use or develop an analysis of counter-intuition.

36 Gibson (1981, 2001: 83, footnote 96).

37 This is developed in Geach (1980), Gibson (1997, 2000, 2000a, 2001).
38 i.e., $P_1{}^1$. See Moschovakis (1974), chapter 7, to which Hintikka refers.
39 Cf. Cunningham (2002) for theological insight on this aspect of infinity.
40 This hypothesis draws on the present chapter and Gibson (1987, 1997, 2000).
41 The value of Δ for Freeman Dyson's (1985: 56) model is: $\Delta = \log 3 - (19/12) \log 2 = 0.001129$.
42 For example see Cachazo *et al.* (2003).
43 Gibson (2000): 166, 170, 181–4, 195, 198, 204, 206, 214–15, 219, 318, 321.
44 For example baryogenesis, examined in Witten (2002).
45 I am grateful to Frank Madsen for suggesting this idea (personal correspondence, February 2000).
46 I am not talking here of some mystical thesis, but of the mystery of what it is to be consciousness.
47 It seems to me that Rush Rhees (1998: 110–18) failed to allow for this in his criticism of Wittgenstein. The latter was not claiming that understanding what is said, is knowing the rule for a use of an expression, but a basis for understanding in the context of use.
48 For example, see Gibson (2000: 152–68, 242–48).
49 See Maor (1987).

5 The quality of creative language

1 Gibson (2001: 40, footnote 37) observes that vague predicates can have precise definition, though it would be wrong to infer from this that the identities of vagueness and logical transparency are equivalent.
2 Sraffa does not use 'counter-intuitive'; see Schefold (1989: 333).
3 Woods 2003: 234.
4 As mentioned earlier, this term 'schizophreniform' is crafted from Hacking's (1995) use.
5 There is a fragmentary similarity between my view and that of Woods (2003: 235–6) here, though I displace paraconsistency as a basis for logic and assume a counter-intuitive realist primacy for truth.
6 Gibson (forthcoming a).
7 A reason for returning to Lewy's view here is that Wittgenstein taught him; his concerns over logical relations go back to issues canvassed by Wittgenstein. Lewy (1976) stands as a sort of *a priori* battle-ground for some of the issues taken up in the present chapter, while I do not adopt Lewy's particular conception.
8 For this use of the term 'Classic' see Kermode (1983).
9 Aspects of the preparation for such analysis are laid out in (Gibson, 2000b) and implemented in Gibson (forthcoming d).
10 A reason for noting this, incidentally, is that Wittgenstein knew Bakhtin's brother Nicholas and was very close to him, often travelling to Birmingham, discussing Mikhail's views in Russian.
11 I am assuming use of the Lewis S5 system as a bridging point from one game to others; see Chihara (1998) for alternatives.
12 See Lewis (1986).
13 The use of 'strange' here reflects and develops from the use in Fleming and Butterfield (1999).
14 See Gibson (2000) and chapter 9 of the present book.
15 See Chihara (1998).
16 For varying ways of mapping such claims, see Chihara (1990, 1998) and Lewis (1986).
17 On the topic of 'thinking more crazily', it is helpful to read Hacking (1998: 1–10); and Gibson (2000) studies this aspect in relation to Socrates' 'bizarreness' or 'strangeness'.

18 For a fine general account see Singh (1997).

19 Tolstikov (1989); he notes that his study was written in 1984.

20 This issue of surveyability is perhaps the reason, I guess, why Turing left Wittgenstein's seminars on the foundations of mathematics, though this does not justify Kreisel's technically expert but often conceptually superficial or inaccurate criticisms of Wittgenstein's views, subsequent to the latter's death; it is also a matter of regret that Kreisel's retraction or qualification of some of his opinions have not been given the same publicity as his negative criticisms (as Marion, 1998 notes).

21 Although Cartwright (1999: 188–91) does not discuss these subjects, her employment of 'bridge principles' could be introduced here, and be of assistance to model possible relations.

22 Timothy Smiley introduced this example to me in 1972.

23 No doubt readers will be aware that 'fuzzy' draws here on the logic and mathematical uses of it, and presupposes for example, Sangalli's (1998) treatment.

24 i.e., of asymptotic topological invariants using Zorn's lemma; see Katok and Hasselblatt (1995: 130); especially proposition 3.3.6. This is required for the proposition that, for every continuous map of a compact metric space, X has an invariant minimal subset. (I thank Robert MacKay for discussion about this.)

25 Many studies should deter people from this conclusion; see for example, Haack (1974). The trend outside of, say, logic, to the opposite view seems similar to ways in which some scholarly institutionalised misdescription of ancient literary sensibility obscures creativity in ancient literary texts, by 'harmonising' the text with a postulated editorial tradition that is taken to be a smoothing out of individualist creativity; so it is not surprising to see that unrealistic contrasts are assumed between science and humanities.

26 The expression 'manifold' roughly is the bedrock residual type for internal and fundamental properties of a field, space and domain, defined by a proposition or set of propositions. (For my purpose, these proposition(s) can be the semantic fields of the narrative.) For formal uses of this term, see for example, variously, Katok and Hasselblatt (1995: 716–18); also see Hasselblatt and Katok (2002). Cf. Hawking and Ellis (1973); for its application to logic in relation to primordial cosmology and philosophy, see Gibson (2000).

27 See Gibson (2000, 2000a, and forthcoming b).

28 For a complementary point of view on this topic, see Prawitz's (1994) helpful study.

29 In an applied linguistic context, research on metaphoric grammar might proceed by starting with Halliday's (1999) research that is related to late Kuhnian analysis.

30 Even if with Hawking and Turok (1998) this was taken to be a 'self-caused' universe; and this would require a heavily transcendent non-surveyability property.

31 It is often assumed that the emergence of human unconsciousness is primeval in date or bound into the same temporal point as the evolution of consciousness. That this may not be so is discussed in chapter 9 of the present book.

32 I have mentioned above (and in Gibson, 1987, 2000) how Frege eliminated tone from natural language as though it were an ineradicable disease. (No doubt there is such tone, especially in dumbing down mass media.) It is interesting to see here that the German of Wittgenstein's colour book, *Bermerkungen uber die Färben* takes up the stem of one of Frege's words for 'tone'. There seems to be some pun here. In his inability to register any logical qualities in the natural language of literature, Frege seemed to have something akin to Charlemagne's incapacity with regard to writing. In this respect, a logician like Frege might be likened to a member of an alien tribe who is colour-blind to certain aesthetic qualities.

33 To follow up this point see Gibson (2000: Part II).

34 I am grateful to Sraffa for discussion years ago, and to Schefold (1989: 333) for the translation of Wittgenstein's remark used here.

35 Elizabeth Anscombe remarked to me, enlarging on her published comment

(Anscombe, 1957) that the references and allusions in Wittgenstein's *Investigations* to the *Tractatus* are like a ghost, momentarily appearing and increasingly fading. Well too bad; perhaps these references either are, or might have been better pictured as, a Samuel 'resurrection' to deconstruct and foil Saul's belief in ghosts, ironising future revival. Namely, I argue, a resurrection in the *Investigations* to a new form of life that transforms the *Tractatus'* usage.

36 In personal discussio\n, Cambridge and London 1993.
37 For which see Gibson (forthcoming b).

6 Virtual reality metaphysics

1 Also see Boler's (1963) study on Peirce's relation to 'realism' via Duns Scotus.
2 Some specialists have claimed that Penrose's argument confuses distinct senses of 'algorithm', though they concede that he has a point; Butterfield (1998) has a much more positive view of his work.
3 Whitehead (1898).
4 See Gibson (2000, chapter 7).
5 Such use of symbolism extends to problematic texts, for example the she-bears in 2 Kings 2: 24, which mysteriously come out of the wood, perhaps embroiled in allusions to cult functions, expounded in Gibson (2000a: 225–37).
6 For example, the Fisher Griess Monster Group in algebra has numbers $8 \times 1Q^{53}$ and sets of at least six figures for each number; these inexplicably coincide with numbers in the Fourier series (for example, 196,884). Conway conjectured that might apply to quantum properties (tessellation) in the opening epoch of the universe.
7 This would be a Hawking (Hawking and Luttrell, 1984) minisuperspace defined by a Euclidean path-integral approach to quantum gravity.
8 As Gibson (2000: chapters 2, 5–7) argues.
9 Cf. Gibson (2000), chapters 3–4.
10 In Cambridge at various times in the 1980s.
11 I first picked up a reference to this from Quine (1969) and was grateful for the opportunity to discuss the matter with Quine between 1971 and 1973.

7 Some resurrection logic

1 See Smith (1998), and the foregoing discussion in chapter 3 of chaos and Mallarmé.
2 I will return to this account later, and now somewhat silently allow for critical issues, though some of these will be examined in the subsequent two chapters.
3 'Syllogism' here is just one group of argument patterns. This term is not synonymous with the Greek *sullogismos*. See Burnyeat (1994), Smiley and Priest (1995), and chapter 10 of the present book.
4 See also Prior and Fine (1977).
5 But we need a more developed conception of the relation of logic to (say, poetic) creativity so as to explore what are the outer and deeper boundaries of logic which are presupposed in our uses of language.
6 Priest (1995) and Woods (2003) explore some of these areas, though many demur from their paraconsistent approach.
7 Cf. Geach 1971: 18–44, 112–14. In abstractionism, both in medieval and modern treatments, features are artificially lifted out of a subject to the detriment of its other properties and in ways that distort the abstractionist product. An effect of this is to commit a modal quantifier shift fallacy (see Gibson 2001: 13–34).
8 See Tarski (1956); in contrast note Frege's more subtle theses, as explained in Dummett (1991a: 294–301).
9 See Gibson (1987, 2000a, 2001, forthcoming a and b).
10 See Gibson (2000: chapter 2).

11 See chapters 5 and 8 of the present book.
12 Cf. French (1996).
13 Another instance may assist illustration: For example the Marxism of Piero Sraffa can be paraphrased into Wittgenstein's picture theory of language, though the former disbelieved the latter's claims. For background, see Kaldor (1986: 615–40).
14 See Sainsbury (1995: 129) and Woods (2003).
15 See Gibson (2000), chapter 4, section 'Causal originality'.
16 Hawking and Turok (1998).
17 Cf. Rees (1995, 1997).
18 See Kretzmann (1999: 74–5).
19 The qualitative topology of maps on to the topology between two differential manifolds (as in Thom, 1989: 335–9) where one manifold relates to our universe and the other to whatever are beyond the space–time boundaries outside General Relativity.
20 The referent of any subject p, such as the resurrection, in this catastrophe system is a closed subspace of a finite codimension. But such a closed subspace can be attached to any other subspace by the catastrophe theory's deformation of the topology. This is rather like a sheet of paper being curved back on itself, by which the two ends are joined together to provide a cylinder. In this way two different apparently discontinuous boundaries can be attached. This can be extended to join two quite distinct sheets or topologies. This formalism can be extended infinitely to enclose qualitatively distinct remote domains. I suggest that one may paraphrase this into Hawking and Turok's (1998) global structure for the conditions comprising the start of the universe. On this analysis a proposition p (e.g. a proposition about creation or about resurrection) is a subsystem of an infinite transcendent manifold.
21 See Thom (1989) in Castrigiano and Hayes (1993: x).
22 Cf. French (1996: 1–22).
23 Wittgenstein's (1961) *Tractatus*.
24 Cf. the Preface in Wittgenstein (1961) and for an account of Sraffa's criticism of Wittgenstein picture theory see Kaldor above.
25 See the end of chapter 2.
26 Cf. Hobson (1982).
27 Hacking (1995) has expanded our problems as well as comprehension of the importance of this study by applying some of its insights to issues in multiple personality (see chapter 9 of the present book).
28 R. Hoffmann (1990) presents a case that counter-intuitive surprise attends inference in this sphere; for example it is traditional science that carbon is unable to form more than bonds; but six bonds have been synthesised.
29 See chapter 2 of the present book.
30 Cf. Oakes (1994).
31 See Part II of Gibson (2000).

8 The semantic logic of 'God'

1 See Rorty (1984).
2 Cf. Dummett (1993: 129–30).
3 Dummett's (1991a: 17) writes of a similarity between problems of the meaning of 'God' and logic: 'Perhaps a polytheist cannot mean the same by "God" as a monotheist; but there is a disagreement between them, all the same. Each denies that the other has hold of a coherent meaning; and that is just the charge made by the intuitionist against the classical mathematician.' We could replace the term 'polytheist' by opposing belief in an angel's role using the term *'lwhym*, so as to adjust this contrast for our purpose.
4 So I do not exclude the possibility of a semantic difference matching the difference in orthography between *'lwhym* in some DSS MSS and *'lhym* in the Hebrew OT,

though my present study attempts to allow either eventuality. For further discussion on the Exodus orthographic issue, see Sanderson (1986), and Skehan *et al.* (1992).

5 See Dummett (1991: chapter 5); Gibson (1981, 2001).

6 e.g. Sanders (1977, 1985).

7 See Nigosian (1993).

8 See Barnes' (1995, 1995a) and Milbank (1997).

9 An analogy to introduce, as well as connect, the issue for future generalisation with other linguistic phenomena could be provided by noting the work in Gibson (1981, 2001), and Gibson (2000, chapter 2). The ossified semantic 'contents' of a proper name when subject to paronomasia are triggered into having a semantic value assigned to it. Normally, of course, the proper name is solely a referring term whose value is to satisfy a given criterion of identity, for example such as that of the bearer of 'YHWH'. When paronomasia is created by the narrative function of a proper name, the mention (and not only use) of, say, the paronomastic thematised explanation of the 'meaning' of 'YHWH' (for example in Exodus 3: 12–15) is concurrent with the use of 'YHWH' as a referring term. I leave aside here the above proposal of an idiomising notion applied to, though I address it in a proper name context, Gibson (1981, 2001).

10 Works by Frege (1969); see Geach (1980), Dummett (1981); for a different approach, see Lewis (1986).

11 Since a logical predicate is not a grammatical predicate, though the categories may sometimes coincide, as to when they do is a matter of disputed interpretation. Barnes (1996) presents a confrontational view of the matter using his interpretation of Aristotle. In respect of the use above, a logical predicate might characterise a function within any grammatical category if its use is a property ascribed to a subject; and this is the case with certain internal properties of the class of nouns such as *'lhym*.

12 This formulation slightly adjusts for the present purpose the theory in Gibson 2000, chapter 2.

13 This subject has not been much developed in philosophical logic, though as noted earlier Jane Heal (1997) has formulated some new insights; also see Recanati (1993); Gibson (1998) and chapter 2 of the present book venture some proposals.

14 This suggestion is a component in a larger investigation. For example a function x^2 has its metaphorisation in any value that it takes, as with 1002. So I am arguing that we may properly view the predicate calculus as a complex set of 'live metaphors', which of course is a radical one and is receiving attention in my other publications, though the new concepts I have offered do not stand or fall with this proposal.

15 See Gibson (1998).

16 See Gibson (1981, 2001: chapters 2–3), for the analysis of sense and reference in Bible usage.

17 Concerning this literary use of 'interiority' see Chinca (1997), which, though defined within the context of Germanist medieval Tristan literary theory, encapsulates the way in which an external mirroring of relations has its point within the inner life, here in use of *'lhym*.

18 See for example, Stern (1995).

19 Even so, of course, the complexity of this sort of question is enormous; see for example Dummett (1991, 1993).

9 Modern philosophy and ancient consciousness

1 See Gibson (2001a: Part I).

2 Although Bouveresse (1995) does not address ancient phenomena, his study of Wittgenstein in relation to Freud is a valuable study that could be thus applied.

3 Cf. Williams's (1978: 248) view of Skorupski's point.

10 Transcendent reason

1 See Hacking (1975).
2 Wittgenstein (1996) 2: 8.
3 I have theoretically lifted the term 'monopole' from physics to construct it as a live metaphor: a counter-intuitive monopole: in astrophysics a *monopole*, predicted by Dirac (cf. Rees (1997: 194–8) and Gibson (2000: 100–7)). So some *terrestrial* physical states are accurately represented as monopole propositions that have a contrary relation to related normal dipole forms, under suitably exotic states of affairs.
4 For research on this arena, see Gibson (forthcoming b).
5 Schutrumpf (1994: 101–2).
6 Aristotle, in *Rhetoric* 1.1.1354a1 ff.
7 Aristotle, *Rhetoric*, 1.1.3, 1354a15–16.
8 Hintikka (1996): 90–6.
9 *Ibid.*, p. 89.
10 I have avoided terming this 'inductive inference', in conformity with, for example, Sainsbury (1991: 9–11).
11 Cf. Garver (1996).
12 This topic can be more explicitly formulated by relatedness logic: cf. Epstein *et al.* (1995: 92–6).
13 See Smiley (1998); I am grateful to the author for discussion on the topic.
14 See Gibson (2000: chapter 1).
15 Cf. Gibson (2000: chapters 3–6).
16 See Gibson (forthcoming b: chapters 2–3) regarding Beckett's *Godot* and *Endgame* with Shakespeare's *Lear*, and Gibson (2000a) for Huwawa plus forest archetypes in the earliest Sumerian versions of *Gilgamesh* as examples of such intertextuality in Baudelaire's poem 'Correspondence'.
17 This concept is advanced in Gibson (forthcoming a) and chapters 4–5 of the present book.
18 Perhaps the basis for a solution is ontology: an ontology which converges into one universal set at the Universe's time t_o, and counter-intuitively reserves an infinite well-ordered domain outside of this closure.
19 Wittgenstein (1996) 2: 67.
20 See Shoesmith and Smiley (1978: 181–6, 214).
21 Anderson and Belnap (1992).
22 Lewy (1976: 15–51).
23 W. and M. Kneale (1984).
24 Lear (1980).
25 Burnyeat (1994).
26 Martin (1986) shows that in the twelfth century 'William's Engine' was already attending to metalanguage interests in entailment, necessity and relevance logic.
27 See Smiley and Priest (1995).
28 Geach (1972).
29 Geach (1998: 580).
30 Geach (1980) and (1972); Geach (1991) argues that a similar confusion attended the development of deontic logic, in which von Wright's original conception in 'Deontic logic' did not have its natural development which would preserve the priority and difference of the subject, while binding the predicative elements and the deontic operator; later work in deontic logic took the role of obligation as a function over whole propositions.
31 Resulting from Frege's (1977) research.
32 See Lear (1980: 11–33).
33 Sorensen (1998: 322).
34 Boethius (1934: 43–5) seems to have been sensitive to similar problems.

35 Haack (1974).

36 For example, one could criticise Frege for his denouncing 'tone' as non truth-functional, and develop a natural logic along the lines of a tree structure to introduce tones as functions, for which see Gibson (1987: 11–14), and Gibson (2001: 48, 157–64).

37 Lear (1980: 11).

38 See Smiley (1998).

39 See Bolzano (1837).

40 Burnyeat (1994: 41–4).

41 Burnyeat (1994) traces this through Quintillion back to Archedemus and Antipater. Cf. Cicero, *Top.* 55 *init*, 56 *init*: 'Not both p and q; q; therefore not q'.

42 Aristotle, *Prior Analytics* 1.1,24b10.24–25.

43 See Burnyeat (1994).

44 Ross (1949: 500).

45 As Burnyeat (1994: 4–5) notes, Aristotle did not develop an account of the omission of conclusion of a syllogism as an *enthymeme*. Hamilton, *Lectures on Logic XX*, castigating the whole notion of the *enthymeme*, adduced that there could be a third order of *enthymeme* – the omission of a conclusion.

46 For example in Mark 2–3, to be examined below.

47 See Burnyeat (1994: 6–7) for textual data; he observes that this reading is from the Aldine of 1495, appears in the commentary (which is usually but perhaps incorrectly ascribed to) Philoponus on the above passage, and both he and Alexander affirm that the *enthymeme* is a syllogism with one premise omitted, with their examples citing a major premise, whereas Ammonius permits suppression of the minor premise.

48 See Wallies (1909).

49 Aristotle's *Rhetoric*, 1.2.14, 1357a32–33; 1359a7–10.

50 Burnyeat (1994: 11–12).

51 For proof of this see Geach (1998: 573–4).

52 Burnyeat (1994: 13).

53 *Ibid.*, p. 14.

54 'More relaxed'; cf. *Metaph.* 6.1, 1025b13, etc.

55 Aristotle's *Rhetoric*, 1396a34–b1.

56 As noted by Burnyeat (1994: 16–17); here Burnyeat has an important examination of the relations of 'example' and επαγωγη in relation to definition.

57 Burnyeat (1994: 22).

58 Aristotle, *Rhetoric* 1394b3–6; traced by Burnyeat to Euripides, *Hecuba* 864–5.

59 See Geach (1971).

60 Cf. Altham (1971) and Lewis (ed.) (1991: 263–5).

61 Aristotle, *Prior Analytics* 1.30 and 2.12.

62 Aristotle, *Prior Analytics*, 2.27, 10–11.

63 Aristotle, *Prior Analytics* 23.15–35.

64 Cf. Lewy (1976).

65 See Levi (1967: chapter 6).

66 Hacking (1975: chapter 5) is an important study on 'signs' that exposes the development of modern uses of probability that can be applied to trace confusions about 'signs' and *enthymemes* in post-sixteenth-century scholarship.

67 It seems clear that the use of this example has an intertextual relation to Isaiah 19: 2.

68 For a start on the literary theory of this where location is a function of ironic argument, see Gibson (1997a; forthcoming b, and chapter 8 of the present book).

69 Cf. Bowie (1993).

70 See Gibson (2000a: chapters 5–7).

71 *Ibid*, and Driver, CML, KERET, I.ii.27–46. Notice how the sick man taking up his bed contrasts with the only Old Testament occurrence of Baalzebub, 2 Kings 1, where it notes that Ahaziah, awaiting news of a cure from Baalzebub, is told by

Elijah that he will not arise from his bed but dying, he shall die, implementing Genesis 3's curse; Mark's irony in the miracle reverses the curse.

72 See Geach (1972).

73 See Gibson (2001); chapter 8 above, and Gibson (1987: 11–14).

74 Dummett (1981), chapter 2.

75 It is not that the author is resistant to new discoveries, since he has developed a logic of counter-intuition – that of how to surprise a logician within the canon of logic's own new results by calculating perhaps neglected inferences from standard logic research.

76 For further analysis see Gibson (1987) and chapter 9 of the present book.

77 Some of the formal work for stipulating these fallacies is to be found in Gibson (2001, Appendix and *passim*).

78 *Ibid.*, pp. 39–99.

79 *Ibid.*, pp. 21–4.

80 *Ibid.*, p. 193.

81 *Ibid.*, pp. 229–31.

82 *Ibid.*, pp. 83–4. This is illustrated by Dahood's rhetorical style in analysis of Hebrew. Here the subjective features of mental patterns are taken to be causal evidence of external linguistic reasoning. I appreciated Dahood's interest in discussing this type of use in his writings; he agreed that he was quite unaware of this pattern of reasoning in them and would have wished to withdraw such reasoning from them. Of course he was aware that this leaves open the question of what would remain if this excision occurred.

83 *Ibid.*, p. 201.

84 An old obvious example is an apt illustration here: 'If you want some poison, then it is on the table' employs 'if' in a non-truth-functional use, since it is on the table even if you do not want it.

85 Tennant (1997).

86 See Bogossian (1989, 1990, 1990a).

87 Cf. Geach (1972: 45–8).

88 Douglas Campbell and I separately formulated related issues by linking Greek terms for 'faith' and 'proof', which views we briefly exchanged in dialogue at the 1998 Florence Conference on Rhetoric, where aspects of the present study had their first airing in a lecture; I appreciated discussion there with him and other scholars present.

89 See Gibson (2000a: chapter 10).

Bibliography

Abusch, T. (1995) 'The socio-religious framework of the Babylonian witchcraft ceremony Maqlu: some observations on the introductory section of the text, Part II', in Z. Zevit, S. Gitin and M. Sokoloff (eds) *Solving Riddles and Untying Knots* (Winona Lake, IL: Eisenbrauns).

Adams, M. M. (1987) *William Ockham*, 2 vols (Notre Dame, IL: University of Notre Dame Press).

—— (1990) 'Ockham's individualisms', in W. von Vossenkuhl and R. Schonberger (eds) *Die Gegenwart Ockhams* (Weinheim: VCH Acta humaniora): 3–24.

Alexander, P. S. (1972) 'The Targumim and early exegesis of "Sons of God" in Genesis 6', *Journal of Jewish Studies*, 23.1: 60–71.

Alfieri, R. (1989) *Guillaume d'Ockham le singulier* (Paris: Minuit).

Alter, R. (1984) *Motives for Fiction* (Cambridge, MA: Harvard University Press).

Altham, J. E. J. (1971) *The Logic of Plurality* (Cambridge: Cambridge University Press).

—— (1991) 'Plural and pleonetetic quantification', in H. A. Lewis (ed.) (1991: 105–19).

Anderson, A. R. and Belnap, N. F. (1975, 1992) *The Logic of Relevance and Necessity*, 2 vols (Princeton, NJ: Princeton University Press).

Anscombe, G. E. M. (1957) *Intention* (Oxford: Basil Blackwell).

—— (1971) *An Introduction to Wittgenstein's 'Tractatus'* (London: Hutchinson).

—— (1975) 'The first person', in S. Guatemalan (ed.) *Mind and Language* (Oxford: Oxford University Press).

—— (1981) 'Aristotle and the sea battle', in *The Collected Philosophical Papers of G. E. M. Anscombe*, I (Oxford: Basil Blackwell).

—— (1981a) 'The intentionality of sensation', in *The Collected Philosophical Papers of G. E. M. Anscombe*, 1 (Oxford: Basil Blackwell).

Aragon, L. (1928) *Traité du style* (Paris: Gallimard).

Aquinas, Thomas (1950–3) *Summa Theologica*: cura et studio Petri Caramello; cum textu ex recensione Leonina quem (Turin: Marietti).

Baker, A. (1975) *Transcendental Number Theory* (Cambridge: Cambridge University Press).

Bakhtin, M (1984) *Problems in Dostoevsky's Poetics* (ed. and trans. C. Emerson; Manchester: Manchester University Press).

Balslev, A. N. (1991) *Cultural Otherness: Correspondence with Richard Rorty* (New Delhi: Indian Institute of Advanced Study).

Barnes, J. (1996) 'Grammar on Aristotle's terms', in M. Frede and G. Striker (eds) *Rationality in Greek Thought* (Oxford: Clarendon Press).

Barnes, M. R. (1995) 'Augustine in contemporary trinitarian theology', *Theological Studies*, 56: 237–50.

—— (1995a) 'De Regnon reconsidered', *Augustinian Studies*, 26.2: 51–80.

Barr, J. (1961) *The Semantics of Biblical Language* (Oxford: Oxford University Press).

Barrett, C. K. (1972) *Essays on John* (London: SPCK).

Beckett, S. (1982) *Ill Seen Ill Said* (London: John Calder).

Beasley, C. and Witten, E. (2003) 'Residues and world sheet instantons', in PUPT–2081, e-Print Archive: hep-th/0304115.

Bell, J. S. (1987) *Speakable and Unspeakable in Quantum Physics* (Cambridge: Cambridge University Press).

Bermudez, J. L. and Millar, A. (eds) (2002) *Reason and Nature* (Oxford: Clarendon Press).

Black, M. (1962) *Models and Metaphors* (Ithaca, NY: Cornell University Press).

—— (1993) 'More about metaphor', in A. Ortony (ed.) *Metaphor and Thought*, 2nd edition (Cambridge: Cambridge University Press): 19–41.

Blackburn, S. (1984) *Spreading the Word* (Oxford: Clarendon Press).

Bleuler, E. (1908) 'Die Prognose des Dementia Praecox: Schizophreniengruppe', *Allgemeine Zeitschrift für Psychiatrie*, 65: 436–64.

—— (1924) *Textbook of Psychiatry*, trans. A. A. Brill (New York: Macmillan).

Boethius, A. M. T. S. (1934) *Philosophiae consolationis libri quinque* (Corpus scriptorum ecclesiasticorum Latinorum v. 67 Vindobonae: Hoelder-Pichler-Tempsky).

Bogossian, P. (2002) 'How are objective epistemic reasons possible?', in J. L. Bermudez and A. Millar (eds) (2002): 15–48.

—— (1989) 'The rule-following consideration', *Mind*, 98: 507–49.

—— (1990) 'The status of content', *Philosophical Review*, 99: 157–84.

—— (1990a) 'The status of content revisited', *Pacific Philosophical Quarterly*, 71: 264–78.

Boler, J. F. (1982) 'Intuitive and abstractive intuition', in A. Kenny, N. Kretzmann and J. Pinborg (eds) *Cambridge History of Later Medieval Philosophy* (Cambridge: Cambridge University Press).

—— (1963) *Charles Peirce and Scholastic Realism: A Study of Peirce's Relation to John Duns Scotus* (Seattle: University of Washington Press).

Bolzano, B. (1837) *Wissenschaftslehre* (4 vols; Prague: Sulzbach); reissued as *Theory of Science*, trans. R. George (Oxford: Basil Blackwell, 1972).

Boolos, G. S. (1998) *Logic, Logic, Logic* (ed. R. Jeffrey; Cambridge, MA: Harvard University Press).

Boolos, G. S. and Jeffrey, R. C. (1989) *Computability and Logic* (Cambridge: Cambridge University Press).

Borthwick, A. (1995) *Music Theory and Analysis* (New York: Garland).

Boukricha, A. (1985) 'The Schrodinger equation with an isolated singularity', in S. Albervio (ed.) *Infinite Dimensional Analysis and Stochastic Processes* (Boston: Reidel).

Bourdieu, P. (2000) *Pascalian Meditations*, trans. R. Nice (Cambridge: Polity).

Bouveresse, J. (1987 *La Force de la règle* (Paris: Editions de Minuit).

—— (1995) *Wittgenstein Reads Freud* (Princeton, NJ: Princeton University Press). Trans. C. Cosman, *Philosophie, mythologie et pseudo-science: Wittgenstein lecteur de Freud* (Paris: Editions de l'éclat).

—— Bouveresse, J. (1997) *La Démande philosophique* (Paris: Editions de l'éclat).

Bowie, M. (1978) *Mallarmé and the Art of Being Difficult* (Cambridge: Cambridge University Press).

—— (1993) *Psychoanalysis and the Future of Theory*. The Bucknell Lectures in Literary Theory (Oxford: Blackwell).

Brontë, E. [Bell, Ellis, pseud.] (1847) *Wuthering Heights* (London: T. C. Newby).

Brooke, G. J. (1994) 'Isaiah 40: 3 and the wilderness community', in Brooke and Martinez (1994): 117–32.

Brooke, G. J. with Martinez, F. G. (eds) (1994) *New Qumran Texts and Studies*. Studies on the Texts of the Desert of Judah (Leiden: Brill).

Brooke-Roose, C. (1999) *Subscript* (Manchester: Carcanet).

Brouwer, L. E. J. (1967) 'On the principle of the significance of the principle of excluded middle', in J. van Heijenhoort *From Frege to Godel* (Cambridge, MA: Harvard University Press): 335–45.

Brown, R. E. (1966) *The Gospel According to John*, Anchor Bible, vol. 29: i–xii (New York: Doubleday).

—— (1977) *The Birth of the Messiah* (London: G. Chapman).

Budd, M. (1995) *Values of Art* (London: Allen Lane, Penguin).

—— (2003) *The Aesthetic Appreciation of Nature* (Oxford: Clarendon).

Burnyeat, M. F. (1994) '*Enthymeme*: Aristotle on the logic of persuasion', in D. J. Furley and A. Nehamas (eds) *Aristotle's Rhetoric* (Princeton, NJ: Princeton University Press) 3–55.

Butler, C. (1994) *Early Modernism* (Oxford: Oxford University Press).

Butterfield, J. (1998) *Consciousness and Human Identity*, ed. J. Cornwall (Oxford: Oxford University Press): 122–59.

Cachazo, F., Seiberg, N. and Witten, E. (2003) 'Phases of N = 1 supersymmetric gauge theories and matrices', in e-Print Archive: hep-th/0301006 (2 January 2003).

Caird, G. B. (1980) *The Language and Imagery of the Bible* (London: Duckworth).

Cajetan, T. de Vio (1959) *The Analogy of Names* (Louvain; Cambridge: Cambridge University Press).

Carr, W. (1981) *Angels and Principalities* (Cambridge: Cambridge University Press).

Carruthers, P. and Smith, P. K. (1996) *Theories of Theories of Mind* (Cambridge: Cambridge University Press).

Cartwright, N. (1999) *The Dappled World: A Study of the Boundaries of Science* (Cambridge: Cambridge University Press).

Castrigiano, D. P. L. and Hayes, S. A. (1993) *Catastrophe Theory* (Reading, MA: Addison-Wesley).

Cavell, S. (1979) *The World Viewed* (Cambridge, MA: Harvard University Press).

Chatton, W. (2002) *Reportatio super Sententias* I, ed. J. C. Wey *et al.*, Studies and Texts, 141 (Rome: Pontifical Institute of Mediaeval Studies).

Chihara, C. S. (1990) *Constructability and Mathematical Existence* (Oxford: Clarendon).

—— (1998) *The Worlds of Possibility* (Oxford: Clarendon).

Chinca, M. (1997) *Gottfried von Strassburg: Tristan*. Landmarks of World Literature (Cambridge: Cambridge University Press).

Chomsky, N. (1995) 'Language and nature', *Mind*, 104: 1–62.

—— (2001) *Beyond Explanatory Adequacy* (MIT Occasional Papers in Linguistics 21; Cambridge, MA: MITWPL).

Cohen, L. J. (1993) 'The semantics of metaphor', in A. Ortony (ed.) *Metaphor and Thought* (Cambridge: Cambridge University Press): 58–70.

Coleman, J. (1996) 'The individual and the medieval state', in J. Coleman (ed.) *The Individual in Political Theory and Practice* (Oxford: Oxford University Press).

Conant, J. (2000) 'Elucidation and nonsense in Frege and early Wittgenstein', in Crary and Read (2000): 174–217.

Conrad, J. (1911) *Under Western Eyes* (London: David Campbell).

Courtenay, W. J. (1992) 'Theology and theologians from Ockham to Wyclif', in J. I. Catto and R. Evans (eds) *The History of the University of Oxford*, vol. II, *Late Medieval Oxford* (Oxford: Clarendon Press).

Craig, E. (1991) 'Advice to philosophers', in *Proceedings of the British Academy*, 76: 265–81.

Crary, A. and Read, R. (eds) (2000) *The New Wittgenstein* (London: Routledge).

Cunningham, C. (2002) *Genealogy of Nihilism* (London: Routledge).

Dallaporta, N. (1993) 'The different levels of connection between science and objective reality', in G. Ellis, M. Lanza and J. Miller (eds) *The Renaissance of General Relativity and Cosmology* (Cambridge: Cambridge University Press): 326–31.

Dalley, S. and Reyes, A. T. (1998) 'Mesopotamian contact and influence in the Greek world', in S. Dalley (ed.) *The Legacy of Mesopotamia* (Oxford: Oxford University Press): 107–24.

Damasio, A. R. (1994) *Descartes' Error: Emotion, Reason and the Human Brain* (London: Macmillan).

Danto, A. C. (1994) *Embodied Meanings* (New York: Farrar, Giroux).

Deleuze, G. and Guattari, F. (1994) *What is Philosophy?* trans. G. Burchell and H. Tomlinson (London: Verso).

Denyer, N. (1995) 'Priest's paraconsistent arithmetic', *Mind*, 104: 567–75.
—— (1998) 'Names, verbs and quantification', *Philosophy*, 73: 619–23.
Derrida, J. (1978) *The Truth in Painting* (Chicago, IL: University of Chicago Press).
—— (1993) *Aporias*, trans. T. Dutoit (Stanford, CA: Stanford University Press).
—— (1996) *The Gift of Death* (Chicago, IL: University of Chicago Press).
—— (1998) *Monolingualism of the Other*, trans. P. Mensah (Stanford, CA: Stanford University Press).
Descartes, R. (1964) *Oeuvres de Descartes*, ed. C. Adam and P. Tannery; revised edition, (Paris: Vrin/CNRS, 1964–76).
Descombes, V. (1995) 'Foreword to Jacques Bouveresse', in Bouveresse (1995).
Dimant, D. and Rappaport, U. (eds) (1992) *The Dead Sea Scrolls, Studies on the Texts of the Desert of Judah*, vol. X (Leiden: Brill).
Dimant, D. and Schiffman, L. H. (1995) *Time to Prepare the Way in the Wilderness, Studies on the Texts of the Desert of Judah*, vol. XVI (Leiden: Brill).
Drury, M. O'C. (1999) 'Some notes on conversations with Wittgenstein', *Portraits of Wittgenstein*, 3, ed. and Intro. F. A. Flowers III (Bristol: Thoemmes Press).
Dummett, M. (1977) *The Elements of Intuitionism* (Oxford: Oxford University Press).
—— (1978) *Truth and Other Enigmas* (London: Duckworth).
—— (1981) *Frege: Philosophy of Language*, 2nd edition (London: Duckworth).
—— (1991) *Frege and Other Philosophers* (Oxford: Clarendon Press).
—— (1991a) *The Logical Basis of Metaphysics* (London: Duckworth).
—— (1991b) *Frege: Philosophy of Mathematics* (London: Harvard University Press).
—— (1993) *The Origins of Analytical Philosophy* (London: Duckworth).
—— (1993a) *The Seas of Language* (Oxford: Clarendon Press).
Duns Scotus, John (1639) *Opera omnia*, vol. VII, ed. L. Wadding, J. Ponce *et al.* (Lyons: Duran).
Dupré, J. (1993) *The Disorder of Things* (Cambridge, MA: Harvard University Press).
Dyson, J. Freeman (1985) *The Origins of Life* (Cambridge: Cambridge University Press).
Earman, J. (2002) 'Bayes, Hume, Price, and miracles', *Proceeding of the British Academy*, 113, ed. R. Swinburne (Oxford: British Academy for Oxford University Press): 91–110.
Ebbs, G. (1997) *Rule-following and Realism* (Cambridge, MA: Harvard University Press).
Eco, U. (1988) *The Aesthetics of Thomas Aquinas* (trans. H. Bredin; Cambridge, MA: Harvard University Press; London: Radius).
Else, G. F. (1957) *Aristotle's Poetics: The Argument* (Cambridge, MA: Harvard University Press).
Emerton, J. A. (1960) 'Some New Testament notes', *Journal of Theological Studies*, NS 11: 329–36.
Epstein, R. L. (1995) *The Semantic Foundations of Logic*, 2nd edition (Oxford: Oxford University Press).
Evans, G. (1982) *Varieties of Reference* (Oxford: Clarendon Press).
Evans, G. R. (1985) *The Language and Logic of the Bible: The Road to Reformation* (Cambridge: Cambridge University Press).
Everett, H. (1973) 'The theory of the universal wave function', in B. S. DeWitt and N. Graham (eds) *The Many-worlds Interpretation of Quantum Mechanics* (Princeton: Princeton University Press).
Fine, K. (2002) *The Limits of Abstraction* (Oxford: Clarendon Press).
Finney, P. C. (1994) *The Invisible God: The Earliest Christians on Art* (Oxford: Oxford University Press).
Fitzmyer, J. A. (1971) *Essays on the Semitic Background of the New Testament* (London: Chapman).
Flint, P. W. (1994) 'The Psalm Scrolls from the Judean desert: relationships and textual affiliations', in Brooke with F. G. Martinez (1994): 31–52.
Floyd, J. (2001) 'Wittgenstein, mathematics and philosophy', in A. Crary and R. Read (eds.) *The New Wittgenstein* (London: Routledge): 232–61.
Fodor, J. (1992) 'A theory of the child's theory of mind', *Cognition*, 44: 283–96.

Forrester, J. (1997) *Truth Games* (Cambridge, MA: Harvard University Press).

Forsman, R. (1992) 'Revelation and understanding', in A. Loades and M. McLain (eds) *Hermeneutics, the Bible and Literary Criticism* (London: Macmillan).

Fowles, J. (1977) *Daniel Martin* (Boston: Little, Brown).

Frege, G. (1952) *Translations from the Philosophical Writings of Gottlob Frege*, trans. P. T. Geach and M. Black (Oxford: Basil Blackwell).

—— (1953) *The Foundations of Arithmetic*, 2nd edition; trans. J. L. Austin (Oxford: Blackwell).

—— (1969) *Nachgel Essene Schriften*, vol. 1, ed. H. Hermes, F. Kambartel and F. Kaulbach (Hamburg: Meiner).

—— (1977) *Logical Investigations*, trans. and ed. P. T. Geach and M. Black (Oxford: Blackwell).

—— (1977a) 'The thought', in *Logical Investigations*, trans. and ed. M. Black and P. T. Geach (Oxford: Blackwell).

French, R. (1996) *The Subtlety of Sameness* (Cambridge, MA: MIT Press).

Garver, N. (1994) *This Complicated Form of Life* (La Salle and Chicago, IL: Open Court Publishers).

—— (1996) 'Philosophy as grammar', in H. Sluga and D. G. Stern (eds) *The Cambridge Companion to Wittgenstein* (Cambridge: Cambridge University Press): 139–70.

Gaukroger, S. (1989) *Cartesian Logic* (Oxford: Clarendon).

Geach, P. T. (1969) *God and the Soul* (London: Routledge).

—— (1971) *Mental Acts*, revised edition (London: Routledge).

—— (1972) *Logic Matters* (Oxford: Blackwell).

—— (1980) *Reference and Generality*, 3rd edition (Ithaca, NY: Cornell University Press).

—— (1991) 'Whatever happened to deontic logic', in P. T. Geach (ed.) *Logic and Ethics* (Dordrecht: Kluwer Academic Publishers: 33–48).

—— (1998) 'On modal syllogisms', in P. A. Schilpp and L. E. Hahn (eds) *The Philosophy of Georg Henrik von Wright* (La Salle, IL: Open Court Publishers): 557–80.

Gensler, H. (1996) *Formal Ethics* (London: Routledge).

Gerrard, S. (1996) 'A philosophy of mathematics between two camps', in H. Sluga and D. G. Stern (eds) *The Cambridge Companion to Wittgenstein* (Cambridge: Cambridge University Press): 171–97.

Geuss, R. (2002) *History and Illusion in Politics* (Cambridge: Cambridge University Press).

Gibson, A. (1976) 'Judges 1: 14: NEB and AV Translations', in *Vetus Testamentum*, XXVI 3: 275–83.

—— (1981) *Biblical Semantic Logic* (Oxford: Blackwell; New York: St Martin's Press).

—— (1987) *Boundless Function* (Newcastle, UK: Bloodaxe; US: Dufour Editions).

—— (1997) 'God's semantic logic: some functions in the Dead Sea Scrolls and the Bible', in *The Scrolls and the Scriptures* (RILP 3. JSPSup. Sheffield: Sheffield Academic Press): 68–106.

—— (1997a) 'Archetypal site poetry', in J. Milbank, *The Mercurial Wood*, Studies in English Literature, Poetic Drama, and Poetic Theory (Salzburg: University of Salzburg Press): vii–xi.

—— (1998) 'Ockham's world and future', in J. Marenbon (ed.) *History of Philosophy*, vol. III (London: Routledge): 329–67.

—— (2000) *God and the Universe* (London: Routledge).

—— (2000a) *Text and Tablet* (Aldershot: Ashgate).

—— (2000b) 'Philosophy of psychotic modernism: Wagner and Hitler', in S. E. Porter and B. W. R. Pearson (eds) *Christian–Jewish Relations through the Centuries* (Sheffield: Sheffield Academic Press, 2000): 351–86.

—— (2001) *Biblical Semantic Logic*, 2nd edition (New York: Continuum/Sheffield Academic Press).

—— (2001a) 'Prologue' in Gibson (2001): xiv–xxxvi.

—— (forthcoming a) *Counter-Intuition*.

—— (forthcoming b) *What is Literature?*

Gibson, A. and O'Mahony, N. A. (1995) 'Le Renversement de Sumer et d'Ur', in *Dedale. Le paradoxe des representations du divin: L'image et l'invisible* 1/2, ed. A. Meddeb (Paris: Editions Maisonneuve et Larousse).

Goldhill, S. (1986) *Reading Greek Tragedy* (Cambridge: Cambridge University Press).

Gombrich, E. H. (1986) *New Light on Old Masters* (Oxford: Phaidon).

Goodman, N. (1978) *Ways of Worldmaking* (Indianapolis, IL: Hackett).

Green, J. B. (1995) *The Theology of the Gospel of Luke* (Cambridge: Cambridge University Press).

Gross, D. J. (1989) 'Strings at superplanckian energies', in M. Atiyah *et al.* (eds) *Physics and Mathematics of Strings*, Proceedings of a Royal Society discussion, London.

Grotius, H. [1625] (1995) *Hugonis Grotii De jure belli ac pacis libri tres: in quibus jus naturae et gentium, item juris publici præcipua explicantur; cum annotatis auctoris, ex postrema ejus ante obitum cura multo nunc auctior; accesserunt et annotata in Epistolam Pauli ad Philemonem* (Buffalo, NY: Hein).

Gulley, N. (1979) 'Aristotle on the purposes of literature', in J. Barnes *et al.* (eds) *Articles on Aristotle*, 4, *Psychology and Aesthetics* (London: Duckworth).

Gunson, D. L. (1998) *Michael Dummett and the Theory of Meaning* (Avebury Series in Philosophy; Aldershot: Ashgate).

Guth, A. (1983) 'Phase transitions in the very early universe', in G. W. Gibbons, S. W. Hawking and S. T. C. Siklos (eds) *The Very Early Universe* (Cambridge: Cambridge University Press).

Haack, S. A. (1974) *Deviant Logic* (Cambridge: Cambridge University Press).

—— (1996) *Deviant Logic, Fuzzy Logic* (Chicago, IL: University of Chicago Press).

Hacking, I. (1975) *The Emergence of Probability* (Cambridge: Cambridge University Press).

—— (1985) 'Rules, scepticism, proof, Wittgenstein', in I. Hacking (ed.) *Exercises in Analysis*; (Cambridge: Cambridge University Press): 113–24.

—— (1995) *Rewriting the Soul: Multiple Personality and the Sciences of Memory* (Princeton, NJ: Princeton University Press).

—— (1998) *Mad Travelers* (Charlottesville, VA: University Press of Virginia).

—— (2001) *Social Constructions of What?* (Cambridge, MA: Harvard University Press).

Hale, B. (1994) 'Is Platonism epistemologically bankrupt?', in *Philosophical Review*, 103 (April) 2: 299–325.

—— (1996) 'Singular terms (1)', in M. Schirn (ed.) *Frege: Importance and Legacy* (Berlin: Walter de Gruyter): 438–57.

Hallden, S. (1949) *The Logic of Nonsense* (Uppsala: Lundequist).

Halliday, M. A. K. (1999) 'The grammatical construction of scientific knowledge', in R. R. Favretti *et al.* (eds) *Incommensurability and Translation* (Cheltenham: Edward Elgar): 85–116.

Hanson, A. T. (1992) 'The treatment in the LXX of the theme of seeing God', in G. J. Brooke and B. Lindars (eds) *Septuagint, Scrolls and Cognate Writings* (Atlanta, GA: Scholars Press): 557–68.

Hardy, G. H. (1910) 'Orders of infinity', in J. G. Leatham and E. T. Whittaker (eds) *Cambridge Tracts in Mathematics and Mathematical Physics*, 12: 1–62.

—— (1929) 'Mathematical proof', *Mind*, 38: 1–25.

—— (1941) *A Course of Pure Mathematics*, 8th edition (Cambridge: Cambridge University Press).

Hasselblatt, B. and Katok, A. (eds) (2002) *Handbook of Dynamical Systems*, vol. 1A (Amsterdam: North Holland).

Hawking, S. W. (1983) 'Euclidean approach to the inflationary universe', in G. W. Gibbons, S. W. Hawking and S. T. C. Siklos (eds) *The Very Early Universe* (Cambridge: Cambridge University Press): 287–96.

Hawking, S. W. and Ellis, G. F. R. (1973) *The Large Scale Structure of Space Time* (Cambridge: Cambridge University Press).

Hawking, S. W. and Luttrell, J. C. (1984) 'Higher derivatives in quantum cosmology: 1. The isotropic case' (Cambridge: DAMPT).

Hawking, S. W. and Turok, N. (1998) 'Open inflation without false vacua', *Physical Letters* B 425: 25–32.

Heal, J. (1995) 'Wittgenstein and dialogue', in T. J. Smiley (ed.) *Philosophical Dialogues* (Oxford: Oxford University Press for the British Academy): 63–83.

—— (1997) 'Indexical predicates and their uses', *Mind*, 102: 618–40.

—— (1998) 'Co-cognition and off-line simulation: two ways of understanding the simulation approach' in *Mind and Language*, 343–64.

Heath, S. C. (1981) *Questions of Cinema* (London: Macmillan).

Hegel, G. W. F. (1969) *Science of Logic*, trans. A. V. Miller (London: Allen and Unwin).

Henninger, M. G. (1989) *Relations: Medieval Theories 1256–1325* (Oxford: Clarendon Press).

Hertling, C. (2002) *Frobenius Manifolds and Moduli Spaces for Singularities* (Cambridge: Cambridge University Press).

Hesse, M. B. (1966) *Models and Analogies in Science* (Notre Dame, IN: Notre Dame Press).

—— (1983) 'Cosmology as myth', in *Concilium: Cosmology and Theology* (Edinburgh: SCM Press).

Hiddleston, J. A. (1999) *Baudelaire and the Art of Memory* (Oxford: Oxford University Press).

Hilbert, D. (1922) 'Neubegrundungen der Geometrie', in Erste Mitteilung, *Abhandlungen aus dem Mathematischen Seminar der Hamburger Universitat*, 1: 157–77.

—— (1925) *Methoden der Mathematischen Physik*, 1 (Berlin: Springer).

—— (1926) 'Uber das Undendliche', *Mathematische Annalen*, 95: 161–90.

Hintikka, J. J. (1962) *Knowledge and Belief* (Ithaca: Cornell University Press).

—— (1994) '"Die Wende der Philosophie": Wittgenstein's new logic of 1928', in S. Teghrarian (ed.) *Wittgenstein in Contemporary Philosophy* (Bristol: Thoemmes Press).

—— (1996) 'The development of Aristotle's ideas of scientific method', in W. Williams (ed.) *Aristotle's Philosophical Development* (Lanham, MD, and London: Rowman and Littlefield): 83–104.

—— (1998) *The Principles of Mathematics Revisited* (Cambridge: Cambridge University Press).

Hintikka, J. J. and Hintikka, M. (1986) *Investigating Wittgenstein* (Oxford: Blackwell).

Hobson, M. (1982) *The Object of Art* (Cambridge: Cambridge University Press).

—— (1990) 'Deconstruction, empiricism and the postal services', *French Studies*, 36, 3: 290–314.

—— (1995) 'What is wrong with Saint Peter's? Or Diderot, analogy and architecture', in W. Pape and F. Burwick (eds) *Reflecting Senses* (Berlin: de Gruyter): 54–74.

—— (1998) *Jacques Derrida: Opening Lines* (London: Routledge).

Hoffmann, R. (1990) 'Molecular beauty', *Journal of Aesthetics and Art Criticism*, 48, 3: 191–204.

Holland, E. (1993) *Baudelaire and Schizoanalysis* (Cambridge: Cambridge University Press).

Holland, J. H. (1998) *Emergence from Chaos to Order* (Oxford: Oxford University Press).

Holopainen, T. M. (1991) *William Ockham's Theory of the Foundations of Ethics*, Publications of the Luther Agricola Society, B20, Helsinki.

Horst, S. W. (1996) *Symbols, Computation and Intentionality* (Berkeley, CA: University of California Press).

Horton, F. (1976) *The Melchizedek Tradition* (Cambridge: Cambridge University Press).

Hume, D. (1935) *Dialogues Concerning Natural Religion* (Oxford: Clarendon Press).

Hunt, G. M. K. (1992) 'Is philosophy a "theory of everything?"', in A. P. Griffiths (ed.) *The Impulse to Philosophise*, Royal Institute of Philosophy Supplement 33, Cambridge.

Hutton, J. (1982) *Aristotle's Poetics* (New York: Norton).

Huxley, A. (1982) 'Discovery: accident or design?', *Proceedings of the Royal Society* B: 216: 253–6.

Jackendorff, R. (2002) *Foundations of Language* (Oxford: Oxford University Press).

Jakobson, R. (1873) *Questions de poetique* (Paris: Seuil).

James, H. (1934) *The Art of the Novel* (New York: Scribner).

Jeffner, A. (1972) *The Study of Religious Language* (London: SCM).

Jonge, M. de (1965) '11QMel and the New Testament', *New Testament Studies* XII (1965–6): 301–26.

Kaldor, N. (1986) 'Piero Sraffa', *Proceedings of the British Academy*, LXXI (1985): 615–40.

Kallel, L. and Naudts, B. (1999) 'Theoretical aspects of evolutionary computing', in L. Kallel, B. Naudts and A. Rogers (eds) *EvoNet Summer School on Theoretical Aspects of Evolutionary Computing* (Berlin: Springer).

Kane, G. (2000) *Supersymmetry* (Cambridge, MA: Helix/Perseus).

Kant, I. (1995) *Kritik er reinen* (Frankfurt am Main: Suhrkamp.

—— (2000) *Critique of Pure Reason*, trans. P. Guyer and A. W. Wood (Cambridge: Cambridge University Press).

Katok, A. and Hasselblatt, B. (1995) *Introduction to the Modern Theory of Dynamical Systems* (Cambridge: Cambridge University Press).

Kay, S. (1990) *Subjectivity in Troubadour Poetry* (Cambridge: Cambridge University Press).

Kearns, K. (1997) *Psychoanalysis, Historiography, and Feminist Theory* (Cambridge: Cambridge University Press).

Kelley, D. J. (1974) '"Modernité" in Baudelaire's art criticism', in F. Haskell *et al.* (eds) *The Artist and the Writer in France* (Oxford: Clarendon): 138–52.

—— (1968) 'Charles Baudelaire's "Salon de 1846"', 2 vols (PhD dissertation, Cambridge University).

Kermode, J. F. (1983) *Essays on Fiction* (London: Routledge and Kegan Paul).

—— (1985) *Forms of Attention* (Chicago, IL: Chicago University Press).

—— (1991) *Poetry, Narrative, History* (Oxford: Blackwell).

Kinnier Wilson, J. V. (1979) *The Rebel Lands* (Cambridge: Cambridge University Press).

Kneale, W. and M. (1984) *The Development of Logic*, corrected edition (Oxford: Clarendon Press).

Knysh, C. (1994) *Ockham Perspectives* (Winnipeg: Ukrainian Academy of Arts and Sciences in Canada – UVAN).

Kolmogorov, A. N. (1965) 'Three approaches to the quantitative definition of information', *Problems in Information Transmission*, 1, 1: 1–7.

Kretzmann, N. (1997) *The Metaphysics of Theism* (Oxford: Clarendon Press).

—— (1999) *The Metaphysics of Creation* (Oxford: Clarendon).

Kripke, S. A. (1974) 'Naming and necessity', *Synthèse*, 27: 509–12.

—— (1982) *Wittgenstein on Rules and Private Language* (Oxford: Blackwell).

Kuhn, T. S. (1999) *Incommensurablity and Translation*, ed. R. Rossini *et al.* (Cheltenham: Elgar).

Lacan, J. (1991) *Le Seminaire de Jacques Lacan, Livre VIII: Le transfert* (Paris: Editions du Seuil).

Lacoue-Labarthe, P. (1994) *Musica Ficta: Figures on Wagner* (Stanford, CA: Stanford University Press).

Lakoff, G. and Johnson, M. (1981) *The Metaphors We Live By* (Chicago: Chicago University Press).

Landy, F. (1983) *Paradoxes of Paradise* (Sheffield: Almond).

Langton, R. (1998) *Kantian Humility* (Oxford: Clarendon).

Lear, J. (1980) *Aristotle and Logical Theory* (Cambridge: Cambridge University Press).

Leick, G. (1994) *Sex and Eroticism in Mesopotamian Literature* (London: Routledge).

Lerner, R. and Mahdu, M. (eds) (1966) *Medieval Political Philosophy* (Glencoe, IL: Free Press; Toronto: Collier Macmillan).

LeVay, S. (1993) *The Sexual Brain* (Cambridge, MA: MIT Press).

Levi, I. (1967) *Gambling with Truth* (New York: Alfred A. Knopf; London: Routledge).

—— (1997) *The Covenant with Reason* (Cambridge: Cambridge University Press).

Lewis, C. I. (1912) 'Implication and the algebra of logic', *Mind*, 21: 522–31.

Lewis, D. (1966) 'An argument for the identity theory', in *Journal of Philosophy*, 63: 17–25.
—— (1976) 'Probabilities of conditionals and conditional probabilities', *Philosophical Review*, 85: 7–315.
—— (1986) *On the Plurality of Worlds* (Oxford: Oxford University Press).
Lewis, E. (1954) *Medieval Political Ideas* (London: Routledge).
Lewis, H. A. (ed.) (1991) *Peter Geach: Philosophical Encounters* (Dordrecht: Kluwer Academic Publishers).
Lewy, C. (1976) *Meaning and Modality* (Cambridge: Cambridge University Press).
Locke, J. (1996) *An Essay Concerning Human Understanding*, ed. K. P. Winkler (Indianapolis, IL: Hackett).
Lovell, B. (1992) 'Reason and belief in cosmology', in *Interpreting the World*, ed. W. R. Shea and A. Spadafora (Locarno/Canton: Science/History Publications USA).
Lyotard, J.-F. (1984) *The Postmodern Condition* (Manchester: Manchester University Press).
Macé, G. (1993) *La memoire aime chasser dans le noir* (Paris: Gallimard).
MacKinnon, D. M. (1974) *The Problem of Metaphysics* (Cambridge: Cambridge University Press).
MacQuarrie, J. (1973) *The Concept of Peace* (London: SCM).
Madsen, D. (1986) *Postmodern Allegory in the Novels of Thomas A. Pynchon* (Leicester: University of Leicester Press).
Magee, J. (1998) *Anicii Manlii Severini Boethii: De Divisone Liber* (*Philosophia Antiqua* LXXVII), ed. J. Mansfield, D. T. Runia and J. C. M. van Winden (Leiden: Brill).
Mallarmé, S. (1914) *Un Coup de Dés* (Paris: Bonniot).
Mann, F. A. (1973) *Studies in International Law* (Oxford: Clarendon).
Maor, E. (1987) *To Infinity* (Boston, MA: Birkhauser).
Marenbon, J. (1987) *Later Medieval Philosophy (1150–1350)* (London: Routledge).
—— (1990) Review of Tachau *Vision and Certitude*, in *Journal of Ecclesiastical History*, 41: 105–6.
—— (ed.) (1998) *Routledge History of Philosophy, III: Medieval Philosophy* (London: Routledge).
Marion, J.-L. (1991) *God without Being*, trans. D. Tracy (Chicago, IL: Chicago University Press).
—— (1998) 'Descartes and onto-theology', in P. Blond (ed.) *Post-Secular Philosophy* (London: Routledge): 67–106.
Marion, M. (1998) *Wittgenstein, Finitism and the Foundation of Mathematics* (Oxford: Clarendon).
Martin, C. J. (1986) 'William's machine', in *Journal of Philosophy*, 83: 564–72.
Matthews, G. B. (1992) *Thought's Ego in Augustine and Descartes* (Ithaca, NY: Cornell).
Maurer, A. (1984) 'Ockham's Razor and Chatton's anti-Razor', in *Mediaeval Studies*, 46: 463–75.
McAleer, M. (2001) 'Simplicity: some views of Nobel laureates in economic science', in Zellner *et al.*, *Simplicity, Inference and Modelling* (Cambridge: Cambridge University Press): 292–6.
McGinn, C. (1984) *Wittgenstein on Meaning: An Interpretation and Evaluation* (Oxford: Blackwell).
—— (1997) *Ethics, Evil and Fiction* (Oxford: Clarendon Press).
McGrade, A. S. (1974) *The Political Thought of William of Ockham* (Cambridge: Cambridge University Press).
Mellor, D. H. (1991) 'I and now', in *Matters of Metaphysics* (Cambridge: Cambridge University Press).
Milbank, J. (1990) *Theology and Social Theory: Beyond Secular Reason* (Oxford: Basil Blackwell).
—— (1997) *The Word Made Strange* (Oxford: Blackwell Publishers).
—— (2003) *Being Reconciled: Ontology and Pardon* (London: Routledge).
Mill, J. S. (1996) 'A system of logic, ratiocinative and inductive', in *Collected Works*, 2nd edition; ed. J. M. Robson, intro. R. F. McRae (London: University of Toronto Press).
Mirimanoff, D. (1917) 'Les antimonies', in *L'Enseignement Mathematique*, 19: 37–52.

Montefiore, A. and Vines, D. (eds) (1999) *Integrity in the Public and Private Domains* (London: Routledge).

Moore, A. W. (1990) *The Infinite* (London: Routledge).

Moreno, C. (1999) *Algebraic Curves over Finite Fields* (Cambridge: Cambridge University Press).

Moschovakis, Y. N. (1974) *Elementary Induction on Abstract Structures* (Amsterdam: North-Holland).

Mothersill, M. (1984) *Beauty Restored* (Oxford: Oxford University Press).

Mottron, L. (1989) 'Rene Thom's semiotics: an application to the pathological limits of semiosis', in T. A. Sebeok, J. Umiker-Sebeok and E. P. Young (eds) *The Semiotic Web* (Berlin: de Gruyter): 91–127.

Nash, J. F. (1951) 'Non-cooperative games', *Annals of Mathematics*, 54, 2: 286–95.

Nedo, M. (1993) *Ludwig Wittgenstein: Wiener Ausgabe, Einfuhrung* (Vienna: Springer).

Neumann, J. von (1925) 'Bine Axiomatisierung', in *Journal für reine und angewandte Matheinptik*, 154.

Newsom, C. A. (1985) *Songs of the Sabbath Sacrifice: A Critical Edition*. Harvard Semitic Studies, Harvard Semitic Museum (Atlanta, GA: Scholars Press).

—— (1992) '4Q374: a discourse on the Exodus/Conquest tradition', in Dimant and Rappaport (1992): 4–52.

Nicholls, S. G., Brownlee, M. S. and Brownlee, K. (eds) (1991) *The New Medievalism* (Baltimore, MD, and London: Johns Hopkins University Press).

Niebergall, K.-G. and Schirn, M. (1996) *The Philosophy of Mathematics*, ed. W. D. Hart (Oxford: Oxford University): 280–96.

Nigosian, S. A. (1993) 'Moses as they saw him', *Vetus Testamentum*: 399–50.

Nitzman, B. (1994) '4QBerakhot (4Q286–290): a preliminary report', in Brooke with Martinez (1994): 53–72.

Oakes, E. (1994) *The Pattern of Redemption* (New York: Continuum Press).

Oakesford, M. and Chater, N. (1998) *Rational Models of Cognition* (Oxford: Oxford University Press).

Ockham, William of (1967–88) *Opera Philosophica et Theologica ad Fidem Codium Manuscriptorum Edita*, 17 vols (St Bonaventure University: Franciscan Institute).

—— (1995) *Epistola ad Fratres Minores*, ed. A. S. McGrade; trans. J. Kilcullen (Cambridge: Cambridge University Press).

—— (2002) *Dialogus*, Latin text ed. and trans. J. Kilcullen *et al.* (London: British Academy).

Offler, H. (1990) 'The "influence" of Ockham's political thinking', in W. von Vossenkuhl and R. Schonberger (eds) *Die Gegenwart Ockhams* (Weinheim: VCH Acta humaniora): 338–68.

Oliver, A. (1999) 'Logical form', in *Aristotelian Society, Proceedings*, New Series, XCIX (London: Aristotelian Society): 247–72.

Oudart, J.-P. (1969) 'La suture', in *Cahiers du cinema*, 211.

—— (1977) 'Cinema and suture', in *Screen*, 18, 4.

Parfit, D. (1984) *Reasons and Persons* (Oxford: Clarendon Press).

Pascal, B. (2000) *Pensées*, presentation and notes by Gérard Ferreyrolles; text by Philippe Sellier following that of Gilberte Pascal (Paris: Librairie générale de France).

Pasnau, R. (1997) *Theories of Cognition in the Later Middle Ages* (Cambridge: Cambridge University Press).

Pears, D. (1982) 'Motivated irrationality', in R. Wollheim and J. Hopkins (eds) *Philosophical Essays on Freud* (Cambridge: Cambridge University Press): 264–88.

Penrose, R. (1994) *Shadows of the Mind* (Oxford: Oxford University Press).

Penrose, R., Shimony, A., Cartwright, N. and Hawking, S. (1997) *The Large, the Small and the Human Mind* (Cambridge: Cambridge University Press).

Phillips, D. Z. (1982) *Through the Darkening Glass* (Oxford: Blackwell).

Pickstock, C. (1997) *After Writing* (Oxford: Blackwell).

Popper, K. R. (1972) *Objective Knowledge* (Oxford: Oxford University Press).

Porada, E. (ed.) (1980) *Ancient Art in Seals* (Princeton, NJ: Princeton University Press).

Porter, S. E. (ed.) (1997) *Handbook of Classical Rhetoric in the Hellenistic Period: 330 BC–AD 400* (Leiden: Brill).

Potter, M. (2000) *Reason's Nearest Kin: Philosophies of Arithmetic from Kant to Carnap* (Oxford: Oxford University Press).

Prado, B. (2003) 'The plane of immanence and life', in J. Khalfa (ed.) *An Introduction to the Philosophy of Gilles Deleuze* (New York: Continuum): 9–25.

Prawitz, D. (1994) 'Logic and philosophy of science' in D. Prawitz and D. Westerstahl (eds) *Ninth International Congress of Logic, Methodology, and Philosophy of Science* (Synthese Library 236, Dordrecht: Kluwer).

Prendergast, C. (1986) *On the Order of Mimesis* (Cambridge: Cambridge University Press).

Priest, G. (1987) *In Contradiction* (Boston, MA: Nijhoff).

—— (1994) 'The structure of the paradoxes of self-reference', *Mind*, 103: 25–34.

—— (1995) *Beyond the Limits of Thought* (Cambridge: Cambridge University).

Prior, A. N. (1968) *Papers on Time and Tense* (Oxford: Clarendon Press).

—— (1976) 'Entities', in P. T. Geach and A. Kenny (eds) *Papers in Logic and Ethics* (London: Duckworth).

Prior, A. N. and Fine, K. (1977) *Worlds, Times and Selves* (London: Duckworth).

Qimron, E. (1992) 'Observations on the history of early Hebrew (1000 BCE–200 CE)' in Dimant and Rappaport (1992): 349–61.

Quine, W. V. (1941) 'Whitehead and the rise of modern logic', in P. A. Schilpp (ed.) *The Philosophy of Alfred North Whitehead* (Chicago, IL: Evanston): 125–64.

—— (1969) *Set Theory and its Logic*, revised edition (Cambridge, MA: Harvard University Press).

—— (1987) *Quiddities* (Cambridge, MA: Belknap Press, Harvard University).

Rangos, S. (1999) 'Between physis and nous: logos as principle of meditation in Plotinus', *Journal of Neoplatonic Studies*, 7.2.

Rawls, J. (1972) *A Theory of Justice* (Oxford: Clarendon Press).

Read, S. (1988) *Relevant Logic* (Oxford: Blackwell).

Recanati, F. (1993) *Direct Reference: from Language to Thought* (Oxford: Blackwell).

Redpath, T. (1990) *Ludwig Wittgenstein: A Student's Memoir* (London: Duckworth).

Rees, M. (1995) *Perspectives in Astrophysical Cosmology* (Cambridge: Cambridge University Press).

—— (1997) *Before the Beginning* (London: Simon and Schuster).

—— (1999) *Just Six Numbers* (London: Weidenfeld and Nicholson).

Renfrew, A. C. (1982) *Towards an Archaeology of the Mind* (Cambridge: Cambridge University Press).

Reynolds, D. (1995) *Symbolist Aesthetics and Early Abstract Art* (Cambridge: Cambridge University Press).

Rhees, R. (1998) *Wittgenstein and the Possibility of Discourse*, ed. D. Z. Phillips (Cambridge: Cambridge University Press).

Richardson, J. (1996) *Nietzsche's System* (Oxford: Oxford University Press).

Robson, E. (1999) *Mesopotamian Mathematics* (Oxford: Clarendon).

Rogers, E. F. (1995) *Thomas Aquinas and Karl Barth* (Notre Dame, IN: University of Notre Dame Press).

Rorty, R. (1979) *Philosophy and the Mirror of Nature* (Princeton, NJ: Princeton University Press).

—— (1984) 'The historiography of philosophy', in R. Rorty, J. B. Schneewind and Q. D. Skinner (eds) *Philosophy in History* (Cambridge: Cambridge University Press).

—— (1996) 'An examination of Sir William Hamilton's philosophy', in *Collected Works*, ed. J. M. Robson and A. Ryan (London: Routledge, and University of Toronto).

—— (1997) 'Religious faith, intellectual responsibility, and romance', in R. A. Putnam (ed.) *The Cambridge Companion to William James* (Cambridge: Cambridge University Press): 84–102.

—— (1998) *Truth and Progress*, 3 (Cambridge: Cambridge University Press).

Ross, W. D. (1949) *Aristotle's Prior Analytics* (Oxford: Oxford University Press).

Rowland, C. C. (1982) *The Open Heaven* (London: SPCK).

Ryan, J. J. (1979) *The Nature, Structure, and Function of the Church in William of Ockham;* AAR Studies in Religion 16 (Missoula, MT: Scholars Press).

Sainsbury, R. M. (1991) *Logical Forms* (Oxford: Blackwell).

—— (1995) *Paradoxes*, 2nd edition (Cambridge: Cambridge University Press).

Salvesen, A. (1998) 'The legacy of Babylon and Nineveh in Aramaic sources', in S. Dalley (ed.) *The Legacy of Mesopotamia* (Oxford: Oxford University Press): 139–61.

Sanders, E. P. (1977) *Paul and Palestinian Judaism* (London: SCM Press).

—— (1985) *Jesus and Judaism* (London: SCM Press).

Sanderson, J. E. (1986) *An Exodus Scroll from Qumran: 4QpaleoExod^m and the Samaritan Tradition*, Harvard Semitic Studies 30 (Atlanta, GA: Scholars Press).

Saslaw, C. (1985) *Gravitational Physics of Stellar and Galactic Systems* (Cambridge: Cambridge University Press).

Sangalli, A. (1998) *The Importance of Being Fuzzy* (Princeton, NJ: Princeton University Press).

Schefold, B. (1989) *Mr Sraffa on Joint Production and Other Essays* (London: Unwin Hyman).

Schiffman, L. H. (1989) *The Eschatological Community of the Dead Seas Scrolls* SBL Monograph Series 38 (Atlanta, GA: Scholars Press).

—— (1995) '4QMysteries^a: A Preliminary Edition and Translation', in Z. Zevit, S. Giton and M. Sokoloff (eds) *Solving Riddles and Untying Knots* (Winona Lake, IL: Eisenbraums): 207–60.

Schuller, E. M. (1992) '4Q380 and 4Q381: non-canonical psalms from Qumran', in Dimant and Rappaport (1992).

Schutrumpf, E. (1994) 'Some observations on the Introduction to Aristotle's *Rhetoric*', ed. D. J. Furley and A. Nehamas (Princeton, NJ: Princeton University Press).

Scott, D. (1988) *Pictorialist Poetics* (Cambridge: Cambridge University Press).

Seigfried, C. H. (1996) *Pragmatism and Feminism* (Chicago, IL: University of Chicago).

Sen, A. (1995) 'Is the idea of purely internal consistency of choice bizarre?', in J. E. J. Altham and R. Harrison (eds) *Making Sense of Humanity* (Cambridge: Cambridge University Press): 19–31.

Shoesmith, D. J. and Smiley, T. J. (1978) *Multiple-conclusion Logic* (Cambridge: Cambridge University Press).

Simon, H. A. (2001) 'Science seeks parsimony, not simplicity', in Zellner *et al.* (2001): 32–72.

Singh, S. (1997) *Fermat's Last Theorem* (London: Fourth Estate).

Skehan, P. W. *et al.* (1992) *Discoveries in the Judaean Desert*, 9: *Qumran Cave*, 4 (Oxford: Clarendon).

Skinner, Q. (1988) 'A reply to my critics', in J. Tully (ed.) *Meaning and Context* (Cambridge: Polity): 231–88.

Skorobogatov, A. (2001) *Torsors and Rational Points* (Cambridge: Cambridge University Press).

Skorupski, J. (1976) *Symbol and Theory* (Cambridge: Cambridge University Press).

Smiley, T. J. (1982) 'The theory of descriptions', in *Proceedings of the British Academy* LXVII: 321–36.

—— (1998) 'Conceptions of consequence', in E. Craig (ed.) *Routledge Encyclopedia of Philosophy*, 2 (London: Routledge): 599–603.

Smiley, T. J. and G. Priest (1993) 'Can contradictions be true?', *Proceedings of the Aristotelian Society*, Supp. 67: 17–33.

—— (1995) 'A tale of two tortoises', in *Mind*, 104, 116: 725–35.

Smith, P. (1998) *Explaining Chaos* (Cambridge: Cambridge University Press).

Sober, E. (1975) *Simplicity* (Oxford: Clarendon Press).

Solomon, R. C. (2002) *Spirituality for the Skeptic* (Oxford: Oxford University Press).

Sorensen, R. A. (1992) *Thought Experiments* (Oxford: Oxford University Press).

—— (1993) 'Infinite decision theory', in J. Jordan (ed.) *Gambling on God* (London: Rowman and Littlefield): 139–59.

—— (1998) 'Logical luck', *Philosophical Quarterly*, 48 (July), 192: 319–34.

Spade, P. V. (1975) 'Some epistemological implications of the Burley–Ockham dispute', *Franciscan Studies*, 35, 13: 212–23.

—— (1982) 'Quasi-Aristotelianism', in N. Kretzmann (ed.) *Infinity and Continuity in Ancient and Medieval Thought* (Ithaca, NY and London: Cornell University Press).

—— (1988) *Lies, Language and Logic in the Middle Age* (London: Variorum Reprints).

—— (1994) 'Medieval philosophy', in A. Kenny (ed.) *The Oxford Illustrated History of Western Philosophy* (Oxford: Oxford University Press).

Spence, S. (1996) *Texts and the Self in the Twelfth Century*, Cambridge Studies in Medieval Literature 30 (Cambridge: Cambridge University Press).

Sraffa, P. (1960) *Production of Commodities by Means of Commodities* (London: Cambridge University Press).

Starobinski, J. (1971) *Les Mots sous les mots: les anagrammes de Ferdinand de Saussure* (Paris: Gallimard).

Stefanovic, Z. (1992) *The Aramaic of Daniel in the Light of Old Aramaic* (Sheffield: Sheffield Academic Press).

Steiner, G. (1989) *Real Presences* (London: Faber).

Stern, D. G. (1995) *Wittgenstein's Language and Thought* (Oxford: Oxford University Press).

Stove, D. (1995) *Darwinian Fairytales* (Aldershot: Avebury).

Striker, G. (1998) 'Aristotle and the uses of logic', in G. Gentzler (ed.) *Method in Ancient Philosophy* (Oxford: Clarendon Press).

Stump, E. (1989) *Dialectic and its Place in the Development of Medieval Logic* (Ithaca, NY: Cornell University Press).

Summerfield, D. M. (1996) 'Fitting versus tracking', in H. Sluga and D. G. Stern (eds) *Cambridge Companion to Wittgenstein* (Cambridge: Cambridge University Press): 100–38.

Sutherland, S. R. (1984) *Faith and Ambiguity* (London: SCM).

—— (1984a) *God, Jesus and Belief* (Oxford: Blackwell).

Tachau, K. H. (1988) *Vision and Certitude in the Age of Ockham* (Leiden: E. J. Brill).

Tait, W. W. (1996) 'Truth and proof: the Platonism of mathematics', in W. D. Hart (ed.) *The Philosophy of Mathematics* (Oxford: Oxford University Press): 142–67.

Tarski, A. (1956) *Logic, Semantics, Metamathematics* (Oxford: Oxford University Press).

Tennant, N. (1978) *Natural Logic* (Edinburgh: Edinburgh University Press).

—— (1997) *The Taming of the True* (Oxford: Clarendon Press).

Thom, R. (1989) *Structural Stability and Morphogenesis*, 2nd edition; trans. D. Fowler (Reading, MA: Addison-Wesley).

—— (1952–4) *The Disputed Questions of Truth [De Veritate]*, trans. R. W. Mulligan, 3 vols (Chicago, IL: Chicago University Press).

Tolstikov, A. V. (1989) 'Fermat's Great Theorem', in *Encyclopaedia of Mathematics*, vol. 3, ed. M. Hazewinkel. [Updated and annotated translation of the *Soviet Mathematical Encyclopaedia*] (Dordrecht: Kluwer): 485–7.

Torre, B. R. de la (1987) *Thomas Buckingham and the Contingency of Futures*, a study and edition of Thomas Buckingham's *De contingentia futurorum et arbitrii libertate* (Notre Dame, IN: University of Notre Dame Press).

Tov, E. (1995) 'Groups of biblical texts found at Qumran', in Dimant and Schiffman: 85–102.

Tuck, R. (1983a) 'Grotius, Carneades and Hobbes', *Grotiana* New Series 4: 43–62.

—— (1983b) 'P. Haggenmacher's *Grotius et la doctrine de la guerre juste* (Paris)', in *Grotiana*, New Series 5.

Vilenken, A. (1986) 'Looking for cosmic strings', *Nature*, 322: 613–14.

Vitanyi, P. and Li, M. (2001) 'Simplicity, information, Kolmogorov complexity and prediction' in Zellner *et al.*: 135–55.

Ulrich, E. (1995) 'The paleo-Hebrew biblical manuscripts from cave 4', in Dimant and Schiffman: 103–29.

von Vossenkuhl, W. and Schonberger, R. (eds) (1990) *Gegenwart Ockhams* (Weinheim: VCH Acta humaniora).

von Wright, G. H. (1983) *Philosophical Logic, Philosophical Works*, vol. 2 (Oxford: Blackwell).

—— (1996) *Six Essays on Philosophical Logic* (Helsinki: Philosophical Society of Finland).

Wada, S. (1986) 'Consistency of canonical quantization of gravity and boundary conditions for the wave function of the universe', *Physical Review*, D: 34.8.

Wallies, M. (1909) (ed.) *Ioannis Philoponi in Aristotelis Analytica posteriora commentaria* (Berolini: G. Reimeri).

Walton, K. L. (1990) *Mimesis as Make-believe* (Cambridge, MA: Harvard University Press).

Weinfeld, M. (1995) 'The angelic song over the luminaries in the Qumran texts', in Dimant and Schiffman (1995): 131–57.

Weirich, P. (1998) *Equilibrium and Rationality* (Cambridge: Cambridge University Press).

White, G. (1990) 'Ockham and Wittgenstein', in W. von Vossenkuhl and R. Schonberger (eds) *Die Gegenwart Ockhams* (Weinheim: VCH Acta humaniora).

White, R. (1982) 'Notes on analogical predication and speaking about God', in B. Hebblethwaite and S. R. Sutherland (eds) *The Philosophical Frontiers of Christian Theology* (Cambridge: Cambridge University Press).

Whitehead, A. N. (1898) *A Treatise on Universal Algebra*, vol. 1 (Cambridge: Cambridge University Press).

Whitehead, A. N. and Russell, B. (1910) *Principia Mathematica* (London: Cambridge University Press).

Wiggins, D. (1980) *Sameness and Substance* (Oxford: Blackwell).

Wiles, A. (1995) 'Fermat's Last Theorem', in *Annals of Mathematics* (May).

Wilkerson. T. E. (1997) *Irrational Action* (Avebury Series in Philosophy; Aldershot: Ashgate).

Williams, B. (1978) *Descartes* (Harmondsworth: Penguin).

—— (1998) 'What could philosophy become?' (Lecture delivered at the University of Surrey Roehampton in the series 'The Present Future').

—— (1999) *Plato: The Invention of Philosophy* (London: Phoenix).

—— (2002) *Truth and Truthfulness* (Princeton, NJ: Princeton University Press).

Williams, D. (1996) *Deformed Discourse* (Exeter: University of Exeter Press).

Williamson, T. (1994) *Vagueness* (London: Routledge).

Witten, E. (1998) 'Magic mystery and matrix' [Josiah Willard Gibbs Lecture Baltimore], in *Notices of the American Mathematical Society*: 1,124–9.

—— (2000) 'Foreword', in Kane: xi–xiii.

—— (2002) 'Comments on string theory' (December 2002) e-Print Archive: hep-th/0212247.

Wittgenstein, L. (1922) *Tractatus Logico-Philosophicus*, trans. C. K. Ogden (London: Routledge).

—— (1941) Handwritten notes by Wittgenstein in his copy of G. H. Hardy (1941) in the Wittgenstein archives, Wren Library, Trinity College Cambridge.

—— (1961) *Tractatus Logico-Philosophicus*, trans. D. F. Pears and B. F. McGuiness, 2nd corrected impression (London: Routledge and Kegan Paul).

—— (1969) *On Certainty*, ed. G. E. M. Anscombe and G. H. von Wright; trans. G. E. M. Anscombe and D. Paul (Oxford: Blackwell).

—— (1974) *On Certainty*, ed. G. E. M. Anscombe and G. H. von Wright; trans. D. Paul and G. E. M. Anscombe, corrected reprint (Oxford: Blackwell).

—— (1975) *Philosophical Remarks*, 2nd edition; ed. R. Rhees; trans. R. Hargreaves and R. White (Oxford: Blackwell).

—— (1977) *Remarks on Colour*, ed. G. E. M. Anscombe; trans. L. L. McAlister and M. Schattle (Oxford: Blackwell).

—— (1978) *Remarks on the Foundations of Mathematics*, 3rd edition; ed. G. H. von Wright *et al.*; trans. G. E. M. Anscombe (Oxford: Blackwell).

—— (1979) *Wittgenstein's Lectures: 1932–35* (from the notes of A. Ambrose and M. Mac-Donald; ed. A. Ambrose; Oxford: Blackwell).

—— (1980) *Culture and Value*, ed. G. H. von Wright; trans. P. Winch (Oxford: Blackwell).

—— (1980a) *Culture and Value*, 2nd edition; ed. G. H. von Wright and N. Nyman; trans. P. Winch (Oxford: Blackwell).

—— (1981) *Zettel*, 2nd ed.; ed. and trans. G. E. M. Anscombe (Oxford: Blackwell).

—— (1993) *Philosophical Occasions: 1912–1951*, ed. J. C. Klagge and A. Nordmann (Indianapolis, IN, and Cambridge: Hackett).

—— (1994) *Vermischte Bermerkungen, Eine Auswahl aus dem Nachlass*, ed. G. H. von Wright *et al.* (Frankfurt am Main: Suhrkamp).

—— (1996) *Notes on Logic*, ed. M. A. R. Biggs, *Editing Wittgenstein's 'Notes on Logic'*, vols 1 and 2 (Working Papers from the Wittgenstein Archives at the University of Bergen, no. 11).

—— (1998) *Philosophical Investigations*, revised re-issued 2nd edition; ed. G. E. M. Anscombe, R. Rhees and G. H. von Wright; trans. G. E. M. Anscombe (Oxford: Blackwell).

—— (1998a) *The Collected Manuscripts of Ludwig Wittgenstein on Facsimile CD-ROM*, The Wittgenstein Archives at the University of Bergen (Oxford: Oxford University Press).

Woess, J. (2000) *Random Walks and Infinite Graphs* (Cambridge: Cambridge University Press).

Wood, D. (1992) *Derrida: A Critical Reader* (Oxford: Oxford University Press).

Wood, R. (1990) 'Ockham on essentially-ordered causes: logic misapplied', in W. von Vossenkuhl and R. Schonberger (eds) *Die Gegenwart Ockhams* (Weinheim: VCH Acta humaniora): 25–50.

Woods, J. (2003) *Paradox and Paraconsistency* (Cambridge: Cambridge University Press).

Wortley, B. A. (1967) *Jurisprudence* (Manchester: Manchester University Press).

Woude, A. S. van der (1965) 'Melchisedech als himmlische Erlosergestalt in den neuge-fundenen Midraschim aus Hohle XI', in *Oudtestamentische Studien*, 14: 354–73.

Wright, C. (1980) *Wittgenstein on the Foundations of Mathematics* (London: Duckworth).

—— (1987) *Realism, Meaning and Truth* (Oxford: Blackwell).

Zellner, A., Hugo, A., Kreuzenkamp, H. A. and McAleer, M. (2001) *Simplicity, Inference and Modelling* (Cambridge: Cambridge University Press).

Zink, M. (1985) *La subjectivité littéraire autour du siècle de Saint Louis* (Paris: Presses Universitaires de France).

Indexes

Name index

Subject index